THE MARINER AND THE MONK

CAPTAIN LA RUE, BROTHER MARINUS, AND
THE RESCUE AT HUNGNAM

PHILIP LACOVARA

CATALINA PRESS

Catalina Press, LLC
Tucson, Arizona
www.catalinabookpress.com
books@catalinabookpress.com

Follow us and our authors on:
Twitter: @CatalinaPress
Facebook: @CatalinaBookPress
Instagram: #CatalinaBookPress

ISBN: 978-1-953721-05-1

To Bob Lunney, who for seventy years has told the story of Captain La Rue, Brother Marinus, the SS Meredith Victory, and the rescue at Hungnam.

CONTENTS

FOREWORD

One of the many pleasures of working at the American Merchant Marine Museum is that one never knows who will walk through its doors. In September 2019, Philip Lacovara made an appointment to research the remarkable accomplishments of the SS *Meredith Victory*. As it so happened, the Museum has a cache of documents and ephemera relating to that ship's master, Captain Leonard La Rue, or Brother Marinus as he later came to be known. The museum also displays the original "Gallant Ship" award given to the vessel, an elegant copper medallion roughly eighteen inches in diameter, depicting a merchant ship. The medallion is mounted on a wooden plaque, with a rectangular bronze plaque below it, which reads:

At the height of the epoch-making evacuation of Hungnam, Korea, by the United Nations Forces in December, 1950, the MEREDITH VICTORY was requested to assist in the removal of Korean civilians trapped and threatened with death by the encircling enemy armies. Most of the military personnel had been pulled out, and the city was aflame from enemy gunfire. Despite imminent danger of artillery and air attack, and while her escape route became more precarious by the hour, the MEREDITH VICTORY set her course through enemy minefields, and although having little food and water, and neither doctor nor interpreter, accomplished the three day voyage to safety at Pusan with her human cargo, including several babies born enroute, without loss of a single life.

The courage, resourcefulness, sound seamanship, and teamwork of her master, officers and crew in successfully completing one of the greatest marine rescues in the history of the world have caused the name of the MEREDITH VICTORY to be perpetuated as that of a Gallant Ship.

Phil Lacovara was not the first such researcher the Museum has welcomed. A number of other people with *Meredith Victory* connections have visited the Museum, which is on the grounds of the U.S. Merchant Marine Academy (USMMA) in Kings Point, New York. Foremost among these is Rear Admiral J. Robert Lunney, USNR (ret.), who was an officer on board that victory ship on Christmas Day of 1950 when it saved thousands of Koreans from certain death at the hands of Communists. Other research requests included one from Dr. Kyungsoon Lee of The National Museum of Korean Contemporary History who organized an exhibit on the Hungnam evacuation on its sixty-fifth anniversary in December 2015. Finally, Phil Lacovara came to the Museum to do research, and has produced this lively and well-researched volume about the mariner behind the Hungnam rescue.

The *Meredith Victory* story has long fascinated me. Some of my interest is personal: my late father-in-law was himself a refugee from Communist oppression in what became known as the Democratic People's Republic of Korea (DPRK). My interest is also intellectual, in that I am a maritime historian who studies the complicated past of the American merchant marine. It has long confounded me that the humanitarian aspects of maritime endeavor have been largely ignored. In my mind, the Hungnam evacuation fits into a pattern of American-flagged ships, manned by civilian crews, transporting oppressed or endangered peoples to safety. In the aftermath of World War II, this could be transporting U.N. relief cargoes to starving populations around the world, or carrying Displaced Persons to a new life in the United States or overseas. Often these evacuations carried vulnerable populations away from a Communist threat during the Cold War, as with the

Meredith Victory. Other examples include Operation Passage to Freedom in 1954, when American ships transported Vietnamese from North Vietnam; or in 1956, when the United States welcomed thousands fleeing the Soviet forces suppressing the Hungarian Uprising; and then Vietnam again in the mid-and late-1970s.

Even when U.S.-flagged ships were not involved, courageous American merchant mariners stepped forward to assist the oppressed. Among these was a young William Bernstein, a Kings Point graduate who volunteered to navigate a refugee ship to Palestine. Loaded with thousands of European Jews, Bernstein and the *Exodus 1947*'s passengers and crew resisted British Royal Navy's attempts to stop them. Tragically, Bernstein lost his life fighting the British boarding party. There were four USMMA graduates on board the *Meredith Victory* at Hungnam: Chief Mate Dino Savastio, class of 1943; Third Officer Alvar Franzon, class of 1944; Junior Third Officer H.J.B. "Burley" Smith, just graduated in the class of 1950; and Third Assistant Engineer Merl Smith, class of 1944. If you haven't heard of them, it may be because they were living the Academy's motto, *Acta Non Verba*, which translates as "Deeds, Not Words."

A merchant fleet can be a force for good in this parlous world, and mariners can take noble actions to save others, even when it risks their lives. American-flagged ships, such as those of Military Sealift Command with their civilian crews, continue to operate relief missions in the aftermath of disasters such as an earthquake in Haiti. Sometimes these relief missions occur closer at home, such as after Hurricane Katrina ravaged New Orleans or even the recent COVID crisis of 2020. The federal government is well aware of this benevolent aspect of sea power. One manifestation of that awareness is a new generation of training vessels that will train future merchant marine officers and serve as humanitarian relief platforms during emergencies. The National Security Multi-Mission Vessels (NSMV) promise to transform maritime training. Furthermore, as the Maritime Administration states, they will support the federal response to national disasters and "will have state-of-the-art hospital facilities, a helicopter landing pad and the ability to berth up to 1,000 people in times of humanitarian need. Alongside its humanitarian capacities, the NSMV has a roll-on/roll-off ramp and container storage allowing it to provide aid to damaged ports." I hope the government finds it appropriate to name one of these vessels after Leonard LaRue, as an inspiration to future merchant mariners.

In *The Mariner and the Monk*, Phil Lacovara examines the moral dimensions of a seafarer. Captain Leonard La Rue defies the merchant mariner stereotypes. Here was a serious, sober, and moral seafarer, a man who did not hesitate to do the right thing, even if it put himself in danger. There is no question that his Roman Catholic faith acted as his moral compass at Hungnam, and that his deep religiosity informed virtually everything he did, eventually leading to his joining a monastic order. In an age where many see religion as a canard, Lacovara provides a powerful example of how it is a force for good in this world, and thus the Church is pursuing the canonization of this former mariner.

Joshua M. Smith
Director, American Merchant Marine Museum
US Merchant Marine Academy
Kings Point, NY

PREFACE

How do you write about a man who never wanted to talk about himself? About a man who had no girlfriend, wife or children, and who only saw members of his family at most once or twice a year? About a man who less than halfway through his eighty-seven years left the world after sailing all of its seas and entered a monastery's walls? But how can you not write about a man whose decency and sense of duty inspired all around him to retell, for almost three quarter of a century, an extraordinary experience they had shared with him all those years before? And how can you not write about an event that saved the lives of more than fourteen thousand men, women and children, and meant that many tens of thousands more would live, and live in freedom?

I first learned of Leonard Panet La Rue through a few paragraphs written in the "Comment and Discussion" section of the February 2019 issue of US Naval Institute *Proceedings*. There, Rear Admiral J. Robert (Bob) Lunney, USNR (Ret.), wrote about an article appearing in *Proceedings* the previous December, "A Christmas Eve Mass for the Living." Bob wrote,

"This moving article by Mr. Fuss brought back memories of the
Hungnam evacuation during the Korean War when our ship, the SS
Meredith Victory, one of the last ships in the harbor, rescued many
North Korean refugees. Under the courageous command of our
captain, Leonard P. LaRue (a veteran of the World War II Murmansk
Run), on 22 December 1950 we commenced embarking North Korean
refugees fleeing from the Chinese communist forces. The constant
naval and gunfire support from Seventh Fleet ... enabled us to embark
more than 14,000 refugees."

Bob concluded, "At the end of the war, Captain LaRue left the sea and
joined the Benedictine Order as a monk, taking the name Brother
Marinus, OSB. Recently the Apostleship of the Sea has taken steps to
have Brother Marinus canonized."

The string of actions—Murmansk, evacuating 14,000 refugees, holy
orders, possible canonization—piqued my curiosity about a man and
event I had never before encountered. Through the magic of the inter-
net, I found Bob Lunney's email address and reached out to him,
inquiring about some of the details. Bob promptly replied. From our
email conversations spanning half a year, and a half-day in-person
interview with Bob and his gracious wife, Joan, in September 2019, I
decided that there really was value to retelling this story.

Leonard La Rue's story crosses many of the mid twentieth-century
touchstones of the sea services. La Rue served in World War II with
Merchant Marine convoys across the Atlantic, including the perilous
"Murmansk Run," and then throughout the Pacific. After the war, his
ships served the booming Latin American trade. After five years of
peacetime service, he again skippered ships in and out of a war zone,
facing mines and in some cases, air attacks, just as he had a half-
decade before. His ship, the SS *Meredith Victory*, supported the
successful United Nations landing at Inchon. The pinnacle of that
service was his involvement in the "Hungnam evacuation," the redeployment of US Army, Marine and Republic of Korea forces following
the historic fight at the Chosin Reservoir, which was accompanied by

the evacuation of tens of thousands of Korean civilians. La Rue served at sea for twenty years across all of these events, yet, little had been published on the man's experiences besides newspaper articles and a somewhat hagiographic book that largely repeated the same anecdotes. There is a lot more to the man's story.

La Rue was respected as a professional and honored as a hero. And yet, midway through his very successful career, he left the sea and chose a different path. Instead of a life where nearly every day brought a different horizon, he spent the greater half of his life among a small community of cloistered monks, living a simple life in a simple world that extended not thousands of miles, but hundreds of feet. By all indications he was supremely happy with his choice, never pining for the good old days at sea and new things not yet experienced. His was a life defined by supreme self-awareness. He knew what, ultimately, was important to him, and what he needed to do, and so he acted. And the experience of his life, both on the sea and at the monastery, so inspired others who learned of his story that in 2019 the Roman Catholic Diocese of Patterson, New Jersey, initiated a "Cause for Sainthood" for "Servant of God Brother Marinus La Rue."

Perhaps that is what is so compelling about Leonard La Rue's story: his life was truly lived according to his sense of duty. When Tom Brokaw popularized the term "Greatest Generation" in 2001 with the eponymous book, we all knew what he meant. These were our friends, our parents, our aunts and uncles; in my case, my grandparents. They came of age under crushing poverty, but they knew their minds, and when the time came to fight fascism, they answered the call by the millions. They sailed our ships, flew our planes, fought in our battles, worked in our factories. Each—by their own service, by how they lived their lives and, in so many cases, died their deaths—created the world we prospered in for the next seventy-five years. Some contributed with grand accomplishments, others with small, but the common thread was a sense of duty, the conviction of each man and woman that they had a duty to perform.

So much has been written about these men and women that "Greatest Generation" has become a cliché, but as these men and women are passing into history, our responsibilities are two-fold. First, we must remember and retell the works of these men and women so they are not forgotten by our children and grandchildren like moments lost in the flood of time. And we must see in our own soldiers, sailors, airmen, and Marines the same sense of duty for the challenges of our present age. And we do.

The opportunity to interview participants in World War I has long since passed. The opportunity has almost passed for World War II. As I write this, my grandfather, a veteran of the Battle of the Java Sea and other clashes of the first few years of our Navy's war in the Pacific, has almost completed his hundred and first year. The veterans of the Korean War are themselves perishable. My new friends who were young men serving on the SS *Meredith Victory* in Korea are well into their nineties, and in a few years they and their fellow merchant mariners, soldiers, sailors, airmen and marines will also have passed to their reward. Our history would be a little less rich if we did not tell the stories of these men and their times with as much fullness as they deserve.

I am not a professional writer. I have written some fiction, and a lot of business and technical documents over the years, but writing history is at once more difficult but immensely more rewarding. The opportunity to research, capture, and convey information in a way that will enlighten the reader is common to any non-fiction writing; however, history and biography require a unique marriage of content and context. The author starting a project like this hopes that there will be a dusty library shelf or a rusty filing cabinet that will hold all of the answers to the questions of "who, what, where, when, how and why" that he or she seeks to answer. Unfortunately, that almost never happens. Researching this book has required a journey to many people and places that have answered many questions but have left a few still a mystery.

Very few of La Rue's letters remain. We can find no diary or journal that he left behind besides entries in ship's logbooks. He gave a few interviews and spoke in public several times. Fortunately, I have found enough information that I believe I have been able to flesh out more about La Rue the man, and to place his actions in an historical context that reflects his concept of duty and his efforts to fulfill that duty. We see a poor, depression-era youth make the most of his education at the Pennsylvania Nautical School. We sail with him through drifting mines, lurking submarines, and attacking aircraft and ships. We live through mutinying sailors and life-threatening storms. We see the personal contacts that started his life down a new path. But before that new path, we experience perhaps the most dramatic rescue of refugees in the twentieth century, and the ongoing reaction of his shipmates and his fellow citizens to that remarkable accomplishment. Even decades later, the *Guinness Book of World Records* credited the *Meredith Victory* with the record for the "Largest evacuation from land by a single ship."

As we follow La Rue's life, the ships themselves become characters in telling his story, sometimes with their own history and quirks. La Rue's Merchant Marine career followed the zenith of the United States Merchant Marine, and he sailed on ships built at United States government expense between 1920 and 1945. I have tried to provide context for the ships as well, since there would be little story without them.

The reader will find this book divided into three parts. The first part, *Mariner*, tells the story of La Rue's early life in Philadelphia and his two years at the Pennsylvania Nautical School. The story then follows his Merchant Marine career during World War II, including his perilous journey above the Arctic Circle to Murmansk in 1942, as well as a wartime circumnavigation or two. The first part concludes with his peacetime journeys to the Caribbean and South America, right up to the start of the Korean War in 1950.

The second part, *Rescue at Hungnam,* sets the context for the Korean War and tells the story of the *Meredith Victory's* participation in the landing at Inchon. It then tells the story of the X Corps' landings on the east coast of Korea and the subsequent push north and west to the Chosin (Jangjin) Reservoir. The famed battle there that followed motivated the redeployment of X Corps out of Hungnam. As the name of this part suggests, many pages are devoted to detailing the massive and effective effort to evacuate 100,000 soldiers and Marines and an equal number of civilians while under constant attack from Chines and North Korean forces. This is the hinge of La Rue's story, and the *Meredith Victory* and her crew figure prominently, but not exclusively. The chapter on Hungnam provides, I believe, the most comprehensive public description of what was called at the time, "the most perfect withdrawal in history." Since the description of military operations is rife with potentially distracting acronyms, etc., the reader who desires additional detail will find it in the endnotes for these chapters. The reader will also find a glossary of abbreviations that may prove helpful.

The third part, *Monk,* tells the story of La Rue's religious vocation, of further honors for the ship and crew, and of tributes to La Rue that continued after his death. Some of those honors and tributes came from the US and Korean governments, including honors sixty years apart from presidents of the Republic of Korea. The narrative concludes with the current activities around a cause for La Rue's sainthood.

A few notes about transliterations of Korean names and words. The author is, unfortunately, not a speaker of the Korean language and must rely on what have been, at times, historical but awkward attempts to translate Korean sounds into pronounceable English words. Many of the place names in the book, such as "Chosin," actually resulted from Japanese transliterations of Korean names into English. I have chosen to use the contemporaneous (1950) English transliterations for historical accuracy, juxtaposing the currently accepted transliteration where I can; for example, Chosin (Jangjin). My apologies to any Korean speakers if this usage is at all jarring.

Finally, one note about the spelling of our subject's name. La Rue's last name was often rendered "LaRue" or "Larue." I have used "La Rue" because that is how he wrote it.

INTRODUCTION

An hour south of Washington, DC, the Potomac River has grown to a lazy, tidal estuary before emptying into the big bay to the east, the Chesapeake. The lands on both sides of the river, which divides Maryland from Virginia, were settled by Scots-Irish immigrants in the seventeenth and eighteenth centuries. By the nineteenth century, the shores were littered with tobacco plantations. In 1917, long after the economics of Southern planting had been altered forever, the US Marine Corps purchased 55,000 forested acres along the river on the Virginia side at Quantico Station and established Marine Barracks Quantico. The site was rural enough for live-fire training, but close enough to the Marine Corps Headquarters thirty-five miles to the north that the commandant and his staff could travel there for the day. As a result, thousands of Marines were trained at Quantico, and the Corps established schools and exploratory commands that developed, among others, amphibious warfare doctrine that was successfully used in the Second World and Korean wars, and the ship-to-shore doctrine for the use of helicopters in the Korean and Vietnam wars.

Today, as the home of the Marine Corps Combat Development Command and the Marine Corps Museum, the only place closer to the heart of the Corps is the old Washington Barracks at Eighth and I Street, SE. Even so, Quantico rarely receives a high-profile, international visitor. Hence, when the newly elected president of an important US ally came there to give a speech before he had even met with the president of the United States; indeed, making it his first stop in the D.C. area, it was big news. The president's aircraft, brightly adorned with his country's red, white and blue flag, would land at Joint Base Andrews to an official welcome. But the president would bypass the halls of power in the District of Columbia and instead cross the Potomac just below the city, not stopping until he arrived at Quantico.

Quantico can be oppressively hot in late June, so when the morning of June 28, 2017, dawned clear and in the low sixties, the organizers of the event smiled. Streets were cleaned and sidewalks swept beyond their usual Marine standard. White folding chairs were arranged in neat rows under the shade of the trees surrounding the location where the president would speak. In front of them was a tall octagon of bronze and black. Carved text on the granite sides and reliefs cast in the bronze told the story of one of the proudest battles in US Marine Corps history.

The newly elected president arrived and was escorted by the Commandant of the Marine Corps, General Robert Neller. The president was, in some ways, an unlikely honored guest. While he had served in his country's military, he had also come to political prominence as a lawyer promoting civil and human rights, with clients spanning the left-leaning elements of his country, including student protesters and union activists. He was also an outspoken advocate for rapprochement with the long-separated, communist half of his nation. He had only run for election to public office for the first time five years before, winning a seat in his country's national assembly. He had won his country's presidency in a landslide just six weeks before he boarded the plane for the United States.

Moon Jae-In, president of the Republic of Korea, rose from his seat in the front row and strode to the podium. Bespectacled and neatly attired in a conservative blue suit and tie, the president began his speech. After thanking the assembled guests, including a few generals and the relatives of men long-ago passed, he turned to the substance of his talk.

"I am filled with special emotion to see you in front of the monument to the Jangjin Reservoir Battle. At last, I am here where I have so dearly wanted to come. It is all the more meaningful for me to start off the first day of my first overseas trip as president of the Republic of Korea here today."

"In 1950, sixty-seven years ago, the US Marines suffered noble sacrifices to defend 'a country they never knew and a people they never met.' The most heroic battle fought by them during the Korean War was the Battle of Jangjin Reservoir. Thanks to the remarkable fighting spirit of those heroes ... the operation to evacuate some 100,000 refugees from Hungnam could be successful ..."

"My parents were also among the refugees aboard the SS *Meredith Victory* at that time.

"The late Captain Leonard La Rue, who was ordered by General Almond to rescue refugees, jettisoned weapons and supplies on the ship to board as many refugees as possible. Loaded with a whopping 14,000 refugees, the ship set sail to freedom and human rights navigating a sea of death teeming with naval mines. The voyage was a perfect success without a single death.

"During the voyage that started on December 23, 1950, from the Port of Hungnam and ended on December 25 when the ship arrived on the Island of Geoje in the sea down south, five babies were born. It was a Christmas miracle! It was the greatest humanitarian operation in history.

"Two years later, I was born on Geoje Island where the SS *Meredith Victory* disembarked the refugees. Had it not been for the valiant warriors of the Jangjin Reservoir Battle and the success of the Hungnam evacuation, my life would not have started. I would not even exist today.

"So, how can I fully express my gratitude for your sacrifice and devotion with any words in any language in this world? Words like respect and gratitude just seem far from enough.

"The story goes beyond my personal and family histories. I am also deeply touched by the love for humanity the US service members showed when they evacuated not just their comrades but also so many refugees from the North at such an urgent moment ...

"My mother once said that US sailors handed out a piece of candy to each refugee as a Christmas gift on Christmas Eve while still sailing southward ...

"The ROK-US alliance was forged with blood in the fire of war like this. It is not an alliance forged simply by signing several papers ...

"Honorable warriors of the Battle of Jangjin Reservoir and their descendants, the journey of the SS *Meredith Victory* towards freedom and human rights sixty-seven years ago must continue hereinafter ..."

President Moon continued for a few more paragraphs, speaking of his anxiousness to work with President Trump to "bring about the dismantlement of North Korea's nuclear program, peace on the Korean Peninsula and, moreover, peace in Northeast Asia," and his desire for Korean unification. Speaking just a few days after the sixty-seventh anniversary of the beginning of the Korean War and with a few of the men who had served in that conflict in attendance, it was clearly an emotional time for all present, not the least for President Moon.

After his speech, the president solemnly presented a wreath of red and blue roses shaped in the "yin-yang" symbol of the Republic of Korea.

The wreath's white silk ribbons reaching almost to the ground read, in English and Korean, "President of the Republic of Korea" on one side and "Alliance forged by the noble sacrifice" on the other. The president also ceremonially planted a "Winter King" hawthorn tree near the memorial as a sign of the flourishing of the ROK-US relationship.

The Republic of Korea's official recognition of Leonard La Rue continued the next year, this time at the location where La Rue spent the second half of his life under a different name and with different duties. On June 1, 2018, the Ambassador of the Republic of Korea to the United States, Cho Yoon-je, dedicated a memorial in front of the chapel at St. Paul's Abbey in Newton, New Jersey. The polished black granite reads in Korean and English, "With respect and gratitude for Brother Marinus who, in the winter of 1950, Korea, led the voyage of miracle." The inscription is signed, "President of the Republic of Korea, Moon Jae-In, June 1, 2018." Later thrust into the ground along-side side the monument were the flag of the Republic of Korea and a less familiar flag, one also with a white background but featuring the Korean peninsula, undivided, in pale blue, the flag of Korean Reunification.

Almost a year after President Moon's visit to Quantico, another speech highlighted Captain La Rue and the events of that Christmas. On June 16, 2018, the US Secretary of Defense, retired US Marine General James J. Mattis, delivered the commencement address at the United States Merchant Marine Academy in Kings Point, New York. General Mattis remarked about the importance of the US Merchant Marine and the need for US-flagged ships. He re-told the fearless accomplishments of merchant mariners during World War II, using his own father, a 1935 graduate of the Pennsylvania Nautical School, as an exemplar.

Towards the end of his speech, General Mattis turned to the subject of ethics.

"We need leaders with a strong sense of ethics today. You need to be a source of strength for your subordinates and you need to be a lifelong learner so you're as strong when destiny does tap you on the shoulder to lead your crew or team through the rocks and shoals of life as you are here today at this point in your life.

"Leonard La Rue had that strength. He also attended the Pennsylvania Nautical School in the 1930s, and like my father he did his sea year aboard the USS *Annapolis*. But he is remembered not for his physical courage in World War II, which he had an abundance of, but for his moral courage in Korea as captain of the SS *Meredith Victory* where he proved to not only be a mariner in the finest tradition of your service, but also a great American listening to his better angels. In the frigid December of 1950, the United Nations command would go back to Huang Nam [*sic*] in what is today North Korea. Enemy soldiers bored down upon a city in flames, the harbor was mined and thousands of refugees swarmed the beaches desperate to escape the climate as they bored down.

"Captain LaRue ordered his SS *Meredith Victory* into shore amidst a storm of war, and he and his crew rescued 14,000 refugees and bore them away safely on a ship. Before they could put in at safe anchorage, five babies were born of his crew and (of) over 14,000 refugees, not a single life was lost. Now there was a leader not concerned with putting it all on the line. He was competent; he was aware of danger and stoically he dealt with it.

"Remember him and don't allow his example to be lost on the compost heap of events."

In General Mattis' colorful words, the tale you are about to read is intended to rescue the story of Leonard P. La Rue, his life and times, from "the compost heap of events."

PART I

MARINER

1

PHILADELPHIA

T he mariner who would circumnavigate the globe lived his first eighteen years within a few square miles of working-class Philadelphia. In the second decade of the twentieth century, the Philadelphia metropolitan area was the second most populous in the nation, behind only its giant neighbor to the north, and the city proper was behind only New York and Chicago in number of inhabitants. The city bustled as a manufacturing and transportation hub, dubbing itself, "The World's Greatest Workshop," and its population grew over the decade as immigrants flooded the city to work in its industries, ranging from tiny bakeries to the nearly 10,000-man Baldwin Locomotive Works in Eddystone.

Leonard Panet La Rue was born on a frigid January 14, 1914, the youngest child of Paul and Isabelle La Rue. Paul Philippe La Rue had been born on January 17, 1875, in Quebec, Canada, and entered the United States through Boston on September 9, 1900.[1] Less than a month later, Paul stood before a district court judge in Boston to swear his intention to "become a citizen of the United States and to renounce forever all allegiance and fidelity to every foreign Prince, State, Potentate and Sovereignty whatsoever, more especially to Victoria, Queen of the United Kingdom of Great Britain and Ireland, whose subject he has heretofore been." On the same day, October 2, 1900, Paul enlisted in the US Army.[2] The enlistment record lists his occupation as "student," and it describes him as five-feet-seven-inches tall, with blue eyes, light brown hair and a ruddy complexion. He was discharged on October 1, 1903, on completion of his service.

On a page where many of his fellow soldiers' service was rated as "excellent," Paul's was described only as "very good," but he must have had other things on his mind because a little over six month later, on April 20, 1904, Paul married Isabelle Catherine O'Brien in St. Joachim's Church in Philadelphia. Isabelle had been born in the town of Port Monmouth, New Jersey, on April 6, 1877, the youngest child of Michael J. O'Brien and Catherine Leonard O'Brien. Michael died sometime before 1900, since the census of that year shows Catherine as the head of the household with her son, Francis, a "Grocery Clerk," and her daughter, Isabelle, the only other residents. Isabelle's older sister, Alice, had married by that time. The census notes that Isabelle could "read, write, and speak English."

With Isabelle by his side and citing his service in the 55th Company of the Massachusetts Coast Artillery, Paul became a US citizen on May 29, 1905.[3] Their address was given as 5028 James Street, Philadelphia, a short walk from the Frankford Arsenal where Paul worked as a machinist and instrument maker, and a half mile from the busy Delaware River. War Department records show that Paul was paid a wage of two dollars per day that year, typical for a time when the average worker earned $0.22 per hour. They would live in that tiny, twelve-foot wide, two-bedroom home for decades with their son Maurice, born in 1905, twin daughters Irma and Isabelle, born in 1907, Paul in 1908, and finally, Leonard, born in 1914. Paul's draft registration of September 12, 1918, describes La Rue's father as a man of moderate height and slim build with blue eyes and light hair, much like later descriptions of his son.

By 1930, even though Maurice and Irma had moved out, the house on James Street was still bursting at the seams. Maurice was living with his wife, Jesse, and their two-year-old son, Eugene, at Jesse's parents' home on Edgemont Street, half a mile to the south. Irma was now living with her new husband, Frank Lambert, in an apartment on Harrison Street, half a mile to the north. Still, Leonard shared the thousand-square-foot house with his parents, brother Paul, sister Isabelle, and Isabelle's new husband, John Hanigan. Perhaps the only time Leonard had to himself was the mile he walked each day to and from Frankford High School.

Docks of Port Richmond on the Delaware River, Philadelphia, PA circa 1925.

For all of its charms, today's Philadelphia does not present itself as a booming seaport. But for centuries before its mid-twentieth-century decline, Philadelphia was one of the busiest ports on the east coast of the United States. *The Philadelphia Inquirer* ran a regular column in the first section of the paper entitled "News of the Ships and Shipping Men." The Philadelphia Department of Wharves, Docks and Ferries advertised, "The Port of Philadelphia Guarantees Satisfaction to Shippers. Philadelphia has: New and Modern Piers; A Broad Policy of

Extension and Improvement; and Direct Connections with Three Great Trunk Railroads which cover all destinations in the United States." The advertisement closed with the familiar maxim, "Philadelphia is the Industrial Workshop of the World." On a typical day, two dozen ships might arrive, sailing from places like Port Arthur, Texas; Norfolk, Virginia; or St. Nazaire, France.

La Rue said later in life[4] that he had, "a powerful 'travel bug' that bit him as a teenager when he heard tales of far-away places" and he always had an interest in travel. For a young man from a working-class family, there were few opportunities to travel internationally besides joining the Navy or the Merchant Marine, so during the second week of May 1932 La Rue joined more than two hundred other young men at the Bourse Building near Independence Hall to take the entrance examination for the Pennsylvania State Nautical School. A school brochure from the time states the qualifications for admission included,

"Only young men of good character, between the ages of 17 and 20 years, residents of the State of Pennsylvania, who are physically and temperamentally fit for a life at sea, and who will appreciate and avail themselves of the instruction given, and submit to disciplinary control as is requisite for their welfare under conditions incident to the life, are acceptable as cadets in this school."

Twenty cadets were typically selected from the applicants taking the tests in May and October, and Leonard P. La Rue joined the class matriculating that May, starting classes immediately after the results of the examination were announced.

The Nautical School was located aboard the USS *Annapolis*, a 1,172-ton gunboat commissioned by the Navy in 1897 that had served in the Spanish-American and Philippine wars. After *Annapolis* was decommissioned in 1919, the Navy loaned her to the school as a floating classroom, dormitory, and working training ship. The ship was moored in the Philadelphia Navy at the south end of Broad Street most of the year, but twice a year she sailed and steamed with the students for months-long cruises to New England, the Caribbean, or Europe. The school's brochure from the time says, "The Schoolship 'ANNAPOLIS' is training young men for responsible positions in the American Merchant Service-teaching them the secrets of mastering the sea." Under "Course of Study and Instruction," it reads,

> "students are instructed in dead reckoning; the method of finding latitude and longitude by the sun, moon, planets and stars; the duties of an officer; theoretical and practical marine engineering; receive practice in a vessel under both sail and steam-in steering, heaving the lead and in handling boats under both oars and sail."

Thanks to an appropriation by the Pennsylvania state government, the Nautical School provided room and board in addition to instruction to the cadets enrolled. The only cost to La Rue's class was an initial fee of $100 at the beginning of the first year, and a $30 fee at the beginning of the second. While this was a considerable amount for a family living on a machinist's wages, the La Rue family was fortunate in one respect; later in 1932, as the Great Depression began to bite, the state legislature cut the Nautical School's appropriation from $100,000 per year to $75,000. Members of the next class would need to pay $125 to attend.

USS Annapolis, *known as "Annie" by the cadets of the Philadelphia Nautical School.*

The Nautical School sought to train cadets coming from a range of socio-economic situations in the near-military discipline expected of an officer in the Merchant Marine. Cadets were expected to dress neatly in their prescribed uniforms as the situation required: blue double-breasted dress wool uniforms worn with a hard-brimmed officer's cap with a white cover, white sailor-style trousers and jumpers worn with a sailor's "dixie-cup" cap, or dungarees and undershirt. They were to wear their hair neatly trimmed, maintain a clean shave and use tobacco in moderation. They were taught to salute the flag and their superiors and to respect and implement a chain of command starting with the superintendent of the Nautical School, through the executive officer to the second-year cadets and below.

Nautical School cadets pose in front of the Annapolis, *1934.*

La Rue and his cadet colleagues attended their two years of school year-round. Classroom and practical instruction took place on the ship, which provided both sails and steam to prepare the graduates for any eventuality, although by the 1930s the chance that a young mariner would serve professionally on a sailing ship were already negligible.

The cadet's daily routine on the ship helped prepare them for the rhythm of a life at sea. Weekdays the routine was largely the same whether in port or on a cruise. "Call all hands," was bugled at six in the morning, with the cadets lashing their hammocks to stow them out of the way, and the mess serving coffee by six fifteen. By six thirty the cadets were already engaged in cleaning their quarters. At seven fifteen they had time to wash up and enter formation to march to breakfast at seven thirty. The colors were raised at eight with attendant honors, and by nine the cadets were engaged in fifteen minutes of physical drill before classes began. Morning classes were complete by eleven thirty, and at noon the cadets entered formation and marched to dinner. Classes resumed at one fifteen in the afternoon and continued until three thirty. At five twenty. they again entered formation and marched to supper. Six thirty to seven thirty were designated as, "Evening study period," but at seven thirty the cadets were allowed time for recreation and to attend to personal needs. Taps was sounded at nine p.m., and the lights went out until six the next morning.

No classes or drills were held on weekends. Saturday afternoon and all-day Sunday were time off, so he would be able to spend that time with his family, attending Sunday mass at St. Bartholomew's Church, about a mile and a half from the family home on James Street. Leave and liberty were granted based on "a cadet's record of good conduct and application."

The performance of each cadet was reported on a monthly report card that rated the cadet on such attributes and subjects of study as: Adaptability and Professional Fitness, Hygiene, Naval Architecture, Practical Seamanship, Rules of the Road, Storage of Cargo, and Third Mate's Questions. The last item was intended to prepare the cadets for the Coast Guard's licensing examination they would take when they graduated. The card also included the cadet's class rank and the number of demerits earned. The minimum passing score in any subject was seventy out of a perfect score of one hundred; the Regulations of the Nautical School stated, "a cadet failing to attain this mark shall be deemed deficient in any of the subjects covered." Along with the facts that all grades were posted on a public bulletin board and sent to their parents or guardians, this ensured that the cadets took their studies seriously.

Demerits could be issued for offenses ranging from whistling or wearing clothing unbuttoned, to assault or "scandalous conduct." A locker with its contents not stowed properly might cost one demerit, a cap worn improperly two, but going swimming without permission would rate twenty-five and an unauthorized absence from the ship, fifty. A total of 250 demerits for a first-year cadet or a total of 200 for a second-year would result in a cadet being, "declared deficient in conduct by the Board of Instruction." The demerits were used, "solely as a record of misconduct." Punishment was separate, and could result in, "confinement, extra duty or drill, deprivation of leave or liberty," and in extreme cases, expulsion from the school.

There was no summer vacation at the Nautical School; rather, the cadets had an extended leave after returning from one of their biannual cruises. These cruises were the highlights of the school year, an opportunity for the cadets to develop their seamanship through hands-on operation of the ship and her systems. The cadets also got the chance to see places they perhaps had read about, almost certainly had never visited, but might likely visit later as professional mariners. In the case of La Rue and his classmates who entered the school in May 1932, their first cruise took them up the east coast of the United States for nine weeks from August to October. The Helm, the Nautical School's yearbook, described the cruise as starting such that "a week of serpentine courses left us a few hundred miles from our destination," but due to a cadet's attack of appendicitis, "we traversed this last leg in jig time. The very beams and planks seemed animated as the ancient engine sent us at full speed up the Thames to land the stricken Cadet at New London."

New London, their, "first liberty in a 'foreign' port," did not impress them much, but the subsequent visit to Provincetown on Cape Cod was more noteworthy,

> "The fair sex of the town were invited to spend an evening tripping the light fantastic upon our gleaming topsides. Though the savage strains produced by the trip engaged for the evening are yet painful to recall, it seemed of no consequence, what with so many damsels quite curious about the more secluded sections of the ship."

They next took in the sights at Gloucester before spending two weeks in Boston. The *Annapolis* docked at the Charlestown Navy Yard next to Admiral Richard E. Byrds's SS *Bear*, which the admiral had just purchased for use in his second expedition to Antarctica, due to take place in 1934.

The *Annapolis* and her cadets sailed for the Caribbean in February, 1933. The ship arrived in St. Thomas, US Virgin Islands, where the cadets enjoyed sightseeing and horseback riding and commented on the beauty of the island. After their stay in St. Thomas they made a short run to Martinique. The Mount Pelee volcano towering over the town of Fort-de-France impressed them, but overall the island struck them as, "the most unsanitary, dirty and uninteresting island of the cruise."

Trinidad impressed them much more, with its sugar cane, cacao, and coffee plantations, and the cosmopolitan city of Port-of-Spain. They rode horses to see the Governor's Mansion and the surrounding gardens, and perhaps La Rue had his first exposure to the Benedictine religious order when he visited the Mount Saint Benedict Monastery, about six miles east of Port-of-Spain, foreshadowing a change in his life twenty years hence. The cadets completed their time in Trinidad by sailing the *Annapolis* down the Gulf of Paria on the western coast to see the Pitch Lake at La Brea, an important resource then being harvested for the heavy petroleum asphalt used for paving. La Rue would visit Trinidad again many time in the years to come as his ships refueled there.

Annapolis *at anchor during a winter Caribbean cruise.*

The *Annapolis* continued south to Willemstadt, Curacao. The cadets' seamanship skills were challenged by the crowded harbor, which required the ship to be moored with anchors bow and stern. They were dazzled by the shopping, even then a duty-free port, and they purchased gifts for their families back home. Turning north, their final stop was at the Naval Station at Guantanamo Bay, Cuba, where they swam and fished, catching barracuda and butterfish. The visit was marred only by a near fatal injury to one of the cadets that required him to be left behind at the Naval Station for medical treatment.

We have no letters from La Rue during these cruises, but other letters provide some color for these cruises. A cadet who had graduated a few years earlier wrote to his mother of his experiences on a similar cruise aboard the *Annapolis*.[5] From Bridgetown, Barbados, he wrote:

"We pulled in here after three of the roughest days sailing I've ever put in. Most of the boots got sick all over again. Any dump would seem nice after the trip from Culebra and this town is real nice which makes it double.

"The limeys who run this town are pretty high hat, but there have been several dances for us and this P.M. there was a swimming and tennis party invited out to Lady Something or other's estate.

"There is practically no harbor here at all, and this old packet rolls at anchor like a decent ship would in a hurricane. There are a good many ships pull in however with tourists and the bumboats are pretty thick. They have some stuffed ignanus [*sic*] and other junk. They peddle flying fish which are very good. No fooling, they really are. They have fins which open out like chicken's wings and extend over half the length of the fish.

"I have been standing throttle watch since St. Thomas and Bill Armstrong has broken a rule on the schoolship by allowing cadets to handle the control entering and leaving ports. It isn't really a rule but they never did it before. It's exciting though. You get nervous as the deuce but it's fun.

"This has been a pretty tough cruise so far but I guess things will break better soon."

For the next several months, the cadets studied back pier-side in the Navy Yard, but on July 6 the *Annapolis* steamed into the Delaware River to begin a journey across the Atlantic. The seas were calm, and after thirteen days the cadets could see Mount Pico on Ilha do Pico in the Azores. As they passed on their way to the port in Ponta Delgada, Ilha do Sao Miguel, a day hence, they spied an unusual mass floating in the ocean that the captain and the other old salts believed was ambergris, a near-mythical substance produced in the digestive tracts of sperm whales and highly valued by perfumers for its ability to stabilize scents. The cadets struggled to bring the malodorous substance aboard, the officers and cadets convinced they would become rich selling their prize. On arriving in Ponta, they were disappointed to learn that the material was simply refuse from the whaling station on Pico, the island they had just passed.

The cadets enjoyed their four-day liberty in the colorful town, even though they did not find much to do. Ponta was a fishing town, not set up to entertain tourists, so no hearts were broken when they left for the four-day journey to Gibraltar. There, only the officers and the first-class cadets took liberty, the second-class cadets assigned to take on coal for the ship's boilers. Apparently, there was more to entertain the cadets than in Ponta. On an earlier stay in Gibraltar, the cadet wrote, "there was no liberty Sunday except for church parties. Two men were in the brig and received 100 demerits for drunkenness. About ten got demerits for the same charge." The next day they began the four-day journey to Marseilles, punctuated by typically rough seas as they rounded "The Pillars of Hercules" and entered the Mediterranean. The earlier cadet wrote, "The Mediterranean is way different from the ocean. The water is blue and there are plenty of white caps no matter how smooth the water is."

Marseilles was their first real taste of Europe, and a month after leaving home they received their first batch of mail. On August 5 the seas were flat as they slowly steamed past the Chateau d'If and moored at the center of the city at the Quai des Belges. There the cadets sat in sidewalk cafes people-watching and drinking champagne (in moderation, no doubt). The earlier cadet had written,

"The chow was good in the city and was fairly cheap, altho' [sic] most every thing else was just about standard price, what you'd pay in the U.S.A. No kidding, this French is fairly easy to talk and it not very hard to order a meal. Trying to parlay what the waiter says to you, however, is a different matter. We went into a place something like Whitmans [referring to the iconic Philadelphia confectioner] for some ice cream (we eat three or four dishes every day) and I called out to the waitress 'quatre glaces' and I guess she thought I spoke the lingo and she runs off a string as long as my arm and then laughed like the deuce when she saw that was about all I knew. We did get our ice cream though."

The cadets endured the Mediterranean summer heat for their three-day steam to steamy Naples. Anchored under the shadow of Mount Vesuvius, the cadets found their week in Italy the most interesting part of the voyage. Their three-day trip to Rome was perhaps the highlight of the cruise. At dawn the cadets boarded a second-class train car and watched as they crossed fields and pastures and passed through mountain tunnels on their way to the "Eternal City." By noon they had reached the *Stazione Termini* and settled in at their hotel, the afternoon free for sightseeing. Not all were impressed with their first taste of Rome. The earlier cadet had written, "the trains are not as good as the Pennsy and contrary to the popular notion they don't tear around at breakneck speeds." Of the Stazione Termini he wrote, "Broad St. Station looks like a palace compared the dump we came in to."

After settling in at the hotel, two cadets to a room, they had a free afternoon to sightsee. The cadets were impressed by the fashionable dress of the civilians and the crisp uniforms of the Fascist police and military, years before they would be at war with them. The earlier cadet wrote, "Everywhere you go you see the Fascists, trains, trolleys, no place without them." A visit to "Il Duce" was planned for La Rue's group, but the cadets were unable to meet with Mussolini due to the premier's schedule. They visited an exhibition of the progress of Italy under Fascist rule, but they were much more interested in the historic scenes. The cadets were underwhelmed by the Tiber, a bare trickle compared to their mighty Delaware and Schuylkill rivers back home. But they loved the quiet of the older parts of the city and the grand public spaces. Like many visitors to Rome, the cadets were struck by the city environments so different and so much older than even their historic Philadelphia. The earlier cadet wrote, "Aside from the public buildings the structures are practically identical, all about four or five stories high and faced with yellow plaster. Inside, most of them have a court, which is very pleasant after the heat of the streets." The cadets toured the Coliseum and the Pantheon and some of Rome's magnificent churches, including Santa Maria Maggiore and St. John Lateran, as well as the Catacombs of St. Calistus on the Appian Way. The highlight for many, no doubt for a devout Catholic like Cadet La Rue, was a visit to St. Peter's and an audience with Pope Pius XI.

Back in Naples, they traveled down the coast to Sorrento and Positano and visited Capri with its Blue Grotto. Even the sweltering heat did not dampen their enthusiasm. Many of the cadets were fascinated with the hulking form dominating Naples, the volcanic mountain Vesuvius. The earlier cadet wrote of a journey up the cone,

> "All we've seen in Italy so far was ruins and such stuff but when you look at the volcano, there's action, and I don't mean maybe. Starting at the bottom ... is a regular trolley. You go about three miles and then they hook a cog wheel pusher on which goes on for two miles. Then it's back to the trolley again till you get within a thousand feet where you take an inclined railway pulled by cable after which you have a ten minute walk and you are at the brink of the old crater. You know how it is now I guess, the new crater within the old one."

Finally, it was time to head back west. They steamed four days to reach Gibraltar, refilled the "Annie's" coal bunkers, and continued on for four days to Madeira in the Canary Islands. Their trip across the Atlantic was largely uneventful aside from heavy weather off the New Jersey coast. After a week's pause in New Castle, Delaware, to paint and refit the ship, the cadets were back home in Philadelphia after three months. They resumed their study pier-side at the Navy Yard over what turned into a bitterly cold winter. What would be their graduation year, 1934, was punctuated by the mid-February death of one of their classmates, Dean K. Madden, from scarlet fever. The ship was quarantined and weekend liberties cancelled for a time, but more importantly, the winter cruise that would have commenced that February, the final one of their academic career, was cancelled.

Leonard La Rue graduated from the Nautical School with a diploma as a deck officer on May 23, 1934. His nineteen classmates divided into twelve deck officers (with certificates of graduation in "Seamanship and Navigation") and seven engineering officers. The Pennsylvania

Board of Commissioners of Navigation, who acted as the trustees of the Nautical School, provided a letter to the local inspectors certifying that, "the bearer, Leonard P. La Rue, graduated honorably from the Pennsylvania State Nautical School ... after a full course of two years in Seamanship and Navigation."

The Nautical School's 1934 yearbook, *The Helm*, was dedicated to the late Cadet Madden. In a letter to the graduates, the faculty advised the graduates,

"Your course of study has fitted you to enter this profession, and from now on ... your life will be as you make it. The Sea brooks no idlers or weaklings and you must always strive to place yourself at the top. Having achieved that pinnacle, hold it."

La Rue's graduation picture is formal, with maybe the slightest hint of a smile, the brim of his cap low over his eyes. *The Helm*'s editors gave his nickname as "Rudy," and they said, "Leonard LaRue is a true Frankford thoroughbred, and he, like his forerunners, has won a place in the hearts of his classmates." They go on to tease, "When 'Rudy' first came on the Schoolship you could hardly get him to talk, but from his Second Class term on he has been constant in his conversation. Does one year on this Schoolship affect one like that, or could it be that he's been smitten by the arrow of Cupid's bow?" In later years La Rue would say, "I never kept company, never came near marriage," so we are left to wonder whether the reference is to a serious courtship that ended, a simple affection, or if he was simply being teased by his classmates for the lack thereof.

We do get some visibility into the man in his youth as the description of Cadet La Rue continued.

"Every day you can hear his crooning voice, which is a sure blues chaser, sung like only one 'Rudy' can sing. And if you are ever disturbed by a loud and boisterous laugh, that is sure to be our Rudy (probably laughing at his own jokes)."

Making light of an affliction that he would suffer all of his life,

"So now let us cast our eyes on the lad pictured above. Here you will see the benefactor of our sea-companions, the Fish. Many times the gallant Cadet has given-er-up his meal that these poor denizens of the deep will not go hungry. 'How can one refuse the longing in a poor fish's eyes,' quotes Rudy in a moment of despair."

La Rue frequently suffered from sea-sickness during his career.

Leonard La Rue's graduation picture in The Helm.

La Rue's entry ends with the affection of his classmates, stating, "we wish our Rudy the best of luck and may he be remembered as one of the best to ever grace the front porch of the Annie." It would seem that the even temper and competence that would mark him as an officer were already evident to his peers.

Since LaRue was now twenty years old, he was eligible to take the initial licensing examinations for his career as a Merchant Marine officer. On May 15 the executive officer of the *Annapolis*, E. J. Kingsland, wrote a letter to the "U.S. Steamboat Inspectors," the representatives of the Department of Commerce who would examine prospective officers. "Gentlemen," the letter begins,

"It is respectfully requested that Cadet Leonard La Rue be allowed to take his third Mate Examination before his graduation. Cadet La Rue will graduate from the deck department on Wednesday, May 23, 1934. He will have completed, at that time, three ocean cruises and the two years-time required in accordance with the rules and regulations of the U.S. Steamboat Inspectors. The courtesy granted to this cadet in the respect will be greatly appreciated."

On May 17 LaRue applied for his license using the Inspectors' Form 866A, "Application for Original License, Department of Commerce, Steamboat Inspection Service." The form reads, "To the U. S. Local Inspectors, Steamboat Inspection Service. Gentlemen: I hereby respectfully apply for the license as 'third #3 Mate unlimited' on the waters of 'Oceans.'" Executive Officer Kingsland and two other instructors from the school signed the form to certify that the applicant, "is a person of temperate habits and of good character, and recommend him as a suitable person to be intrusted [sic] with the duties of the station, as above, for which he makes application." His "Application and Certificate of Physical Examination," Form 935A (27th edition) describes a young man five-feet-eleven-inches tall, weighing 150 pounds, with light-colored hair and blue eyes. The form admonishes that, "Epilepsy, insanity, senility, acute venereal disease or neuro-syphilis, badly impaired hearing, or other defect that would render the applicant incompetent to perform the ordinary duties of an officer at sea are causes for certification as incompetent." Following the examination, the physician noted the applicant as "competent."

On May 26, 1934, Leonard P. La Rue received his "License to Mate of Ocean or Coastwise Steam and Motor Vessels ... having given evidence to the undersigned ... that he is a skillful navigator and can be intrusted to perform the duties of 'Third' Mate on Steam and Motor Vessels of not over 'any' gross tons, upon the waters of 'Oceans.'" On the thirty-first he also received his "Certificate of Service to Able Seaman." He was now a licensed officer in the United States Merchant Marine.

La Rue began his career immediately. Unlike in a navy, where a sailor or officer is assigned to a ship by higher authority, in the Merchant Marine a mariner contracts to work on a particular ship on a voyage-by-voyage basis. By tradition, and in the United States by federal law since 1790, a merchant mariner signs a "Ship's Articles of Agreement," usually just called "Ship's Articles," "Shipping Articles," or simply "Articles." The Articles form a contract between the officers and crew serving on the ship, and the operator of the ship. A modern set of articles provides an example of what young Leonard La Rue would have committed each time he joined a ship.[6] Titled "United States of America Shipping Articles," the document "Articles of Agreement Between Master and Seamen in the Merchant Service of the United States" is followed by the name of the ship, official number, port of registry, class of ship, and registered tonnage gross and net.

The next section identifies the "Operating Company on This Voyage," and is followed by the statement, "IT IS AGREED between the Master and seamen of the [blank], of which [blank] is at present master, or whoever shall go for Master, now bound from the port of [blank] to [blank]." Parenthetically the Articles note, "Here the voyage is to be described, and the places named at which the vessel is to touch, or cannot be done, the general nature, and probably length of the voyage is to be stated." On a normal commercial voyage in peacetime, the ports of call would ordinarily be spelled out, but during wartime this section might just state a general destination, such as on Articles that La Rue signed almost a decade later as "a point in the Pacific Ocean to the westward of San Francisco and thence to such ports and places in any part of the world as the Master may direct or as may be ordered by the United States Government or any Department, Commission or agency thereof."

The next section spells out the general contract with those signing. Here the language has certainly evolved over the centuries, but the intentions are the same,

"For a term not exceeding [blank] calendar months. The seamen agree to conduct themselves in an orderly, faithful, honest and sober manner, and to be at all times diligent in their respective duties, and to be obedient to the lawful commands of the master, or of an individual who lawfully succeeds the master, and of their superior officers in everything related to the vessel, and the stores and cargo of the vessel, whether on board, in boats, or on shore. In consideration of their service by the seamen to be performed, the master agrees to pay the crew, as wages, the amounts beside their names respectively expressed, and to supply them with the following provisions: at least 3 meals daily that total at least 3,100 calories, including adequate water and adequate protein, vitamins and minerals, in accordance with the United States Recommended Daily Allowance."

Merchant mariners signing Articles.

The Articles continue,

"It is agreed that any embezzlement, or willful or negligent destruction of any part of the vessel's cargo or stores, shall be made good to the owner out of wages of the person guilty of the embezzlement or destruction. If an individual holds himself or herself out as qualified

for a duty which the individual proves incompetent to perform, the
individual's wages shall be reduced in proportion to the incompetency.
It also is agreed that if a seaman considers himself or herself to be
aggrieved by any breach of this agreement or otherwise, the seaman
shall present the complaint to the master or officer in charge of the
vessel, in a quiet and orderly manner, who shall take the steps that the
case requires." There is blank space below for "any other stipulations
... to which the parties agree, and that are not contrary to law."

The master signs below, "IN WITNESS WHEREOF," with his identi-
fying information, and then the members of the crew each complete a
line that lists: name and signature, capacity (job on the ship), wages
per month, birthplace, date of birth, reference number, place of signing, date of signing, time at which to be on board, and next of kin
name and address. The master initials each line. When a voyage is
complete, or a crew member leaves for any other reason (illness,
misconduct, etc.), a second line is completed for each member listing
the "Particulars of Discharge": place for leaving the ship, date of
leaving the ship, cause for leaving the ship, time of service in days,
wages earned, deductions, balance of wages paid in discharge. The
mariner and master sign and date each line.

Once completed, the Articles are carried aboard the ship as a record of
the crew's origin and as proof that they joined the ship voluntarily.
The latter might seem a minor point, but in the eighteenth and early
nineteenth centuries, when it was common for both merchantmen and
warships to "impress" unwilling men into service, the Articles had
particular value.

These were the terms and conditions under which freshly licensed
Third Mate La Rue would join the crew or "sign on to" a ship.[7] The
nation was still deep in economic depression and there was no point
in staying in Philadelphia beyond saying goodbye to his family. By the
month after graduation and receipt of his license, he was serving as an
Able Seaman (AB) aboard the tanker SS *Francis E. Powell* of the Atlantic
Refining Company on a regular run between the oil terminals in Texas

and the refineries in Philadelphia.[8] Eight years later the *Powell* would fall victim to a submarine, sinking off the North Carolina coast, but AB La Rue was long gone from the ship. In 1935 he served as quartermaster aboard the SS *Columbia* of the Panama Pacific Steamship Line and the SS *Steelmaker* of the Isthmian Steamship Line. The crew list for the *Columbia* described La Rue as having "fair" eyes and complexion, and a height of five foot six, perhaps displaying a lack of attention on the part of the scribe. His mother is listed as "Next of Kin," with her address the house on James Street.

In June 1935, within a year of graduation, he had progressed to third mate of the *Steelmaker*, serving in that position for the next three years aboard two other ships of the Isthmian Line. What duties would Third Mate La Rue have performed as his ship steamed from Texas, Panama or Honduras? The *Merchant Marine Officers' Handbook* lists the duties of third and junior third officers, including: navigation; compiling weather reports; inspecting the condition of bridge equipment, lifeboats, capstans and fire-fighting equipment; and ensuring flags are properly hoisted while in port.[9] The third mate may also be assigned paperwork duties by other officers of the deck department or the chief engineer. Like the other officers, the third mate would stand watch on the bridge when the ship was at sea, or a security and fire watch when the ship was in port. As the "low man on the totem pole," the third mate would do whatever his seniors instructed him to do.

Over the next three years, he served as second or third mate on ships sailing for Standard Fruit, Seatrain, Black Diamond, Sword, American Export, and Lykes Brothers. He served as third mate aboard the Black Diamond Lines' SS *Black Hawk*, leaving New York on June 24, 1939, sailing to Antwerp, Belgium and Rotterdam, the Netherlands. La Rue signed off the ship when she returned to New York on August 29. During the next trip, as the *Black Hawk* was again returning from Rotterdam about six weeks later, she would rescue thirty-nine crew members of the French oil tanker *Emile Miguet* when the tanker was torpedoed off the coast of Ireland by a German submarine, an *Untersee-boot* or "U-boat."

On the eve of the United States' entry into World War II, Third Mate La Rue was finishing his second voyage aboard the Lykes Brothers' SS *Cranford*. On his first voyage in March 1941, *Cranford* had carried a load of coal from the port of Baltimore to Lisbon, Portugal, and had been delayed on her return as she rendered aid to another freighter, the SS *Kentucky*. Before she made port again, Lykes Brothers received a letter from H. Harris Robson, Director, Emergency Shipping of the United States Maritime Commission.

"The President of the United States," the letter began, "pursuant to provisions of Public Laws Nos. 11 and 23 (77th Congress), has directed the United States Maritime Commission to acquire for national defense purposes, the services of at least 2,000,000 tons of merchant shipping and to make such cargo space immediately effective in accomplishing the objectives of national defense."

The letter continued,

"In accordance with the President's directives you are requested, upon arrival of the ... SS *Cranford* at their last North Atlantic ports on or about ... May 31 ... to discharge all cargo and not load any further cargo on said vessels preparatory to making the vessels available for accomplishing the objectives of national defense (details of which will be given you later) ..."

SS *Cranford*.

That June, *Cranford*, with La Rue aboard, began serving under charter to the British Ministry of War Transport for service between US Atlantic ports and ports in South Africa (Cape Town) and India (Karachi). Before returning to the US, *Cranford* had loaded a full cargo of salt from Jamnagar, on the west coast of India, for transport to Calcutta, at almost the same latitude on the east coast. As profitable as that might have been for the owners, it is easy to imagine how unpleasant the loading of that cargo must have been, in the dead of summer, for the Indian stevedores, the men of the *Cranford*, and the officers supervising them, including Third Mate La Rue.

The ship arrived in New York from India with a load of jute on December 7, 1941, just as the Japanese attacked Pearl Harbor. As the war began for the United States, La Rue completed his duties and was released from the ship on December 26. He immediately applied to the Steamboat Inspection Service's successor organization, the Bureau of Marine Inspection and Navigation, for a license as a second mate, but he soon cancelled the application and applied instead for chief mate. He must have requested a recommendation from the captain of the *Cranford*, Captain James Henry Donlon, because on February 13, 1942, E. A. Jimison, manager of the Marine Division at Lykes Brothers, sent a letter to La Rue at the house on his parents' new home on Disston Street, which La Rue now listed as his permanent address. "Dear Mr. La Rue," the letter began,

> "This will confirm that you were employed on the SS 'Cranford' in the capacity of Junior Third Officer from June 18 to July 22 , 1941 and as Third Officer from July 23 to December 26, 1941; during which period your services in the above capacities were entirely satisfactory to Captain Donlon. It is not possible for Captain Donlon to write you as he has just sailed for sea on an extended voyage."

It was indeed an extended voyage. On June 30, 1942, the *Cranford* was 250 miles east of Barbados returning from Cape Town, South Africa, laden with 6,600 tons of chromium ore and 1,600 tons of cotton when she was struck by a single torpedo fired by a U-boat.[10] The torpedo struck the starboard side fifteen feet below the waterline, flooding the number two and three holds. Laden by her heavy cargo, the ship sank in three minutes. Two of the survivors were taken aboard the submarine for medical treatment. Following treatment, the survivors were given some matches, a towline (to tie the life rafts together) and two cans of water and deposited back in the ocean with their fellow survivors. The Germans also provided them with course and distance to Barbados. Later in the war, no such courtesies would be extended to the crews of torpedoed ships. The captain of the submarine did deny them food, as they were near the end of their own voyage and running short of supplies themselves. The survivors were picked up by a Spanish tanker, the *Castillo Alemenara*, about two hours later and landed in Curacao, Spain's official neutrality and political alignment with Germany having protected the tanker from the submarine lurking nearby. Among the eleven officers and men that were lost in the sinking of the *Cranford* were Captain Donlon and Hynne Jorgensen, La Rue's replacement as third mate.

2

WAR

Whether it was Third Mate La Rue's previous good service, the exigencies of the new wartime situation, or both, Leonard La Rue received his license as chief mate, "'any' gross tons, upon the waters of 'Oceans,'" on January 30, 1942. On February 11, he joined the crew of the SS *Mormacmar* of the Moore-McCormack Lines, beginning a professional relationship with "Mooremack" that would last the next dozen years, the remainder of his Merchant Marine career.

Moore-McCormack Lines was founded on July 9, 1913, by Albert V. Moore and Emmett J. McCormack. Emmet McCormack was born in Brooklyn, New York, in September 1880, the only child of Mary and Joseph McCormack, both Irish immigrants. His father, an engineer on a seagoing tugboat, died when he was just fourteen, requiring him to enter the workforce to support his mother. A born extrovert, as a young man he worked as a messenger for four shipping-related companies at the same time, using the ferry between the Brooklyn and Manhattan waterfronts to carry messages for his employers. After a while, McCormack moved from the waterfront to the ships themselves, working as a deckhand on a towboat and, as his natural exuberance came into play, as a salesman for the ship's services. His ambition was likely enhanced by the fact that, by the turn of the century, Emmet was living with his new wife in a house he shared with his mother and three boarders. It was not long before McCormack was working full time selling dunnage (inexpensive materials like scrap wood and jute mats used to secure and protect cargo in the ship's hold) and coal to fuel the ships plying New York's crowded waterfront. By 1905 McCormack had formed Commercial Coal Company to supply bunker coal to the growing proportion of steamships replacing sail in commerce.[1]

Albert Voorhis Moore Jr. was born in Hackensack, New Jersey, on September 21, 1880, the youngest child and only son of Albert Voorhis and Catherine (Lozier) Moore. Perhaps as the result of having five older sisters, young Albert developed into a quiet, careful, methodical young man. Where Emmet had married at eighteen, Albert did not marry Margaret Sterling until he was almost thirty-two. His early professional career was among businessmen and merchants in the shipping industry, developing a reputation as an expert in matching cargo and customers to available ships and shippers. His choice of career was no doubt influenced by the fact that his father owned a share in several ships, his uncle owned and captained his own ship, and his grandfather had also been the master of a ship. Moore and McCormack became acquainted through a coal contract Moore granted through his employer, Tweedie Trading Company, to McCormack's company.[2]

McCormack's ambition extended beyond the Commercial Coal Company. In 1911 he formed a ferry company that ran two ships between Brooklyn and Staten Island at a time when the ferry fares ranged from five cents for individual passengers, to fifteen cents for a passenger with a handcart, to ninety-five cents for a wagon with four horses. By comparison, a motor truck was a bargain at eighty cents. Finally, in 1913, McCormack and Moore formed the Moore and McCormack Company, Incorporated. They soon chartered their first ship and began what would be a major focus of their business, trade into the Caribbean and the Atlantic coast of South America. Their first ship, the SS *Montara*, carried a load of dynamite from the DuPont factory in Wilmington, Delaware, to Rio de Janeiro, Brazil. McCormack later joked that, "it was a fifty-fifty proposition. Either we would be launched in the shipping business on a very profitable charter or we would be minus a ship."

By 1920 Moore-McCormack had added Bahia and Santos in Brazil and the Rio de la Plata ports of Montevideo, Uruguay, and Buenos Aires, Argentina, to their South-American routes, along with a regular passenger run between New York and ports in Southampton, England, and Stockholm, Sweden. In 1923, Moore-McCormack was awarded management of the American Scantic line by the United States Shipping Board. American Scantic had begun operations in 1918 and had pioneered routes from New York to Denmark, Sweden, Poland, Finland, and Russia (Leningrad); indeed, the first US-flagged shipping vessels to carry cargo to and from Leningrad were on the American Scantic line. Commodore Robert C. Lee, who joined Moore-McCormack in 1920, cultivated relations with the new Soviet government with the result that Moore-McCormack became an agent for the Soviet shipping agency "Amderuta" and the Soviet "Amtorg" trading company. Moore-McCormack recognized the potential of the Baltic routes, which were otherwise underserved by US shipping companies because of the high costs (a round trip could be more than ten thousand miles and take more than two months), and by 1927 they had completed negotiations with the Shipping Board to purchase the American Scantic Lines outright. By the eve of World War II, Moore-McCormack and its subsidiaries boasted a truly international service with destinations ranging from ports on the Gulf of Mexico, the Caribbean, the Baltic, and the Pacific. Their experience in Russia would prove to be particularly useful.

The SS *Mormacmar* of the Moore-McCormack Line was launched in 1920 by the Los Angeles Shipbuilding Company as the SS *Culberson*.[3] The *Culberson* was 424 feet long with a beam of fifty feet and a rating of 8,800 deadweight tons and 5,453 gross tons.[4] Her three-cylinder triple-expansion steam engine gave her a design speed of 10.5 knots. The owner of the ship was the United States Shipping Board, formed by an act of Congress in 1916,

> "to establish a United Stated Shipping Board for the purpose of encouraging, developing and creating a naval auxiliary and naval reserve and a Merchant Marine to meet the needs of the commerce of the United States with its territories and possession and with foreign countries; to regulate carriers by water engaged in foreign and domestic comer of the United States for other purposes."

The Board funded the construction of ships, which were then leased or chartered by shipping lines, relieving them of the cost of capital for ship construction and allowing them a "pay as you go" method for increasing capacity. Under a "Bareboat Charter," the Shipping Board maintained title to the ship but the shipping line covered all of the direct costs of operating the ship; that is, salaries, maintenance, fuel, insurance, etc., but not depreciation, which was borne by the Shipping Board (and in turn, the US taxpayer). During wartime, because it would be nearly impossible to obtain insurance for a ship operating under threat of enemy action, the preferred agreement was a "General Agency Agreement" or GAA, under which the Shipping Board retained title, insured the vessel, made repairs and improvements, and paid the shipping line a fee for operating the ship, from which the shipping line covered salaries, maintenance, fuel, overhead and profit. In 1936, the Shipping Board would be succeeded by the United States Maritime Commission, which took on the same responsibilities.

The Shipping Board initially assigned *Culberson* to McCormick and McPherson for management and operation.[5] During slack shipping demand it was not unusual for a line to lease a ship from the Shipping Board just for a single cargo, so the assets of the Shipping Board frequently moved from lessee to lessee. By 1926 she was being operated by Moore and McCormack. In 1930 she went to C. H. Sprague, but by 1938 she was back in Moore-McCormack's hands and renamed the *Mormacmar*.[6]

With war looming, the freighter's speed and reliability became a special concern. Correspondence between the D. S. Brierley, the director of maintenance and repairs for the Maritime Commission, and Moore-McCormack shows that due to installation of a new, streamlined rudder, the *Mormacmar* was capable of maximum speeds of between twelve and thirteen knots, depending on displacement.[7] The previous year Brierley had approved refurbishment and modifications to permit the triple-expansion steam engine propelling the *Mormacmar* to generate its rated 3,500 horsepower. In addition, the commission had paid to installed a radio direction finder as well as modern high-frequency radio equipment on the ship to replace the antiquated spark-gap equipment the ship had carried since launch. All of these improvements would be essential if *Mormacmar* were to survive in the increasingly dangerous environment for neutral ships carrying cargo between neutral ports, much more so to Allied ports.

SS *Mormacmar* in her pre-war Moore-McCormack Lines colors. American flags painted on her hull identify her as a neutral ship.

And the environment was indeed getting dangerous. On September 3, 1939, British Prime Minister Neville Chamberlain announced that, as a result of Germany's attack on Poland, following their earlier invasion of Czechoslovakia, "...this country is at war with Germany." As the prime minister's words wafted through the ether over the BBC, forty-nine of Germany's fifty-seven U-boats were at sea prepared to take the war to his island nation. During World War I, German U-boats had sunk almost thirteen million tons of shipping, almost nine million tons during 1917 alone, nearly crippling Great Britain. This time the German Navy, the *Kriegsmarine*, intended to succeed where it almost had before.[8]

The prime minister had finished addressing his nation a little over eight hours earlier when the 13,500-ton British-flagged passenger liner *Athenia*, steaming 200 miles west of the Hebrides Islands on her way to New York, was struck amidships by a single torpedo fired from the U-30. Immediately, her shattered compartments flooded, and the ship slowly sank by the stern until she disappeared into the depths the next morning. Some 1,300 of her passengers and crew were rescued, but 118 died, including twenty-two Americans. Before the end of the month, U-boats would send another 140,000 tons of British shipping to the join *Athenia* at the bottom of the Atlantic. It was but a taste of things to come. During the next year, 1940, Axis U-boats, aircraft, mines, and surface ships sank nearly four million tons of shipping, almost six hundred thousand tons in June alone. Britain's shipyards could not keep pace.

As the German Army, the *Wehrmacht*, turned its attention west following the conquests of Czechoslovakia and Poland, the situation became more acute. On October 10, 1939, Grand Admiral Erich Raeder, commander in chief of the Kriegsmarine, advised Hitler that intelligence suggested Britain would seize Norway. Britain could then control the approaches to the North Sea, Germany's access to the Atlantic from the Baltic. It could also threaten German moves in Sweden and deny Germany their vital supplies of Swedish iron ore. Germany began Operation *Weserubung* in early April 1940 with landings along the Norwegian coast at Narvick, Trondheim, Bergen, Kristiansand, Oslo and Egersund. The Allies fought back, with the Royal Navy engaging the invading forces off the coast from Narvick to Bergen, and the British landed their own forces near Narvick and Trondheim to try to force the Germans out, but it was too little, too late. By early June, Britain had evacuated all of their forces from Norway, ceding control of its 1,600-mile-long coast to Germany. Germany now had countless fiords in which to hide its commerce raiders, such as the "pocket battleships" *Scharnhorst* and *Gneisenau*. It also now had airfields on which to base aircraft to threaten Allied commerce in the North, Norwegian, and Barents seas.

The situation for the Allies was no better to the south. Germany began its push into the low countries and France on May 10, 1940, with General Gerd von Rundstedt leading forty-six German divisions against a small Belgian force in the Ardennes and sixteen divisions of French infantry and (horse) cavalry. At the same time, German transport aircraft dropped parachute battalions over strategic airfields, bridges, and other targets in the Netherlands, including The Hague, Rotterdam, Dordrecht and Moerdijk. German armor and infantry followed into Holland, and the disorganized Dutch defenders were quickly overwhelmed. The Netherlands surrendered to German forces on May 14.

Around the same time, Rundstedt's divisions had routed Allied forces in Belgium and were thrusting deep into France. By May 27, Belgium was forced to sue for peace. Britain had provided thirteen divisions for a "British Expeditionary Force" to augment the French and Belgian armies in their defense against Germany. Those British forces now joined their hosts with their backs to the English Channel. Between May 26 and June 4, 1940, 338,000 British and French troops trapped at Dunkirk were evacuated by a diverse flotilla. Royal Navy warships, private yachts, tugboats and fishing trawlers sailed the ninety miles from the British port of Dover, around dense minefields laid in the English channel, to Dunkirk and back, rescuing the troops from certain capture or death. The fabled evacuation foreshadowed an even more successful exodus from the coast of Korea in which La Rue would participate a decade later.

General von Rundstedt's soldiers marched into Paris on June 14, and the French government, under the leadership of World War I hero

Marshall Henri Philippe Petain, began armistice negotiations. As Germany and France negotiated their armistice, the remaining British troops in France that were not already prisoners of the *Wehrmacht* were being evacuated from ports in Brittany. By 11:35 AM on June 25, when the armistice officially took effect, most of the remnants of the British Expeditionary Force had been returned to Britain, but British, Czech, and Polish soldiers and French civilians continued to trickle out of France until mid-August. By the time the British had finished their retreat, they had lost 66,000 men killed, wounded, or taken prisoner.

Where did this leave the United States? Political isolationism and the privations of the Great Depression meant that there was no great groundswell to become involved in another war in Europe. The US Armed Forces had suffered more than 116,000 fatalities during World War I, albeit with more than half of that total due to the Spanish Flu epidemic of 1918. Another 320,000 were wounded in combat or sickened by the flu but recovered. President Franklin D. Roosevelt was an internationalist and an anglophile, but he recognized that national politics on this issue were not tending in his direction. Over the course of the 1930s, he signed multiple pieces of legislation declaring US neutrality, but he skillfully used the increasingly fraught situation in Europe to position the United States to support what would become the Allied cause.

The vote counts in the Senate and the House of Representatives demonstrate both Roosevelt's patient molding of political opinion and the increasing fraught international situation. Roosevelt initially opposed the strictures of the Neutrality Act of 1935 but signed it when the Act passed with large, veto-proof majorities; for example, the final Senate vote on the bill, Senate Joint Resolution 173 (74th Congress) incorporating amendments from the House of Representatives, passed by seventy-nine votes in favor to two against. Signed into law by Roosevelt on August 31, the bill prohibited the export of "arms, ammunition and implements of war" from the United States to foreign nations at war and as insurance required armament manufacturers to apply for licenses before exporting their products. Congress renewed the act on February 29, 1936, and extended the restrictions to loans for waring nations (or "belligerents," in Roosevelt's words.)

During 1937, in response to the outbreak of the Spanish Civil War in 1936, and the increasingly strident rhetoric and actions from Nazi Germany and Fascist Italy, Congress passed another series of Neutrality Acts, again with overwhelming voting margins. In January, Senate Joint Resolution 3 (75th Congress), "A Joint Resolution Prohibiting the Exportation of Arms, Ammunition and Implements of War from the United States to Spain," passed by a vote of eighty-one to zero in the Senate and by a vote of 377 to twelve in the House. In March, Senate Joint Resolution 51 (75th Congress), the "Neutrality Act of 1937," passed by a vote of sixty-three to six in the Senate, and 377 to twelve in the House.

The 1937 Neutrality Act banned US citizens from traveling on the ships of belligerent nations, and prevented American ships from carrying arms to a belligerent even if the arms were from a third party. It also prohibited the arming of US merchant vessels. But in tacit recognition that the United States might eventually have to choose sides, the new act permitted, at the discretion of the president, the sale of "commodities" besides armaments to belligerents as long as they paid immediately (without credit or "cash and carry") and the material was transported on non-US ships. This was an important concession to President Roosevelt and to the reality of the situation in Europe, where Britain, France, and other European nations were facing looming threats from Germany. Two weeks before the final bill was passed, the Senate voted down an amendment to strip the president of the discretion to choose which commodities could be sold to the belligerents by a vote of twenty-four to forty-eight. The president signed the act and it became law on May 1.

Like the Neutrality Act of 1935, the act of 1937 required reauthorization after two and a half years, and the world situation had become far more perilous when the time for its renewal approached in 1939. Germany had marched into Austria on March 12, 1938, uniting the 6.7

million Austrians to their 68 million German co-linguists. Debate on renewal of the act began early in 1939, with the House taking their first vote in June, just three months after Germany had seized Czecho-slovakia.

As debate continued into the fall, Germany invaded Poland, with the result that the Allied powers of France and the United Kingdom declared war on Germany on September 3, 1939. After a series of amendments, the House voted to pass what would become the final pre-war Neutrality Act, House Joint Resolution 306 (76th Congress), voting on November 3 by 243 to 172 to accept the results of confer-ence with the Senate, much closer than the previous tallies. There was a wide view in Congress and across the country that US involvement in the war was probably inevitable, but there was still no rush to join it. Bowing to the new realities, the act, which took effect on November 4, 1939, removed the embargo against selling arms to belligerents, allowing the US, at some risk to its shipping, to supply the war-making of the Allied powers of Britain and France.

The impact of the loosening of restrictions on the belligerents, which in practical terms meant the United Kingdom, were clear in the trade statistics of the time.[9] The annual value of exports from the United States to the United Kingdom averaged about 500 million dollars in the period 1935-1939, but in 1940 they suddenly doubled to more than a billion dollars. Exports to Britain rose to 1.6 billion in 1941, 2.5 billion in 1942, 4.5 billion in 1943, and 5.2 billion in 1944 before dropping again in 1945 as the war wound down.[10] All of these arms and armaments, food stuffs, oil, and raw materials would be carried in ships, and as the British Merchant Marine came under stress from Nazi aircraft, surface ships and U-boats, the US Merchant Marine would need to pick up the slack.

World War I had painfully demonstrated the effectiveness of U-boats against merchant vessels, even when the latter were armed and prop-erly crewed with lookouts. The introduction of the convoy system by the British in June 1916 dramatically reduced the loss of merchant ships. The US Navy's *Escort Manual* (1941) defined a convoy as, "A number of naval auxiliary vessels or merchant vessels, or both, assembled and organized for an operation, or for passage together, and usually escorted by one or more combatant vessels and aircraft."[11] The convoy relied on the speed, maneuverability, sensors (radar and sonar) and armaments of the escorts to thwart attacks or destroy the attacker.

U-442 running on the surface in front of its victim, a burning tanker.

In the case of Atlantic convoys, the threat included surface raiders, aircraft and the ubiquitous U-boats, although in practice it was only U-boats that could threaten a convoy for its entire voyage between US and Canadian ports on one side of the Atlantic, and the UK and Europe on the other. The *Escort Manual* characterized the German submarine as, "a good sea boat. On the surface it has a long cruising radius, a maximum speed of 17-21 knots, guns for use against surface and aircraft, and radio capable of long range transmissions." The speed of the submarine on the surface, powered by its diesel engines, was particularly noteworthy, since the maximum speed of the merchant ships in a convoy was rarely more than twelve knots, at least for the first few years of the war. There was little chance a merchant ship could outrun a surfaced submarine. Even with its decks awash (to present a lower profile to lookouts or gunners), the submarine could make fourteen knots. On the other hand, the submarine, "submerged has a low speed (2 knots) cruising radius of 90 miles," running on its storage batteries, "and a submerged endurance of about 45 hours lying on the bottom." Only the effective use of armed escort vessels could keep submarines and other attacking craft from sinking the slow and unarmed or lightly armed merchant ship.

This was the world facing La Rue and his fellow merchant mariners in early 1942. Even if US forces were not yet fighting in Europe, both Britain and the Soviet Union were engaged in a death-struggle with the Axis powers. In the Pacific, the US Navy was licking the wounds it had suffered at Pearl Harbor and along with the US Army was trying to fend off the Japanese invasion of the Philippines. Even before the US entered the war, Congress had voted in mid-October, 1941, to amend the Neutrality Act of 1939 to permit the arming of merchant ships, something specifically forbidden since the passage of the 1937 act.

The previous November the Maritime Commission had scheduled *Mormacmar* to enter a dry-dock in Baltimore, Maryland, on April 8 for "Degaussing and Installation of Defense Features." Even as late as December 4 the Maritime Commission had reconfirmed that schedule, but after the US entered the war on December 8, the schedule was moved up and she instead immediately went to Norfolk for installation of the degaussing coils and guns.[12] Degaussing involved the use of electric coils installed inside the hull to neutralize the magnetic field generated by the steel of the ship so as to reduce her vulnerability to magnetic influence mines. Unlike a "contact" mine that relied on the physical contact between a ship's hull and a mechanical detonator to trigger the explosives in the mine, a "magnetic" mine could be laid deeper and in less-dense fields but still be triggered by a ship's presence to explode with devastating effect. The British had pioneered the development of magnetic mines during World War I, with the US and Germany launching their efforts between the wars.[13] By World War II, this version of the "weapons that wait" had become a major threat to surface ships and submarines.

Installation of the degaussing coils was completed on the twenty-eighth of January. Arming the ship proceeded in parallel, with the ship's guns successfully test-fired on February 2. As would be the pattern for the entire war, US Merchant Marine ships like the *Mormacmar*, operated by commercial shipping lines employing civilian crews, would be supplied with US Navy "Naval Armed Guard" crews. The crews, typically eight to thirty enlisted men (depending on the armaments on the ship) under the command of an ensign or a lieutenant (junior grade), added what little defensive component a merchant ship carried. The Navy Department's *General Instructions for Commanding Officers of Naval Armed Guards on Merchant Ships* (Fourth Edition) tells the commander of the Armed Guards that,

"He is the master's military advisor and is specifically charged with the vessel's armed defense.[14] He has exclusive control over the military functions of the Armed Guard ... the master commands the vessel and is charged with her safe navigation and the safety of all persons on board. The Armed Guard is subject to the orders of the master only in matters pertaining to the general organization of the ship's company. The Armed Guard will not be required to perform any ship duties ... Armed Guard commanders must not permit their men to be utilized as messengers, deck hands, gangway or cargo hold watchmen, or the like."

That being said, one of the roles of the Armed Guard was to provide security to the ship while in foreign ports, which might include manning anti-aircraft machine guns to repel attacks by air.

The Navy recognized the potential for conflict on board the ship due to the parallel lines of authority of the master and the commander of the Armed Guard. The *Instructions* point out,

"In order to carry out effective defense of the vessel it is essential that the commander of the Armed Guard and the master of the vessel thoroughly understand their relative responsibilities and authority.

The ship must be defended by every means possible. It is emphasized that the ship's master is by law in full command of the ship, which authority is in no manner restricted by the instructions referred to."

But it continued,

"The authority to open fire quickly is delegated to the Armed Guard commander by reason of strict military necessity since attacks may develop suddenly day or night. There is no situation where either the master or the Armed Guard should delay firing on the enemy."

Balancing military necessity with the master's ultimate control of and responsibility for the ship, the *Instructions* noted,

"The Armed Guard officer is directed to consult with the master on matters of procedure which may vary with circumstances, and which may not be clearly defined in these orders. Arbitrary conduct and independent actions by the Armed Guard officer in matters where the master has cognizance would tend to lessen respect for the master of the ship, an officer who by law, tradition and experience, is entitled to certain prerogatives."

This discussion concluded with the anodyne,

"Both Armed Guard officers and masters are enjoined to compose personal differences, should any exist, to the end that harmony and concerted action may save the ship and promote the interests of the United States."

The Armed Guard was responsible for maintaining a lookout independent of the ship's navigational watchmen to search for submarines, threatening surface ships, and aircraft. The *Instructions* explain, "The safety of the ship depends as much upon a proper lookout as it does on the protection afforded by the guns." The directive adds, "if lookouts are alert and see a submarine in time to permit report, maneuver and gunfire before the torpedo is fired, there is small chance the attack will succeed." This was true because the torpedoes of the time, lacking the internal acoustic homing of modern torpedoes, were designed to follow a straight course once fired and to maintain a preset depth. Any evasive action by either the targeted ship or the targeting submarine (while itself came under fire) could upset the torpedoes' aim-point. For this reason, Armed Guard lookout watches were stood at the guns, "so that the guns may be brought into action immediately upon sighting the enemy."

Typical Naval Armed Guard complement: eighteen sailors, two petty officers and a lieutenant junior grade.

The lookouts were supplied with binoculars to improve their ability to discern targets and were given specific instructions for their duty at night:

"Lookouts should be selected with due regard to keenness of vision at night. It should be noted that men of equal vision in daylight do not by any means make equally good lookouts at night ... Lookouts should be at their station 15 minutes before taking over so that their eyes may become accustomed to darkness."

The lookouts were to use more than just their vision:

> "There should be no noise or talk on the bridge or on deck which might interfere with the lookout's hearing. He must listen as well as look. At night, lookouts should be instructed to listen for sounds of Diesel motors such as produced by a submarine operating on the surface or charging batteries."

On a moonlit night, lookouts were warned to be, "particularly vigilant on the side of the ship away from the moon as the submarine would probably attack from that side to get a silhouetted target."

Hours of lookout, manned from noontime sunlight to midnight darkness, in heat, cold, rain and snow, exhausted the discipline of even the most dedicated sailors. "Lookouts must be assigned a definite arc and confine themselves exclusively to watching this arc. Relaxation of vigilance must not be tolerated. Constant supervision of lookouts is essential." Just how taxing was the job of a lookout could be seen in the dictum, "Lookouts should never stand a watch longer than 2 hours for submarines and 1 hour for aircraft."

Since time was always of the essence, lookouts would signal a threat by sounding the ship's general alarm system, with a specific sequence depending on the specific threat. The standard signals late in the war were: one long and one short ring for a submarine on the starboard side, one long and two short rings for a sub on the port, and one short and one long ring for an attack from the air. Whatever guns had a view of the threat would commence firing immediately, since the lookout watch-standers were also the gun crews, and they stood their watches at their guns. For the *Mormacmar*, these consisted of: a single four inch/50-caliber gun mounted aft on the ship centerline and supplied with 100 rounds of ammunition, four .50-caliber Browning machine guns mounted port and starboard on the forecastle (bow) and on the aft end of the boat deck with a total of 4,200 rounds, and two .30-caliber Browning machine guns mounted port and starboard on the bridge with 6,000 rounds of ammunition.[15] In actual combat, the

Armed Guard would rely on the master to provide some of his crew members to pass ammunition from the ship's magazines to the guns as the ammunition in the ready-service boxes at the guns was depleted. The guard crew were also issued four .45-caliber M1911A1 pistols with 240 rounds of ammunition, presumably to help secure the ship in port and perhaps even to pacify an unruly crew. The Armed Guard crews were instructed not to wear the pistol while on watch at sea.

Sailors manning a .50 caliber machine gun in a convoy. Black spots are towed barrage balloons.

The one other defense the ship had, besides its Armed Guards and their weapons, was maneuver to disrupt the enemy's decision-making and targeting. The *Instructions* say,

"Whenever anything resembling a submarine is sighted it is extremely important that the course of the ship be changed instantly in compliance with doctrine. Change of course upsets the submarine's arrangements for firing a torpedo, and gives the ship time, which is very important. In cases where the lookout sights something that is not instantly seen from the bridge, the same rule should hold-change course at once and investigate afterwards."

These rules did not apply in convoys, because a single ship maneuvering among the others brought the immediate danger of collision. Here, the ship would have to rely on its own defenses and those of its escorts.

Anticipating that the armed-guard crew would frequently operate far from naval facilities, the armed-guard crews were supplied with tools, paint and paint brushes, grease and grease guns, and other materials to maintain their guns and mounts. The crews were issued their own lifejackets, gas masks, and goggles. Item number one on the inventory was always, "BAG, canvas, weighted," to be used by the Guard for the disposal of classified material to prevent its compromise in the event the ship were to be boarded by the enemy or sunk intact.

Disposal of sensitive material notwithstanding, the Armed Guards were instructed to fight to the last. The *Instructions* stated in bold type,

"There shall be no surrender and no abandoning ship so long as the guns can be fought. In case of casualty to members of the gun crew the remaining men shall continue to serve the gun. The Navy Department considers that so long as there remains a chance to save the ship the Armed Guard should remain thereon and take every opportunity that may present itself to destroy the submarine."

This tenacity would be needed soon. On January 31, 1942, *Mormacmar* joined sixteen other vessels that were, "allocated to load at Boston or Philadelphia for Archangel."[16] *Mormacmar*, her officers and men, including her soon-to-be Second Mate Leonard La Rue, were going to cross the North Atlantic, the Norwegian Sea and the Barents Sea to resupply Soviet Russia.

3

MURMANSK

The northern Russian city of Murmansk was founded as a harbor and rail spur in 1915 to take advantage of the fact that, even though it is located two degrees above the Arctic Circle, the comparatively warm North Atlantic Current keeps the waters of the Barents Sea around the Kola Peninsula ice free year-round. This includes the Kola Inlet, where Murmansk sits, and the approaches to the White Sea to the southeast of Murmansk, with its port of Archangelsk, known in English as Archangel. The city lies almost 700 miles due north of St. Petersburg (the Soviet city of Leningrad), but it seems even further from the wealth and opulence of Peter the Great's capital, which is now the headquarters of that great exporter of Russia's wealth of natural gas, Gazprom OAO. Unlike St. Petersburg, there are no palaces here, no grand state buildings painted in pale blue or cheerful, bright yellow; only a moldering palace of culture and an iconic Stalin-era railway station still sporting the red star of the Soviet Union on its spire. To the west of the train station lies the riverine southern strand of Kola Bay and its massive docks. Where their predecessors unloaded hundreds of ships during the "Great Patriotic War," today the massive docks host Chinese bulk-cargo ships loading Russian coal scooped from enormous mounds hidden, perhaps in embarrassment, behind two-story fences. Lines of waiting hopper cars outside the fence filled with the black stones give away the secret.

The docks of Murmansk today.

On a hill north of the center of the city stands guard an enormous, stylized, concrete soldier, "Alyosha," built in 1974 as a monument to the "Defenders of the Soviet Arctic during the Great Patriotic War." A twenty-minute walk southeast down the hill from Alyosha leads to the Russian Orthodox Church of the "Savior on the Waters." Built after the Soviet era and consecrated in 2000, it recognizes the close but often fatal embrace between Murmansk and the Barents Sea, which lies a scant thirty kilometers up Kola Bay. Down a concrete staircase from the church is a lighthouse-shaped building that anchors the "Memorial to Sailors who Died in Peacetime." Resting solemnly to its side is the salvaged sail of the Russian nuclear submarine *Kursk*, which in August 2000 sank in the nearby Barents Sea with the loss of her entire crew of 118 men.

Murmansk is filled with memorials. The city hosts a monument to the "Frontier Guards of the Soviet Union" and a monument to the "Anti-Hitler Coalition." There is a memorial to Soviet and Russian fishermen and merchant seamen, and a monument to the all-important codfish. There is even a memorial to the legendary cat "Semyon," who was lost by his owners during their vacation to Moscow but who dutifully made his way back to Murmansk over the course of six years. In front of the dock where the retired nuclear-powered icebreaker *Lenin* floats for visiting tourists, there is a monument to the "Dockworkers Killed in the Great Patriotic War." But there is not a single memorial in all of Murmansk to the thousands of US, British, Canadian, and other allied merchant mariners, who drowned or froze in those frigid waters bringing the supplies for those dockworkers to unload.[1]

Perhaps there are still hard feelings about 1918. With the Great War raging in the West and the Bolshevik revolution flaring throughout Russia, US, British, and other allied troops (sailors, soldiers and marines) landed in Murmansk and Archangelsk, hoping to keep Russia in a war the Bolsheviks had dismissed as irrelevant to them, a war between capitalists. Needless to say, the intervention did not end well, and the surviving allied troops were evacuated a year later, leaving the poorly led White Russian troops to fend for themselves against the Bolsheviks.

In Murmansk there's a monument for that, too—the "Monument for the Victims of the Intervention."

———

THE "MURMANSK RUN," as the convoys were called, began in mid-1941 following the collapse of the Molotov-von Ribbentrop pact establishing goodwill between Germany and the Soviet Union. While both sides were certainly biding their time until hostilities would be inevitable, Germany broke the pact first by invading eastern Poland, the Ukraine, and the Baltic States (the latter which had already been seized by the Soviet Union as part of the agreement). Britain and the United States quickly acceded to Soviet demands for supplies to aid its war efforts against Germany. The ports of Murmansk and Archangelsk, along with Vladivostok on the northern Pacific and Odessa and Sevastopol on the Black Sea, were the only Soviet ports with sufficient capacity to aid the war effort. Among these, Vladivostok was hampered by the poor condition of the ten-thousand-kilometer rail line that crossed Siberia and almost the whole of the Soviet

Union before reaching the armies fighting in the west. In addition, only Soviet ships could carry cargo to Vladivostok, so close to the Japanese home islands, since the Soviet Union was not at war with Japan. Cargo unloaded in Iranian ports on the Persian Gulf could also reach the Soviets, but it was similarly hampered by distance and poor rail connections. By far, Murmansk most effectively placed the ammunition, trucks, tanks, and other supplies where they were needed (the western Soviet Union), as they arrived from where they were produced (the US, Canada, and the UK).

The heavily armed German battleship *Tirpitz* at anchor in a Norwegian fjord.

Naval planners balanced natural and man-made challenges when routing convoys to Murmansk or Archangelsk. The most direct route from ports in North America or the west coast of Britain would have taken the convoys south of the Faroe Islands, paralleled the coast of Norway and then turned south at the Kola Peninsula for Kola Bay and Murmansk or the White Sea and Archangel. But German control of Norway meant that, in addition to the submarine threat, German surface raiders lurking in Norwegian fjords and German aircraft launching from Norwegian airfields along the coast could threaten a convoy along its entire route. The most dangerous surface raider in Norway in early 1942 was the battleship *Tirpitz*, some 49,000 tons and armed with eight 15-inch guns. *Tirpitz* threatened not just convoys passing Norway, but the British fleet in the North Sea, so the movements of *Tirpitz* and her sister ships required a constant reallocation of British surface forces in the area. British destroyers would be no match for her primary armament. In northern Norwegian bases such as Tromso, Germany deployed more than sixty bombers, primarily Junkers Ju-88s and Heinkel He-111s, and thirty Ju-87 "Stuka" dive bombers, capable of attacking the convoys. These threats were in addition to the ever-present U-boats. Four U-boats were deployed to the area in early 1942, but that number rose steadily until 1943 saw a peak of forty German submarines in Norway and its vicinity.[2]

Type VIIC U-boats return to their base at Narvik, Norway, after attacking a convoy bound for Murmansk.

Arctic weather added another dimension to the challenge. In summer, with the ice receding to the north, convoys could be routed well north towards the Svalbard Islands, 560 miles from the North Cape of Norway. Indeed, Spitsbergen, on the southern end of the Svalbard, offered an anchorage for refueling convoys during the summer. But the long arctic summer days, when the sun never truly set, made the ships of the convoy readily visible to searching aircraft and submarines. The arctic winter brought the gift of almost day-long nights, but also the southward march of the ice, which forced the convoys back towards the Norwegian coast. And the ice was not just a threat on the water.

Winter blizzards could coat the decks and superstructures of a ship so thoroughly that, without constant chipping and breaking of the ice (some ships were issued baseball bats for the purpose), the decks would become impassible, the guns unusable, and the ships unstable. There was no easy season for the Murmansk run.

These considerations led to the convoys being routed first north-northwest from the UK to Iceland, and then northeast from Iceland as far north through the Norwegian Sea as the ice conditions permitted towards the Barents Sea and the Kola Peninsula. Britain sent the first convoy to northern Russia in August 1941. The six cargo ships and an escort of "Operation Dervish" left Liverpool on the twelfth and anchored in Hvalfjordur, Iceland, an eighteen-mile-long fjord just north of Reykjavik, on the twentieth, leaving Iceland the next day.[3] Over the course of their journey they were escorted by various combinations of nineteen different ships, including the aircraft carrier *Victorious*. The convoy arrived in Archangelsk ten days later, unmolested by the Germans. On August 19, the British launched Operation Gauntlet, which centered on evacuating Norwegian civilians and Russian miners from Spitsbergen, leaving a British defensive force in their place. The Russians were repatriated through Archangelsk, and the Norwegians returned to Britain without significant contact with the Germans. A week later, the UK launched Operation Strength, with the aircraft carrier *Argus*, protected by a cruiser and three destroyers in flotilla, transporting Hawker Hurricane aircraft to Archangelsk for use by the Soviet air force. Again, the transit was largely uneventful.

The next convoy set the pattern that would continue for much of the war. Designated by the British as "QP-1," the six ships that had arrived as "Dervish," joined by seven Russian cargo ships, steamed from Archangelsk on September 28. Escorted at various times by a collection of trawlers, mine-sweepers, destroyers, and cruisers, the convoy enjoyed an uneventful journey and arrived in the Orkneys on October 10. An eastbound convoy, designated PQ-1, left Hvalfjordur on September 29 and arrived in Archangelsk without contact with the enemy on October 11.[4]

So, the pattern progressed, with convoys leaving east or westbound every week or ten days, but the convoys' good luck could not hold. On December 17 two British minesweepers steaming from Murmansk to meet convoy PQ-6 were attacked by German destroyers, but with little effect. The convoy made it safely to Murmansk. However, PQ-7A was not as lucky. Just two merchant ships escorted by a pair of trawlers, the duo were unable to rendezvous with a pair of minesweepers detailed to escort them into Murmansk. The two then became separated in bad weather and on January 2, 1942, one of the ships, the British freighter *Waziristan*, was sunk by a combination of a German aircraft's bombs and a U-boat's torpedo. The new year was off to a rough start for the Murmansk run. Before long the Germans would get serious about stopping convoys steaming to Murmansk.

On the other side of the Atlantic, in a country now urgently mobilizing for the war it had tried to avoid joining, 28-year-old Leonard La Rue, his fresh chief-mate license in hand, joined the *Mormacmar* at a dock at the Army Base in South Boston. He boarded a vessel that, according to a recent report to the Maritime Commission, was in generally good condition despite more than twenty years of hard service, with the officers' cabins freshly painted and the galley "clean." The ship was armed and degaussed. As La Rue assumed his duties as second mate (the ship already had a chief mate), the ship was loading cargo in anticipation of joining an eastbound convoy in short order. Following standard procedure for a newly appointed second mate, La Rue would have reported to the master immediately upon boarding. Perhaps the master would have instructed La Rue to help supervise the loading and stowage of cargo, which included tanks, trucks, and fighter aircraft loaded in the holds, along with five hundred barrels of incendiary white phosphorus stowed on the deck. As time permitted, he would have inspected the vessel, becoming familiar with her spaces and equipment, with particular attention to the aft of the vessel. He would have had special responsibility for navigation, and so he would have inspected the navigation equipment, inventoried the charts, and reported to the Master that all charts and equipment were on hand for the journey ahead.

Mormacmar sailed from Boston at 1600 on February 18 on what the officer in charge of the Armed Guard, Ensign Harrison Smith, USNR, called, without exaggeration, "an eventful voyage."[5] On February 6, while the ship was still loading cargo, Ensign Smith,

> "deemed it necessary to call upon the services of the F.B.I., Navy, Army, and Coast Guard Intelligence to remove from the ship four of the ship's crew for drunkenness, incompetency, insubordination, threatening to kill various members of the ship's company and for causing general unrest among the crew."

Considering the plain division of responsibility between the master and the commander of the Armed Guard, it is hard to imagine why Ensign Smith felt the need to take control of the crew situation unless he felt it was something the master could not handle.

Perhaps the master's inability or unwillingness to discipline the crew explains an occurrence a few days into the actual sailing. At 1800 on the nineteenth, just twenty-four hours after sailing, the ship received a distress broadcast from the unescorted British ship *Empire Seal*. The *Empire Seal*, carrying 4,500 tons of steel from New York to Belfast via Halifax, had been torpedoed by the U-96 off Sable Island, sixty miles ahead of *Mormacmar* on her course for Halifax. *Mormacmar* immediately changed course for Portland, Maine, avoiding the location of the U-boat and arriving there on February 20. Correspondence between Moore-McCormack lines and the Maritime Commission characterized the diversion as "for minor repairs," but without further elaboration, Ensign Smith records, after approving of the captain's decision not to risk the ship and her cargo to a lurking submarine, that during the short stay in Portland the "captain was relieved of his command." Whatever the reason, *Mormacmar* sailed from Portland on the twenty-second under command of a new master, Captain W. H. Senior, on its way to Halifax to join convoy HX-177. As if the officers and men of the *Mormacmar* needed a reminder of the hazards ahead, the ship passed a burning wreck that had been torpedoed just outside Halifax.

Elderly but proud in fresh camouflage paint, HMCS Niagara swings on a mooring before escorting PQ-13.

On February 25, 1942, *Mormacmar* took her position at the left rear corner of the convoy as HX-177 left Halifax for the journey east. Joining her was just one more American ship, her sister ship *Mormacrio*, in position dead ahead in the convoy, along with eighteen British ships, three Norwegian vessels, and one Dutch ship. The convoy left Halifax in the company of Canadian naval escorts, including the Bangor-class minesweeper HMCS *Chedabucto*, the Flower-class corvettes HMCS *Lunenburg* and HMCS *The Pas*, and the Town-class destroyer HMCS *Niagara*. With the convoy steaming east at a speed of ten knots, the sixteen-knot limitation of the minesweeper and corvettes might not have seemed a limitation, but the thirty-seven-knot speed of the *Niagara* could prove very useful in chasing down a U-boat. *Niagara*, a World War I vintage, Wilkes-class, US Navy "four-piper" destroyer launched in 1918, had been given to the United Kingdom in September 1940 as part of the "Destroyers for Bases" program that granted the United States ninety-nine-year leases on military bases located throughout the British Empire in exchange for badly needed ships. *Niagara* was no stranger to fighting U-boats, having participated with British air and naval forces in the capture of

U-570 south of Iceland in late August 1941. Still, the convoy hugged Nova Scotia and the southern coast of Newfoundland.

By March 1, HX-177 had cleared Newfoundland and Canadian waters, starting her northeast run towards the UK. A new group of escorts that would endeavor to protect the convoy the rest of the way across the Atlantic took over. HX-177 said goodbye to *Chedabucto, Lunenburg, The Pas,* and *Niagara* and welcomed the Flower-class corvettes *Barrie, Chambly, Mayflower,* and *Rosthern.* Along with the Canadian corvettes, the US Coast Guard cutter *Ingham* and the US Navy *Gleaves*-class destroyer *Niblack* joined the convoy to replace the departing *Niagara.* The *Niblack* would provide the thirty-seven-knot speed the other ships lacked if it needed to chase down a U-boat. *Ingham* would sight and sink a U-boat in December and when she would finally be decommissioned in 1988, she would be the last US warship in commission to have sunk a U-boat.

The valiant Coast Guard cutter *Ingham* enjoying typical North Atlantic weather close abeam a merchantman.

Even at a convoy speed of ten knots, *Mormacmar* already had trouble keeping up. The convoy had entered heavy weather, and at 2130 on March first *Mormacmar* suffered a "breakdown in the engine room" that caused her to drop behind the rest of the convoy. With the ship now alone and drifting on the Atlantic, the Armed Guard, assisted by lookouts from the crew, went to general quarters on guard for submarines until the ship resumed course and speed at 2330. The relaxation was short lived, for an hour later several of the barrels of phosphorous broke loose as the ship rolled in the storm. The lids of the wayward barrels popped off and their contents immediately ignited in contact with the waves breaking over the deck, which started a large fire. The combined efforts of the Armed Guard and the ship's crew were needed to extinguish the fire and re-secure the barrels, all while risking being washed overboard. After several hours of strenuous effort with the ship now pointed into the wind and waves, they successfully re-secured the cargo and *Mormacmar* resumed course, rejoining the convoy two days later on March 4.

The next few days were uneventful, but on the eighth of March the crew's lack of discipline highlighted before in Boston became apparent once more.[6] A member of the crew broke into the ship's "Slop Chest," a store of clothing, tobacco, and other items that would be sold to the crew during a voyage, with the cost debited against their wages. Apparently, *Mormacmar* had more than the usual items in her Slop Chest, for what was stolen was a case of rum, with the result that three able seamen became drunk and could not stand their watches. The usual penalty for the offense of failure to stand watch was for the seamen to be docked two-days wages, so they might have considered their revelry worthwhile. Whether the actual thief was identified and penalized is not recorded.

On the following day, the convoy reached their anchorage in Lock Ewe, Scotland, and said goodbye to their American and Canadian escorts. Loch Ewe, or "Echo Lake" in Gaelic, is on the northwestern-most corner of Scotland, a long, deep inlet providing shelter from the prevailing winds. Low hills surround the Loch, with a vista typical of the lonely Scottish Highlands, well suited for raising sheep, fishing from her shores, and sipping strong drinks. Britain had chosen this location to allow convoys to reform before continuing their passage to Russia because the Loch was out of range of German Air Force (*Luft-*

waffe) bombers operating from coastal Norway, and it provided protection from the German naval forces ranging to the northeast. Here the convoy could gather its stragglers and refuel. Ships that had sailed up the coast from Southampton and Liverpool could join their fellows for the passage east. The masters of the merchant ships could meet with the convoy commodore and his staff to review the sailing plan and any changes to signals or codes, and plans of evasion and zig-zag. A lucky crew might motor ashore in the ship's boat for drinks at the only pub in the only town on the Loch, the eponymous Aultbea Inn.[7] But most would rest quietly, hoping the boom and net across the mouth of the Loch was keeping the U-boats away from the juicy targets swinging on their anchor chains.

The next day the convoy, now twenty merchant ships and designated by the British as PQ-13, sailed for Iceland in the company of her new escorts, the British destroyers *Sabre, Saladin,* and *Lamerton* and the Polish destroyer *Blyskawica*. At 1930 the next day, one of the escorts sighted a possible submarine, and destroyers dropped depth charges on the target for an hour, without apparent result. But in any event, none of merchant ships were attacked. Two days later, on the thirteenth, the convoy again hit heavy weather, and the *Mormacmar*, with her five hundred barrels of combustible deck cargo, had to slow and drop out from the convoy, pointing her bow into the seas to give her crew, augmented by the Armed Guard crew, the opportunity to re-secure the cargo once again. Twenty-four hours later the ship was able to rejoin the convoy and sailed with it into Hvalfjordur Fjord on March 15.

PQ-13 rested at Hvalfjordur for three days, but the time was hardly restful. The stress of the passage and the bad attitudes among the crew that had surfaced in Boston before sailing reappeared in a near-mutiny on the *Mormacmar*. On the morning of the sixteenth, the union delegates of the deck, engine, and steward departments presented Captain Senior with a list of complaints. Like most American ships of the time, the unlicensed crew were represented by the Congress of Industrial Organizations, and while the union had taken a wartime no-strike pledge, there was nothing to prevent the union delegates in each department from confronting the master of the ship with their grievances. Boatswain Robert McElroy and Able Seamen Andrew Mahon and Francis W. Durbin alleged that the lifeboats were unseaworthy, the deck cargo not secure, the general alarm system ineffective, and the water and food they were provided poor. Captain Senior and Chief Mate Roberts inspected the ship and determined to their satisfaction that the complaints were groundless aside from the stowage of the deck cargo, which was being re-secured by the deck department while at anchor.

Ships at anchor in Hvalfjordur, Iceland.

Unsurprisingly, the captain's appraisal of the situation failed to satisfy the union delegates, and they requested to go ashore to make their complaints to the US Consul in Reykjavik, as was their right under their labor agreement. But the naval authorities in Reykjavik had forbidden any officers or crew from leaving the ships save the master, so Captain Senior agreed to take their complaints to the consul himself. Aside from trying to restore some level of harmony between the officers and men, the master was surely aware that he could be fined as much as five hundred dollars for not addressing a legitimate complaint of the crew regarding seaworthiness or the adequacy of food or drink. Later that day, Captain Senior presented the complaints in writing, signed by McElroy, Mahon, and Durbin, to the American Vice Consul in Reykjavik, A. G. Heltberg, but assured the consul that, aside from the stowage of the cargo, which was being addressed, the complaints were groundless. Consul Heltberg and the captain conferred with the US Naval authorities in Reykjavik, who told them in no uncertain terms that the ship would sail with the next convoy and if the captain could not handle the situation on board the ship, the Navy would.

At 0830 on March 17 the union delegates approached the captain and asked about the consul's decision regarding their grievances. When apprised of the decision, the delegates called the crew together, both on and off duty, and organized a strike on the ship. With the crew refusing to turn to for duty, and preparations still needed for sailing the next day, including the all-important re-stowing of the perilous deck cargo, Captain Senior dispatched Junior Third Officer Griswold to the vice consul with a letter explaining the situation. The fact that the master chose to remain on the ship and sent one of his officers ashore in contravention of the Navy's instructions highlights how seriously he took the discontent.

Griswold returned from the consul's office at 1400 accompanied by Lieutenant Commander Frank T. Kemmer, USCG, who was in command of ten fully-armed US Marines. Commander Kemmer investigated and agreed with the captain that the complaints were largely baseless and signed a statement in *Mormacmar's* official log to that effect. Faced with the official dictum and ten men with rifles, the crew relented and returned to duty. At 1500 Kemmer and the Marines left the ship accompanied by Captain Senior, who was to attend the convoy conference ashore that afternoon. There, the master was informed that the convoy would get underway for Murmansk at 0630 the next morning, March 18. When the captain returned to the ship, he determined the deck cargo was still not properly secured and ordered the chief mate to have the deck department turn to at 1900 to finish securing the cargo. When the hour arrived, the deck department again refused to work.

On questioning Bosun McElroy and the deck department's CIO delegate, the men claimed that they were speaking for the entire deck department and the department would not turn to unless the captain declared an emergency, which would have required the entire ship's company to assist the deck department in re-stowing the cargo. The captain refused. Given that the ship was scheduled to sail in less than ten hours, it might be surprising that the master did not declare an emergency and grant the deck department the help they wanted. Perhaps given the problems of discipline the ship had experienced before he had assumed command three weeks earlier in Portland, during the Atlantic crossing, and now in Iceland, the captain chose not to accede to demands he feared might escalate later. Maybe he just didn't want to pay overtime. However, when the men refused to relent despite being reminded of the seriousness of refusing an order (an offense which could be punished by up to three months in prison), the captain had no choice but to ask the Navy again for help.

Just before midnight, Lieutenant Commander Kemmer returned to the *Mormacmar* with his detachment of Marines. No doubt tired of this nonsense and now losing sleep, he lined up the entire deck department and questioned them about whether they would return to work. All but eight agreed to turn to, and Kemmer took the intransigent eight ashore under guard. Following questioning by the port director, a US Navy captain named B. R. Alexander, five of the eight subsequently relented and were returned to the ship, leaving Bosun McElroy and Able Seamen Mahon and Durbin in the Navy brig.

As the convoy sailed on schedule the next morning the *Mormacmar* still rode at anchor. At 1300, Captain Alexander called Captain Senior ashore and informed him that the *Mormacmar* was to sail and catch up to the convoy if at all possible. Senior responded, "Give me the men and the ship will sail." The port authorities followed through, for within a few hours they had hired three Icelandic sailors to replace the three Americans in the brig. The authorities took them to the American Consulate to sign them onto the ship, gathered their gear, and raced them out to the *Mormacmar* by speedboat. The ship weighed anchor at 1600 and with her engine running at maximum revolutions, *Mormacmar* rejoined the convoy the at 0730 next morning, March 18.

As the three crew members sat in the Navy brig in Iceland, the convoy continued on its somber journey towards northern Russia. The escort out of Hvalfjordur consisted of a ragtag assortment of ships, including the converted whaler *Sulla*, the trawlers *Blackfly* and *Paynter*, and the British E-class destroyer *Eclipse* and F-class destroyer *Fury*. After *Mormacmar* rejoined the convoy on the eighteenth, the early journey was uneventful. Once the convoy crossed seventy-one degrees north latitude (the lattitude of the North Cape), lookouts aboard *Mormacmar* started to see floating mines. Ironically, although there is no record of any ships in PQ-13 striking mines, *Eclipse* and *Fury* would both meet their demise later in war (*Eclipse* in 1943 and *Fury* in 1944) following mine strikes, highlighting how deadly these simple weapons could be.

The critical naval situation around the North Cape of Norway had led Britain to deploy a significant task force in the Norwegian Sea to deter German attacks against both the convoy and shipping closer to the UK itself. By March 1942, the Germans had deployed the battleship *Tirpitz* along with the cruisers *Admiral Scheer*, *Prinz Eugen* and *Admiral Hipper* to Trondheim, Norway. Five German destroyers and nineteen U-boats were known to be operating in Norwegian waters. In response, the British deployed the battleships *King George V*, *Duke of York*, the aircraft carrier *Victorious*, and almost twenty cruisers and destroyers in an attempt to respond to any sortie by these raiders from their refuges in the Norwegian fiords. Closer to PQ-13, *Lamerton* rejoined the convoy between March 23 and 25, accompanied by the British cruiser *Trinidad*.

On March 25 the convoy ran into "a typical North Atlantic gale," in the words of Ensign Smith, causing the convoy to spread out so that by the twenty-seventh, *Mormacmar* was able to remain in a group consisting of just five ships of the original convoy. The rest of PQ-13 spread over 150 miles east to west in the seas between the Northern Cape and Bear Island, the latter a major land feature midway between the Cape and Svalbard. By the twenty-eighth, the weather had cleared enough for German aircraft flying from Norway to search for the convoy, and *Mormacmar* went to general quarters at 1240 as a German aircraft flew in a wide circle around the ship, well outside the range of the ship's .30- and .50-caliber machine guns.

Less than two hours later, the Luftwaffe found a target. At 1425 the Panamanian-flagged SS *Raceland*, about ten miles astern *Mormacmar*, broadcast an SOS saying she had just been bombed by a German aircraft and was sinking, with the crew manning the lifeboats. Later that day, the British-flagged *Empire Ranger*, about 100 miles ahead of *Mormacmar*, radioed that she was being attacked. The next morning, as the ship passed *Empire Ranger*'s last known position, the crew of *Mormacmar* and her Armed Guard scanned the sea searching for the ship or her crew in the water, but they were gone. German destroyers had already reached the location of the sinking and rescued some sixty-one survivors from the British ship. It was later believed that the Germans learned of the planned movements of the convoy from some of the survivors and as a result early on the twenty-ninth one of the German destroyers, the Z-26, was able to find another ship, the Panamanian-flagged *Bateau*, and sink her.

The battle for the convoy, now about 150 miles northwest of Murmansk, was in full swing. Around the time the *Bateau* was being attacked on March 29, *Mormacmar* and the ships around her, now the core of the convoy, were joined ahead and on her flanks by four destroyers, with the cruiser *Trinidad* ranging ahead. At 1015 the ships steamed into heavy fog, and just five minutes later Ensign Smith and his shipmates on *Mormacmar* could hear "loud reports," with Smith thinking the deck cargo had once again broken loose. *Mormacmar* soon realized that the destroyers were firing at an enemy abeam her, where the visibility was judged less than two thousand yards. *Trinidad* and the *Eclipse* were seeking to hold off the German destroyers by engaging them in a close-fought surface battle. The sounds of explosions became louder and more frequent, with German shells landing in the water off *Mormacmar's* port side. One impacted close enough to blow the lock off the cabin door of one of the ship's officers.

The British eventually got their revenge on the Z-26 by damaging her badly and knocking her out of the fight, but an errant torpedo fired from *Trinidad* swam back to the cruiser and exploded directly below her bridge, forcing the ship to make its way to Murmansk alone. By 1100 the battle was over for now and *Mormacmar* secured from general quarters. An hour later, *Mormacmar* and the convoy passed the *Trinidad*, which was listing "six or seven degrees to port" with "smoke pouring from amidships ... There were numerous other holes along her port side received from the German destroyer's 5.9" guns."

A convoy sailing through ice in the Barents Sea.

What remained of PQ-13 continued sailing eastward, encountering ice most of the evening of the twenty-ninth, some of which "stove in a few plates" on *Mormacmar's* bow. On the thirtieth the convoy finally turned south to approach Kola Bay from the northeast, but the threat was not over. At 1945 that evening, the convoy was just twenty miles from Murmansk when "an unidentified aircraft flew overhead in the overcast skies ...We went to General Quarters immediately" as Russian antiaircraft guns on the hills surrounding Kola Bay began firing and Russian fighter aircraft searched for the target, careful to avoid friendly fire. Ensign Smith continued his account,

"A few minutes later a large bomber flew directly overhead in the now clearing skies. It was still twilight. None of the escorting vessels used their guns. A few minutes later the same plane came out of a cloud at an altitude of approximately 2,000 feet, off our port quarter, and released two bombs. The first one hit not more than 100 yards off the quarter, and the second was a very near miss. We were the only ship to open fire but since we had only .30 and .50 caliber machine guns our effective fire was not very great."[8]

By all indications, *Mormacmar* was very lucky to avoid the bombs that had doomed two of her compatriots. Indeed, her sister ship, *Mormacsul*, would be sunk by the Luftwaffe off the North Cape less than eight weeks later as part of convoy PQ-16, the Germans' warmup to the doomed PQ-17.[9] The only damage to *Mormacmar* from the near miss were three broken bearing caps on her propeller shaft. Two more ships would be sunk on the March 30, this time by U-boats, the British-flagged *Induna* by the U-376, and the American-flagged *Effingham* by the U-435.

A survivor of the *Induna* described what it was like to be in a lifeboat in the Barents Sea:

"After the ship had gone we could see nothing of the port lifeboat as there was a high sea running and it was all I could do to keep our boat head on to the seas, the men rowing as hard as they could ... There were 32 of us in the boat which we found very cramped ... It was bitterly cold during the night and the six or seven bottles of whisky which were in the boat were passed round, ... unfortunately, some of the men drank a great deal ... most of the men who drank the whisky died in their sleep that night. We put their bodies over the side of the boat, without removing their clothes ... My feet were wet all time ... We rowed in spells to keep ourselves warm, but our hands were so numb that it was all we could do to hang onto the oars."

Mormacmar and the surviving ships of PQ-13 finally made the port at 0130 on March 31. The survivors of *Induna* would spend two more days at sea before rescue by a Russian minesweeper.

Arriving pierside was an accomplishment, but now La Rue and *Mormacmar* had to survive Murmansk itself. Lying above the Arctic Circle, Murmansk struggled to rise above its roots as a rough fishing camp. A single-track rail line ran from Murmansk the length of Karelia to Petrozavodsk on Lake Onega, then south to Leningrad. The Assistant US Naval Attaché to the Soviet Union assigned at Murmansk, Commander Samuel B. Frankel, later wrote in a secret dispatch to Washington that, after some improvements,

"Estimate port can offload 500 tons daily but past experience has shown inability of railroad to handle the amount results in congestion [on] docks and deceleration of discharge. Railway clearance capacity not over 400 tons daily under favorable circumstances and latter not experienced this year due to shortage [of] cars bombing of like and like contributory causes."[10]

Since each ship that arrived in the port would carry several thousand tons of supplies, the ships of a convoy could reside in Murmansk for several weeks until all of them could be emptied and a convoy reformed for the trip back west.

Because the port had such strategic importance to the Soviet war effort and it was well within the range of Luftwaffe air bases in northern Norway, German aircraft regularly bombed the port and its environs. During the month *Mormacmar* stayed in Murmansk, her Armed Guard responded to sixty-five air-raid alerts. *Mormacmar* weathered these attacks largely unscathed. Ensign Smith noted as the result of near misses in port that, "two of my 4"/50 projectiles were torn from the cartridge case and the small metal bands that cover the percussion caps in the ready service boxes were bent." The Armed Guard crew even received partial credit for shooting down several German aircraft, but not all the members of PQ-13 were so lucky. Two members of the convoy, the British *New Westminster City* and *Empire Starlight*, were sunk at their berths by German bombers on April 3.

Freighters offloading in Murmansk.

The problem of Luftwaffe attacks on Murmansk seemed to frustrate the British and Americans more than the Soviets. The obvious solution would have been to bomb the airstrips from which the attacking bombers were launched. In a secret letter sent on April 5 to the Commander of US Naval Forces Europe in London, Frankel said,

"Russian General Staff will not give Golovko [commander of the Soviet Northern Fleet][11] enough bombers because they think our convoy supplies are drop in the bucket compared with their great industrial output. Golovko does not have a single long-range bomber that can reach Banak[12] and his twenty long range fighters are not enough to cover slow moving convoys for the long daylight voyage from Kola Inlet to a reasonable distance from coast. Locally the Hurricanes and air defenses are quite adequate but attacks from enemy aerodromes 50 miles away cannot be prevented."[13]

There were inadequate forces to maintain a continuous air cover over Murmansk, and the short flight time from the Norwegian airfields meant that there was little warning when an air raid approached the city or a convoy at sea.

Murmansk after repeated *Luftwaffe* incendiary attacks. Note the many ships at anchor opposite the piers in the distance.

Regarding convoy escort, Frankel's note continued, "Russian destroyers now being used but believe maintenance poor and officers unaccustomed to long sea trips. Cannot be counted on to keep their promised assistance to convoys. Golovko willing but understaffed." High level contacts between US/British and Soviet officials reinforced the opinion that, "getting convoys safely in and out of north Russian ports should be a joint British and American responsibility."

The Brits and the Yanks were largely on their own.

German incendiary attacks had burned whole swaths of the wood-constructed city of Murmansk, making the crews stay in a cold, dark, foreign city all the more dismal. A British naval officer wrote of the privations following sustained German attacks,

> "Quite recently two provision shops have blossomed out into most appetizing windows displaying hams, sausages and fish, made of wood. They avoid the charge of acquiring one's roubles [*sic*] under false pretense by having nothing on sale within whatever ... Otherwise the only things to draw one's eye are crude war posters."

Regarding diversions for the hundreds of sailors spending weeks in Murmansk, he wrote,

> "The social life appears to be confined to Clubs, in Murmansk there are four, one army, two navy and an International sailor's club. Only the latter has made the slightest attempt at extending hospitality to the British and American Missions here, and during convoys, it is rather to be avoided ... Occasional traveling concert parties ... mediocre, visit a hall in one of the clubs and charge an extortionate number of roubles for a very hard seat."

Some of the crew were no doubt able to entertain themselves with black-market vodka, gambling, and perhaps local companionship. For Second Mate La Rue, who did not drink, gamble, or by any indications choose to avail himself of sailors' other typical shore-side entertainments, Murmansk was likely a hard place to spend a month.

At least the sailors had a bunk on their ship. For those whose ships had been sunk out from under them, the situation was even bleaker. Commander Frankel wrote in June 1942,

> "During the period February 1 to June 30, 1942, the Office of the Assistant Naval Attaché at Murmansk has in cooperation with the

British Mission in Northern Russia taken care of approximately 300 survivors from ships under the United States or Panamanian flags. These men were quartered and fed by the Soviet authorities and food and clothing were either obtained from the local stores or from British or American Maritime sources. All injured were admitted to Soviet hospitals and given treatment until such time as they were considered fit for travel and then assigned to vessels for return to the United States."

He continued, highlighting the continued threat in both directions of the Murmansk run,

"No seaman was assigned transportation until he was capable of looking after himself in the event of a marine disaster. At the present time there are 11 survivors from American vessels in Northern Russia all of whom are in hospitals or receiving treatment in rest camps. Two American seamen have been buried in Murmansk, 25 seamen are missing at sea or died and were buried at sea."

On April 28 the return convoy, designated QP-11, finally formed up in the approaches to Kola Bay. Of the 18 ships that had left Reykjavík, five had been sunk en route and two pierside in Murmansk. After unloading, four of the survivors of PQ-13 had already joined an earlier convoy, QP-10, which had sailed on April 10. One ship would sail with QP-12 on May 21 and another, the British tanker *Tobruk*, would not sail until QP-14 on the thirteenth of September, where she would be joined by survivors of the most famous convoy of the Murmansk run, the ill-fated PQ-17, that would be leaving Ryekjavik on June 27. So, on this April morning, *Mormacmar* was joined by four ships that had traveled with her in PQ-13: the US-flagged *Eldena* and *Dunboyne* and the Panamanian-flagged *Gallant Fox* and *El Estero*. Aboard *Mormacmar* were twenty-two additional officers and men being repatriated back to the US, survivors of PQ-13's *Effingham*, which had been torpedoed and sunk on March 30. Eight more ships rounded out the convoy, including a lone Soviet-flagged merchant ship, *Tsiolkovsky*.

These thirteen merchant ships were matched with fifteen escorts initially led by two Soviet destroyers, the British destroyers *Amazon*, *Beagle*, *Beverley* and *Bulldog*, four British minesweepers and an assortment of British trawlers and corvettes. QP-11 steamed for two days on a course northeast of Kola Inlet, turning westward only after crossing seventy-three degrees north latitude. The Soviet destroyers and the British minesweepers returned to Murmansk and the Soviet Naval base at nearby Polyarny to be replaced on the thirtieth by the British cruiser *HMS Edinburgh* and two more British destroyers, *Foresight* and *Forester*. Unknown to her escorts, QP-11 had already been detected the day before by German U-boats and aircraft. Not long after *Edinburgh* had taken her position at the head of the convoy she was torpedoed by U-456. The torpedo struck her stern and blew a large section away, but she retained propulsion on her port shaft and slowly started her way back to Polyarny, escorted by *Foresight* and *Forester*. Unbeknownst to the Germans, *Edinburgh* had been loaded with a large quantity of gold bullion in Murmansk in partial payment to the British for war supplies delivered to the Soviet Union, and the British did not want that treasure on the bottom of the Barents Sea.

At 0440 on May 1, the convoy was approximately 130 miles due north of the North Cape when a quartet of four-engined Luftwaffe bombers approached the convoy from its port quarter (the southeast), flying just 150 feet above the sea surface. *Mormacmar* was apparently the first to see the aircraft, for her gunners opened fire with their .30- and .50-caliber machine guns before the destroyers on her port side had seen the aircraft. Intense fire by the Armed Guard caused the bombers to change course to avoid *Mormacmar*, and a torpedo aimed for the ship passed astern. The aircraft circled QP-11 and reattacked from the starboard, but without effect, the rest of the ships now fending them off with concentrated antiaircraft fire. Their weapons expended, three of the aircraft flew back in the direction of Norway, with one orbiting for about two hours, keeping watch over the convoy before the ships steamed into a snow squall and visibility was lost.

HMS Edinburgh, *missing part of her stern.*

If the men of *Mormacmar* and the other ships in the convoy thought they were out of danger, the afternoon of the May 1 was to prove otherwise. The Kriegsmarine had dispatched several destroyers, the *Schoemann*, Z 24 and Z 25, to finish what U-456 had started with Edinburgh. At 1257, *Mormacmar* went back to general quarters when she received a signal (presumably by Aldis lamp, a spotlight with manually operated shutters for sending Morse code using pulses of light, rather than by radio) that German ships were near. The four remaining escort destroyers formed up on the port side of the convoy and started laying a heavy blanket of smoke, obscuring the Germans' view of the merchant ships now turning forty degrees to starboard, away from the attackers. The British destroyers fired on the Germans for several minutes, and the combination of intense gun fire and heavy smoke appeared to be holding the enemy at bay when at 1329 the *Tsiolkovsky*, six hundred yards off *Mormacmar's* starboard beam, was torpedoed and disappeared beneath the waves within five minutes. *Mormacmar* had dodged another torpedo.

A convoy spotted from a *Luftwaffe* aircraft, the unfortunate PQ-17, just two
months after QP-11. Of the thirty-five merchant ships of PQ-17 that left
Hvalfjordur on June 27, only ten would reach their destination ports in the
Soviet Union.

The destroyers resumed firing at each other ten minutes later, but now
the Germans turned their attention to searching for the crippled *Edinburgh*. As the Germans raced to the east, by 1500 the British
destroyers had now interposed themselves astern the convoy, three
thousand yards behind *Mormacmar*, still laying smoke in an attempt to
limit the Germans' ability to acquire targets among the merchantmen.
As a result, while the Germans fired into the convoy, their three-shot
salvoes were landing not on the ships but in the empty water between
them. Despite some near misses, none of the ships were hit. Again, at
1600, shells rained down on the convoy, but without effect. By now,
QP-11's turn to starboard had driven the convoy into an icefield, but
by 2025 the convoy had escaped this threat, re-formed, and continued
on her way west.

If the threat from ice and German destroyers was receding, other
threats were not. Late on the evening of the first, escorting destroyers
commenced depth-charge runs close aboard *Mormacmar*, shaking the
ship but not revealing a submarine. The next morning, May 2, the
men of *Mormacmar* rose to see a German aircraft orbiting high above
the convoy, out of antiaircraft range, relaying QP-11's position to the
Kriegsmarine. At 0940 destroyers dropped depth charges to *Mormacmar's* starboard, and for two hours in the early afternoon they

dropped depth charges to port, but no oil slick, wreckage, or stricken submarine on the surface could be seen. No torpedoes were aimed at the dozen survivors of the convoy either.

Coast Guard cutter *Spencer* drops depth charges on a U-boat during an attack on an Atlantic convoy in April 1943.

The same could not be said for HMS *Edinburgh*, that same day engaged with her escorts hundreds of miles east in a battle with the three German destroyers. Despite gunfire from *Edinburgh* so intense that it eventually sank the *Schoemann*, the destroyer got her revenge when one of her torpedoes struck the cruiser amidships, nearly cutting her in two. The dying cruiser was finally sent to her rest by one last torpedo, this time fired by her compatriot, *Foresight*, taking her dead and her cache of gold eight hundred feet down to the bottom of the Barents Sea. Most of the four and a half tonnes of gold bars she carried would be salvaged, but not until forty years later.

As if the threat from U-boats were not enough, late that night the importance of alert lookouts was driven home when one of the men on *Mormacmar's* bow, despite standing his watch in a blinding snowstorm, spotted a mine floating ahead of the ship. The ship was able to change course to avoid its two hundred pounds of explosives by just three feet. The next day, despite passing more mines floating close aboard, *Mormacmar* and the other members of QP-11 were heartened to see Allied patrol aircraft flying overheard in place of the dreaded Dorniers and Focke-Wulfs. By midday on the fifth, the ship spotted the coast of Iceland, but it was almost a day and a half before the convoy was at anchor again at Hvalfjordur.[14]

On May 13 *Mormacmar* sailed from Iceland in the company of four of her convoy-mates, *Dunboyne, El Estero, Eldena* and *Gallant Fox,* joining seven other merchantmen and two American escorts. The convoy steamed south for three days to join the westbound Atlantic convoy ON-94, which had sailed from Liverpool the day before bound for Halifax. Comprising forty-five ships, ON-94 was a sign of things to come. Larger, denser convoys with plentiful escorts and as much air cover as could reach from Canada, Greenland, the UK, and Iceland, or could fly from escorting aircraft carriers, would eventually win the Battle of the Atlantic for the Allies. The two American destroyers returned to Reykjavik and the four British destroyers accompanying ON-94 assumed responsibility. Escorts dropped depth charges on suspected U-boats on the thirteenth, eighteenth, and nineteenth, but no attacks nor submarine wreckage appeared.[15]

The voyage continued to be largely uneventful compared to *Mormaca-mar's* previous wartime adventures. On May 20 the convoy came under the protection of US patrol aircraft based in Newfoundland, but on the morning of the twenty-second, the convoy steamed into a fog so thick that the convoy became separated. When the fog briefly lifted on the twenty-fourth, only nine merchantmen and two destroyers were in sight. When once again fog settled over the convoy and rendered it unsafe to enter Halifax, the commodore elected to avoid the port and instead continue straight for New York. Since it was essential to continue radio silence but the fog was too thick to use an Aldis lamp, the ships of the convoy used their ship's whistles to send messages in Morse code during the day, and similarly by flashing their running lights at night. On the twenty-fifth ON-94 received warning of a submarine ahead and altered course. When the fog finally lifted at 1800 on the twenty-sixth, the convoy, now down to seven ships and two destroyers in *Mormacmar's* vicinity, was abeam the tip of Cape Cod. The destroyers proceeded to Boston, and *Mormacmar* arrived in New York at 1100 on May 27.

Ensign Smith and members of his Armed Guard detachment were recommended for award of the "Operation and Engagement Star" for their service on PQ-13. The citation read, in part:

"The Convoy carrying vital war supplies was first attacked by submarines, aircraft and surface raiders when it reached a position of the northern part of the Scandinavian Peninsula about four days out of Murmansk. Four attacking enemy destroyers were sunk. On 28 March 1942 a pack of German submarines attacked the convoy but were repulsed by fire from the escort vessels and the merchant ships. Three of the attacking submarines were sunk or severely damaged. The Convoy was repeatedly attacked by torpedo planes, by Stuka and level-flying bombers. During the thirty days the ships of the Convoy were in Murmansk, there were 110 air alarms and actually 54 bombing attacks. Several of the attacking planes were shot down by concentrated fire from ships in port."[16]

Commander Frankel was awarded the Distinguished Service Medal for his "exceptionally meritorious service" as the Assistant Naval Attaché in Murmansk during 1942. He went on to serve in various intelligence roles after the war, as director of the Naval Intelligence School, Deputy Director of the Office of Naval Intelligence, and Chief of Staff of the Defense Intelligence Agency, retiring as a Rear Admiral.

For the officers and men of the *Mormacmar*, having lived through the same danger on the high seas as the Naval Armed Guard, and probably more danger in port than the Assistant Naval Attaché, there were no medals. More so, Captain Senior elected to withhold from the majority of the crew the one-hundred-dollar per man bonus that the

Soviet trading company Amtorg provided him for making the Murmansk run. The War Shipping Administration's General Counsel, responding to a question on the matter from the Administration's Director of the Division of Maritime Labor Relations, responded with a carefully crafted non-answer on the subject:

> "If, as contended on behalf of the Master, the money was given to the Master for distribution to such of his crew as in his sole discretion he saw fit, then those of the crew who did not share in the distribution have no cause for legal complaint. If, however, the money was given to the Master upon the condition that each member of the crew was to receive $100, then those of the crew who did not receive their share have a right of recovery from the Master."

Despite protestations from the crew and threats of lawsuits, the Maritime Commission and Moore-McCormack Lines upheld the master's decision and only certain of the crew, and likely all of the officers, received the bonus.

The voyage might have been over, but the saga of the three disaffected sailors seized from *Mormacmar* dragged on through much of 1942. McElroy, Mahon, and Durbin remained in the brig in Reykjavik for more than two months, only being repatriated to the United States in the end of May. After a preliminary hearing on June 11, the men were tried in late June on charges of failure to obey orders and failure to perform their duties before an administrative court of the Bureau of Marine Inspection and Navigation, which had recently been absorbed into the Coast Guard. The master's testimony reiterated the events of March 16-17. McElroy defended himself by asserting he was just reflecting the sentiment of the deck department, which felt it was overworked, and due to injury and illness, was understaffed to accomplish the re-stowage of the cargo before sailing from Iceland. Able Seaman Durbin accused the captain of using "foul and obscene language to him." He said that, despite his role as a CIO union delegate, Captain Senior, had "refused to listen to the various complaints that were made from time to time." On the other hand, all of the men, along with their witnesses, admitted that they had not done any work during the almost five hours between when the master had ordered the cargo restowed and the arrival of the shore guard.[17]

The three defendants were convicted, and their certificates as able seamen were suspended for thirty days, a rather minor punishment reflecting a wartime-nation's need for merchant seamen.[18] The entire affair was a poor reflection on the crew and their master. John Donovan, assistant counsel for the Maritime Commission, who attended the trial, commented,

> "In my opinion, Mr. Robert McElroy, boatswain, Mr. Francis W. Durbin, A.B., and Mr. Andrew Mahon, A.B., were the ring leaders in refusing to carry out the orders of the master or allowing other members of the crew to perform their work. The other members of the crew who were arrested were also equally at fault for in refusing to carry out instructions to re-fasten the deck cargo. I think the discipline aboard the vessel was very poor." He added, "It was strongly intimated by the boatswain and other members of the crew that there were continuous disorder and differences of opinion between the Master and the Chief Officer. It might be mentioned, however, that at the hearing the Chief Officer substantiated and corroborated everything the Master testified to."[19]

Throughout all of this drama, La Rue is never mentioned. While he was licensed as a chief mate, he had signed onto *Mormacmar* as second mate. Aside from duties delegated from the chief mate, he probably would have focused on navigation and left crew matters to his superiors. But he certainly observed whatever dynamic was at work between the master and his chief mate, and between them and the crew, and taken aboard lessons that would serve him when he was in command of his own ship a year hence. The burden of disciplining a crew resides with the master, who had the power to dock wages, the usual punishment for a minor infraction. But for major infractions, the master could order a crewman confined in irons until the ship reached a port where the American Consul could take the subject into custody for further prosecution.

After the near-mutiny in Iceland and the constant danger of the passage from weather, torpedoes, guns, mines, and bombs, what a relief it must have been for the officers and crew to arrive in New York. Forget the weeks in a hard, narrow bunk or sagging pipe berth, the plain food, duty that alternated from the bone-chill of the deck to the steamy heat of the engine room or the deckhouse. A bed ashore, welcoming bars and female companionship, the chance to spend some wages, and blow off some steam beckoned. Late spring on the streets of New York, even in wartime, must have seemed like a seaman's heaven.

For the more family oriented, like Leonard La Rue, it was the opportunity to visit loved ones—a taxi to Penn Station in Manhattan, a few hours in a Pennsylvania Railroad Pullman car to travel the length of New Jersey, a cloud of steam and a "whoosh" of air brakes as the train stopped at the Pennsylvania's 30th Street Station in Philadelphia. Maybe his family met him at the train and used a bit of their precious, rationed gasoline to drive him back to the house on Disston Street. Maybe he took a taxi, or the trolley. But there is no doubt La Rue saw his parents and whatever siblings were close by when he returned from Murmansk.

4

AROUND THE WORLD

By June 12 the officers and men signed back onto *Mormacmar* had assembled on her decks, for the ship sailed for Philadelphia, probably for a minor refit of her defensive arms at the Philadelphia Navy Yard. By the nineteenth the ship was back in New York, preparing for another extended voyage. She sailed on June 22, with a deck cargo of aircraft and general cargo stowed below, again bound for the Soviet Union. But this time, she would be serving her Russian allies from the south, through the Persian Gulf.

The ship was now commanded not by Captain Senior but Captain Frank V. Westerlund. Aboard was a new Armed Guard crew led by Lieutenant (junior grade) Hiram Royal Mallinson in command of twelve enlisted men.[1] The .50-caliber machine guns had been removed and replaced with four 20 mm Oerlikon cannons with 4,800 rounds. Firing a round almost twice the diameter and three times the mass, the Oerlikon had a much greater range and effectiveness against attacking aircraft than the guns she replaced, and had become standard anti-aircraft armament on all US Navy ships in addition to merchantmen. It was later replaced, in turn, by the even more potent Bofors 40 mm cannon. The 4"/50 was still aboard with ninety-six rounds, along with the two .30-caliber Browning machine guns on the bridge wings, supplied with 7,000 rounds. Four .45-caliber Colt 1911A1 pistols with 150 rounds completed the Guard's armaments.

The 20 mm Oerlikon cannon added extra punch.

Mormacmar started her journey by working her way alone down the Atlantic Coast before joining a convoy, the crew and Armed Guard alert to the danger all around. U-boats had operated in the western Atlantic for more than a year, preying on British and other allied and neutral shipping supporting the British war effort. But when Germany declared war on the United States, one of the first practical effects was for the Kriegsmarine to send U-boats to prey on US ships leaving US ports.

Initially, the Commander in Chief of the United States Fleet, Admiral Ernest J. King, had resisted the formation of convoys along the US coast, citing a shortage of suitable escort vessels and, it was said, allowing his strong dislike for the British to ignore their advice. But after months of U-boats ranging up and down the east coast, sinking or damaging eleven ships in January, another eleven in February, twenty-four in March, and twenty-five in April, some within sight of horrified civilians on the shore, the pressure was too much.

Oil tankers plying the routes from the Gulf of Mexico and the Caribbean up the Atlantic coast were the U-boats' richest targets. Indeed, one of the first victims was the SS *Francis E. Powell,* the first ship on which La Rue had sailed professionally. The *Powell* was steaming east of the Outer Banks of North Carolina, loaded with petroleum from Port Arthur, Texas, when she was sunk by a single torpedo fired by the U-130 on January 27. Amidst months of sinkings and developing fuel shortages as the tankers were forced to stay in port until they had escorts, King finally relented. The Navy pieced together an escort force of Coast Guard cutters, commandeered fishing trawlers, civilians in the Civil Air Patrol flying civilian aircraft to watch for submarines along the coast, Navy and Army Air Force aircraft, and the occasional Navy destroyers. The first such convoy leaving Norfolk for Key West, KS-500, sailed on May 14.[2]

A tanker burns after being torpedoed along the Atlantic coast.

The *Mormacmar* anchored at Lewes, Delaware, at the mouth of Delaware Bay, at midnight on the first day at sea, June 22, waiting to join the convoy from Norfolk, denoted KS-514. The following day she made the mouth of the Chesapeake Bay and anchored there between Virginia Beach and Norfolk. Captain Senior and Lieutenant Mallinson attended the convoy conference and re-boarded the ship, waiting for *Mormacmar* to take her place in the convoy. When the convoy steamed into the Atlantic at 0455 on June 26, U-boats were waiting. First to suffer was the 7,256-ton Norwegian ship *Tamesis*, torpedoed by U-701 late in the day. An escorting destroyer dropped depth charges two thousand yards off *Mormacmar's* starboard beam, but there was no sign that the sub was struck and they suspended their attack. The crew of the *Tamesis* took to their lifeboats but when the ship remained afloat the next day, they returned to her and beached her at Hatteras Inlet. Next to fall to the elusive U-701 was the 6,985-ton tanker *British Freedom*, torpedoed a thousand yards off *Mormacmar's* starboard beam around 1100. Almost immediately, her empty tanks filled and she healed to an alarming forty-five degrees, but by flooding her tanks on the opposite side she was able to reclaim an even keel and return to port. *Mormacmar* went to general quarters, and the Armed Guard manned their guns for an hour. A patrol aircraft believed it had spotted a submarine, and the destroyers made a series of depth-charge runs over the spot where they suspected the submarine would be. Before long, an oil slick and debris were spotted on the surface, and the attacks were halted. Later that afternoon an escort plane dropped still more depth charges on another suspected submarine.

Whether the explosives dropped into the Atlantic by aircraft and destroyers sunk a submarine, a submarine tricked them, or there was ever a U-boat there at all when the depth charges were dropped, we do not know. If a U-boat were sunk, it was not the U-701, which escaped that day and went on to sink the 14,000-ton tanker SS *William Rockefeller*, whose burning hulk *Mormacmar* and the convoy probably passed soon after.[3] Kriegsmarine records do not show a submarine sunk on that date and that place, the closest being U-158 three days later west of Bermuda. But in any event, U-701 did not have long to live. She would be sunk just ten days later when she succumbed to depth charges dropped by a US Army Air Force A-29 Hudson off Cape

Hatteras, taking thirty-nine of her forty-six-man crew with her to the bottom.

The ships of KS-514 continued their route south, arriving in Key West, Florida, on July 2. Between Cape Hatteras and Key West, *Mormacmar* went to general quarters five times, as suspected submarines were spotted and the convoy's escorts raced around attempting to sink the attackers or drive them off. The convoy only averaged a little over seven knots for the 1,140 miles from the Chesapeake Bay to Key West, less than half the maximum speed surfaced of a Type VIIC like the U-701 and her "Atlantic Submarine" sisters; so it is possible that the convoy was attacked by the same U-boat more than once, shadowing the convoy and racing into position to attempt a firing solution.

Dodging German torpedoes on the way to Key West was one thing, but dodging shoal water and friendly mines in the designated anchorage was another. Here the *Mormacmar*'s officers and crew had to bear the responsibility for the protection of the ship they normally ceded to escorts in the convoy and the Armed Guard. The Navy had created a protected anchorage at Key West, using nets and minefields to prevent submarines from approaching and attacking ships at anchor. This was not an idle effort; even before the US entered the war, Germany had made an intensive effort to restrict the flow of oil to Britain by attacking oil tankers at the ports of Aruba, Trinidad, and Curacao and those crossing the Caribbean itself. Less than three weeks before KS-514 had arrived in Key West, the US Coast Guard cutter *Thetis* had sunk a submarine on the surface to the southwest of the key.

Lieutenant Mallinson tells of the near chaos associated with negotiating that anchorage at night.

"Anchored 12 miles north of Key West on the night of July 2nd, inside the nets and mine fields after much maneuvering. There was difficulty in making buoys, and avoiding collision with other ships which were likewise drifting about seeking safe anchorage on a dark night in mined, shoal waters. It was difficult to determine whether to come in further and risk grounding, or anchor as we were and take the chance of being attacked, so far as we knew outside the nets. We had no pilot aboard, and could not make contact with any Coast Guard or Naval Control vessel to inquire about safe anchorage."

Evidently, all the ships managed to anchor without incident.

On the evening of Independence Day, fourteen ships of the convoy, now designated WAT-2, left Key West for its next stop, Trinidad. The convoy sailed through the Windward Passage (between the islands of Cuba and Hispaniola) and southeast towards the coast of Venezuela. Along the way *Mormacmar* received five radio reports of suspected U-boats, but there were no attacks. Over the nine-and-a-half-day passage from Key West, there was little for the escorts to do besides keep a sharp lookout. Escort and merchantman alike could see the remnants of previous submarine attacks in the empty rafts and lifeboats that were sighted along the way. After verifying them to be empty, the flotsam was sunk to avoid wasting rescuers' time in the future. The floating debris gave the destroyers' gunners useful target practice.

The convoy arrived in Trinidad at 0100 on July 14. *Mormacmar* and the rest of the ships filled their tanks with the heavy Bunker C fuel oil their boilers needed and which the refinery processed from the tarry Trinidadian and Venezuelan crude. Their tanks full for the month-long journey, the convoy left Trinidad after sunrise on the sixteenth, bound for Cape Town, South Africa. Within a few hours *Mormacmar* received a warning in the form of the Panamanian-flagged tanker *Beaconlight*, torpedoed and beached in shallow water north of Trinidad. Her attacker, U-160, had already left the area and escorts found no sign of the submarine.

The second day out of Trinidad, the convoy dispersed, each ship proceeding unescorted at its best speed, relying on lookouts and the skill of the Armed Guard to defend the ship from isolated U-boats prowling the mid-Atlantic. To be ready for action, the Guard test-fired their guns. They must have been pleased, and the crew of *Mormacmar* relieved, when they scored two hits out of four rounds fired at floating wreckage two thousand yards distant using the 4"/50. *Mormacmar* steamed northeasterly to a point five hundred miles west of the Cape Verde Islands to avoid U-boats prowling South America's Atlantic coast. She then turned south-southeast for Cape Town.

The journey carried its share of mysteries. Lieutenant Mallinson noted, "Suspicious vessels were sighted on two consecutive days and battle stations sounded without incident." That summary downplays the tension of one of the incidents. At 0715 on July 25, lookouts sighted what they initially suspected was a German raider six hundred yards off the starboard beam, and Mallinson called his men to battle stations. *Mormacmar* changed her course, but the unidentified ship matched the course change. It was only after a second course change that the ship continued past *Mormacmar*. Left unsaid is how the navigation watch and the Armed Guard lookouts allowed the other ship to get so close, although Mallinson explains the event by saying it was "Probably confused by the storm," so the ship must have appeared out of a nearby squall. It is also unsaid why the Guard did not fire on it at six hundred yards if they thought it were a raider, particularly after she had matched *Mormacmar*'s course change.

On July 27 another event occurred, this one potentially more serious. Lieutenant Mallinson reports,

"we received S.O.S from SS STELLA LYKES-torpedoed-position 0640 N 2505 W. This was 93 miles from our present position. Master without my knowledge altered course and headed ship for position given by STELLA LYKES. When more than halfway to destination informed me of actions and asked for advice. Advised him this might be a trap; that he head back on course, and make sure of getting ship safely and speedily to destination. Master disregarded advice, stating it is the tradition of seamen to go to the aid of those in distress. Doubled all watches and advised Master to declare a state of emergency and post all hands on watch. This was complied with. Arrived at given position shortly after dark and found no trace of survivors."

The *Stella Lykes* had indeed been torpedoed by a submarine, U-582, killing a crewman below and starting a fire on deck. The crew, including the Armed Guard, abandoned ship but the *Stella Lykes* refused to sink. An hour after the first torpedo flooded her engine room, U-582 fired another into the other side of the ship, but still she refused to sink. The submarine surfaced and fired more than 150 rounds at the ship from her deck guns, but still the ship floated in defiance. In desperation, the U-boat crew boarded the hulk and set demolition charges in the holds, which finally loosened her grip on the surface, and mid-afternoon that day *Stella Lykes* settled to her grave on the bottom of the Atlantic.

The U-582 took the captain of the *Stella Lykes* and her chief engineer captive. As with the *Cranford*, sunk a month earlier on the other side of the Atlantic, the U-boat gave the survivors some supplies and directions to the nearest land. The crew, less the oiler killed by the torpedo and the captive master and chief engineer, made landfall in Guinea eleven days later, fifty men in a single lifeboat. The Allies would get their revenge in October when U-582 would fall prey to depth charges dropped by the RAF while she was on patrol southwest of Iceland.

The position given by *Stella Lykes* was probably correct, as it corresponded with the position logged for the sinking by the U-boat. *Mormacmar* missed her because it was dark when she arrived, *Stella Lykes* had already sunk, the U-boat was gone, and her survivors were already drifting east, away from the wreck site. Lieutenant Mallinson was right to be concerned; even if the SOS was not a trap, it meant that a U-boat was in the vicinity. Only by sheer luck did the *Mormacmar* miss an encounter with U-582. Indeed, when *Mormacmar* reached Cape Town, the senior US Navy officer in the port admonished Captain Senior, "never to alter course to act as a rescue ship."

And there were other U-boats in the area. The British SS *Tekoa*, 580 miles southwest of Monrovia, Liberia, radioed in an SOS on July 31 that she had spotted a periscope. Since *Mormacmar* was nearby, the skies were clear, and the moon was full, Lieutenant Mallinson doubled the watch. *Tekoa* was not sunk that night. Three days later, the American SS *Harry Luckenbach* radioed that she had seen a periscope at a position 250 miles south of the border between Liberia and Ivory Coast, about 860 miles from the original report. She also would survive the encounter. Whether the lookouts on both ships were highly efficient and the U-boats could not get into position to make a torpedo hit, or the lookouts were jittery and saw something else, we do not know.

Mormacmar reached Cape Town at 1030 on August 13. It was a short stay, just long enough to run the ship over the degaussing range to verify her magnetic signature was sufficiently low (it was) and anchor overnight. The next evening, she steamed south out of the anchorage and began her long journey up the Indian Ocean along the coast of Africa and back across the equator.

The Royal Navy and Royal Air Force made their presence known around the UK's African colonies. On August 16, she was challenged by a British battleship and also by a British patrol aircraft. She was challenged by another British aircraft seven days later. On the twenty-third, the lookouts heard, but did not see, an aircraft flying over them in low clouds, which did not drop lower to identify or challenge the ship. After the second flew over a day later without challenging the ship, Mallinson became suspicious and the Guard went to general quarters, but no attack followed and the Guard went back on their regular watch.

By now the ship was between Mozambique and Madagascar, hugging the African coast, with her next stop scheduled for Mombasa, Kenya (East Africa in 1942). *Mormacmar* received a radio broadcast of a "suspicious craft" at a location dead ahead on her current course. She altered heading to make a shortcut to Mombasa, but when the warning was rescinded, she resumed her original course to make her scheduled arrival at the anchorage. She anchored on the twenty-sixth and was bunkered at anchor. She still had almost three thousand miles to travel as she crossed the Arabian sea and traversed the length of the Persian Gulf.

The next day *Mormacmar* weighed anchor and started her final leg northeast. She received multiple reports of submarines as she crossed the Arabian Sea, unescorted as before. The SS *Palma* reported a submarine on the surface at a position a hundred miles south of them on September 1.[4] Two days later,[5] they received a message broadcast from the SS *British Genius* steaming in the Gulf of Oman, which reported "sighted periscope" and five minutes later sent "British Genius missed torpedo." The punctuation symbols of International Morse Code do not include an exclamation point, but one might imagine a bit of relief on the part of the sender, and perhaps, the receiver. The 8,553-ton tanker's luck continued for the rest of the war.

Mormacmar covered almost three thousand miles in less than eleven and a half days as she arrived at her destination, the northern Persian Gulf, on September 7. Thus, began an ordeal that would illustrate just why the Allies were so committed to sending supplies over the hazardous Murmansk route. Inadequate facilities for the number of ships and the amount of cargo arriving, unskilled labor hired on for the emergency and then poorly supervised, and limited transportation from the port areas conspired to make what would have been less than a week in any modern port into a multi-month affair. And even in September, the men on the ship would face daily temperatures that could reach 135 degrees in the shade, with the deck rising to two hundred degrees in the sun, burning the men's feet through their thin-soled shoes.

Mormacmar anchored at the mouth of the Shatt al-Arab, the wide estuary formed where the Tigris and Euphrates rivers meet 120 miles north of the head of the Gulf. For its southernmost sixty miles, it also comprises the border between Iraq and Iran. After two days, there was enough space in the river for *Mormacmar* to steam the forty miles to Abadan, Iran, where she could unload her deck cargo, eight Douglas A-20B attack bombers, as well as spare parts. Even though dock space was free, she was forced to anchor in the river until September 11, when the bombers were finally unloaded.

On the fourteenth she departed for Bushire, Iran, 140 miles south of the entrance of the Shatt al-Arab on the eastern shore of the Persian Gulf. *Mormacmar's* engineers took the opportunity to replenish her fresh-water supplies by pumping water from the river as she made her way south. Once she entered the Persian Gulf, she encountered a dust storm so fierce that she was forced to anchor, unable to navigate the unfamiliar waters. For two days *Mormacmar* swung at anchor, blowing her fog horn regularly to warn any ships approaching in the gloom. When the storm finally cleared, she made her way the short distance to Bushire, but found that there was no space at the docks for the ship. Lieutenant Mallinson related,

"Anchored seven miles off Bushire, and commenced unloading lend lease cargo for Russia onto dhows and lighters. During the three weeks of unloading there was much petty thievery of cargo by coolie stevadores [*sic*] and particularly the boatmen who were caught on numerous occasions taking tires, sugar, truck parts, etc., to a smugglers village rather than transport the cargo to the UKCC docks and there be checked."

One can visualize *Mormacmar* swinging at anchor, a hot wind blowing across the decks even in September, a light wisp of smoke from her funnel as a boiler steams for the ship's cranes and winches and for electricity to light the holds below, the local traders smiling as the cargo is lowered onto their decks, the deck crew laughing at the irony of risking their lives for this.

By the twenty-ninth of September, *Mormacmar* had finished unloading the cargo due for Bushire but she still had another three thousand tons to unload, this time at Khorramshahr, about five miles further up the Shatt al-Arab from Abadan. En route to Khorramshahr, she received orders to anchor at the mouth of the river and await further orders, as there was no room at the docks and no spare lighter capacity to unload the ship at anchor. She waited more than three weeks at anchor before the orders to proceed up river arrived, but no sooner had *Mormacmar* reached Khorramshahr than she received further orders to anchor and wait for an available berth. She waited another week before she could finally begin unloading her cargo on October 30, a process not complete for another three weeks.

Crowded docks at Khorramshahr.

While we do not have the ship's logs, Lieutenant Mallinson's report hints that the crew of the ship and the Armed Guard were enjoying liberty while in the Shatt al-Arab and perhaps enjoying it too much. Two members of the Armed Guard were hospitalized at the sick bay at the Royal Naval Base in Korramshahr for venereal disease. Mallinson records, "Originally exposed at Abadan, Sept. 11th, and Korramshahr, Oct. 20th. Source of infection-prostitutes. Neither men reported to C.O. [commanding officer] after exposure or used prophylaxis issued to them." They were released after a few days, with treatment to continue aboard the ship. Mallinson himself was hospitalized for two weeks in Abadan for "acutely infected dermatitis of the ankles." We might suspect the men of *Mormacmar* were similarly afflicted with diseases, venereal and otherwise. According to Mallinson, "Commanding Officers ... should emphatically warn their crew of the great prevalence of venereal disease in Persian Gulf ports. Nearly all ships had crew members with V.D. in some form or other." Perhaps related to the activities the crew were seeking, he continued, "In most Persian Gulf ports members of Armed Guard crews should carry side arms when on liberty at night, and should remain in groups as much as possible. There have been many instances of unprovoked assault by Arabs and Persians, particularly in native quarters." It does not take much imagination to envision devout Muslim men strongly objecting to bored, lecherous foreigners seeking out alcohol and feminine pleasures in their neighborhoods.

On November 21 *Mormacmar* finally started on her route to leave the Persian Gulf, ten weeks after arriving. By now, the men had been away for more than five months and had received no mail that whole time. The ship's "slop chest," the small stores that sold everything from toothpaste and cigarettes to underwear and dungarees, was emptied. Two men from another ship's Armed Guard had been released from the hospital and added to *Mormacmar's* complement, having missed their ship's sailing due to medical treatment, one for venereal disease and one for "sand fly fever."

The first leg was brief, just to Abadan to bunker for the long journey ahead. Tanks filled, she left Abadan on the twenty-third and arrived at Bandar Abbas, on the Strait of Hormuz, around noon on the twenty-fifth, awaiting the formation of a convoy for the onward journey, not westward, but eastward to India. By this time, many of the men onboard the ship were suffering from malaria, and the officers took advantage of the time in Bandar Abbas to have the men examined and treated. But there was not much time, for following a morning convoy conference on the twenty-seventh, the ship sailed in convoy from Bandar Abbas at 1320. On November 29 *Mormacmar* left the convoy to steam to Colombo, Ceylon (now Sri Lanka) alone.

Mormacmar arrived in Colombo on December 6, staying just a day but long enough to off-load one of the men transferred aboard at Korramshahr, who was now gravely ill with malaria and dysentery, and to take aboard 3,600 rounds of ammunition for the 20 mm Oerlikon guns. She left Colombo around noon on the seventh, and almost immediately the 20-mm guns were manned, for she was frequently visited by aircraft flying overhead, going to battle stations for air attack seven times over two days. The threat now was now not from Germany, but from Japan, probably the first time La Rue and his shipmates would be threatened by that Axis power, but not the last. Fortunately, the heavy aircraft cover was British, and no shots were fired.

On the twelfth, *Mormacmar* received a radio broadcast from the SS *Mulbera*, a British liner that had the distinction of having hosted King George VI, then the Duke of York, while on his honeymoon 1924. The *Mulbera* broadcast that she had sighted a periscope at a location directly on *Mormacmar's* current heading. *Mormacmar* changed course five degrees, constrained by the coast to her port side, and doubled up the watch because she would reach the vicinity of the sighting around dawn the next morning. Neither *Mulbera* nor *Mormacmar* ended up being attacked.

On December 14 *Mormacmar* picked up a pilot to handle navigation in the tricky currents and sand bars of the Hooghly River and carefully picked her way to Calcutta (now Kolkata), India, arriving at her dock at 2011. Perhaps *Mormacmar's* official welcome to Calcutta was an air raid warning the next morning, which fortunately only lasted ten minutes before the all-clear was sounded. The crew could have been forgiven if they feared they were going to live through another perilous time in port like Murmansk, albeit with the inhabitants wearing thin cotton and saris rather than wool and furs, and with the rising sun on the airplane's wings instead of black crosses. And they would have been correct. Over the next week, as *Mormacmar* took on a load of hemp, jute and tea, the port came under attack on four moonlit nights.

Hooghly docks, Calcutta, with ships waiting at anchor in the river.

In fact, *Mormacmar* had the honor of being in Calcutta on the first night the city had actually been bombed during the war, December 20. Japanese planes bombed for over an hour, striking the city and the dock area, fortunately causing few casualties and only slight damage to the ships in the harbor and to their cargo. They also attempted, unsuccessfully, to destroy the locks on the Hooghly south of the harbor. The locks, designed in the late nineteenth century by British engineers and constructed with Indian labor, retained enough water behind them to allow large ships to make it to Calcutta, the heavily silted river otherwise being too shallow. If the locks had been damaged or destroyed, it could have stranded the twenty ships in the harbor, leaving them proud on the mud. If the tons of high explosives dropped over the city didn't make enough of an impression on the inhabitants, the Japanese dropped leaflets saying, they "would bomb every night until the New Year and then every day." Despite the relative lack of damage and casualties, the bombings so unnerved the local populace that the stevedores refused to work at night following the first night's attacks.

As in Murmansk, *Mormacmar's* Armed Guard, augmented by the ship's crew, fought back, joining an American and an Australian ship on either end of her in firing at the attacking Japanese. Most of the aircraft were at high altitudes, and the gunfire was ineffective, but *Mormacmar's* 20-mm guns damaged a low-flying Japanese aircraft enough that an RAF Hurricane was able to overtake it and shoot it down. Bombing resumed on the evening of the twenty-first, and on the twenty-second, hundreds of civilians were killed when a bomb was dropped on a market near the harbor. That same night the Japanese dropped leaflets promising to bomb the city on Christmas Eve.

By the twenty-third the ship was fully loaded and ready to depart, but, like the stevedores before, the tugboat crews now refused to work at night and the ship had to wait another day for a suitable tide. Ironically, there was no air raid on the twenty-third, but early on the morning of the twenty-fourth, Calcutta was bombed heavily, including the docks and oil facilities. Fortunately for *Mormacmar*, she was already anchored south of the city and far from the damage. That did not prevent her from bringing her 20-mm anti-aircraft guns into action. This brought another occurrence of crew insubordination aboard the ship. One of *Mormacmar's* able seamen had previously been dismissed from general-quarters duty as standby loader of one of the 20-mm guns for failure to follow orders. During action on the twenty-fourth, as the guns were being fired at attacking Japanese bombers, that individual refused repeated orders to clear an area he was obstructing near the gun. When he refused, Lieutenant Mallinson told him to get below or he would shoot him. The lieutenant had to strike the man on his head with the butt of his service pistol before he finally complied.

Mormacmar steamed from her anchorage south of Calcutta at 0944 on the morning of the twenty-fourth, bound for Colombo. The ship spent Christmas 1942, at sea, alone and unescorted, with the British planes flying overhead again the only reason for the crew to go to general quarters. When *Mormacmar* arrived back in Colombo on the morning of New Year's Day, 1943, the able seaman who had been disciplined by Lieutenant Mallinson with the butt of his .45 was joined by the union delegates of the deck, engine, and steward departments in petitioning the crew to refuse to sail with Mallinson on board. The US naval attaché in Colombo made clear in no uncertain terms that the crew was obligated to follow the instructions of the officer in charge of the Armed Guard during general quarters. The matter was quickly dropped by the time the ship steamed out of Colombo the next evening, bound for Freemantle, on the west coast of Australia.

The passage from Colombo to Freemantle was without danger from ship or aircraft, but this time the threat came from the sea. *Mormacmar* encountered a gale blowing from the southeast, her direction of travel, that slowed her to six knots, the old ship pounding in the seas. She made Freemantle at 1701 on January 16, staying just twenty-four hours to take on fuel and water before leaving for Wellington, New Zealand. By the twenty-third, *Mormacmar* was steaming through the treacherous Southern Ocean south of Tasmania when the rudder post came loose in its bushings and the rudder started to vibrate severely, forcing the ship again to reduce her speed. In addition, her after peak tank, located in the hull just ahead of the rudder and screw, started to leak.

Both of these developments must have been extremely troubling to the men aboard *Mormacmar*, since they hinted at incipient structural failure. The ship had in fact suffered cracks in her stern frame, popped rivets, and severe damage to her tail shaft (the last section of her propeller shaft) during heavy weather off Boston in October,1939.[6] *Mormacmar* had been dry-docked to repair the damage in April, 1940; perhaps there had been additional damage to the stern of the ship that was just manifesting now. Since the peak tank, used for trimming the ship, was also frequently used for storing fresh water, her boilers and crew could be endangered if the tank became contaminated with sea water.

On January 30, just as *Mormacmar* reached Wellington, she encountered hurricane-force winds and seas so high they smashed her starboard lifeboat. Fortunately for Second Mate La Rue and the rest of her crew, she was at rest in Wellington harbor by the next morning. The crew made temporary repairs to her rudder post and her after peak tank, leaving Wellington early on the afternoon of February 5 for Balboa, Panama, and the western entrance to the Panama Canal. But a day later, she was forced to turn back when the leak in the tank reappeared, with the tank losing thirty-five tons of water over half a day. By February 8, she was back in Wellington, and her master and Moore-McCormack's agents in New Zealand were making arrangements for the ship to enter dry dock for permanent repairs. The next day, in order to lighten the ship prior to entering the dry dock, the crew and Wellington stevedores unloaded 2,133 tons of her 6,000 tons of cargo and stored it in a warehouse next to the dock. Four million pounds lighter, she entered the dry dock in Wellington for permanent repairs on February 11. By the twentieth, the repairs were complete, and she was able to float out of the dry dock and return wharf side to start reloading her cargo for the long journey home.

Two days later, *Mormacmar's* bad luck reappeared when a fire started in her offloaded cargo, the bales of jute still stored in the warehouse next to her. Members of the crew and the Armed Guard rushed to fight the fire, and the ship was quickly repositioned on the wharf so that the craft would not be damaged by the flames. By the time the Wellington Fire Brigade had extinguished the fire the next morning, 1,966 chests of tea, 785 bales of burlap, and 737 bales of hemp and jute were damaged or destroyed.[7] The undamaged balance of the cargo was reloaded, and the ship steamed out of Wellington for the last time on the morning of February 25, with a Royal New Zealand aircraft escorting because of reports of a submarine operating in the Cook Strait. The loss of the cargo, about seven hundred tons in all, became the subject of legal proceedings between the consignees and Moore-McCormack lines that stretched all the way into the 1950s.[8]

The repairs in the Wellington dry dock were apparently successful, for the ship averaged eleven knots on her 6,755-mile journey northeast across the Pacific to the Canal Zone. Traveling alone and zig-zagging in attempt to thwart any submarines (presumably Japanese, since they were still in the Pacific), the trip was uneventful until *Mormacmar* approached the coast of South America, when for the first time since leaving Wellington she went to battle stations as an aircraft approached on the afternoon of the eighteenth. The all-clear sounded a short time later when the aircraft was identified as American.

Two days later the ship actually engaged in combat with a suspected submarine for the first time since *Mormacmar* had left New York the year before. In flat seas 120 miles west of the northern coast of Ecuador, lookouts sighted a possible periscope two thousand yards off the starboard beam, which was visible for about twenty seconds before disappearing. The ship turned to present the smallest aspect to a possible torpedo attack and when the suspected periscope reappeared, the Armed Guard opened fire with the 4"/50. After adjusting their aim, they believed they hit just below the periscope with their fifth round. The target disappeared and did not reappear. Whether it was, in fact, a submarine is unclear.

Mormacmar reached Balboa, Panama Canal Zone, at 1100 on March 22 and anchored for the night to await her turn to cross the canal. She weighed anchor at 0844 the next morning and by 1747 she was in the Atlantic, anchoring at Cristobal to await a northbound convoy. On the morning of the twenty-fifth, she joined the fifteen other merchant ships and eight escort ships of convoy ZG-26 bound for Guantanamo Bay. The trip was uneventful; indeed, over the entire four-year history of the ZG convoys and their southbound (Guantanamo to Cristobal) GZ equivalents, not a single merchantman was lost. The convoy arrived at Guantanamo around noon on the twenty-ninth. The next morning, she joined convoy GN-50 bound for New York. This voyage was also largely uneventful, although earlier on the day the convoy arrived in New York, the escorts were required to drop depth charges three times on suspected submarines. Despite the minor excitement, *Mormacmar* arrived at her berth in New York on the evening of April 7, 1943. *Mormacmar*, her officers and men, including Second Mate La Rue, had sailed around the world, 41,200 miles over 291 days.

Her cargo unloaded, La Rue said goodbye to the SS *Mormacmar* for the last time on April 24[9] and took the train to Philadelphia. It was no doubt a great relief to visit his family and sleep in his parents' home instead of a bunk aboard ship, but the time was not all leisure. On May 5 he sat for his examination for master at the Philadelphia offices of the Bureau of Marine Inspection and Navigation. Captain Wester-lund had written La Rue a highly competent letter of reference, saying "Mr. LaRue has proved himself at all times to be sober, industrious and conscientious in his duties and it gives me great pleasure to recommend him to anybody requiring his services."[10] On May 11, 1943, Chief Mate La Rue received his final license as a merchant mariner, "Master of Steam and Motor Vessels of not over 'any' gross tons, upon the waters of 'Oceans.'" That license in hand, Leonard La Rue was joining a newly-built ship, the SS *Joseph M. Medill*, as chief mate.

5

LIBERTY

One of the great stories of World War II, and one of the secrets of the Allied victory, was America's massive and successful industrial mobilization. Compared to its pre-depression peak in July, 1929, US industrial production had dropped in half by mid-1932, when Leonard La Rue began his studies at the Nautical School. By mid-1937, production had rebounded before declining again precipitously later in the year and into 1938. Thanks to the Lend-Lease policy and the various efforts of the Roosevelt administration to support the Allies, by the time Germany invaded Poland in September, 1939, industrial production had climbed again to 1929 levels.[1] Even today, the scale of the industrial accomplishment is astonishing. By the end of the war in 1945, United States factories had produced 88,410 tanks and self-propelled guns, 257,000 artillery pieces, 324,750 aircraft, 2,400,000 jeeps and trucks, 2,600,000 machine guns, and forty-one billion rounds of ammunition.[2]

Transporting all this war-making capability and the nine million soldiers and Marines who would use it to bring violence to the enemy required a huge merchant marine fleet. At the beginning of the war, more than ninety percent of the ships of the fourteen million gross tons of US merchant fleet were more than twenty years old. Before the war was over, the US would build thirty-four million gross tons of new merchant ships.

A Liberty ship is launched at Delta Shipbuilding, New Orleans, LA, one of eighteen yards that built them.

The SS *Joseph M. Medill* was an exemplar of American industrial genius; she was a "Liberty Ship." As with the rest of the massive production of war goods, the key to producing ships faster than they could be sunk, even during the Kriegsmarine's "Happy Time" of the U-boat war, was standardization across multiple shipyards. The Liberty ship design was based on a British design of 1939, with minor changes to make the ship faster to construct by using welded rather than riveted plates and as few complicated curves in the hull as possible.[3] The crews of the Liberty ship lived in a single "house" rather than one amidships and one at the stern, and the ships had decks of steel rather than wood. Other small changes were made to improve habitability, safety, and access. With these changes, the design was approved by the Maritime Commission, and shipbuilding started in January, 1941. The first ship, SS *Patrick Henry*, was launched on September 27, 1941. Her keel had been laid on April 30, so she had taken five months to construct. Once production ramped up on US entry into the war, Liberty ships would routinely slide down the builders' ways less than a month after keel-laying; one, *Robert E. Peary*, most famously in fewer than five days.

Cutaway view of a Liberty ship showing its five holds.

Like all 2,710 Liberty ships constructed, the *Medill*, Maritime Commission hull number MCE-1523, was 441 feet, six inches long overall, with a beam of fifty-seven feet. Rated at 7,176 gross tons, her 2,500-horsepower, triple-expansion steam engine was fed by two oil-fired, water-tube boilers, and her single screw could drive the ship at eleven knots. Piston-type steam engines as opposed to steam turbines were chosen because of a shortage of the specialized manufacturing capability for the finely machined and balanced rotors. There was an expectation that turbines would be needed in vast numbers to power warships, where the turbines' power would be essential for high speed. Most of the ships built were, like the *Medill*, designed for standard break-bulk cargo and designated EC2-S-C1. Tanker and troopship variants used the same hull but with modifications for their particular service and carried different designations.[4]

Named after the nineteenth-century publisher of the Chicago Tribune who served as mayor of the city after the great Chicago fire, the SS *Joseph M. Medill* had been built in the Wainright Yard of the J. A. Jones Construction Company in Panama City, Florida, one of several brand-new shipyards set up by the Maritime Commission specifically to produce Liberty ships. Over the life of the building program, from 1941 to 1945, Liberty ships would be produced at eighteen different ship yards, from Portland, Maine, to Portland, Oregon, many building ships for the first time. The *Medill*, whose keel was laid on September 28, 1942, was only the fifth ship the yard had built out of the seventy-four it would launch.[5] As the ship neared completion, the Maritime Commission advised Moore-McCormack in a letter dated April 15, 1943,

> "we assume you would wish to assign to this vessel licensed officers and department heads whose experience and ability are known to you, and probably former employees of your company ... the Master, Chief Engineer, Chief Mate and First Assistant Engineer should be assigned to the payroll of the SS JOSEPH M. MEDILL immediately ... when the vessel has substantially advanced they shall proceed to the yard to join the vessel."[6]

Among those assigned was Leonard La Rue.

La Rue took the train down to Panama City and signed onto the *Medill* on May 15. With her new crew on board, she completed sea trials to the satisfaction of the Maritime Commission on May 30, and the next day, valued at $1.75 million, she was officially delivered to the care of the Moore-McCormack Lines. In addition to her normal complement, *Medill* also carried on her first sailing deck and engineering cadets from the Merchant Marine School in New Orleans.

Idealized image of a Liberty ship at sea.

The need for shipping was critical, so as soon as the *Medill* was delivered, she and her crew went to work. In April the War Shipping Administration had scheduled *Medill* to steam to Cuba to load a full cargo of sugar for delivery in Britain, but a month later plans had changed, so instead on June 2 she made the overnight trip to Tampa, Florida, to load 4,200 tons of potash, also bound for the UK.[7] She completed loading and sailed on the fourteenth for Key West to join a northbound convoy, KN-247, which sailed on the eighteenth. Six days later, after an uneventful journey, they were in New York, waiting for a convoy to form for the journey across the Atlantic. On June 30 *Medill* joined HX-246 bound for Liverpool.[8] Reflecting the changes in convoy composition in the year and a half since La Rue had first convoyed across the Atlantic in HX-177, HX-246 comprised twenty-two US ships, nineteen British, nine Norwegian, and a ship each flagged from Belgium, the Netherlands, Poland, Iceland, and Panama. When the convoy sailed from Halifax on July 3, she was joined by a further six British and two American ships, as well as a ship from Greece. At St. John's she was joined by two more American and a British ship, and the nearly seventy ships of the convoy slowly made their way in zigzags across the sea. Aside from a few days of fog and a pair of collisions between merchantmen (one in fog, one inexplicably in clear weather), the convoy made good time and arrived at Liverpool on July 14 intact.

On July 24, her unloading of the potash complete, the *Joseph M. Medill* joined convoy ON-194 for the return trip across the Atlantic. This was another enormous convoy comprising thirty-nine American ships, twenty-two British and a mix of Dutch, Norwegian, French, Polish, and Panamanian ships, bringing the total leaving Liverpool at eighty-four ships plus nine escorts. As usual, the escorts leaving Britain would be replaced as the convoy approached the Canadian coast. Again, in stark contrast to a year earlier, no ships would be lost to enemy action on the return journey to New York. The SS *Joseph M. Medill* arrived back in New York on August 7, 1943.

Chief Mate La Rue took just that one voyage on the *Joseph Medill*, for on his return from the UK, Moore-McCormack assigned him as chief mate aboard the MS *Mormacdale*. The *Mormacdale* had been completed in February, 1942, by the Pennsylvania Shipyard, Inc. of Beaumont, Texas. She was one of forty-six type C-1A ships built by the Maritime Commission under a prewar contract to expand the US merchant fleet and make it more competitive by the use of more modern, economical ships. The C-1A was 412 feet long with a sixty-foot beam. She was rated at 6,976[9] gross tons and 11,000 tons displacement, and her propulsion was diesel rather than steam; indeed, she was the only non-steam powered ship on which La Rue ever served. Two 2,000-horsepower, two-stroke, Nordberg diesels turning at up to 220 RPM drove a single screw through electro-magnetic clutches and a single reduction gear. The unique propulsion system meant the ship could be underway quickly from "cold iron," and since the engines could be independently clutched and un-clutched from the shaft, one could be run forward and one in reverse, with the engines clutched in and out for precise control of the ship's motion. Running together, the 4,000-horsepower gave the ship a speed of fourteen knots.[10]

SS *Mormacdale* during her sea trials.

Chief Mate La Rue joined *Mormacdale* on September 12, 1943, in Norfolk, Virginia. The ship had just returned from more than six months at sea, with multiple stops in the Persian Gulf and India, but unlike *Mormacmar*, which had rounded the Cape of Good Hope and crawled up the east coast of Africa, *Mormacdale* had passed through the Panama Canal and crossed the Pacific.[11] She would do that again with Chief Mate La Rue aboard.

At 1700 on the September 18, *Mormacdale* started her journey, ultimately bound for Milne Bay, New Guinea.[12] Taking advantage of her speed, she traveled independently up the coast to Quonset Point, Rhode Island, arriving on the twentieth. Three days later she departed for New York, arriving at 0600 on the twenty-fourth. *Mormacdale* left her berth at 0420 on the twenty-fifth and joined convoy NG-388 bound for Guantanamo Bay, forty-five merchantmen, and five escorts who protected the convoy as it covered the 1,300 nautical miles at a leisurely eight knots. NG-388 arrived Guantanamo Bay on the morning of October 2, and at 1300 the next day, *Mormacdale* set out for Balboa, Panama Canal Zone, in the company of eight other merchant ships and three escorts.[13] The convoy arrived in Cristobal on the seventh, and *Mormacdale* anchored with the other ships, the master going ashore at 1130 for orders. By 1235 she had weighed anchor and begun her trip through the canal, reaching Balboa at 1700, where she anchored for the night and the crew took liberty before the long passage across the Pacific.

A 0730 on October 8, *Mormacdale* weighed anchor to cross the big ocean, able to use her thirteen-plus knot speed to motor independently to Espiritu Santo, New Hebrides. With no sightings of enemy aircraft or submarines, the days were repeated cycles of watches and drills, but as she approached the South Pacific and the Islands of Micronesia, she began to receive reports of enemy submarines and aircraft on the route ahead. On October 25 there was one report of a submarine, on the twenty-eighth two reports of hostile aircraft and submarines, and sub reports again on the twenty-ninth and thirtieth, but the ship never even saw a periscope. On the thirty-first the lookouts began to see aircraft, but fortunately for *Mormacdale*, they were

American patrols. By 1230 on November 1, *Mormacdale* was anchored
in Palikula Bay, Espiritu Santo, New Hebrides (now Vanuatu).

Ships at anchor in Palikula Bay, Espiritu Santo. Not a bad place to wait.

Once in Espiritu Santo her rapid progress stopped. The ship swung at
anchor for almost an entire month, awaiting orders to proceed. What
had been an island paradise of jungle and white-sand beaches was now
a busy naval and air base. Warships and merchantmen anchored in the
bay, some showing damage from their latest encounter with the
Japanese. Aircraft landed and took off from the six-thousand-foot
landing strip US Navy Seabees had carved out of the jungle. The men
stood watch, maintained their equipment, took liberty in the town.
Unlike the Persian Gulf, where La Rue and the men of *Mormacmar* had
suffered at anchor, the temperatures hovered only between the low
seventies and high eighties Fahrenheit; warm during the afternoon
peak, but more comfortable for sleeping, albeit steamy, after the daily
afternoon rains. For some of the crew, it was certainly better to while
away the war at anchor in a protected harbor than to brave aircraft and
submarines on the high seas.

While Chief Mate La Rue performed his duties in Espiritu Santo, early on a cold winter's morning his mother was crying. Leonard's father, Paul Philip La Rue, sixty-eight years old, died on November 5 from kidney failure. It is unknown when La Rue was informed of his father's passing, given his remote location at the time. It is possible Moore-McCormack was able to route a message to him. Back in Philadelphia, Paul was buried on November 8 in St. Dominic's Cemetery, next to the church and just two miles from where his widow would continue to reside for the time being on Disston Street.

Finally, on November 26, *Mormacdale's* master was summoned ashore to the port director's office to receive routing instructions and orders to the next port. She weighed anchor at 0600 the next morning and started for New Guinea in the company of a destroyer escort. By 0530 on December 1, *Mormacdale* was close enough to New Guinea to be challenged by a friendly patrol vessel. She anchored in Milne Bay later that day, her cargo waiting patiently in her holds.

Men of the Royal Australian Air Force watch swimmers race in Milne Bay.

If Chief Mate La Rue and the officers and men of the *Mormacdale* were frustrated with the delay in the New Hebrides, there was much more to come in New Guinea. Indeed, the ship lay at anchor eighty-four days before being instructed to unload her cargo. How did the officers and men occupy themselves for almost three months? The terrain is beautiful and today Milne Bay is a major diving attraction, but in wartime, with a congestion of ships and the ubiquitous threat from malaria, it is hard to imagine much recreation besides swimming next to the ship.

Japanese air attacks added some excitement. On the morning of December 6, a reconnaissance plane was observed over the bay, and shore-based anti-aircraft guns fired on it (the Armed Guard had been instructed by local authorities not to fire unless the ship was actually attacked.) There was another air-raid alert later in the day, but the men on *Mormacdale* couldn't see an aircraft, and none of the guns fired. Christmas came and went uneventfully, as did New Year's Day, 1944. On January 7, the officer in charge of *Mormacdale's* Armed Guard advised his men to stop swimming in the bay because of sharks; the restriction was lifted two weeks later when the sharks had moved on. The crew of the ship had been swimming in the bay the whole time despite the danger.

January 8, though, brought a bonus, as the master was able to bring back from shore a large bag of mail, the first mail the ship had received. Still, the days droned on with nothing for the men to do but stand their watches, take an occasional liberty ashore, swim, and watch the rest of the world pass by. On February 5, the ship moved for the first time since the first of December the previous year. She didn't move very far, just seven hundred yards, but it was seven hundred yards closer to shore, and since the ship did not have a motor whaleboat, it would make it much easier to get ashore either with her own boats or by hitching a ride from one of the passing Navy motor launches.

The days dragged on. The ship received another bag of mail on February 10, including Christmas packages that had been mailed months ago. On the nineteenth, friction between the ship's bosun and members of the Armed Guard crew boiled over, leading to an intervention by the officer in charge and the *Mormacdale's* master. Unlike the events on the *Mormacmar*, this matter was resolved without further drama. On February 24, the ship moved again, this time in an apparent sign of progress, to an anchorage off the docks at Gama Dodo, a US Navy receiving station built as a way-station for arriving sailors and troops. By the afternoon, she was actually alongside the dock. Now, perhaps, the ship would be unloaded, and *Mormacdale* could make her way home.

Photo taken from an Allied aircraft showing some of the ships keeping *Mormacdale* company at anchor in Milne Bay, February, 1944.

It was not to be. The next day another merchant ship tied up alongside *Mormacdale* and stevedores were still nowhere to be found. On the morning of the twenty-seventh, La Rue's ship was sent away from the dock to accommodate an incoming ship with a higher-priority cargo. As *Mormacdale* made her way from the dock to her anchorage (without a pilot), she went aground on a coral reef about a mile from the dock at Gama Dodo and seven hundred yards from the nearest shore, her stern in eighty feet of water but the forward part of the ship aground to the number three hold. The ship did not appear to be taking on water, but despite the aid of boats from around the bay, she was unable to work herself loose. Rather than tear out the bottom of the ship, on the twenty-eighth, the master was able to arrange for stevedores (probably US Navy Seabees) to partially unload the cargo onto lighters while she was aground to lessen the weight in the ship and refloat her.

On the twenty-ninth a US Navy fleet tug arrived to attempt to pull *Mormacdale* off the reef. It was unsuccessful. Work began the next day to empty the forward holds (number one and number two). The holds emptied, when the tug again attempted to pull the ship off the reef on March 3, this time it was successful. *Mormacdale* motored to an anchorage where divers examined the hull for any damage and found none.

On March 8 *Mormacdale* was permitted to return to the dock at Gama Dodo with the intention of unloading the balance of her cargo. But before all her holds could be emptied, she was again banished from the docks on March 12, this time to accommodate a refrigerated ship carry meat, fruits, and vegetables. Perhaps the master exercised some influence, maybe the local Navy officials took pity on the *Mormacdale*, or perhaps they were just getting tired of the ship, but in any event, *Mormacdale's* unloading resumed on March 13, while she was at anchor, the cargo being lowered again onto lighters. The next afternoon, she was permitted back to the docks, and by the seventeenth, all her cargo had been unloaded at the dock except for a load of steel plate that would be unloaded onto another ship in the bay.

Her entire cargo finally unloaded, on March 19 *Mormacdale* received orders and routing instruction to proceed to Brisbane, Australia. She weighed anchor at 0830 the next morning and made her way unescorted. Aside from target shooting by the Armed Guard, punctuated by a ruptured cartridge in one of the ship's 20-mm guns, the voyage was uneventful, but the now empty ship rolled uncomfortably in the heavy seas. By the twenty-second she was inside Australia's Great Barrier Reef, rendering the threat from submarines negligible, and so the watch was relaxed. The seas had calmed by the twenty-fourth, and that evening she anchored at Brisbane, waiting for a dock. On the twenty-seventh a berth opened and *Mormacdale* took her spot on Dalgetty's Wharf to load cargo for the return to the United States.

Now the men had a real liberty port, and they took advantage of it. Chief Mate La Rue no doubt took his turn, sightseeing in the capital of the Australian state of Queensland, probably gawking at General MacArthur's headquarters in the AMP building, maybe visiting a museum. Back on the ship, the *Mormacdale* shifted to a different dock to take on additional cargo, the colorfully named "Abattoir Wharf."

Her cargo fully loaded and the hatches replaced and secured over the holds, *Mormacdale* left Brisbane for her trip across the Pacific at 0630 on April 1. As before, the ship motored across the sea by itself, relying on zig-zagging and speed to avoid submarines. Three days out, she spotted an aircraft approaching, but it was identified as friendly. Three days later they spotted a lone ship off the port bow on a reciprocal course, but she was identified as a US Liberty ship; still, the gun crews stayed at their stations until the ship was well past. The same pattern repeated on the fourteenth, again with a Liberty ship. The ship sailed through some rough weather, but nothing that slowed her down, and on April 29 *Mormacdale* entered the harbor at San Pedro, California, arriving at a berth at the terminal dock. The master gave the order to secure the engines at 1100. *Mormacdale* was back in the United States and if she had not quite traveled around the world, she and Chief Mate La Rue had traveled about 13,000 miles over 222 days.

La Rue deserved a little time ashore. After he signed off the *Mormac-dale* effective May 7, he would have certainly taken the train across the country to Philadelphia to comfort the widowed Isabelle and visit the grave of his recently deceased father. For a few months he stayed close to home, perhaps to support his grieving mother. Starting on June 6, he served in a series of shore positions as night master or relief master on various ships in New York harbor, which allowed him frequent trips back to Philadelphia.

On September 7, Leonard La Rue, licensed as a master for more than a year, finally got his command. The SS *Smith Thompson*, US Maritime Commission hull number MCE-654, was a Liberty ship named after an early nineteenth century Secretary of the Navy and Associate

Justice of the Supreme Court. She had been completed in October, 1942, by the California Shipbuilding Corporation of Los Angeles, California, and turned over to Moore-McCormack for operation. Since being put in service in November 1942, she had already been to New Zealand, India, Australia, the UK, Algeria, Italy, Morocco, and Malta.

Captain La Rue led his ship, loaded with general cargo and carrying 350 troops, out of Norfolk, Virginia, on September 12. The *Smith Thompson* joined sixty-four other merchant ships and fourteen escorts comprising convoy UGS-54, bound for Gibraltar. Despite an average speed of only 9.5 knots, the convoy had no contact with either the Kriegsmarine or the Luftwaffe, and it arrived in Gibraltar on the twenty-eighth. After a short stay in Gibraltar, the *Thompson* proceeded in the convoy to Augusta, Sicily, just north of Syracuse, arriving on October 5. The ship joined Convoy AH-71 and made the four-hundred-mile trip to Bari, on Italy's Adriatic coast, arriving on the seventh.

Mers El Kebir, Algeria, in the foreground, with Oran in the distance.

Her cargo and troops unloaded and ballast taken on in their place, the *Smith Thompson* left Bari on October 13 for the sixty-five-mile trip to Brindisi, Italy, where on the fifteenth she joined convoy HA-72 for

Augusta. From Augusta she sailed with Convoy GUS-55. The convoy stopped and picked up ships in Bizerte, Tunisia, and Oran, Algeria, so that by the time it left Gibraltar on October 22, it comprised sixty-six merchantmen, almost half of them Liberty ships, along with eight destroyers and a destroyer escort. With the Allies in control of North Africa, Sicily and Malta, and the Battle of the Atlantic essentially won, the return trip was as uneventful as the trip east, and the *Thompson* reached New York on November 6.

The *Smith Thompson* left New York for Norfolk on November 20. There she loaded general cargo and fifty troops bound for Marseille, France. On December 1, she joined 104 other merchant ships and eight escorts in Convoy UGS-62, bound for Oran. Again, the trip was uneventful, and the convoy arrived on the eighteenth. The next day she joined twenty-one other merchantmen and two escorts in Convoy ON-27 to make the seven-hundred-mile journey to Marseille. Again, it was an uneventful journey and she arrived at Marseille on the twenty-second.

Captain La Rue and his crew spent Christmas 1944 in Marseille. By the twenty-ninth, the cargo had been unloaded and she proceeded independently back to Oran carrying 318 Free French troops, arriving in Oran on New Year's Eve. The French troops left the *Thompson* in Algeria to join their countrymen in celebrating the New Year. On January 2, 1945, Captain La Rue and his crew joined the seventy-eight other merchant ships and eight escorts in Convoy GUS-63.

Unlike the last few journeys across the Atlantic, this one experienced an enemy attack. After a brief stop in Gibraltar, the convoy had made its way through the Straits of Gibraltar on January 3. Just before six that evening, within sight of the northeastern-most point in Africa, Cape Spartel, Morocco, the SS *Henry Miller*, an American Liberty ship also operated by Moore-McCormack[14] and ahead of the *Thompson* in the convoy, was torpedoed by the U-870. The ship did not sink, but some of her crew were removed by a US warship and the remainder sailed her back the short distance to Gibraltar, where she would be scrapped after the war. Destroyers dropped depth charges, but the U-870 got away. She did not have long to live. The US Army Air Force bombed Bremen on March 30, 1945, and caught U-870 and five of her sisters at dockside. For the convoy, the rest of the voyage was uneventful and the *Thompson* arrived safely at her berth in New York on January 20.

Life aboard a ship, its speed, course, location, and major events, are recorded in a "log book." Within the wheelhouse will be the "Deck Log," which records most of these details. Since the Deck Log is filled in by hand, for many ships the Deck Log will be retyped as a "Smooth Log," which captures the information in a more readable format. The engine room may maintain its own "Engine Log," recording demands for propeller revolutions or ship's speed, changes in boiler or engine operation, major malfunctions or maintenance events, etc. Most of these log books for ships operated seventy or eighty years ago by now-defunct shipping lines have long since been lost. While there are almost no log books extant for ships on which Leonard La Rue served, there are a few "Official Logs" in archives around the country belonging to the National Archives and Record Administration. One of them is the "Official Log-Book" of the SS *Smith Thompson*, dated "11/9/1944." This book encompasses Leonard La Rue's first voyage as master of his own vessel. Unlike the Deck Log, the Official Log primarily contained records of the crew, their behavior, punishments, injuries, deaths (for passengers, as well), births (presumably only of passengers), and other information that could be required to demon-strate that the ship and her crew were operated within Coast Guard regulations.

One of the first sections of the Official Log is entitled, "List of Crew and Report of Character." Here the master rated each of his subordi-nates, from the chief mate to the greenest ordinary seaman or wiper, on "Conduct" and "Ability." The log instructed the master to use a standard nomenclature: "V.G." for "Very Good;" "G" for "Good;" "M" for "Middling;" and "I" for "Indifferent." The master may also write notes, or refer the reader to a page where disciplinary actions would be noted. Almost all of La Rue's first crew were rated V.G. for conduct and V.G. or G for ability. A few stand out, however. For the conduct of Messman Bradley C. Small, La Rue noted "At sea V.G. in port appears to be a rumhound." The assessment seems well-founded. The log noted that, at 7:20 p.m. on October 10, 1944, in Bari, Italy, "Bradley C. Small, messman, removed from ship for continual drunkenness by U.S. Army Provost Marshal." At eight p.m. on October 12, "Bradley C. Small returned aboard by military police." The log noted the master's judgment and punishment: "As Bradley C. Small, Messman, was aboard ship Oct. 9 and 10 in a drunken condition and was unable to perform his duties I fine him 2 days' pay on wages and bonuses." This amounted to $5.84 in lost pay but ten dollars in lost bonus. Messman Small's response to the charge and punishment was, "There is nothing I can say," the typical response when a crew member was caught patently in the wrong.

La Rue's first signed entry as master in an Official Log.

For another man, instead of ratings he noted, "Obstinate, lazy and shiftless, troublemaker." Neither of these men sailed with La Rue on the *Smith Thompson* again. It would seem that Captain La Rue had learned from his experiences on *Mormacmar* and elsewhere that the crew needed a strong hand in discipline, tempered with fairness. Officers who served with him in Korea repeatedly emphasized that quality in La Rue's leadership.

For his second voyage as master, La Rue rated the conduct of all of his crew V.G. with one exception: one Leendert J. Van Loon. Following his note, we find that, in the captain's words, "Leendert J. Van Loon, A.B., was placed in irons and confined for neglect of duty, refusal to turn to, disobedience of lawful commands of master and chief officer," on January 16, 1945. A day later, La Rue wrote, "Leendert J. Van Loon, A.B., stated that he would return to work and obey the lawful orders of the master, was, therefore, restored to duty." The captain noted at the bottom of the page,

> "The conduct of Leendert J. Van Loon, A.B., has been above reproach up until the above occurrence took place. It has been noted recently that his actions have become a trifil [sic] erratic and it is my opinion that he may be suffering from a mental disorder. Leonard P. La Rue Master."

The comment reflected La Rue's sincere concern for the well-being of his crewman.

Captain La Rue signed off the SS *Smith Thompson* on January 29 and took some time with family in Philadelphia. On April 24 he signed aboard the SS *George B. McClellan*, a Liberty ship built by the Richmond Shipbuilding Corporation, a division of Henry J. Kaiser's Permanente Metals Corporation. Named after the Civil War general and Democratic presidential candidate, the *McClellan* had been completed in June 1942 as US Maritime Commission hull number MCE-322, just one of the almost 1,200 Liberty ships the six Kaiser yards would build. By the time La Rue took command, the *McClellan* had already been once to the Caribbean, three times to the UK, and five times to the Mediterranean, each voyage including multiple stops carrying cargo among nearby ports. In the now closing days of the war, she had just a few more runs to complete.

La Rue joined the ship in Norfolk, Virginia. The ship steamed from Norfolk on May 1 and spent the next two weeks visiting ports along the mid-Atlantic, taking on cargo, briefly joining convoy NK-684, one of the New York-Key West convoys, stopping in Wilmington, North Carolina, to load cargo, and then sailing on to Charleston. She steamed out of Charleston on May 8, "VE-Day," the day to celebrate the capitulation of Germany and the end of the war in Europe. She arrived in New York on the twelfth loaded with 3,100 tons of tobacco, flour, and military vehicles, to join the eastbound convoy, HX-356, the next day. Even as Germany had surrendered, a small amount of bureaucratic inertia and a large amount of caution that not all German forces, particularly U-boats, had gotten the message, or accepted it, kept the convoys going a little longer. The last convoy for the UK would be HX-358, sailing from New York just ten days later.

The forty-five ships of HX-356 sailed on May 13, accompanied by just four escorts. The convoy arrived in Liverpool, England, on May 27. The Armed Guard and the ship's crew had maintained their watches, but there was nothing to defend against now besides collisions with other ships in the convoy. Her holds emptied and the ship ballasted with sea water, *McClellan* steamed on the thirty-first for Le Havre, France, on the coast of Brittany, to load 377 US Army officers and their men. After a brief delay waiting for the men to arrive, the *McClellan* turned for home with her cargo of victorious soldiers, arriving in Newport News, Virginia, on June 19. It took less than two hours for the men to gather their duffels and weapons, and march down the *McClellan*'s gangplank onto their country's soil for the first time in many months, and for some, many years. A day later, the SS *George B. McClellan* was back at her berth in New York, a city still living in the afterglow of the VE celebrations Captain La Rue and his crew had missed.

6

VICTORY

I f the war in Europe had been won and Americans and their allies could celebrate, there was still the prospect of more bloody fights in the Pacific. By the end of March, Iwo Jima had been captured at the cost of 28,649 Americans killed or wounded, and more than 20,000 dead Japanese.[1] By the end of June, Okinawa had been captured at the cost of almost 50,000 Americans killed or wounded, more than 110,000 Japanese soldiers killed and the loss of perhaps another 100,000 Japanese civilians. The ferocity of the Japanese resistance even three hundred miles from the tip of Kyushu, the southernmost home island, convinced Allied war planners that a massive invasion force, as many as five million men, would be required to force Japan to capitulate.[2] And just as it had been throughout the war, it was primarily the Merchant Marine that would deliver the men and supplies to where the battles would be fought. Merchant ships were already repatriating men and materiel from Europe back to the United States for staging before shipment on to west coast ports. Before long they would be continuing their voyage westward across the Pacific.

Captain La Rue signed off as master of the SS *George B. McClellan* on July 7 and the next day signed on as master of the SS *Whittier Victory*. The *Whittier Victory*, US Maritime Commission hull number MCV-798, was a brand-new transport being completed at the California Shipbuilding Corporation (Calship), the same yard that had built the *Smith Thompson*. When she was launched at 5:30 p.m. on June 20, she was the 448th ship Calship had slid down the ways; the *Whitter*, however, was not a Liberty ship, but a Victory ship. The hulls were the same basic size, 455 feet long overall with a sixty-two-foot beam, since they had to use the same builders' ways and dry docks built for the construction and repair of the Liberty ships. The hull was reshaped to make it more streamlined to take advantage of the steam turbines now available to power them to a speed of at least fifteen knots (compared to eleven on a Liberty). The *Whittier Victory* and the rest of the Victory ships built at Calship were in the VC2-S-AP2 configuration, with 6,000 horsepower steam turbines. Multiple manufacturers were now building turbines for the Victory ships; Whittier's were built by Allis Chalmers. The gross and displacement tonnage were slightly increased, 7,612 and 15,200 tons for the Victory compared to 7,176 and 14,245 tons for the Liberty, respectively. Because deck cargo (aircraft, tanks, trucks, etc.) had proven so important, the main deck was configured to provide a more useful area outboard the hatches compared to the Liberty ships. Those hatches accessed five holds with a total capacity about 10,000 cubic feet higher than the Liberty.

In addition to being faster, the Victory ships also were designed to remedy some of the deficiencies identified in the Liberty's systems and crew accommodations. Pumps, blowers and windlasses were now powered electrically rather than by steam, easing maintenance. The Liberty ships had been designed to accommodate fewer than fifty men but often sailed with more than eighty aboard, depending on the size of the Armed Guard. The Victory ships were built with accommodations for sixty-two officers and men in the midships house and a further twenty-eight in the house located on the aft (quarter) deck.[3] The captain's cabin, formerly located on the same deck as the wheelhouse and blazingly hot as the tropical sun beat down on the open deck above, was relocated to the cabin deck where other officers' cabins were located. Other changes better organized berthing for the crew, as well as their galleys and messing. All in all, the Victory was a better ship than the Liberty, and far more useful to shipping companies after the war.

Calship outfitting newly completed Victory ships. Victory ships were mass produced in the same yards that had cranked out Liberty ships. U.S.S.R. Victory in the foreground, launched in April, 1944, was a slightly faster AP3 configuration with 8,000 horsepower turbines.

Whittier Victory, named after Whittier College[4] in Whittier, California, was the forty-ninth Victory ship built at Calship.[5] Little did Captain La Rue know at the time, but five years later he would command the fiftieth, the *Meredith Victory*.[6] It would be an understatement to say that ship would figure prominently in his life. The SS *Meredith Victory* was launched three days after *Whittier Victory* and the two ships occupied adjacent outfitting berths. They were joined by sister ships the SS *Pacific Victory* and SS *Wabash Victory* for a "Million Dollar Open House" at Calship on Sunday, July 1. According to the *Wilmington Press-Journal*, "The vessels are 10,500-ton cargo ships built by Calship for the United States Maritime Commission." Perhaps reflecting the optimism that the end of the World War was truly in sight, the *Press-Journal* continued, "They are the type of vessel which will be the backbone of America's postwar Merchant Marine." Visitors were, "permitted to tour the main deck and boat deck of the vessels" and were "able to reach vantage points" where they could "look into holds and quarters of the ships. Guns on the after side of the midship house" were available for "inspection by visitors," of which the organizers expected eight thousand per hour. The event was arranged to help sell war bonds to continue financing the war, and even the fifty company employees who volunteered to escort visitors through the ships committed to buy the bonds.[7] If the static displays and the enthusiasm of the Calship employees didn't seal the deal, Calship planned to launch the *Amarillo Victory* into the Cerritos Channel in front of the shipyard during the open house.

SS Whittier Victory *steaming empty in Norfolk, 1945.*

Calship completed outfitting the *Whittier Victory*, and on July 15 she was delivered to the Maritime Commission, and on the same day by the Maritime Commission to the War Shipping Administration. Moore-McCormack assumed operational responsibility, and Captain La Rue assumed command. On July 24 the *Whittier Victory* left Los Angeles for San Francisco. The War Shipping Administration advised Moore-McCormack that the *Whittier Victory* had been "assigned to the Army for her initial voyage. It is requested that you contact Vessel

Movement Staff, Water Div., Ft. Mason for further instructions." The articles the crew signed instructed Whittier Victory for its "Voyage Number 1" to proceed to "a point in the Pacific Ocean to the westward of San Francisco and thence to such ports and places in any part of the world as the Master may direct or as may be ordered or directed by the United States Government or any Department, Commission or agency thereof."

Whittier Victory sailed for the Philippines on July 27, sailing north of the Hawaiian Islands, north of the Marshalls, and south of Guam, landing at San Fernando, La Union, on the western side of the island of Luzon. On September 5 the *Whittier Victory* was between Guam and Palau when, eight thousand miles away, Isabelle Catherine La Rue, Captain La Rue's mother, died from cardiac arrest in St. Mary's Hospital, Philadelphia. She was sixty-eight years old, the same age as her husband when he had died the year before. La Rue and his ship didn't dock in San Francisco until sixteen days later.

But by the time *Whittier Victory* had arrived at her destination in the Philippines, the war was already over. The fighting in the Pacific had been taken to the Japanese home islands as B-29 "Superfortresses" had burned almost all of its major cities by dropping thousands of tons of magnesium-filled incendiaries. Still, Japan fought on.

As the Navy, Army, and Marine Corps were planning for "Operation Olympic," the planned November 1945 invasion of Kyushu that was to throw fourteen divisions against the southernmost Japanese home island, a secret weapon delivered by fewer than a dozen men stole their thunder with a thunder all its own. Before the sun rose on August 6, a B-29 bomber named *Enola Gay* rumbled down the mile-and-a-half runway on Tinian Island for the 1,500-mile flight to the city of Hiroshima, located 420 miles southwest of Tokyo on the island of Honshu. At 9:15 local time, cruising four and a half miles above the city, *Enola Gay* dropped a single bomb just ten-and-a-half-feet long and twenty-nine inches in diameter. After all of the millions of tons of explosives dropped on the Axis, contained within the five-ton cylinder falling to earth were two pieces of uranium-235 totaling just 140 pounds. About forty-five seconds later, when the bomb had fallen to less than two thousand feet above the city, those two pieces of uranium were shot together inside a gun barrel and Hiroshima and fifty thousand of her inhabitants instantly ceased to exist, with thousands yet to die over the following days and months.

Japanese soldier walking through the ruins of Hiroshima.

Even as reports reached Tokyo of this terrible, new American weapon, the militarists dominating the Japanese government refused to surrender. Their obstinance was answered three days later, when, shortly after noon on August 9, a second weapon, this time a five-ton melon-shaped bomb carrying less than fourteen pounds of plutonium-239, was dropped by the B-29 *Bockscar* over the Mitsubishi plant in Nagasaki, six hundred miles southwest of Tokyo on the island of Kyushu. Clouds over Kokura, the primary target, had spared that city the destruction that Nagasaki now suffered.

The Japanese cabinet once again debated meeting the terms the Allies had laid out in the Potsdam Declaration of July 26, which required unconditional surrender and the complete disarmament of all Japanese military forces. Emperor Hirohito listened quietly to hours of heated debate and early on the morning of August 10 he made the decision to "bear the unbearable" and surrender to the Allies. That morning the foreign ministry transmitted Japan's willingness to surrender to the Allies, conditioned on retaining the emperor as head of state. On August 12 the Allies accepted the surrender, making clear that the emperor's role would henceforth only be ceremonial. As the most militaristic factions within the Japanese government still resisted the idea of surrender and attempted a coup, the emperor chose to remove any chance of insurrection by addressing his nation by radio. On August 15 the Japanese people for the first time heard the reedy voice of Emperor Hirohito, speaking in a highly formalized Japanese few could fully understand, tell them that the struggle was over. Resistance to the surrender fizzled out none too soon, since a third nuclear weapon could have been employed on Japan on the seventeenth or eighteenth of August to force the issue.

The fission weapons that forced Japan's capitulation were years in the making, but only a tiny minority of Americans knew of their existence before headlines, like "Atom Bomb Fury Hits Japan," appeared in US newspapers a few hours after the destruction at Hiroshima. It had started with a letter from famed physicist Albert Einstein[8] to President Roosevelt on August 2, 1939, alerting the president that, based on recent advances in the physics of nuclear chain reactions, "it is conceivable-though much less certain-that extremely powerful bombs of a new type may thus be constructed. A single bomb of this type, carried by boat and exploded in a port, might very well destroy the whole port together with some of the surrounding territory." The letter continued, "However, such bombs might very well prove to be too heavy for transportation by air." In response to Einstein's letter, Roosevelt formed a committee, the Advisory Committee on Uranium, to assess the prospects for such a device. The committee shortly granted six thousand dollars to a small research group working at Columbia University under the direction of Italian physicist Enrico Fermi[9].

As progress advanced and the United States entered the war, Fermi and his group moved to the University of Chicago to expand their research and escape the potential vulnerability of the Atlantic coast. On December 2, 1942, as La Rue and the *Mormacmar* were steaming through the Arabian Sea on their way from the Persian Gulf to Colombo, Ceylon, forty-eight men and one woman witnessed the first controlled, self-sustaining nuclear reaction in an experiment set up in a squash court under the stands of the university's abandoned football stadium.

A year later, more than 100,000 men and women would be working on the "Manhattan Project," creating materials and designs needed for a working nuclear bomb. They worked at locations around the country, including Los Alamos, New Mexico, Hanford, Washington, and Oak Ridge, Tennessee, but few knew precisely why they were building the enormous structures and the machines they contained. Early on the morning of July 16, 1945, as Captain La Rue was asleep in his cabin aboard the brand-new *Whittier Victory*, a brilliant light illuminated the mountains around Socorro, New Mexico, as the scientists of the Manhattan Project demonstrated the first nuclear fission weapon (in this case using plutonium, rather than uranium). By the end of the war, the project had cost 1.9 billion dollars (about $27 billion in 2020 dollars), or about half the cost of all the Liberty ships built.

There are no Armed Guard reports extant for *Whittier Victory*, but it is entirely likely that *Whittier Victory* sailed on her return voyage from the Philippines with her guns manned, since no one could be certain this early after the official Japanese surrender that there were no rogue submarines or unrepentant *Kamikaze* pilots still seeking to wreak vengeance on an American ship. As it happened, the greater threat turned out to be mines. La Rue had steamed under the threat of mines all the way back to early 1942 on the Murmansk run. The last US merchant ship to be sunk by a torpedo was lost off Okinawa on August 10, but ships were being damaged and sunk by mines, whether floating or moored in fields, all the way through the end of 1945.

All told, during the war 9,521 US merchant mariners had been killed outright, drowned, died of their wounds, or died as prisoners of war out of the 243,000 men that served. The fatality rate of one in twenty-six, almost four percent, was higher than that of any of the US armed services during the war.

If the war was over, the demobilization was just beginning. After having arrived back in San Francisco at the end of September, by the ninth of October *Whittier Victory* was again loading military cargo, this time for the Navy. She sailed for Okinawa on October 15. On her return it is likely that the Armed Guard had sailed their last. This was certainly the case by the following February. *Whittier Victory* sailed from Manilla on February 6, 1946 and, with a stop in Colombo, arrived in Beira, Mozambique, to load five thousand tons of chromium. The American Consul in Durban, South Africa, seeking passage for US nationals, was advised that the *Whittier Victory* could accommodate eighteen passengers, provided the Coast Guard issued a waiver permitting her to do so. This many could only have been carried if some were accommodated in the former Armed Guard quarters in the ship's aft house. The Coast Guard granted the waiver on March 6, but when the ship arrived in Cape Town, the demand for passage back to the US was so high that Captain La Rue requested an a second waiver to permit the ship to carry an additional six passengers for a total of twenty-four. This waiver was also granted, since the ship still carried all the life-saving equipment for her full complement of sixty-two plus the twenty-eight members of the Armed Guard, and because "all but three" were single males.

When the ship arrived in New York on April 1, among the passengers was the Rev. William B. Coppens, a Catholic priest of the Missionary Oblates of Mary Immaculate, who was bound for Boston to visit his dying mother. Father Coppens had been serving as a missionary to South Africa's Zulu and before that as a chaplain in the British Eighth Army commanded by Field Marshall Bernard Law Montgomery. La Rue, whose Catholic faith was always foremost, certainly used the opportunity to visit with his passenger, perhaps exchanging stories about their travels and their service, presumably attending masses Father Coppens said while onboard the ship. When Mary C. Coppens died on April 29, she was surrounded by her four sons, all, like William, priests of the Oblates of Mary Immaculate.[10] One can imagine that the purpose of Father Coppens' journey was particularly poignant for Captain La Rue given his mother's recent death while he was at sea the year before.

Whittier Victory *in Moore-McCormack colors.*

On July 25, 1946, Moore-McCormack and the Maritime Commission changed the terms of *Whittier Victory*'s charter, a "redelivery" from General Agency Agreement to International Bareboat, so the line could use the ship in its own commercial service. Now in the Atlantic, *Whittier Victory* shifted to one of Moore-McCormack Lines' specialties, carrying cargo and occasional passengers between ports on the East Coast of the United States such as Newport News, Philadelphia, New York, and Boston, and ports in South America. During one of those trips, pictures taken by Bob Cochran, third engineer on the *Whittier Victory*, show Captain La Rue on liberty with some of his officers, the men dressed in civilian clothes, sightseeing in Sao Paolo or swimming from a Brazilian beach. The pictures highlight that, while La Rue was not a heavy drinker or a womanizer, he was also not a loner or a misanthrope. He satisfied his love of travel by stepping off the ship when he could, and not always by himself.

La Rue, facing camera, on the beach in Brazil, 1946. Facing away is one of his officers on the Whittier Victory, *Ed O'Regan.*

La Rue, second from left, with some of his officers in Sao Paolo, Brazil, 1946.

During one of the voyages on that route, La Rue met a passenger who would prove to be very influential on his future. In December 1946, *Whittier Victory* embarked a group of Benedictine[11] monks during a stop in Trinidad. The monks, on their way back to their home, the Monastery of St. Benedict in Bahia, Brazil, had been visiting their brother monks at the Mount St. Benedict Monastery in St. Augustine,

Tunapuna-Piarco, Trinidad. The Mount St. Benedict Monastery had been founded by monks from Bahia's monastery in 1912, which, in turn, had been founded in 1581, the earliest monastery in the Americas. Among the Benedictines was a priest, the Rev. Vicente Lautenschlager. Father Lautenschlager was born in Switzerland in 1889, joined the Benedictines in 1918, and was ordained a priest in 1923. Captain La Rue and Father Lautenschlager struck up a friendship during the two weeks and apparently spoke of many subjects, notably their shared Catholic faith. Perhaps La Rue mentioned he had visited the Mount St. Benedict Monastery more than a decade earlier, during his Caribbean cruise as a young cadet at the Pennsylvania Nautical School.

Captain La Rue bids farewell to Rev. Vicente Lautenschlager, OSB, in Bahia, Brazil, December, 1946.

Bob Cochran took a picture on the day the Benedictines disembarked in Bahia. La Rue, in dark trousers and white, short-sleeved shirt, is shaking the hand of an older man dressed in the black habit of the Benedictines, on his head the black *cappello romano* worn by Catholic priests at the time. On the back of a copy of the picture La Rue wrote,

"Father Vincente Laudenstlager [sic], a German-Swiss who joined the Benedictines in Brazil. He was a passenger from Trinidad back to Brazil. On leaving the ship, we shook hands. He told me this was no vocation. I don't know if he meant me or was speaking generally."[12]

Later, we will see the impact of their friendship.

By the end of January 1947, the *Whittier Victory* had steamed almost 37,000 nautical miles. The Maritime Commission conducted a "Final Guarantee Survey," assessing the physical condition of the ship and whether any warranty claims needed to be made against Calship or the vendors of her various components and systems. Seventy-Eight items were identified, mostly minor, and the survey committee declared the ship in "very good condition." This was as much a reflection on the master's leadership and his oversight of the chief engineer and the deck department as on the builder's quality.

The US Merchant Marine had left its war footing and was returning to a commercial environment that in some ways was the same as prewar, in other ways different. Europe was in ruins, and many of the cargoes carried in US bottoms were for humanitarian relief to keep starvation at bay. On the other hand, South America was almost entirely untouched by the war. An advertisement in *Time* magazine on February 17, 1947, brought the point home:

"From Pearl Harbor to V-J Day, Moore-McCormack Lines operated more than 150 ships, lost 11 vessels, transported 754,239 troops and carried 34,410,111 tons of war cargo. To discharge such responsibilities in time of crisis, America's Merchant Marine must be kept strong in peace-as in war."

For much of 1947, *Whittier Victory* continued her routes between the US and South America. On March 6, 1947, *Whittier Victory* sailed from New York bound for Trinidad. She arrived in Trinidad on the eleventh just long enough to bunker and sailed the same day for the River

Platte, 4,500 miles away. She arrived in Montevideo, Uruguay, on March 23.

Evidently, some of the crew enjoyed their time in Montevideo more than they should have. On March 28 two members of the engine department missed their assigned watches when they were absent without leave, overstaying their time ashore on liberty. They were fined two days' pay each. The ship's chief electrician was absent without leave on March 31. His statement, "was not awakened in time to come back to the ship," failed to sway Captain La Rue, who fined him two days' pay as well.

The chief electrician had additional punishment to follow. On April 2 he reported to the chief mate, who functioned as the medical officer on the ship, that he had a sore in a very sensitive area of his body as the result of "sexual exposure 3 days previously." When the organ swelled to a distressing degree on April 3, the man was taken to a hospital in Montevideo where he was treated and released. On the seventh and eighth, the chief electrician failed to turn to for his duty because he had gone back ashore and checked himself into the hospital without informing the master. La Rue fined the man four days' pay for his failure to stand his watches on those two days.

Medical complaints from the crew, whether from injury, illness, or shore-activities, were common. While the *Whitter Victory* was midway between Trinidad and Montevideo, one of the crew reported not feeling well and showed signs of chicken pox. By the time the ship reached Uruguay, the diagnosis had been changed to smallpox, and the man was isolated until he could be transferred to a hospital in Montevideo. One man was excused from duty twice because of asthma. Another was excused for back strains. It is noteworthy that men who had normal medical ailments were routinely excused from duty and not fined if they could not stand a watch. But the man who had violated the trust of the master and his shipmates was punished even beyond what his body was already doing to him.

The ship remained in port before sailing for Buenos Aires, Argentina, on April 13. *Whittier Victory* arrived the next day in Buenos Aires, 120 miles up the Rio de la Plata, and this time she stayed in port for a month and a half, discharging the vast majority of her cargo (the ship's draft went from twenty feet forward and twenty-seven feet aft when leaving Trinidad to twelve feet forward and fifteen feet aft leaving Buenos Aires). On May 31 she left Buenos Aires due for Trinidad, which she reached on June 11, again staying less than a day to bunker before making for Philadelphia, which she reached on June 16. By the thirtieth she was back in New York, leaving that port for Belem, Brazil. On September 19 she left New York to bunker in Trinidad and continue on to Montevideo, repeating the cycle.

As on previous voyages, the temptations in South American ports seem to have been too much for many of La Rue's crew. Several crew members failed to turn to for their watches following time ashore or drinking binges aboard the ship. Several men even failed to board the ship before she had to sail, rejoining the ship at a later port. La Rue dutifully described their offenses and fined them, occasionally adding some color to the description of the offense. In the port of Paranagua, Brazil, he said of one, he was "absent without leave Monday, Dec. 22nd and because of his self-admitted debauchery, did not turn to Dec. 23rd. For this offense fined two days' pay for each day. Total fine imposed $25.60." The log records the AB's reply as "I can't say nothing about it."

The beginning of 1948 brought one of the odder events in Captain La Rue's career. On this trip, rather than returning to New York from Brazil, the *Whittier Victory* had instead crossed into the Pacific through the Panama Canal in mid-January and arrived in Long Beach, California, on Wednesday, January 28. She then sailed on the thirtieth for San Francisco and from there to Vancouver, British Columbia, to offload a cargo of coffee and load a cargo of flour for delivery to Cartagena, Colombia, on the Atlantic coast of South America.

As *Whittier Victory* prepared to depart for San Francisco on February 16, a strong winter gale moved in with high winds and heavy snow. The ship had been scheduled to move up the Strait of Georgia to Powell River to load five hundred tons of wood pulp, but apparently that was not enough cargo to risk being stranded by heavy weather. Perhaps she was already overdue, since the San Francisco papers were reporting her expected arrival that day. In any event, the *Whittier Victory* departed the Lapointe terminal in Vancouver on the evening of February 16 and, as she made her way west in blowing snow toward the Strait, she collided with a "boom" of logs under tow, severing part of the tow and setting the logs adrift. *Whittier Victory* continued into the Strait of Georgia and out to sea on her way to San Francisco. The *Whittier Victory* was not alone in her misfortunes. Another ship, the *Lake Winnipeg*, struck a different tow of logs that night.

The next day, February 17, the largest headline above the fold on the front page of the *Vancouver Sun* read, "Drifting Log Booms Menace Small Boats," with the subheading, "Freighters Smash Tows in Snowstorm." The article begins, "Tossing logs in the wind-wracked lower Strait of Georgia menaced fish boats and other small craft this afternoon. The logs were cut loose from their tows by two freighters which sliced into them during a blinding snowstorm Monday night." As the article described traffic accidents and downed telephone lines caused by the storm, it continued,

> "Cliff Towing Co.'s *Sea Son* lost between seven and eight sections of logs, which went adrift and had not been found by searching vessels. Towers Towing Co.'s tug *Celmor* lost eight sections of logs, some of which were recovered, in a mishap with a second freighter. Murray Cliff at Cliff Towing Co. said today that at least ten tugs and their booms were menaced off Point Grey when one freighter-believed to be the U.S. ship *Whittier Victory*-seemed to go 'berserk' for nearly two hours in the snow storm. Both Cliff and an official of Straights Towing Co., whose *Eldoma* was among the tugs 'menaced,' said the freighter was 'inside the bell buoy off Point Grey where it shouldn't have been.'"

What exactly happened that night? Clearly, the visibility was very poor. The *Whittier Victory* almost certainly did not have radar, since the bulky, operator-intensive sets of the day were installed only on warships that had the space and manpower to accommodate them. There were no global electronic navigation systems like GPS or Loran in 1948. The Decca radio navigation system was in limited use, but by all indications not employed at that time in Vancouver, and in any event, it is highly doubtful that the ship was equipped with a Decca receiver. The most sophisticated navigational system aboard the ship was a gyrocompass and a radio-direction finder, the latter of limited use when the range to the transmitter was short. As such, she would have mainly relied upon dead reckoning and visual sights of charted landmarks to establish her position, perhaps with a little help from the fathometer. The marine traffic lanes entering and leaving Vancouver from the south hug the land to the east (Lulu Island), and with the heavy winds, perhaps she misjudged her turn into the Strait, turning to the south too soon and entered the northbound lane. She certainly did not turn inside the buoy to the northwest of Point Grey or she would have rapidly entered shoal water and grounded.

Did the master and crew know they had collided with the boom? In case of collision at sea, a ship is obligated to stand by and render aid, if needed. There is no evidence this was done. Perhaps, in the blinding snowstorm and high winds, the *Whittier Victory* simply thought she had collided with logs set adrift in the storm. Or maybe she never knew she'd hit them.

Suffice it to say, the events of February 16, 1948, had no lasting effect on Captain La Rue's career. The *Whittier Victory* continued on to San Francisco and sailed from there to Cartagena on March 2. Despite the fact that the M. R. Cliff Tugboat Company filed a claim for $20,000 against the *Whittier Victory* on February 20, claiming the ship "carved through a boom towed by Cliff's tug *Sea Son* and set a number of sections adrift," La Rue remained in command of the ship until he delivered her to the Maritime Commission's Reserve Fleet at Mobile, Alabama, on June 9 of that year and out of service with Moore-McCormack.[13] Like many Victory ships, *Whittier Victory* would be reactivated in 1950 for service during the Korea War, leased under Bareboat Charter for commercial shipping during the mid-1950s, sent back to the Reserve Fleet, reactivated in the mid-1960s for service during the Vietnam War, and then sent back to the Reserve Fleet before being scrapped in 1993.

Whether it was a slap on the wrist because of the incident in Vancouver[14] or the lack of a suitable command at the time *Whittier Victory* entered the Reserve Fleet, La Rue's next service was aboard the SS *Uruguay*, not as master but as first officer.[15] The *Uruguay* had been built for the Panama Pacific Steam Ship Company in 1928 by the Newport News Shipbuilding and Dry Dock Company, one of three sisters: the *California* (later renamed the *Uruguay*), the *Pennsylvania* (renamed the *Argentina*), and the *Virginia* (renamed the *Brazil*). At 601 feet long overall and eighty feet in beam, the ship was rated at 20,237 gross tons, the largest ship on which La Rue ever served. Her twelve boilers[16] powered steam-turbine electrical generators, which in turn powered electric propulsion motors propelling her through twin screws to a speed of 18.5 knots. Designed to carry 519 passengers, the ship also had holds fore and aft and extensive refrigerated stores for the transportation of fresh fruits and vegetables. In *Time* magazine Moore-McCormack Lines advertised "Fresh Plums, out of Season," thanks to the "reestablishment of luxury cruises to Brazil, Uruguay and Argentina." The advertisement showed the precious produce being unloaded from the refrigerated hold of the *Argentina*.

Moore-McCormack Lines had chartered the ships from the Maritime Commission in 1938 after the commission had received them as part of a transaction involving the new ship SS *America*. Moore-McCormack renamed the ships, reflecting their use on "Good Neighbor" routes to South America, and successfully operated them south until the war, when they were converted to troop ships for use by the War Shipping Administration. As USAT (US Army Transport) *Uruguay*, she made multiple trips to India, Australia, New Zealand, and, eventually, Japan. After the war, she and her sisters, after having carried nearly half a million troops, were converted back from troop ships to passenger liners, renovated and redecorated at a cost to the Maritime Commission of almost $8 million ($88 million in 2020 dollars) each.

After a nine-day proving cruise in early February 1948 to Nassau in the Bahamas and Havana, Cuba, she resumed her prewar service to South America on February 12. "The Good Neighbor Fleet is Back," heralded an ad from 1948.

"Completely rebuilt, modernized and restyled, the 33,000-ton luxury liners of Moore-McCormack's Good Neighbor Fleet bring back to South American travel all the comforts and pleasures that characterized their prewar service, together with smart new decorations and furnishings. They will establish a regular schedule of fortnightly departures with the fastest, largest ships in service to South America, calling at Rio, Santos (port for Sao Paulo), Montevideo, Buenos Aires and Trinidad, and resuming 38-day luxury cruises."

A cheerful image of the Uruguay used in a 1948 Moore-McCormack advertisement.

Signing aboard the *Uruguay* on September 9, 1948, First Mate La Rue counted navigation as high among his responsibilities. La Rue was well suited to the role, having navigated these waters during the war and then many times afterwards as master of the *Whittier Victory*.

Even more so than a cargo ship, a passenger ship holds to a fixed schedule for her sailing dates, since passengers rely on these dates for embarking and disembarking, excursions and other land activities. The ship sailed from New York on September 10 for Bahia, Brazil. She sailed from Bahia for Rio de Janeiro on the twentieth, Brazil, from Rio for Santos, Brazil, on the twenty-third, from Santos for Montevideo, Uruguay, on the twenty-fifth, from Montevideo to Buenos Aires, Argentina, on the twenty-eighth, from Buenos Aires back to Montevideo on October 1, from Montevideo back to Santos on the second, from Santos back to Rio on the fourth, from Rio for Trinidad on the sixth, and after bunkering in Trinidad, homeward on the thirteenth. By October 18 the *Uruguay* was pier-side in New York again. The ship repeated the cruise with departures from New York on October 22, December 3, January 14, 1949, February 25, and April 8.

When the ship returned from the April cruise on May 16, La Rue signed off the *Uruguay* for his next command. How he had felt about not being master aboard the *Uruguay*, we do not know. At a time when the salary for the master of a C-2 or Victory ship was $675 per month and the third in command (second mate on the cargo ships) was earning about fifty percent of the master's wages, the same position on a ship twice the displacement was probably paying comparably to his previous master's salary. Was he being groomed by Moore-McCormack lines for command of one of these ships in the future? We do not know.

The duty aboard the ship must have been enjoyable, for he stayed aboard for six cruises. The accommodations and food were almost certainly better than he experienced aboard his cargo-ship commands. While the *Uruguay's* passengers dined on "Consomme Santos Dumont" and "Filet of Sole Dieppoise," First Mate La Rue enjoyed

"Rice Jambolaya, Creole Style" and "Broiled Veal Chops, Diablo Sauce." Every ship had a steward department, but while on a cargo ship it might consist of a steward, a cook, and a few assistant cooks and messmen, aboard *Uruguay* some forty men were aboard just to prepare food, including bakers, a butcher, a fish cook, a roast cook, and a sous chef, in addition to waiters to serve the passengers and messmen to serve the crew.

La Rue made good use of his time when he was not on watch. *Uruguay* had an instructor on board who provided Spanish lessons for the crew. La Rue took twenty-three of the twenty-four lessons offered, charging the $5.75 ($0.25 per lesson) cost to his slop account. Needless to say, the masters under which he served on *Uruguay*, Captains A. P. Spaulding and A. W. Pierce, rated both his conduct and ability "V.G."

Captain La Rue received his next command as master of the Liberty ship SS *Deborah Gannett* on May 26, 1949. The ship was named after Deborah Sampson Gannett, a woman who had served for a year and a half as a man in the Continental Army during the American Revolution until her actual gender was discovered. The *Gannett*, Maritime Commission number MCE-2620, was launched on April 11, 1944, at Bethlehem Steel's Fairfield shipyard in Baltimore by a distant relative of her namesake, Sally Gannett, daughter of newspaper publisher Frank E. Gannett. She was among the 385 Liberty ships built at Fairfield, starting with the very first Liberty, SS *Patrick Henry*, launched in December 1941. The *Deborah Gannett* sailed from Houston on May 29 with a load of grain bound for Europe for aid under the Marshall Plan, and when she returned in July, Captain La Rue was off to his next assignment.

On July 15 La Rue signed on as master of the SS *Mormacwren*. The "*Wren*" had been built as part of the Maritime Commission's prewar shipbuilding program, like the *Mormacdale*, but she was a larger, "C-2" ship, 6,214 gross tons, 460 feet long and sixty-three feet in beam. Her sleek hull and steam turbines gave her a design speed of 15.5 knots. Maritime Commission hull number 1184 was completed on June 14,

1944, by the Moore Dry Dock Company at Oakland, California, as the SS *Eagle Wing* and delivered by the Maritime Commission to the Waterman Steamship Corporation for charter. The ship passed to Moore-McCormack in 1946 and after operating the ship in bareboat charter, Moore-McCormack Lines purchased it from the Maritime Commission on January 14, 1947, for $957,818. Renamed *"Mormacwren,"* Moore-McCormack must have been highly satisfied with the ship, for she remained in their fleet for almost twenty years before she was sold to the Sperling Steamship and Trading Company.[17]

Captain La Rue joined the ship in Norfolk, where *Mormacwren* had steamed on July 7. A few days later, the ship sailed for Recife, Pernambuco, Brazil, before returning to US ports. She would repeat that route, well familiar to La Rue, three more times while he was in command, sailing from New York to Pernambuco on October 19, again just after the beginning of 1950, and again on March 10. When *Mormacwren* arrived back in New York around May 5, La Rue signed off the ship for the last time. His next command, arising in July, would be by far his most significant.

PART II

RESCUE AT HUNGNAM

7

WAR AGAIN

The headline on the front page of the *Arizona Republic* newspaper on June 25, 1950, declared, "58 Lost in Plane Disaster," the crash of a Northwest Airlines DC-4 into Lake Michigan during a storm the day before, what it called "the Western Hemisphere's worst air disaster." Other top stories were "Early Jap Settlement is Forecast," describing progress made in negotiating a treaty with Japan that would end the five-year postwar occupation, and a story about the control of a fire in northern Arizona that had endangered three million acres of forest.

At the very bottom of the front page was a story that began and ended with a single column, entitled, "South Korea Invaded by Reds from North." The Associated Press story began,

"Communist forces from North Korea invaded South Korea at dawn Sunday on a wide front and U.S. military advisers feared it was the long-expected invasion." The brief article continued, "Attacks rolled up at 11 points or more along the 38th parallel which divides this country at the forefront of the cold war between East and West."

Map of Korea showing major cities and the pre-invasion division.

The invasion of South Korea by forces from the North did earn top billing on the front page of that Sunday's *Boston Globe*. "Soviet Korea Wars on U.S.-Supported Republic," the headline blared. The United Press International story begins,

"The Russian-sponsored North Korean Communists invaded the American-supported Republic of South Korea today and their radio followed it up by broadcasting a declaration of war. The attacks started at dawn. The northern Pyongyang Radio broadcast a declaration of war at 11 a.m. (9 p.m. E.D.T., Saturday). North Korean forces attacked generally along the border, but chiefly in the eastern and western areas, in heavy rain after mortar and artillery bombardment started around 4 a.m. ... The extent and purpose of the attacks remained unclear for hours after the first fragmentary reports of the invasion were received. But shortly after noon, the Communist's radio at Pyongyang, the northern capital, said war had been declared effective 11 a.m."

For much of America, North Korea's invasion of South Korea was a surprise. The talk that June was of labor unrest, Joe DiMaggio's batting slump, and Gloria Swanson having left retirement to star in a motion picture scheduled for mid-summer release called *Sunset Boulevard*. Americans were enjoying a strong economy, a welcome change after the deep post-war recession in 1946 and the uneven economic growth over the following years.

But among military and foreign-affairs circles, the broader international security situation had been of foremost concern. On June 10 President Truman, speaking to a crowd in St Louis, in his home state of Missouri, had asserted, "With a cynical disregard for the hopes of mankind, the leaders of the Soviet Union have talked of democracy-but have set up dictatorships." No doubt with the Berlin Blockade of 1948 on his mind, along with ongoing provocations in Berlin and divided Germany, Truman focused on the problem of Eastern Europe. He claimed that Soviet leaders were "turning the school children of Eastern Germany into the same kind of pitiful robots that marched into hopeless battle for Hitler." He further asserted that the Soviets refused to participate in the work of the United Nations, forced representatives of "free nations" out of satellite states, and was maintaining the "largest peacetime armed force in history, far greater than it needs for the defense of its own boundaries."

Even if Truman did not mention it, Korea was a subject of great concern to some in the US government. On June 24, a day before the invasion, syndicated columnist Robert S. Allen reported on testimony before a senate committee the preceding week regarding aid to the Republic of Korea. That Saturday his column began, "The chances are good that South Korea will get $100,000,000 in special Marshall plan aid, but the Senate appropriation committee will not be enthusiastic about it when reporting the giant omnibus bill next week." During testimony on the appropriation, Michigan Republican Sen. Homer Ferguson responded to the skepticism of a Democratic colleague, saying, "The situation is obvious to anyone who had looked into the area ... If Russia marches into Korea with her own army or the Chinese army, the Koreans are helpless. Everybody knows that." Sen. Ferguson only had to wait a day for his prescience to be rewarded.

Where had this all come from? The end of World War II had left the Allies jubilant and the Axis in ruins, but the world was no more stable. Less than ten months after V-E day, as former British Prime Minister Winston Churchill made his famous "Iron Curtain" speech on March 5, 1946, at Westminster College in Fulton, Missouri, the relationship between the United States, Britain, and France on one side, and the Soviet Union and its client states in Eastern Europe and Asia were hardening.

The Yalta Agreement, the result of negotiations in February, 1945, between Soviet Premier Joseph Stalin, Prime Minister Winston Churchill and President Harry S. Truman held in the resort of Yalta on the Crimean Coast, attempted to lay out an architecture for post-war security. It formed the international organization known as the United Nations. It established surrender terms and occupation for Germany.

The second section, entitled "Declaration of Liberated Europe," laid out the conditions under which governments would be re-established in the nations through which the Allies and Axis had fought. The agreement among the Allies stated,

> "They jointly declare their mutual agreement to concert during the temporary period of instability in liberated Europe the policies of their

three Governments in assisting the peoples liberated from the domination of Nazi Germany and the peoples of the former Axis satellite states of Europe to solve by democratic means their pressing political and economic problems ... rebuilding ... must be achieved by processes which will enable liberated peoples ... to create democratic institutions of their own choice. This is the principle of the Atlantic Charter-the right of all people to choose the form of government under which they will live ... By this declaration we reaffirm our faith in the principles of the Atlantic Charter, our pledge in the Declaration by the United Nations and our determination to build in cooperation with other peace-loving nations world order, under law, dedicated to peace, security, freedom and general well-being of all mankind."

Churchill, Roosevelt and Stalin with their aides at Yalta in February 1945.

It sounded good. But Stalin was intent on skillfully using facts on the ground, support for insurgent movements, espionage, and assassination to satisfy his ambition to expand communist control over national governments, with the Soviet Union in the lead. The presence of Soviet troops across Eastern and Central Europe, in nations from the Baltic States to the eastern half of Germany, facilitated the overthrow of existing nationalist or non-communist provisional governments and the formation of communist governments closely aligned with Moscow. The United States and Britain, weary from years of war, could only discourage communist movements outside of Soviet control in countries such as Italy, France, and Greece by funding center-right parties and supporting other movements, both overtly and covertly, sympathetic to democracy and Western ideals. And in places where they were unwilling to do even that, they were reduced to protesting Soviet actions in the newly formed United Nations, where the Soviets either boycotted the sessions or used their veto in the Security Council to prevent substantive actions.

In 1948 matters in occupied Germany, and in particular, divided Berlin, reached a near-war intensity. As part of the Yalta Agreement, Berlin had been divided after the war into sectors controlled by the Soviet Union, Britain, France, and the United States, with the former German capital firmly inside Soviet occupied eastern Germany. The Soviets became unnerved by the US economic aid to the occupied western half of Germany occupied by the US, Britain, and France, and by the three powers' creation of a new currency, the Deutsche Mark, for use in western Germany and their occupied areas of Berlin. These actions occurred in the context of tit-for-tat irritations and responses between the Soviets and the three powers, including the Soviets limiting rail service and air corridors to the western part of Berlin through Soviet-controlled Germany.

Since West Berlin resided within Soviet-controlled eastern Germany, the Soviets believed they had leverage with the three powers and they used it. What started in January as harassment, with Soviet soldiers stopping trains passing from western Germany into eastern Germany bound for Berlin for document checks, rapidly escalated in March into the restriction of rail traffic. The three powers responded by increasing cargo flights to supply their personnel in Berlin. In June, as the

Deutsche Mark was introduced as the currency in the western sectors of Germany and Berlin, the Soviets responded with increasing restrictions on land and water transport until, on June 24, all rail, road, and canal transportation between western Germany and Berlin was halted. In just over a month, the western-controlled sectors of Berlin would be in danger of running out of food and fuel.

With the three-powers' inability and unwillingness to force the issue militarily, and the United States' unwillingness to use nuclear weapons, the British and Americans launched their first great triumph of the Cold War, the Berlin Airlift. US and British aircraft landing (and taking off) every three minutes delivered food, coal, and other supplies for ten months until the Soviets lifted the blockade on May 12, 1949. By that time, the Anglo-Americans had delivered almost 2.4 million tons of supplies in what was viewed as a great victory in standing up to Soviet aggression. The afterglow in the West didn't last four months, because on August 29, the Soviet Union tested their first nuclear weapon, raising the stakes in the East-West confrontation.

As the Soviet Union had tried to fill the vacuum left by the collapsing Wehrmacht in Europe, so it strove for the same advantage as the Japanese Empire collapsed across Asia. The final section of the Yalta Agreement, "Agreement Regarding Japan," appearing almost as an afterthought, sought the Soviet Union's entrance into the war against Japan, saying,

> "The leaders of the three great powers ... have agreed that in two or three months after Germany has surrendered and the war in Europe is terminated, the Soviet Union shall enter into war against Japan on condition that: ... The former rights of Russia violated by the treacherous attack of Japan in 1904 shall be restored ..."

The Soviets, still smarting from Russia's defeat during the Russo-Japanese war of 1904, insisted on, among other things, possession of the Kuril Islands, the return of parts of Sakhalin Island occupied by Japan since 1904, and certain rights in China.

On August 8 the Soviet Union declared war on Japan, and on August 9, on the absolute last date in accord with the Yalta Agreement[1] and two days after the nuclear bombing of Hiroshima, the Soviet Union invaded the Japanese-controlled rump state of Manchukuo (Manchuria) with 700,000 men. On the same day, the Soviet Union performed an amphibious landing on Sakhalin Island, whose southern tip is just twenty-five miles from the northern point of the Japanese island of Hokkaido.

While the Yalta Agreement never mentioned it, there was one more item Stalin had on his agenda regarding Japan. Starting with the Cairo Conference of December 1943, the Allies had agreed that, as part of surrender, Japan would lose all of the territory it had seized since its drive for expansion began in 1894. In addition to large areas of mainland China, during the early part of World War II Japan had seized but since been expelled from Thailand, Burma, Singapore, Malaysia, the Philippines, the Dutch East Indies, New Guinea, and dozens of smaller islands. But following the Sino-Japanese War of 1894-95, Japan had also seized Formosa (Taiwan) and parts of Korea from a weak Qing Dynasty. Japan completed the seizure of Korea in 1910, instituting an ongoing policy of colonization. As part of its occupation, Japan labored to show it had a centuries-long history in Korea.

With the Soviet Union invading Manchuria in force, the United States suddenly realized that the Soviet Union could easily invade the whole of the Korean Peninsula in short order as Japan surrendered. Quickly, the War Department developed the concept of a partition that would divide the peninsula more or less evenly between areas occupied by the Soviet Union and the United States, but would leave two-thirds of the population as well as the capital, Seoul, under US control. When Japan surrendered unconditionally on August 15, the United States shared with the Soviet Union a draft of "General Order Number 1" detailing the surrender of Imperial forces to local Allied commanders. Paragraph 1.b. of the order read,

"The senior Japanese commanders and all ground, sea, air and auxiliary forces within Manchuria north of 38 north latitude and Karafuto shall surrender to the Commander in Chief of Soviet Forces in the Far East."

Paragraph 1.e. read,

"The Imperial General Headquarters, its senior commanders, and all ground, sea, air and auxiliary forces in the main Islands of Japan, minor islands adjacent thereto, Korea south of 38 north latitude, and the Philippines shall surrender to the Command in Chief, U.S. Army Forces in the Pacific."

Stalin requested some changes to the Order, all of which were acceptable to the United States, and none of which related to Korea, which at that very moment was being invaded by the Soviets via amphibious landings in the northeastern Korean port of Seishin (Chongjin), just sixty miles west of the Soviet border at the Tumen River. Two days later the Soviet forces had completed their landing, establishing a beachhead 260 miles northeast of the point where the eastern Korean coast meets the 38th parallel.

As Soviet forces marched south through Manchuria towards the Yalu river, the dividing line between China and Korea, why did they not continue south, join up with the Soviet amphibious landings, and take all of Korea before US forces could oppose them? Perhaps Stalin wanted United States agreement to seize part of the northern Japanese home island of Hokkaido, close by the newly Soviet island of Sakhalin. Perhaps he simply saw no need to confront the United States at that time. Stalin was a master of the long-game. Simple geography suggested that the United States would soon tire of occupying lands so far from home. The Soviet Union, bordering Korea to the east and occupying Manchuria to the north, could bide its time and use its influence in the North to conquer the South. In that sense, he joined the United States in considering the division of Korea at the 38th parallel as temporary, although with unification coming from a different direction.

The Japanese flag is lowered and the US flag is raised following the surrender of Japanese forces south of the 38th parallel. The soldiers are standing in front of the General Government Building in Seoul, where the surrender took place on September 9, 1945.

Part of the Soviets' influence would come from Korean communists that the Soviet Union repatriated into its half of the peninsula, and from one communist in particular. Thirty-three year old Kim Il-sung had been born as Kim Song-ju in a hamlet outside of the what is today the capital of North Korea, Pyongyang. When he was eight years old, young Kim migrated with his parents to Manchuria. The official North Korean hagiography of the Kim dynasty credited the family's anti-Japanese activities for the move, but it was more likely simply to escape a famine moving across the land. Kim Song-ju does appear to have become involved in anti-Japanese activities as a teenager in Manchuria, and before he was twenty he had joined the Manchurian Communist Party. In 1935 the twenty-three-year-old Kim was serving in the leadership of a communist-led anti-Japanese guerrilla group that was attacking colonial forces in Manchuria when he changed his name to Kim Il-sung, meaning, "Become the Sun."

Within two years Kim Il-sung was leading a division of the Northeast Anti-Japanese Army, and his name was becoming better known within Chinese communist circles. Following a minor military success by Kim's division, the Japanese redoubled their efforts against the partisans and Kim was forced to retreat across the Amur River into the Soviet Union. Having now caught the eye of Soviet officials, Kim Il-sung received training by the Soviets and was commissioned a captain in the Soviet Army.

While Kim Il-sung could claim to be a Korean patriot, from the time he arrived with Soviet troops back in Korea for the first time in almost two decades, he was also a creature of the Soviet Union. For example, Kim spoke poor Korean, having left for China as a child, and he had to relearn the language while in in Pyongyang. As Kim consolidated his primacy among his fellow Korean communists who had accompanied him in September 1945, the Soviet Union provided financial backing, weapons, trucks, and T-34 tanks. The Soviets trained Korean officers and provided all the essentials for an army capable of holding the ground north of the 38th parallel, and, indeed, for moving south in force.

Kim Il-sung, at center, in Pyongyang, in 1946.

Within weeks of the Japanese surrender, US military officials recognized that the division of Korea was untenable and its politics far more complicated than they had realized. A top-secret message sent on September 18 from MacArthur's headquarters in Tokyo to the War Department in Washington minced no words as it began,

> "The general situation in southern Korea at present is compared to a powder keg ready to explode upon application of a spark. The splitting of Korea into two parts for occupation by force of nations operating under widely divergent policies and with no common command is an impossible situation."[2]

The memo cited widespread unrest among Japanese soldiers, colonial officials, and the newly liberated Koreans. While Seoul was quiet thanks to the present of United States troops, to the south, outside the reach of US forces,

> "the Japanese are understood to be looting and intimidating the Koreans, who hate the Japanese with a bitterness unbelievable and would wreak dire vengeance on all Japs, civilians and soldiers alike, were United States Forces not present."

With such hatred for the occupying Japanese, the United States was faced with the conundrum that removing the incumbent Japanese from their senior positions in the Korean bureaucracy would cause the collapse of basic services. The memo commented that,

> "The Koreans themselves have for so long a time been down-trodden that they cannot now or in the immediate future have a rational acceptance of this situation and its responsibilities. There has been a misconception also as to how immediate their independence is to be and as to how quickly the Japs will be thrown out."

The Soviets were not helping matters. Under the heading of "Russian activity," the memo stated,

"Based on reports of persons interviewed and eye-witness accounts of result, the Russians have vandalized, pillaged and looted indiscriminately areas south of 38 degrees where they have visited. Infrequent crossings below 38 degrees have been made, otherwise the line has been respected. Political agents have left their thoughts throughout our area and political agitators have begun parades, demonstration and other propaganda to disrupt our work and to discredit the United States before Koreans."

If the Soviets were not helping, neither was the press. The memo continued,

"The newspaper correspondents covering Korea as a group have behaved badly. They arrived by air after our landing, most of them from Japan with no knowledge of the local situation and without orientation took advantage of the American uniform to run rampant over the area, committing acts of personal misbehavior that troops have been forbidden to do. There is reason to believe that by open sympathies with Korean radicals some of them have incited Korean group leaders to greater efforts at agitation for overthrow of everything and to have the Koreans take over all functions immediately. Before they got any glimmer of conditions as they existed, they were highly critical of all policies of the Nation, of General Headquarters, and of this headquarters relating to the occupation. This latter condition is now rectifying itself slowly as they begin to see the picture."

In an aside that might have come two decades later on another Asian peninsula, that section of the memo concluded,

"One group arrived by air one afternoon, filed stories that evening and left the next morning, feeling that they knew all about the Korean occupation."

US officials had viewed the division of Korea as a short-term expedient until negotiations could lead to a national government, but even this early, the dividing lines that would shape the two Koreas going forward were clear. The memo continued,

> "Already political parties with so called leaders are being born in emotion. Some are Communist and other support the Chungking Provisional Government. G-2[3] [Army intelligence] is investigating many political parties which have recently mushroomed. However, manifestations indicate the desirability of bringing in the Provisional Government and such persons as Kim Koo and Syngman Rhee and others of his groups. Some of the older and more educated Koreans despite being now suspected of collaboration are conservatives and may develop into useful groups."

Just as in Germany, expediency would sometimes take the place of objective justice.

Syngmnan Rhee (left) and Kim Koo.

The two men mentioned in the memo would be pivotal to the future of South Korea. Syngman Rhee was born in Hwanghae[4] Province in western Korea on April 26, 1875. He was educated both by Confucian scholars and American Methodist missionaries, and became politically active. Rhee was imprisoned when he was just twenty-two for demonstrating against the Korean monarchy. When he was released from prison seven years later, he traveled to the United States, balancing his further education with political activities aimed at currying US support for Korean independence. Rhee earned a bachelor's degree from George Washington University in Washington, D.C., a master's degree from Harvard and a PhD degree from Princeton. He returned to Korea in 1910, but he soon came to the attention of the Japanese and fled back to the United States before he could be imprisoned. Rhee spent most of the next three decades in the United States, lobbying US Government officials for support, developing relationships with other advocates for Korean independence, and jockeying for power among them. By the end of the war, Rhee was recognized by the United States as the leader of the non-communist Korean expatriates.

If Rhee was the consummate politician, Kim Koo (also rendered in English as Kim Ku or Kim Gu) was the consummate man of action. Born on August 29, 1876, as Kim Changahm in the town of Haaeju in Hwanghae Province (the same part of Korea as Rhee), he did not have the educational advantages of Rhee. Despite having studied the required Confucian literature, in 1892 Kim failed in his attempt to join the Korean civil service. The next year he joined an organization opposed to foreign occupation, changing his name to Kim Changsoo, and over the next two decades he was involved in multiple attacks against Japanese officials, including an assassination. He was imprisoned several times and tortured severely, to the point of even attempting suicide. While in prison for the last time, he changed his name to Kim Koo.

In 1919 he left Korea for Shanghai, China, where he became involved with the Provisional Government of the Republic of Korea, co-founded by Syngman Rhee. Kim served in several positions in the Provisional Government, including president from 1926 to 1927. By 1931 he was involved again with violence and assassination as founder of the Korean Patriotic Corps and later the Korean Liberation Army. After decades in exile, Kim Koo returned to Korea from Shanghai after the Japanese surrender in 1945.

For Korea, the next five years were a story of which no participant could have been proud. The Allies developed an agreement in December 1945 that the United States, the Soviet Union, the Republic of China, and the United Kingdom would maintain a trusteeship over

Korea for up to five years. The political perceptions among Koreans identified in the September memo guaranteed the trusteeship would not be popular, and both Kim and Rhee opposed it. Rhee, having lived for so long in the United States and fluent in English, was both more familiar and less threatening than the rest of the fractious Korean leadership in exile, and under American influence he assumed a place of pre-eminence in the south. He took his case for Korean independence directly to the US government, even to the point of returning to the United States for four months starting in December 1946 to promote his ideas among the president and other American policymakers.

In the north, the Korean communist leadership and their Soviet backers formed the Provisional People's Committee in February 1946, headed by Kim Il-sung. Meetings between Soviet and US officials regarding conditions for unifying Korea and the establishment of Korean sovereignty floundered during May 1946 because, in President Truman's words, "the two sides could not agree on the Korean parties and social organizations to be consulted" regarding the formation of a government. The US side held that "representatives of all democratic Korean parties should be consulted," while the Soviet Union held that, "all Koreans who had spoken or written against the Moscow Agreement [the product of December 1945 foreign ministers conference that had established the framework for establish a provisional democratic government in Korea] should be excluded." That exclusion would have included Rhee, who refused to participate in talks between the US and the Soviet Union, as well as Kim Koo. The next round of talks, held in May 1947, were no more productive.

Finally, in September 1947, the United States put the matter of Korea to the United Nations. On November 14, with the Soviet Union boycotting, the General Assembly passed Resolution 34 calling for the formation of a "United Nations Temporary Commission on Korea ... for the purpose of facilitating and expediting ... participation by elected representatives of the Korean people." The resolution recommended that the elections be "held not later than 31 March 1948 on the basis of adult suffrage and by secret ballot to choose representatives ... regarding the prompt attainment of the freedom and independence of the Korean people and which representatives, constituting a National Assembly, may establish a National Government of Korea."

It further recommended that,

"immediately upon the establishment of a National Government, that Government should ... (a) constitute its own national security forces and dissolve all military or semi-military formations not included therein; (b) take over the functions of government from the military commands and civilian authorities of north and south Korea; and (c) arrange with the occupying Powers for the complete withdrawal from Korea of their armed forces as early as practicable and if possible within ninety days."

Finally, the resolution called upon "all Members of the United Nations to refrain from interfering in the affairs of the Korean people during the interim period ... and thereafter to refrain from any and all acts derogatory to the independence and sovereignty of Korea."

These were fine words and an admirable aspiration, but the boycott by the Soviets guaranteed that elections for a single government in Korea would not occur. Syngman Rhee argued for elections to proceed in the south in any event, while Kim Koo refused to contemplate elections that did not include the north. Elections for a Constitutional Assembly were held south of the 38th parallel on May 10, 1948. Syngman Rhee's National Association for the Rapid Realization of Korean Independence (NARRKI) won a plurality with 26.1 percent of the vote, followed by the Korean Democratic Party with 13.5 percent. Kim Koo and his supporters boycotted the election and formed the Korean Independence Party. When the Constitutional (National) Assembly cast votes for president on June 20, Syngman Rhee won a landslide with 180 votes of the 196 cast. Kim Koo won thirteen, even though he had enjoined his supporters not to vote for him. The NARRKI candidate won the voting for vice president on the second round, beating runner-up Kim Koo.[5] On August 15 President Syngman Rhee's Republic of Korea accepted sovereignty from the United States occupation forces. Three weeks later the North declared the Democratic People's Republic of Korea, with Kim Il-sung as prime minister.

Responding to actions in South Korea, on December 12 UN General Assembly Resolution 75 declared, "there has been established a lawful government (the Government of the Republic of Korea) ... that this Government is based on elections which were a valid expression of the free will of the electorate of that part of Korea ... and that this is the only such Government in Korea." While the resolution laid out a series of diplomatic steps to remove the "barriers to economic, social and other friendly intercourse caused by the division of Korea," it was clear to all that peaceful reunification would first require rapprochement between the United States and the Soviet Union. For the time being, as with the two Germanys, there would be two Koreas.

While Korea was undergoing its traumas in the first half of the twentieth century, the giant neighbor to the north had been enduring its own. China had struggled under the weakening rule of the Qing dynasty. That dynasty finally collapsed in 1912 following a military revolt inspired by the reform movement advocated by Chinese doctor Sun Yat-sen, founder of the nationalist Guomindang[6] party. A series of military leaders unsuccessfully attempted to form a strong central government, one even installing the last male heir of the Qing dynasty, eleven-year-old Puyi. That government also failed. With a weak central government, continued foreign occupation of coastal areas, and brutal warlords ruling a countryside filled with impoverished peasants, the country was ripe for revolution.

As members of the Guomindang struggled to form an effective central government, other concepts of political reform, namely Marxism, were gaining ground. A Chinese translation of Karl Marx's *Communist Manifesto* became available in 1906. The 1917 Bolshevik revolution in

China's neighbor, Russia, resonated with some intellectuals in China. As a largely agrarian, politically retrograde nation with a weakening central government, they saw analogies to their own country and the promise, in theory, of a movement that would remove power from landowners and capitalists (particularly foreign capitalists in the coastal "concessions") and empower the workers and peasants. In 1919, a young graduate of a teacher's college in Hunan who was working at Beijing University joined the university's Marxist Study Group, founded the year before. His name was Mao Zedong.

Mao was born on December 26, 1893, into a prosperous farming (peasant) family in Shaoshan, Hunan, China. Even before college, Mao read extensively from books and pamphlets regarding nationalism, the weakness of the Chinese government, and revolution in general. After various abortive attempts to start a career, he found himself at the First Normal School in Changsha, Hunan. Mao became involved with radicals on the faculty and among the students, and started writing for a radical newspaper in 1917. After graduation that year, he traveled to Beijing and met other radicals while supporting himself by working in the university's library.

In 1919 Mao returned to Changsha to teach in a primary school, but his political activities only intensified. He was involved in several radical publications but also submitted articles for more mainstream publications, all while watching international developments. Like many Chinese, Mao bristled at one of the settlements of World War I wherein German territories in Shandong, rather than being returned to China, were instead granted to Japan. Protest followed protest, and in 1921 radicals in Shanghai founded (with the help of advisors sent by Lenin) the Communist Party of China, with Mao shortly organizing the party in Hunan and assuming the role as local party secretary.

Often forgotten now is that, in the early 1920s, even as it was providing support for the Communist Party of China, the Soviet Union was also providing significant support to Sun Yat-sen's Guomindang. Lenin believed that the communist revolution in Russia would only succeed if it spread; that is, if there were more communist nations that together could spread communism and oppose external efforts to roll-back the revolutionary gains. With wide support among the Chinese military and a head-start in organizing nationalists, the Guomindang appeared a more likely avenue than the nascent Communist Party of China for overthrowing the old power structure. Mao and other leading communists, urged on by the Soviets, even joined the Guomindang, seeking to leverage its military strength, turn its politics leftward, and eventually seize control. Even Zhou Enlai, the future premier of the People's Republic of China, served as deputy to Chiang Kai-shek, the eventual leader of the Guomindang.

But the marriage of convenience died with Guomindang victories against warlords across much of China in 1927. With half the country now under Guomindang control, the nationalists outlawed the Communist Party of China and in some cases, most famously in Shanghai, massacred their erstwhile allies after taking the city. Leaders of the Guomindang recognized that the communists posed a threat to the wealthy Chinese who funded the Guomindang, and their ultimate vision for China diverged from that of the Communist Party. Guomindang forces under Chiang Kai-shek continued their progress in unifying China into the early 1930s. Then, on September 18, 1931, Japan invaded Manchuria, halting the Guomindang's progress and introducing a new dynamic into Chinese politics.

Mao and his fellow communists continued in their attempts to develop the Communist Party, but not without infighting, fratricide among communists, and clashes with the armies of the Guomindang. Thousands died at the hands of their fellow communists before Chiang turned his attention from skirmishes with the Japanese to exterminating the communists. In October 1934, one hundred thousand communists and soldiers of the People's Liberation Army (PLA) broke out of their encirclement in the southwest corner of Jiangxi province. Under Mao's leadership, they, marched six thousand miles over a circuitous route towards Shaanxi province in the northwest. The eight thousand survivors of the "Long March" who arrived in

Shaanxi a year later, augmented by additional communist soldiers, launched guerrilla attacks against the Japanese. They had also created the founding myth of the People's Republic of China. For the rest of his life, Mao's leadership of the Chinese Communist Party would never again be in doubt.

Mao knew that the PLA alone could not defeat the Japanese, and despite continued skirmishes with forces of the Guomindang, the two sides uneasily joined forces at the end of 1937 to turn their focus solely against the occupying Japanese forces. By the middle of 1938, Mao commanded half a million men, and communist successes against the Japanese served the additional purpose of planting communist leadership in liberated villages. The communists generally treated the peasants well, distributed land, and proved more popular with the rural population than the imperious, urban-born officers of the Guomindang.

With the surrender of the Japanese, the communists and the nationalists could turn their attention back to each other. The Soviet invasion of Manchuria gave the communists an advantage not just in territory but in captured Japanese weapons and stores. The PLA was also better led and enjoyed higher morale than the Guomindang's numerically superior forces. Despite a "Treaty of Friendship and Alliance" between the Soviet Union and the Guomindang signed on August 14, 1945, less than a year later the communists were again at war with the nationalists. The PLA made major gains through superior tactics (mobility versus defending fixed positions) and massive defections from the Guomindang Army to their ranks. In January 1949, a desperate Chiang asked for mediation by the US and the Soviet Union, and the latter actually urged Mao to agree, not wanting a confrontation in China with the United States. But Mao refused, trusting in his own capabilities, and on October 1, 1949, with the remnants of the Guomindang chased off the Chinese mainland and onto the island of Formosa (Taiwan), he declared the founding of the People's Republic of China.

Just a few days before Mao made his formal announcement in Beijing, his new capital (and China's former imperial capital), Americans were shocked by something even more momentous for their security. On September 24, 1949, the New York *Daily News* screamed in a headline with two-inch tall letters, "Soviets Have A-Bomb Secret." The Soviet Union detonated a plutonium fission weapon codenamed "Device 501" on the morning of August 29, 1949, over the arid plains near Semipalatinsk in the Kazakh Soviet Socialist Republic. Aided by the details provided covertly by Manhattan Project scientists Klaus Fuchs and Theodore Hall, the device was an almost exact copy of the Fat Man implosion-type bomb that had destroyed Nagasaki a little over four years earlier.

Mao, at left, in Moscow to celebrate Stalin's 70th birthday, December, 1949.

The United States was not yet aware of the extent of the spy ring that had delivered nuclear secrets to the Soviet Union and would cost Americans Julius and Ethel Rosenberg their lives less than four years later, but US government officials knew the Soviet Union would eventually solve the challenge of nuclear weapons. Estimates for when that would occur ranged from mid-1950 at the earliest, to sometime during 1953 as the most likely. As early as late 1945, efforts began within the War Department to figure out how to determine if and when the Soviet Union tested a nuclear weapon. Using US nuclear tests to rule out candidates, including optical, acoustic, magnetic, ionospheric, and even seismic sensing, the detection of trace products of nuclear fission in the atmosphere, an unexpected and unwelcome reality of atmospheric testing, proved to be the most suitable.

The US Air Force added filtration equipment aboard its regularly operating WB-29 weather aircraft, modified versions of the bombers that had dropped the two nuclear bombs on Japan. The filters were capable of capturing individual particles of "fission products," unstable elements normally absent from the atmosphere but generated during the nuclear fission reaction and ejected high into the air currents where the WB-29s might cross. They could also capture particles of un-fissioned fuel, uranium-235 or plutonium-239. The filter-equipped WB-29s had been flying for less than a year when, on September 3, 1949, the filters removed from an aircraft flying from Japan to Alaska showed abnormally high radiation. Additional flights and other, ground-based methods for detecting fallout confirmed that something had deposited radioactive particles into the air that could not be explained by natural phenomena. While some officials, including Secretary of Defense Louis Johnson, refused to believe it was a Soviet nuclear device, chemical analysis confirmed the US Government's worst fears, as it even provided details of the weapon's construction, suspiciously similar to that of "Fat Man."

By September 23, the evidence that the Soviets had detonated a nuclear weapon was overwhelming. That morning President Truman, knowing that United Press International was about to break the story and that Soviet Foreign Minister Andrei Vyshinsky was scheduled to address the UN General Assembly later in the day, released a statement to the press, which began,

"I believe the American people, to the fullest extent consistent with national security, are entitled to be informed of all developments in the field of atomic energy. That is my reason for making public the following information. We have evidence that within recent weeks an atomic explosion occurred in the U.S.S.R."

And there it was. The United States no longer had a monopoly on nuclear weapons.

If the United States was concerned about developments in China and the Soviet Union from a vantage thousands of miles distant, South Korea, less than two hundred miles from the coast of China across the Yellow Sea or from Manchuria along the peninsula, was *very* concerned. Just three months after declaring the Republic of Korea, President Rhee sent a message to President Truman that began,

> "In the light of the recent developments in China, I should like to remind your Excellency, that the Korean people are deeply concerned over the reported withdrawal of the American troops from Korea soon. In view of the fact, that we do not feel our security forces adequate at this time to defend the country against a major onslaught from without and within, I have requested that a military and naval mission of the United States be established in Korea now, to help train and equip our defense forces as fast as possible. The Communist successes in China have released large forces of the Communist Army for potential invasion of South Korea ... continued reports that the so-called People's Republic of Korea intends to remove from its 'temporary capital' in Pyongyang to Seoul indicate that the Communists are attempting to create alarm and panic ... in the south. While recent planned uprisings in two southern districts have been crushed the remnants of the disloyal forces continue to disturb the peace by murder and arson, wherever possible."

In spite of the UN General Assembly's dictum for occupation troops to leave Korea, President Rhee had no interest in that withdrawal occurring on his side of the 38th parallel.

Given the tense situation in Germany, where the United States was nose-to-nose with the Soviet Union, the Truman administration had other priorities for US troops. The newly formed National Security Council, in a top-secret report to the president on April 2, 1948, entitled *The Position of the United States with Respect to Korea*, concluded that, "it should be the effort of the U.S. Government through all proper means to effect a settlement of the Korean problem which would enable the U.S. to withdraw from Korea as soon as possible with the minimum of bad effects."[7] Around the time Rhee was composing his missive to Truman, the US Army had requested that the State Department, "confirm the date of 15 January 1949 as the date for the completion of the withdrawal from Korea." The State Department pushed back, saying it would be, "premature and prejudicial to the interests of the U.S. to enter into the final and irreversible stages of the troop withdrawal ... before the UN General Assembly has had an opportunity ... to consider the Korean problem." A month later, UN General Assembly Resolution 75, which had declared, "there has been established a lawful government (the Government of the Republic of Korea)," also recommended, "the occupying Powers should withdraw their occupation forces from Korea as early as practicable." The Army now wanted to withdraw remaining forces from Korea, consisting of just a reinforced regimental combat team, fewer than seven thousand five hundred men. MacArthur considered the small force, "will be subject to possible destruction in the event of a major attack on this vulnerable salient. The force ... must be considered a liability rather than an asset."

Deliberations regarding the disposition of the remaining US troops in Korea continued into 1949. On February 28, 1949, the Central Intelligence Agency presented a top-secret report entitled, *Consequences of US Troop Withdrawal from Korea in Spring, 1949*.[8] The summary began,

"Withdrawal of US forces from Korea in the spring of 1949 would probably in time be followed by an invasion ... by the North Korean People's Army possibly assisted by small battle-trained units from Communist Manchuria. Although it can be presumed that South Korean security forces will eventually develop sufficient strength to resist such an invasion ... It is unlikely that such strength will be achieved before January 1950. Assuming that Korean Communists would make aggressive use of the opportunity presented them, US troop withdrawal would probably result in a collapse of the US-supported Republic of Korea ..."

"In contrast, continued presence in Korea of a moderate US force, would assist in sustaining ... the Koreans themselves to resist any future invasion once they had the military force to do so ..."

The Department of the Army's Intelligence Division dissented from the CIA's conclusions. In an appendix included at the back of the CIA's report, it stated,

"The Intelligence Division does not believe that US troop withdrawal would be a major factor in the collapse of the Republic of Korea ... The Intelligence Division believes that an invasion of South Korea by the North Korean People's Army is a possibility at present ... rather than a probability."

The dissent continued,

"The People's Army ... does not have, of itself, the preponderance of strength of South Korean military forces which would be required to ensure victory ... Further, it is the belief of the Intelligence Division that political and economic factors other than the presence of absence of United States troop will have a decisive influence over the future course of events in Korea."

With the benefit of hindsight, it is clear that both sides only saw part of the picture. The Army, in particular, seems to have put too much confidence in the quality of the 65,000 Korean troops it was helping to train, and too little in the capabilities of the North Koreans. The National Security Council, revisiting the Korea matter in March 1949, seemed more sanguine, assessing the strength of the fully equipped South Korean Army at 50,000 while the equivalent North Korean strength was 56,040 but adding, "In Manchuria, furthermore, there are reported to be other Korean units in service with Chinese Communist forces or in training that equal or exceed the combined army and security forces now in north Korea" or another almost hundred thousand men under arms.[9]

The NSC debate reflected the reality that the US force in Korea was too small to be useful in defense, but too large to be sustained given the shrunken Army budget and the requirements for soldiers outside the Korean peninsula, particularly in Germany. Accordingly, the NSC recommended to the president, "Preparations for withdrawal of remaining United States occupation forces ... should be undertaken to permit completion of the withdrawal on or about but not later than 30 June 1949." The report concluded with the face-saving,

> "In publicly announcing the withdrawal of its remaining occupation forces from Korea, the U.S. should make it unmistakably clear that this step in no way constitutes a lessening of U.S. support for the Government of the Republic of Korea, but rather another step in toward the regularization by the U.S. of it relations with that Government and a fulfillment on the part of the U.S. of the relevant provision of the GA [General Assembly] Resolution of December 12, 1948."

The president took the NSC's advice. At the end of May, the United Press circulated a story from Seoul that,

> "Top American officials refused to comment today over persistent reports that the withdrawal of American troops from South Korea would be in full swing by mid-June and probably completed by the end of July. But GI's made no secret of the withdrawal."

Two days later, according to the Associated Press, "The army department staff said no date had been set for the withdrawal of remaining troops of the U.S. 5th Infantry regiment stationed in Korea." But a month later the AP reported that on June 30, "The US Army announced ... that it has completed withdrawal of troops from Korea 'in accord with the United Nations resolution.'" The Army announcement was just as the NSC had recommended.

As the troops were being withdrawn that June, on June 7 President Truman asked the Congress for $150 million in aid for the Republic of Korea, fulfilling another of the NSC's recommendations. Both the House and the Senate Foreign Relations committees approved the president's request and the Senate approved the full amount on October 12, but the full House initially authorized nothing for Korea. When Truman finally signed an aid bill on October 29, it provided funding of just $30 million. Aside from training support and the presence of US ground forces in Japan and naval forces in the Sea of Japan, the Koreans were on their own.

As 1950 opened, the international shocks of the Berlin Blockade, the Soviet nuclear bomb, and the fall of China to communist forces seemed to be fading into the background in favor of a status-quo normalcy. On the second page of New Year's Day's *Boston Globe*, a reader would have seen, next to a Jordan Marsh advertisement taking the balance of the page, Otto Zausmer's syndicated column proclaiming, "The unfounded war hysteria of a year ago has subsided and there seems little likelihood of a clash of arms between Russia and this country."[10] One would have had to read all the way to page fifty-six to find a mention of Korea in a political context, and here it was part of an historical overview of the first half of the century. A reader of the *Chicago Tribune* would find a sentence on page two mentioning congressional debate on aid for Korea, but would have to read all the way to page thirty-nine to find anything at all even remotely substantive. Korea is never mentioned in the 120 pages of New Year's Day's New York *Daily News*. For the time being, Korea was off the American people's radar.

It seemed it was off the Truman administration's radar as well. On January 12, 1950, Secretary of State Dean Acheson gave a speech at the National Press Club in Washington, D.C. Entitled simply, *Speech on the Far East*, it began defensively, asking, "I am frequently asked: Has the State Department got an Asian policy?", clearly a reaction to the administration having "lost" China the year before. After discussing China, historic Russian interests in northern China, and the defense of the now-disarmed Japan, he made the fateful statement that has bedeviled historians of the Korean war ever since. "The defensive perimeter runs along the Aleutians to Japan and then goes to the Ryukus ... The defensive perimeter runs from the Ryukus to the Philippine Islands." Whether he intended to or not, Acheson had just defined US interests running in an arc at least a hundred miles east of Korea, excluding the entire peninsula.

The final paragraph of the speech appeared to drive this point home,

> "So after this survey ... I believe, ... that there is a new day which has dawned in Asia. It is a day in which the Asian peoples are on their own, and know it, and intend to continue on their own ... We are their friends. Others are their friends. We and those others are willing to help, but we can help only where we are wanted and only where the conditions of help are really sensible and possible."

Was economic and military aid to South Korea no longer "sensible and possible"? The renewal of the Korean aid program was foundering in Congress due to ongoing distress with the administration's actions in Asia. Commenting on discussion of the $120 million requested for Korea, on January 18 the Independent News Service circulated a story that said,

> "Opposition to further economic aid to Korea in the absence of a substantial China assistance program was expressed by Representatives ... They charged that the administration's abandonment of China and Formosa would make it a 'waste of money to stay in Korea.'"

Debate and a vote on the measure was scheduled for the next day.

On the nineteenth, the United Press story on the house vote began,

"The House rejected today 193 to 191 the administration's $120,000,000 aid-to-Korea bill in the first Congressional turndown of a major administration foreign policy measure since 1939. The action, a shock to Democrats who had confidently predicted its passage, came after a four-hour debate during which Republicans attacked the administration's Far East policy. A GOP group ... said the aid would be 'money down a rathole' because Communists might overrun U.S.-controlled South Korea 'at any time.'"

Ominous as this might have been for the South Koreans, it was now "below the fold" news if it even made it onto front pages more concerned with the recent one and a half-million-dollar Brinks robbery in Boston, US recognition of Francisco Franco's government in Spain, and a statehood vote for Hawaii.

The intelligence community continued to assess the situation in Korea, but their efforts leading up to the invasion demonstrate the classic contrast between assessing capabilities and determining intentions. On June 19 the CIA's Office of Reports and Estimates published ORE 18-50, *Current Capabilities of the Northern Korean Regime*.[11] The report noted, "The intelligence organizations of the Department of State, Army, Navy and the Air Force have concurred in this report. It contains information available to CIA as of 15 May 1950." The report stated,

"Although the northern and southern forces are nearly equal in terms of combat effectiveness, training and leadership, the northern Koreans possess a superiority in armor, heavy artillery, and aircraft. This, northern Korea's armed forces, even as presently constituted and supported, have a capability for attaining limited objectives against southern Korea, including the capture of Seoul."

This "capability" would be demonstrated just six days later when the North's forces crossed the 38th parallel, even as the report further asserted, "despite the apparent military superiority of northern over southern Korea, it is not certain that the northern regime, lacking the active participation of Soviet and Chinese Communist military units, would be able to gain effective control over all of southern Korea."

However, the report also noted,

"Trained and equipped units of the Communist 'People's Army' are being deployed southward in the area of the 38th Parallel. 'People's Army' and Border Constabulary units there equal or surpass the strength of southern Korean army units similarly deployed. Tanks and heavy artillery have also been moved close to the Parallel in recent months."

Still, no great alarm was raised in Tokyo or Washington.

The capability was there, but would Stalin really risk confrontation with the United States? In the end it really didn't matter because Kim Il-sung forced the issue by launching the invasion himself.

8

INCHON

Within hours of the invasion, US military officials in Korea and at the Tokyo headquarters of the Commander in Chief of US forces in the "Far East" (CINCFE) had enough intelligence reports to understand it was not a minor skirmish or a simple guerrilla action aimed at harassing the South. The invading force was estimated at four divisions, including seventy tanks, and there appeared to be coordinated air attacks against Seoul's Kimpo airfield, and an amphibious landing in the vicinity of Samchok, about 120 miles east-southeast of Seoul. In a top-secret communication with Washington within hours of the initial attacks, CINCFE was asked, "What is your estimate of the objective of current NK effort?"[1] The command's response was unambiguous,

"There is no evidence to substantiate a belief that the north Koreans are engaged in a limited objective offensive or in a raid. On the contrary, the size of the North Korean Forces employed, the depth of penetration, the intensity of the attack, and the landings made miles south of the parallel on the east coast indicate that the north Koreans are engaged in an all-out offensive to subjugate South Korea."

President Truman was at his home in Independence, Missouri, when the invasion began, Saturday night in Missouri, Sunday morning on the battlefields. Cutting short his vacation, he left for Washington Sunday afternoon, but before he boarded the plane he told reporters that the situation "could be dangerous but I hope it is not," and he admonished them not to be "alarmist." When his aircraft arrived in Washington, it was met at the airport by the solemn visages of Secretary of State Dean Acheson, Secretary of Defense Louis A. Johnson, and Under Secretary of State James E. Webb. They accompanied Truman to Blair House,[2] where he met with them, the Joint Chiefs of Staff (JCS), Director of Central Intelligence Roscoe H. Hillenkoetter, and other advisors, from eight p.m. until almost eleven that evening.

Paul W. Ward, writing in the *Baltimore Sun*, summarized the strategic concerns facing Truman and his advisors:

"... how to keep the conflict from involving the United States militarily and precipitating a third world war without thereby risking: 1. Loss of strategically located Southern Korea ... to the forces of Sovietism ... 2. Loosing a shock wave throughout the rest of non-Communist Asia that would seriously diminish, if not erase, the chances of keeping Indo-China, Burma, Siam, Malaysia, India, Pakistan, the Philippines, and Japan from eventually throwing in their lot with the Communists. 3. Encouraging the Communists to strike next at Formosa or even Yugoslavia or Iran if the West's response to their Korean move-regarded by some authorities here as merely their first military probing operation with such ends in view-is not convincingly firm."

What would come to be called in the 1960s the "domino effect"[3] was foremost on their minds.

News of the invasion caused the US to request the president of the United Nations Security Council, Sir Benegai Rau of India, for an emergency meeting that Sunday. The council met at two p.m. that afternoon in its temporary headquarters, the former Sperry Gyroscope plant in Lake Success, (Long Island) New York. At the end of a four-hour session, by a nine-to-zero vote, with Yugoslavia abstaining and the Soviet Union boycotting the session because the council members included the government of Nationalist China, the council passed a resolution that began, "The Security Council, Recalling the finding of the General Assembly in its resolution of 21 October 1949 that the Government of the Republic of Korea is a lawfully established government," it continued,

"... Noting with grave concern the armed attack upon the Republic of Korea by forces from North Korea, ... Calls upon the immediate cessation of hostilities; and calls upon the authorities of North Korea to withdraw forthwith their armed forces to the thirty-eighth parallel ... Calls upon all members to render every assistance to the United Nations in the execution of this resolution and to refrain from giving assistance to the North Korean authorities."[4]

With a favorable decision in hand, President Truman instructed the CINCFE, General Douglas MacArthur, to hurry military supplies to the aid of South Korea, but, initially, there was no instruction to commit US forces. The supplies would have to be flown from bases in Japan to airfields potentially under fire, since a US Air Force C-54 had already been bombed on the ground at Kimpo airfield outside Seoul by North Korean aircraft. MacArthur was instructed to use US Navy and US Air Force aviation assets to protect the air base both to accommodate incoming supplies and to facilitate the evacuation of American non-combatants from Korea. CINCFE sources indicated that South Korea only had a ten-day supply of ammunition, so the priority was to fly small-arms, mortar, and artillery shells as soon as possible. In the meantime, US Ambassador John J. Muccio ordered the evacuation of all non-essential US personnel and dependents from Seoul. The city was in immediate peril, with the City of Chunchon, sixty miles northeast of Seoul, and the town of Kaesong, forty miles to the northwest, having fallen within the first hours of the invasion.

On June 27 Truman ordered "United States air and sea forces to give the Korean government troops cover and support" as the Security Council met again and by a seven to one vote (Yugoslavia voting against and India and Egypt abstaining) went further than the day before. The US-proposed resolution was phrased so that it, "recommends that members of the U.N. furnish such assistance to the Republic of Korea as may be necessary to repel armed attack and to restore international peace and security in the area." The vote came at 10:46 p.m. with the Soviets again boycotting the proceedings.[5] Nevertheless, Truman now had international cover to use US forces and any other help he could get to try to expel North Korea from the South.

While the international backing may have been welcome, the reality on the ground was dismal. South Korean soldiers were being pushed back all along the North Korean line of advance, with Seoul increasingly endangered. US Air Force F-80s, and WW II-era B-26s and F-51 Mustang fighters were engaged in strafing and bombing the invading forces, but they were few in number. Almost two thousand US and foreign nationals were trying to escape to Japan, with transport aircraft doing what they could under fire, the rest leaving by ship from Korean ports. Travel was difficult for the foreign refugees since terrified Korean civilians were already clogging roads south.

By the twenty-eighth, Seoul had fallen, along with the strategic Kimpo airfield. Republic of Korea (ROK) troops retreated before the advancing Korean People's Army (KPA) and when ROK sappers destroyed the bridges over the Han River to slow the North Korean advance, they trapped a significant part of the remaining ROK troops to await their capture. Bad weather meant that US aircraft could not provide support to troops on the ground, only engaging a few DPRK aircraft in air-to-air engagements, claiming eight aircraft shot down. While the ROK attempted to set a new defensive line at Suwon, just 20 miles south of Seoul, it must not have been reassuring that President Rhee and his government had set up a temporary capital in Taejon (Daejon), halfway down the peninsula from the 38th parallel.

The next day marked the first use of US B-29s, flown from Guam, to bomb Kimpo airfield and try to deny its use to the communists. More significantly, General MacArthur flew to Korea from his headquarters in Tokyo to assess the situation firsthand. MacArthur was accompanied by several senior officers who would have a prominent role in the fight to come, including Major General Edward M. Almond, his chief of staff, and Major General Charles Willoughby, his long-time intelligence chief (G-2). The president, through the JCS, instructed MacArthur to use forces under his control to expel the North Koreans from South Korea. The top-secret message, sent with emergency priority, expresses the gravity of the situation facing the president and the JCS. The message began,

"This directive consolidates, broadens and supplements existing instructions governing your actions with regard to situation in South Korea and Formosa. In support of resolutions of United Nations approved on 25 June ... and 27 June ... You will employ naval and air forces to the Far East Command to provide fullest possible support to South Korean forces by attack on military targets to as to permit these forces to clear South Korea of North Korean forces. Employment of army forces will be limited ... except that you are authorized to employ such ... service forces as to insure the retention of a power and air base in the general area Fusan-Chinhae."

MacArthur could use naval and air forces, but no ground forces except those needed to maintain a logistics hub to support ROK troops in a location that would soon be familiar to Americans as Pusan (Busan today).

The message continued,

"By naval and air action you will defend Formosa against invasion or attack by Chinese Communists and will insure that Formosa will be used as a base of operations against the Chinese mainland by Chinese Nationalists."

This represented a distinct change in policy, since the United States had not previously made a commitment to defend Formosa against attacks from the PRC. MacArthur's orders were accompanied by a public request by Truman to the Nationalist forces on the island to "cease all air and sea operations against the mainland."

Regarding naval forces, the message stated,

> "Seventh Fleet is assigned to your operational control. CINCPAC [Commander in Chief Pacific] and CINCPACFLT [Commander in Chief Pacific Fleet] will support and reinforce you as necessary and practicable."

On the date of the message, the Seventh Fleet, under the command of Vice Admiral Arthur D. Struble and based in the Philippines, consisted of the 27,000-ton aircraft carrier *Valley Forge*, the heavy cruiser *Rochester*, six destroyers, two destroyer escorts, three submarines, a seaplane tender, an oiler and a high-speed transport ship. CINCFE already controlled the light cruiser *Juneau* and four destroyers, all based in Japan and under the command of Vice Admiral C. Turner Joy, who would exercise tactical control over Admiral Struble.

The next section of the message would be relevant far sooner than anyone would think.

> "You are authorized to extend your operations into Northern Korea against air bases, depots, tank farms, troop columns and other such purely military targets, in and when, in your judgement, this becomes essential for the performance of your missions ... or to avoid unnecessary casualties to our forces. *Special care will be taken to insure that operations in North Korea stay well clear of the frontiers of Manchuria or the Soviet Union.*" [italics the author's]

The penultimate paragraph dealt with logistics and points to the mobilization of cargo ships that would now be required.

"You are authorized to send to Korea any munitions and supplies from resources at your disposal which you deem necessary. You will submit your estimates of amounts and types of aid required from sources outside your control."

The final paragraph highlighted the grave geopolitical consequences this conflict portended.

"The decision to commit United States air and naval forces and limited army forces ... does not constitute a decision to engage in war with the Soviet Union if Soviet forces intervene in Korea. The decision regarding Korea, however, was taken in full realization of the risks involved. If Soviet forces actively oppose our operations in Korea, your forces should defend themselves, should take no action to aggravate the situation and you should report the situation to Washington."

The president was treading carefully and reserved the ultimate responsibility for a conflict that could, with the Soviet Union now possessing nuclear weapons, escalate dangerously.

So, the president had now given the authority to MacArthur to try to expel the North Koreans from the South, albeit with a short leash, but would he get the resources he needed? Even without the authorization to use US ground troops in any substantive way, the Senate, perhaps seeing the writing on the wall, tried to help. Gerald Griffin, writing in the *Baltimore Sun*, put it this way:

"In an unusual, unanimous vote the Senate today stamped its approval-76-0-on the bill extending the present military draft law until July 9, 1951. The Senate's vote completed congressional action on the bill and sped it on its way to the White House for President Truman's signature. Yesterday the House indorsed it, 315-4."

Elsewhere, the Military Sea Transportation Service was beginning the first elements of the massive sea mobilization that would be required to carry weapons, armor, supplies, and if authorized, ground troops to Korea. The Navy dispatched the 27,000-ton aircraft carrier *Philippine Sea*, the 13,000-ton heavy cruiser *Toledo* and two destroyer divisions (eight ships) from the west coast to Pearl Harbor for possible duty. The 11th through 14th Naval Districts, representing San Diego, San Francisco, Seattle and Pearl Harbor, respectively, instituted near-wartime security measures, eliminating civilian visits to the ports and their ships except on official business.

As the Defense Department tried to keep out of a shooting war with the Soviet Union, the State Department suddenly had its hands full with them on the political front. The Soviets, who had boycotted the Security Council's meetings on Korea because of the failure of the council to seat Mao's government in place of Chiang Kai-shek's, called the votes on the twenty-fifth and twenty-seventh illegitimate, citing the UN Charter to assert that the Security Council could only, "take a decision on an important issue if unanimity is expressed by all five permanent council members, namely-U.S.A., Britain, France, U.S.S.R. and China." The USSR had not been in attendance. Also, since seven votes were required to pass a resolution, including the five permanent members, and the Chinese vote had been placed by the Nationalists, the "decision of the Security Council on the Korean problem has no legal force."

Given the strong support from France[6] and Britain, the latter already sending the 13,000-ton aircraft carrier *Triumph* and the cruiser *Belfast*, among other ships of its Far Eastern fleet, the United States chose to ignore Russia's protestations. This was made easier as the Soviet government's subsequent statements continued to condemn US inter-vention but pointedly noted, "The Soviet Government adheres to the principle of the impermissibility of interference by foreign powers in the internal affairs of Korea." The Soviets would not "call off" the invasion, but neither would they become overtly involved.

CINCFE wasted no time implementing the rules of engagement as specified by the JCS. On June 30, General Almond told reporters that

American aircraft were "operating against their (North Korean) air force wherever they are. That might be in North Korea or in the territory they have taken in the south." Almond did not give further details, but DPRK radio broadcast that Pyongyang had been bombed the preceding evening. At the same time, President Truman, in an exchange with the press, said, "We are not at war," accepting the characterization of the fighting as "a police action." The president refused to answer a question about the possible introduction of US troops into the fighting in Korea.

That question was answered the next day in Pusan, where members of the 1st Battalion of the 24th Infantry Division were hurriedly arriving from Itazuke Airbase in Japan. The initial force consisted of two rifle companies reinforced by two 107-mm mortar platoons, one platoon equipped with 75-mm recoilless rifles, six "bazooka" teams and four 60-mm mortars. The ROK lines had crumbled at Suwon, and the US troops were to be sent by train almost two hundred miles north in an attempt to hold the approaches to Taejon. By the time the US troops started to land, the KPA was forty miles south of Suwon. With the South Korean troops fleeing and the roads not secured, the route was clear for the North all the way to Taejon, if not to the end of the peninsula. The only thing slowing the advance at all were US aircraft, effective against trucks and armored vehicles, less so against masses of troops. But the ability of US fighters to operate depended on clear skies. US B-29s could use radar to penetrate the clouds, but the capability to discern targets on the ground with the technology of the day was as much art as science, and while their payload was certain to the hit the ground, what it struck was always in question.

The next day, July 2, the KPA forces paused to regroup north of Suwon. The Korean peninsula features a mountainous spine along its east, but the land westward south of Seoul enjoys wide plains filled with rice paddies, the adjoining terrain well suited for an army to advance in force along its flat roads. Forward elements of the KPA had reached far south of the city, but the mass of troops were still about ten miles north, and the 24th Infantry troops were preparing to defend the plain between Suwon and Taejon, a tall task for fewer than a thousand soldiers with no armor and limited anti-tank weapons. The pause ended the next day as four columns of the KPA pushed south, two columns flanking the town, not yet close enough for contact with US troops. US B-29s continued to attack targets in the north, including the Yonpo airfield (codenamed K-27), 135 miles north of the 38th parallel.

On the fifth, the 24th Infantry had its first contact with the KPA, firing their weapons at a column of forty tanks approaching their position on the road about two miles north of Osan, thirteen miles south of Suwon. The Americans stopped seven of the tanks and temporarily halted the column, but when their ammunition ran out after seven hours of fighting (each soldier was only issued 120 rounds for his M1 rifle with no resupply), they were forced to retreat, leaving their tubes behind but taking the breechblocks and sights so they couldn't be used by the enemy. Casualties were heavy, with almost a fifth of the men wounded and one of the infantrymen, Pvt. Kenneth Shadrick of West Virginia, became the first American killed in ground combat in Korea.

In the air and on the water, a different kind of combat continued. US B-29s continued bombing targets in the north, including four suspected submarines in port near Pyongyang. Fighters strafed and bombed the KPA armor and troop concentrations when they could find them under the overcast. At a press conference, the commander of US forces in Korea, Major General William F. Dean, implored assembled reporters to, "help me pray for fair weather." At sea the US Navy, aided by ships of the British Commonwealth, enforced the naval blockade around Korea imposed a week earlier. As hard as it was to prevent the DPRK from resupplying and reinforcing its army over land, the United States was adamant that they would receive no support in troops or supplies by sea. Colorfully quoted in the Associated Press, Rear Admiral John M. Higgins, responsible for the blockade on the east coast of Korea, "declared any North Korean troop movements on the east coast, 'are by land, by God, and not by sea.'"

Destroyers patrolled the coast with radar that was probably unable to see small boats but sensitive enough to see medium and large ships, so his boast was probably true in the main.

Seven thousand miles from the fighting, the UN Security Council met to internationalize the effort CINCFE was making to reverse the North Korean invasion. On July 7, by the same 7-0 vote, with Egypt, India and Yugoslavia abstaining and the Soviet Union still boycotting, the Security Council passed a resolution that said,

> "having determined that the armed attack upon the Republic of Korea by forces from North Korea constitutes a breach of peace ... Welcomes the prompt and vigorous support with governments ... have given ... to assist the Republic of Korea in defending itself ... Recommends that all members providing military forces ... make such sources ... available to a unified command under the United States; Requests the United States to designate the commander of such forces; Authorizes the unified command ... to use the United Nations flag in the course of operations against North Korean forces ..."

For the first time in its less-than five-year history, the United Nations was authorizing an international military operation, albeit against a government that was not at that time recognized by the organization.[7]

On July 10 MacArthur received a secret message from the Joint Chiefs of Staff making it official, informing him that he had been,

> "designated by the President of the United States as commander of military forces assisting the Republic of Korea which are placed under the unified command of the United States by members of the United Nations in response to the resolution of 7 July of the Security Council ... The United Nations flag will be used only in operations against North Korean forces and will therefore not be used in connection with your mission with respect to Formosa."

The man who was the CINCFE and now the Commander in Chief, United Nations Command (CINCUNC), Douglas MacArthur, had spent almost all of his 70 years in a uniform. He was born at Little Rock Army Barracks on January 26, 1880. His father, Arthur MacArthur Jr., was a captain who had served with distinction during the Civil War, eventually receiving the Medal of Honor for his valor. Young Douglas followed his father and mother, Mary Pinkney (Hardy) MacArthur, to a succession of postings in the western United Sates until his father was assigned to duty in Washington, D.C. and then San Antonio, Texas. During the latter assignment, the thirteen-year old Douglas attended the West Texas Military Academy, with an eye towards eventually attending the US Military Academy at West Point. MacArthur eventually earned an appointment to West Point and performed with distinction, graduating first in his class in 1903, accepting a prestigious commission into the Corp of Engineers.

MacArthur's father was by now a major general, responsible for the Army's Department of the Pacific, so it is not surprising that the younger MacArthur's first posting was to the Philippines, beginning a long relationship with that vast US protectorate. While it certainly did not hurt to have a father in such a high position in the Army, MacArthur rose quickly, thanks to his audacity, physical courage, and an outsized ego to accompany both. He served with distinction in the Philippines, during the Veracruz campaign in Mexico, where he was nominated for (but did not win) the Medal of Honor, and in World War I. His performance during the World War earned him two Distinguished Service Crosses, seven Silver Stars, and promotion to brigadier general.

After the war, MacArthur served as Superintendent at West Point, married a wealthy heiress, and was assigned to the Philippines as commander of the Military District of Manilla. For the next decade, he served in the Philippines several times before returning to the US and being named Army Chief of Staff with the rank of general. MacArthur served as chief of staff for five years during which he was criticized, unfairly as it happened, for clearing the protesting "Bonus Army" veterans from the National Mall under orders from President Hoover. Following his tour as chief of staff, he returned to his old haunts in Manilla, this time in charge of forming the army of the new Commonwealth of the Philippines. President Quezon of the Philippines granted him the rank of field marshal, which no doubt appealed to MacArthur's vanity, already legendary within the military and beyond. MacArthur retired from the Army in 1937 but stayed on as an advisor in Manilla.

War with Japan was on the horizon when, in the summer of 1941, President Roosevelt called the Philippine Army into federal service and recalled MacArthur to active service at the rank of lieutenant general and the title of Commander US Army Forces Far East. After the Japanese attack on Pearl Harbor, MacArthur was promoted to general and assigned the defense of the Philippines. MacArthur's defense was undistinguished. He was slow to make decisions, unwilling or unable to coordinate with air and naval component commanders, and overall ineffective. Like many of his superiors, he apparently did not anticipate the scale and effectiveness of the Japanese air attacks and amphibious landings, but his performance on the ground during the three months before he was forced (by circumstances and the orders of the President Roosevelt) to relocate to Melbourne, Australia, did him no credit. A month later Roosevelt appointed him Supreme Commander Allied Forces Southwest Pacific Area, and his headquarters was moved to Brisbane.

The rapid Japanese advances soon allowed MacArthur to go on the offensive, where he was better suited. He also was able to use his political skills to cultivate Australian politicians, important because Australia initially provided the majority of this ground forces. After early setbacks in Papua, New Guinea, MacArthur's strategy of only attacking strategic locations occupied by the Japanese eventually paid off, aided in no small measure by the steady destruction of the Japanese Navy by forces under the direction of Admiral Chester Nimitz, Commander in Chief Pacific Ocean Areas. After fierce fighting, New Guinea fell in 1944 and the Philippines followed by the middle of 1945.

By this time MacArthur had been chosen to lead the bloody invasion of Japan, but he was spared this duty, as we have seen, thanks to two nuclear explosions and the Soviet invasion of Manchuria. He instead accepted the Japanese surrender on September 2 aboard the battleship *Missouri* in Tokyo Bay. But his service was not yet over, as he was assigned to lead the occupation and pacification of Japan.

By all indications MacArthur performed his duties in Japan in a highly effective, if morally expedient way. He protected Emperor Hirohito, a living symbol of the Japanese state, and thereby facilitated the Japanese people's acceptance of their new status by rewriting history to absolve the emperor of blame for the war. Almost six thousand men were tried for war crimes in Asia, with more than four thousand convicted and nearly a thousand sentenced to execution, but the emperor and the imperial family were excluded from prosecution. But on the other hand, in the less than five years between the Japanese surrender and the Korean invasion, MacArthur had formed, with the acquiescence of Emperor Hirohito, modern, democratic Japan. The price paid was an historical white-washing of the Imperial role in the colonization of Asia and the atrocities committed by the Japanese colonial rulers and their armies.

As the days of July ticked by, the KPA continued to push down the peninsula. On July 17, after days of fighting the 24th Infantry Division, the KPA forced their way across the Kum (Geum) River, eighty miles south of Seoul, and threatened Taejon five miles further south. On the same day, three days after President Rhee had placed all ROK armed forces under the control of CINCUNC, MacArthur in turn delegated the control of ROK ground forces to General General Walton H. Walker, commander of the US Eighth Army based in Yokohama, Japan. General Walker, whom MacArthur had delegated operational control of all US Army forces in Korea the week before, moved his headquarters from Taejon to Taegu (Daegu), eighty miles further to the southeast, at the same time. He asked the 24th Infantry to hold Taejon until he could move additional forces (the 1st Cavalry Division) into place. The 24th Infantry was only able to hold onto Taejon until the twentieth before retreating southward.[8] The KPA were now halfway down South Korea.

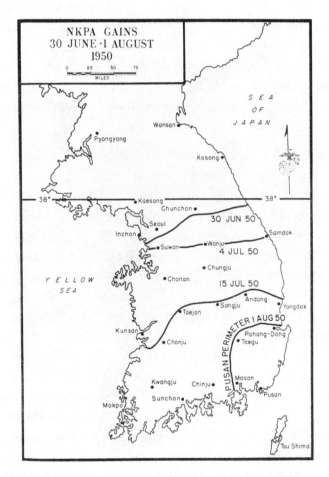

The KPA had captured almost the entire peninsula by the end of July.

The challenge facing MacArthur in mid-July 1950 was in some ways familiar from six or eight years before, and he sought a similar solution. The 450-mile long peninsula was, in essence, more than three-quarters of an island, and thus he could employ the tactics he had used during the island-hopping campaigns in World War II. Needless to say, the land connections at now-communist China and the Soviet Union could not be used to introduce friendly troops. Accordingly, MacArthur and the CINCFE staff began looking for opportunities for an amphibious landing on the peninsula. On July 23 CINCFE's planners distributed for review among the headquarters staff three options for what was referred to as "Operation CHROMITE." The first, Plan 100-B, called for a landing at Inchon (Incheon), the port immediately to the west of Seoul. The second, 100-C, specified a landing at Kunsan (Gunsan), about a hundred miles south of Inchon, and the third, 100-D, called for a landing near Chumunjin-up (Jumunjin-eup), almost due east of Seoul on the east coast of Korea.[9]

It is not clear that there was ever a serious alternative to Plan 100-B, the landing at Inchon. Brig. General William S. Fellers, USMC, commander of the Troop Training Unit at Naval Amphibious Base Coronado (California) and one of his subordinates, Colonel Edward H. Forney, USMC, who was commander of the unit's Mobile Training Team Able, were attending the "American Colony 4th of July party" in Tokyo when they were told by Major General Almond to attend a special conference at CINCFE headquarters. As Colonel Forney described later in a top-secret report,[10] the conference consisted of staff officers of the Command and the two Marines. He related,

"We were informed that it was General MAC ARTHUR's decision that, as soon as possible, United Nations Forces would land at INCHON and cut the Communist supply lines in the vicinity of SEOUL and recapture the city of SEOUL. It was proposed that if the regiment of Marines could not be made available for this operation, that the 1st Cavalry Division would perform this operation. On the next day I was assigned to the 1st Cavalry Division as G-5 (Plans). As such I had considerable knowledge of the objective area for the 1st Cavalry Division landing."

Another element in the choice of landing site, unknown to the two Marines, was MacArthur's appreciation for the optics of a quick recapture of the ROK's capital, Seoul. A landing at Inchon had the potential to accelerate Seoul's recapture, leaving it in the hands of the enemy for only two, or worst case, three months. This discussion would figure into MacArthur's meeting in Tokyo on July 23 with two members of the JCS, Army Chief of Staff General J. Lawton Collins and Chief of Naval Operation Admiral Forrest P. Sherman. Collins strongly favored Plan 100-C as providing the most immediate relief to the besieged Pusan perimeter, while MacArthur recognized, besides the political value of a landing to the north, a northern landings critical ability to severe the KPA's supply lines to their forces in the south.

Colonel Forney continued in his report,

"It was readily apparent to the naval forces involved that the landing at INCHON required highly trained forces and a well coordinated operation. The decision against the Cavalry Division landing at INCHON was finally reached about 10 July 1950."

While the Army had performed many amphibious evolutions during World War II, these had been preceded by considerable training, which the peacetime 1st Cavalry Division had not enjoyed. Amphibious landings under fire were an organic part of US Marine training, so, subject to availability, the first assault would be made by Marines, with Army units landing "administratively" (not under enemy fire) after the beachhead and port were secure.

Even at this early date, with the military situation on the ground still evolving, MacArthur wanted a landing at the earliest possible time. Colonel Forney related,

"The dates for the INCHON operation are fixed by tidal conditions in the INCHON area, the date 15-19 September was definitely fixed by General MAC ARTHUR because he felt any date beyond September would lead to the possibility of a winter campaign in KOREA, which, at that time, he was concerned with avoiding because the troops were not properly trained for a winter campaign. All efforts were then devoted to getting the operation underway so that it could be launched on 15 September."

Even as the JCS was not fully convinced about the location, CINCFE proceeded with planning the invasion. CINCFE instructed its component commanders, including the commander of 7th Fleet's Amphibious Group One, Rear Admiral James H. (Jimmy) Doyle, to plan for the invasion on the fifteenth. Admiral Doyle was assigned as the attack force commander. The 1st Marine Division, assembling in Kobe, Japan, from its base at Camp Pendleton, California, won the assignment for the landing. Major General Oliver P. Smith, 1st Marine Division commanding general, would assume control from Doyle, "at such time as the Landing Force has been landed ashore, the beachhead secured, and Commander Landing Force informs Commander Attack Force that he is ready to assume responsibility for further operations ashore." That the 1st Marine Division headquarters only assembled in Japan during the last ten days in August shows how tight was the timeline. On September 6 MacArthur received approval from the JCS to proceed with Plan 100-B.

Seventh Fleet's *Operational Plan 9-50* highlighted some of the challenges for an amphibious assault at Inchon using large landing craft called "LSTs" (ships that could be beached bow-on to the shore and disgorge their vehicles and men directly ashore using self-contained ramps):[11]

> "The area for the landings experiences one of the largest ranges of tides in the world-over 31 feet. Waters are restricted with many off-lying reefs, shoals and small islands. Due to the extensive mud flats surrounding the landing areas, plus the fact that in some cases the troops must land over existing sea-walls, a tidal height of 23 feet is necessary for landing craft and height of 29 feet is necessary for LST. These limitations restrict the number of days which are suitable for

landing, and also restrict the time available for unloading operations on any one day. The approaches to INCHON are narrow and tidal currents in the transport and gunfire support areas vary between 2 and 3 knots at maximum ebb and flood. The time of landing must be at or near high tide. The distance to the objective area through narrow channels dictates a daylight approach for all but selected groups."

The versatile LST, a World War II innovation. A shallow, flat hull allowed the ship to beach bow-on and load using a ramp behind the doors in the bow.

There were more than just hydrographic challenges. The *Operational Plan* continued,

"An initial landing will be made on WOLMI-DO to secure the island prior or the major landing. This step is essential because of the commanding position of the island in relation to the INCHON shoreline."

The solution was,

"On D day at L hour, BLT [a Battalion Landing Team, about 1200 men full strength] of Marines will land in assault on WOLMI-DO to seize the island prior to additional landings. L hour will be on the early morning high tide about 0630."

The rest of the invasion would proceed after the WOLMI-DO landing, with

"the principal landings ... made on RED, YELLLOW and BLUE beaches at INCHON by the 1st Marine Division ... H hour for these landings will be on the afternoon high tide about 1700. This division will then seize a beachhead in the INCHON area. The beachhead will be expanded rapidly to seize KIMPO airfield and the HAN river line West of Seoul. The advance will be continued to seize and secure the city of SEOUL, the terrain commanding SEOUL and an area to the SOUTH. The 7th Infantry Division reinforced plus X Corps troops will land administratively from second and third echelon convoys in the city of INCHON at a time to be designated after D day ..."

General MacArthur chose his chief of staff, Major General Edward M. "Ned" Almond, to command X Corps, with his appointment official on August 26. Marine Major General Oliver P. Smith, commander of the 1st Marine Division and Major General David G. Barr, commander of the 7th Infantry Division, would report to the Corps commander. Colonel Forney was assigned as Almond's deputy chief of staff.[12]

As planning for the invasion proceeded, the situation in the south continued to deteriorate. After the collapse of Taejon, the KPA continued their progress down South Korea until the beginning of August, when UN forces held what became known as the Pusan Perimeter, a rough arc stretching from just west of Masan on the south coast, north to Waegwan, northwest of Taegu, and then north and east to Pohang-dong on the eastern coast.

Over the course of the next six weeks, as battles between KPA and UN forces would shift parts of the perimeter five or ten miles in either direction, several factors enabled it to hold. First, this far south the KPA's logistics support was becoming tenuous. Further, Walker now had a concentration of troops with which to hold his lines. And when the lines got too close to Taegu and Walker proposed withdrawal, MacArthur told him in no uncertain terms that withdrawal was out of the question; there would be "no Dunkirk, there will be no Bataan" in General Walker's words. Summarized by the press as "stand or die," Walker's words had the desired effect, even if they were not relished by every soldier.

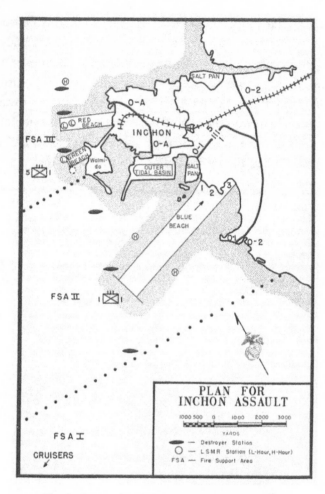

Plan for the assault at Inchon. Note the initial attack on
Wolmi-do, which guarded the approaches to the harbor.
Meredith Victory and the other transports supporting the
second echelon would have anchored to the southwest.

Launching of the SS Meredith Victory, *July, 1945. Note the oil wells surrounding the Calship shipyard.*

When Captain La Rue signed aboard the SS *Meredith Victory* on July 28, 1950, the ship would have seemed very familiar. Like the *Whittier Victory*, the *Meredith Victory* had been built by Calship in Los Angeles as hull number MCV-799, the builder's number 449, as noted earlier, the next in line after *Whittier Victory*. Named after Meredith College in Raleigh, North Carolina, the *Meredith Victory* was delivered to the Maritime Commission on July 24, 1945, just six days after the *Whittier Victory*. She was virtually identical to *Whittier Victory* right down to her Allis-Chalmers turbines. She was immediately placed with the American President Line under the command of Captain Wilton I. Davis for wartime operation under a General Agency Agreement, sailing from Los Angeles on July 30 for Port Hueneme, just up the coast, arriving on the same day. After loading war materiel, she sailed on August 8 for Eniwetok[13] in the Marshall Islands, arriving on the September 2. She carried cargo and personnel to Saipan, Guam,[14] Tinian, and back to Saipan before leaving on September 19 for Los Angeles. She arrived back in Los Angeles on October 2. Like the *Whittier Victory*, when she left port the United States was at war with Japan. By the time she returned, the war was over.

With the end of hostilities and the demobilization of forces, *Meredith Victory* entered bareboat charter in August 1946 for South Atlantic Steam Ship Line and a year later with the Isthmian Steam Ship Line. Like the *Whittier Victory*, she entered the Reserve Fleet, but two years later than her sister-ship, on June 15, 1950, and in the James River, near Newport News, Virginia, rather than Mobile, Alabama. Just a month later she was being reactivated for service in Korea under "time charter" to Moore-McCormack Lines.

There had been some administrative changes between the end of World War II and the beginning of the Korean conflict. Where the War Shipping Administration managed the cargoes and routing of merchant ships during World War II, the Military Sea Transportation Service (MSTS) now had cognizance over the *Meredith Victory* and her fellow Merchant ships. The United States Maritime Commission had been replaced by its successor organization, the United States Maritime Administration.

Joining La Rue aboard *Meredith Victory* on July 28 were a combination of old salts and new graduates, with many having been trained at the US Merchant Marine Academy at Kings Point, New York. Chief Mate Dino Savastio was a 1943 graduate, Third Officer Alvar "Swede" Franzon was a 1944 graduate, and Junior Third Officer Henry J. B. "Burley" Smith and Third Assistant Engineer Merl Smith (no relation) were fresh, 1950 graduates of Kings Point. Another member of the crew, Purser James R. "Bob" Lunney, responsible for the ship's payroll, and customs and other ship's documents, had served in the US Navy in the Pacific during the closing days of World War II. After the war he returned home to attend college, working summers on Moore-McCor-mack ships, and he was due to attend Cornell Law School that fall. Law school would have to wait.

There was no time for the arriving officers and men to get better acquainted, for *Meredith Victory* steamed out of Norfolk on the same day, the twenty-eighth, bound for the Panama Canal. There is no extant copy of *Meredith Victory*'s Deck Log or Sailing Orders, but at fifteen knots she would have reached the eastern entrance to the Canal in about five days. Eight or nine more days to Oakland has her arriving at the pier on August 10 or 11. On August 3, while the men were at sea, the Pentagon had announced that US troop strength in Korea would increase by seventy thousand. The *Meredith Victory* would not be alone going to Korea. Each division of eighteen thousand men required nine ships just for the troops. The division's jeeps, trucks, armored vehicles, and artillery required another seventeen thousand tons of sea lift. Providing weapons, ammunition, food, and other supplies would require another forty-two thousand tons of lift every thirty days. The MSTS was going to need more ships, so the Maritime Administration announced it would reactivate another forty-six ships from the Reserve Fleet, forty-five Victory ships and one C-4, bringing the total number of reactivated ships to 123. Forty of the newly reactivated Victory ships would, like the *Meredith*, be operated by commercial shipping lines.

Dockside at Oakland, the crew commenced loading her cargo for the Pacific, the exact destination a mystery since the ship did not yet have orders. They loaded ten M4 Sherman tanks, 250 two-and-a half-ton trucks, and 150 tons of ammunition and other ordnance bound for the war.[15] On August 16 Captain La Rue and Purser Lunney traveled by cab across the bay to San Francisco, to the Moore-McCormack Lines office at 140 California Street and the Military Sea Transportation Service offices at 33 Berry Street, to pick up their sailing orders.

"Under the terms of charter," the orders began,

> "your cargo and supplies properly stowed, and when ready for sea, your vessel is to leave this port on 16 August 1950, or as soon afterward as practicable, and proceed to Yokohama, Japan, where you will report to the Deputy Commander, Military Sea Transportation Services, Western Pacific, Tokyo, Japan, for the discharge of your cargo.

Upon completion discharge, and when directed by Deputy Commander ... you will return west coast port designated by him."

The orders continued,

"Diversion of your vessel may be required from above destination by the Deputy Commander ... into the Sasebo/Pusan area. Upon diversion you will report by dispatch to Commander, Task Element 96.50 via Deputy Commander ... your estimated time of arrival at one of the following points: Point JUPITER 33.070 North Latitude 129.1600 East Longitude, or KIPPER 32.3300 North Latitude 128.3000 East Longitude. In reporting estimated time of arrival, use only the name of 'reporting point.'"

Point JUDITH corresponded to a location in the strait between the Japanese Island of Fukue-ima and Hirado-shima on Kyushu, about twenty miles from Sasebo, while Point KIPPER corresponded to point off the western tip of Fukue-ima about fifty miles closer to Korea. Both were about seven hundred nautical miles or about two days sailing from Yokohama and less than half a day's sail from Pusan. Task Element 96.50 was the naval Escort Element of the Navy's Japan-Korea Support Group (96.5).

Along with the sailing orders would have been the "Voyage Instructions Folder," eight or nine sheets with details typed in among mimeographed blue text. La Rue would have signed the first sheet certifying that he had received enclosures, including a numbered copy of the "NCSORG[16] Merchant Master's Manual" and that he understood, "fully the degree of security that must be given these documents, and the instructions contained therein." The next page would detail the route positions in latitude and longitude describing the great circle[17] for the 5,336-mile voyage to Yokohama.

The next page would give the estimated time of arrival (ETA) in Yokohama, about thirteen days hence at a seventeen-knot speed of advance. Paragraph 8 exhorted,

"You must keep strictly to your assigned route and make every effort to stay exactly on your dead reckoning position. You must always strive to arrive at your scheduled time. Changes therefrom will be made only for reasons of safety to your ship. YOU ARE AT ALL TIMES RESPONSIBLE FOR THE SAFE NAVIGATION OF YOUR SHIP." [emphasis in the original]

The final pages provided the communication plan, dates, and locations for radio contact, using codes and call signs, to keep NCSORG apprised of the ship's position and updated ETA.

When Captain La Rue and Purser Lunney left the Moore-McCormack offices, La Rue told the cabbie not to take them directly back to the ship, but rather to stop at Old St. Mary's Cathedral, on the corner of California and Grant streets on the edge of Chinatown. Inside the church, La Rue, knowing Lunney was also a Catholic, asked him to join him in prayer, "for the men and for the ship." They were on their way to war and both men, particularly La Rue, understood what that meant.

What would the *Meredith Victory* and her sisters be facing? The MSTS, in its *Operation Plan 1-50*, issued August 15, 1950, described the "Enemy Forces." It said,

"A state of war does not exist. Differences in ideology between Communism and Democracy, and the efforts of the former to expand, cause a state of world tension. Disturbances in Korea, tantamount to war, are now in progress between a Northern (Communistic) faction and a Southern (Democratic) faction (the Korean Republic), in which the United States, as a member of the United Nations, is giving active support to the Southern faction, creates a 'stepped-up' need for sea transportation of personnel, and material in quantities and of types not provided by normal shipping requirements. There is a potential enemy having formidable capability on land, in the air, and at sea. Attacks on shipping and mining of coastal waters and focal points, either before or immediately after commencement of hostilities, may be expected.

Attacks on ships at sea by torpedoing without warning, on ships in harbors, and minelaying by covert means are also potential enemy capabilities. Master of vessels shall be particularly alert and take necessary precautions for the security of their vessels. Sabotage is to be expected and countermeasures are to be deployed."

Meredith Victory loaded and under way.

For the men themselves, somewhat offsetting the risks was a bonus system for merchant mariners similar in concept to that implemented during World War II. Once a ship crossed the International Date Line (the 180th meridian) westward, the entire crew, officers and men, received an additional $2.50 (about $27 in 2020 dollars) per day as it entered a "bonus mine area." The bonus ended when the ship passed back across the same line eastward. There were additional bonuses for more dangerous areas. For example, each time a ship entered the waters around Pusan, she entered "Bonus Area V"[18] and the crew was eligible for an additional bonus equal to one-hundred-percent of salary for each day the ship spent in the Bonus Area.[19]

While *Meredith Victory* was at sea, planning continued for the landing at Inchon. As expected, the tides preoccupied the planners. September 15 would feature a particularly high tide, 31.2 feet at high water, but only 0.5 feet at low water. On September 27, the high tide would reach twenty-seven feet, but the next tide approaching thirty feet would not be until the twelfth of October. Because of the tidal range, the harbor was ringed by stone seawalls that rose, on average, sixteen feet above the mud of the bay, which became extensive mud flats when the tide went out. The landing craft needed a tide of at least twenty-three feet to clear the mud flats and reach the walls. Even with the high tide, ladders would still be needed for Marines to scale the wall. The men of the 1st Marine Division, by now all arrived from California to Kobe, built ladders from aluminum and wood for each landing craft.

When the *Meredith Victory* arrived at anchor in Yokohama Bay in the waning days of August, the first movements for the Inchon invasion were just days away. But amidst the preparations, something more ominous was developing. Typhoon Jane was heading for Japan. The strongest storm to hit Japan since 1934 struck Kobe on September 3 with winds peaking at 110 miles per hour. The 7,733-ton *Tatsuharu Maru*, due to sail for San Francisco, sank after snapping her anchor chain and striking a floating dry-dock. Seven US ships snapped their mooring lines, but suffered less damage due to the efforts of their crews. Before the storm crossed into the Sea of Japan and lost strength, the typhoon killed 250 Japanese around Osaka, Kobe, and Kyoto and wrecked thousands of houses, but despite the damage there were no reports of casualties among the landing force assembling in Kobe.

As the Marines in Kobe dried out their supplies and resumed loading onto the transports and LSTs that would carry the 1st Marine Division into battle, *Meredith Victory* left her anchorage in Yokohama to discharge the cargo she had brought from Oakland and to load additional thirty-ton Sherman tanks and two-and-a-half-ton ("deuce and a half") trucks weighing nine tons a piece into the holds. What did not fit below was chained to the deck. On September 11 she left Yokohama, with 120 GIs from the 7th Infantry Division staking out territory under the canvas tops of the trucks chained to the deck.

An hour out of port, Captain La Rue opened his orders and read the destination: Inchon. *Meredith Victory* joined eighteen other transports of the Second Echelon Movement Group, including seven troop transports, carrying the almost 25,000 men of the 7th Infantry Division. The division, which had been less than half-strength just six weeks before, was the beneficiary of almost six thousand officers and men arriving in Japan ostensibly as replacements for the Eighth Army. In addition, CINCFE had ordered Lieutenant General Walker to send Korean recruits to augment the 7th Division. More than 8,600 Koreans joined the Americans sailing for their homeland that day in September. The rest of the transports, a mixture of C-2, C-3, and Victory ships like the *Meredith*, along with a British "Empire" freighter, carried the division's vehicles, guns, ammunition, and supplies.

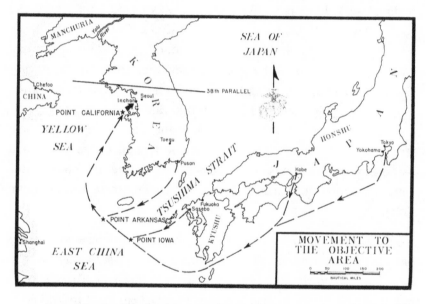

Routes taken by elements of the Inchon landing force, with the *Meredith Victory* departing from Yokohama.

Preceding the 7th Infantry Division had been the 1st Marine Division and its supporting elements, starting with the slowest first. Tugs towed a water barge and small landing craft[20] from Tokyo on September 5 and from Kobe on September 7. Medium landing craft[21] left Tokyo on the eighth and LSTs and other craft carrying the Marines' tracked, amphibious vehicles[22] sailed from Kobe on the ninth. More LSTs sailed from Pusan on the eleventh, the same day the troop transports with the bulk of the 1st Marine Division left Kobe; and troop transports from Pusan carrying the 5th Marine Regiment of the 1st Marine Division, reluctantly released from duty on the Pusan Perimeter by General Walker under orders from General MacArthur, sailed on September 13 and 14.

On September 13 another hurricane, Typhoon Kezia, roared across southern Japan with winds of sixty-seven miles per hour, striking the islands of Honshu and Kyushu. The storm claimed fifteen lives along with the historic Kintai Bridge in Iwakuni, its five wooden arches swept away by the swollen Nishiki River. The storm struck the Second Echelon as the convoy from Yokohama was crossing south of Kyushu at ten knots into the Sea of Japan.

None of the ships had easy going that night. For the *Meredith Victory*, on station at the right rear of the formation and top heavy with tanks and trucks on its deck, the fifty-foot swell and the sixty-mile-per-hour wind from the port quarter rolled the ship alarmingly. Junior Third Officer Burley Smith was in the process of relieving Second Mate Al Golembeski from his watch when the two officers watched with considerable concern as the ship rolled to starboard and hung healed over. Chains securing the deck cargo started to break, with several tanks sliding until they stopped against the starboard bulwark. The ship slowly righted itself and resumed rolling back to port, some of the trucks now sliding across the deck, the shrouds from the ship's cranes cutting into their canvas roofs and injuring the soldiers inside. Top heavy with loose cargo, *Meredith Victory* was in danger of capsizing.

Before he could call the captain in his cabin a deck below, Smith found that La Rue had already braved the violent rolls to climb the ladder and was standing beside him. Silently timing the waves and the motion of the ship for a few moments, La Rue calmly ordered the helmsman, "Hard left rudder," and told Smith to order "Full ahead" on the engine-order telegraph. No one spoke as the ship slowly turned through the perilous point where the seas were on the beam. When the ship steadied on course with a small angle to the wind and waves, the captain ordering "Slow ahead" to keep the *Meredith Victory* pointing into the sea, waiting out the storm as it moved past. In the moment, the junior third mate would have turned the ship to starboard, in the direction of the tanks loose against the bulwark, but La Rue, with almost two decades at sea and months of stormy weather under his belt, knew that the time saved in getting the ship around into the wind and out of the quartering sea was most important. Reflecting on the decision almost seventy years later, Smith pointed to this event as an example of Captain La Rue's calm under pressure and expert seamanship.[23]

As the storm passed a few hours later and the winds and seas calmed, the *Meredith Victory* resumed her course for Inchon. *Meredith Victory* arrived at her assigned anchorage three hours late, but with her cargo and crew intact. The men did not know that the day before the *Meredith Victory* had suffered her trials, the troop transports and cargo ships that had left Kobe carrying most of the 1st Marine Division had turned back in the face of the storm, sure they could not steam through safely. Admiral Doyle had met the ships as the *Mount McKinley* was working her own way through the storm from Sasebo, ordered them turned around, and led the force around the worst part of the typhoon. Doyle later said Typhoon Kezia was one of the worst he had ever encountered.

As the Second Echelon was working its way up the western coast of Korea, UN forces were executing naval bombardments and air strikes both for the actual invasion at Inchon, and for diversions elsewhere along the coast. On September 13, destroyers anchored close offshore to draw fire from shore batteries on Wolmi-do so the batteries would identify their positions and be destroyed by counter-battery fire. Several destroyers were damaged by shore fire using this tactic and the destroyers withdrew mid-day, with the bombardment resumed by US and British cruisers, their longer-range guns allowing them to anchor further off shore. Pausing only to let Marine F-4U Corsairs flown from the escort carriers *Sicily* and *Badoeng Strait* bomb the emplacements, the cruisers resumed their bombardment until late afternoon. The next day the Corsairs struck again, followed by naval gunfire from the cruisers, this time directed at targets on the mainland as well as Wolmi-do. Pausing for another run by the Corsairs, the cruisers, now joined by the destroyers off Wolmi-do, resumed their bombardment, this time without return fire from the island.

The cruiser USS Toledo *firing at targets around Inchon. The island of Wolmi-do rises in the distance.*

Early on D-day, the fifteenth, Marine F-4U Corsairs again attacked KPA positions on Wolmi-do with napalm and rockets, blackening the hillsides. Leaving nothing to chance, just before the 3rd Battalion, 5th Marines reached Wolmi-do at 0633, three rocket-launching landing craft[24] poured their rockets onto "Green Beach" and the hillsides above. The preparations had worked, as the Marines encountered very little resistance, just occasional small-arms fire, and in less than half an hour, an American flag was flying at the crest of Radio Hill, the top of the island. Scattered fighting continued as the Marines secured the rest of the island, including a lighthouse on Sowolmi-do, a tiny rock island connected by a causeway to Wolmi-do. By noon the two islands were secure at the cost of just seventeen Marines wounded in action.

Now the focus could turn to the main event, the landings on the mainland at Red Beach, just north of Wolmi-do, and Blue Beach, to its south. Mid-afternoon, the cruisers and destroyers offshore resumed their bombardment of targets near the beaches, and for three hours they pulverized any potential enemy cover they could find near the beaches. Marine Corsairs joined the onslaught on Inchon, ranging deeper from the shore than the ships could reach, ready to strike any threats as far as twenty-five miles inland from the landing sites. As the time for the landing, H-Hour, neared for the two mainland beaches, Marines started their careful climb down rope nets hung from the troop ships and into the landing craft that would take them ashore. The slow tracked amphibians[25] left first, followed by faster landing craft.[26] As they neared the beach, the ships offshore halted their bombardment at 1705, and on cue the rocket-launching landing craft sent thousands of rockets onto the beaches, ending their salvos just minutes before the first Marine ascended a ladder from the deck of a landing craft and stepped onto the seawall at 1731. The landing at Inchon had begun.

Landing craft (LCVPs) carry Marines to the shore. LSTs and other transports are in the background.

Marines use ladders, some made by the Marines themselves, to scale the seawall.

Early on September 16 MacArthur sent a secret message to the JCS from the *Mount McKinley* by way of his command in Tokyo. It begins,

"During the night of 15-16 Sept the First Marine Div further consolidated its positions in Inchon and to the south thereof, meeting only sporadic resistance. Coordinated attacks this morning all link up the two wings of the Div. [those landing at Red and Blue beaches.] ROK Marines, attached to the First Marine Div, are clearing up the northern half of the city of Inchon...Preparations for the landing of heavy equipment and supplies progressed throughout the night. The high tide this morning will provide the first use of the inner harbor of Inchon for this purpose. Operations continues exactly on planned schedule."

On September 16 the elements of the Second Echelon started landing, soldiers of the 7th Infantry Division climbing down the sides of their ships onto waiting landing craft.[27] *Meredith Victory* was summoned from her anchorage into the harbor to use her cranes to lower her cargo of tanks and trucks onto landing craft that moored alongside. The troops who had endured the storm and the days at sea under canvas were happy to get ashore. The 7th Infantry Division was assigned to cover the right flank of the 1st Marines as they pushed towards Seoul.

Transports off Inchon, mingled with warships, waiting for the tide to come
back in. Wolmi-do is in the center.

The *Meredith Victory* was still at Inchon on the eighteenth to witness
two Soviet-made North Korean Yak-9 fighters attack the heavy cruiser
Rochester, 7th Fleet commander Vice Admiral Struble's flagship, and
HMS *Jamaica*, participants in the surface bombardment a few days
before. Bombs dropped from one of the Yaks caused minor damage to
Rochester and a strafing run by the other caused three casualties on
Jamaica but cost the pilot his life when gunners on *Jamaica* shot her
down. Merl Smith, watching from *Meredith Victory's* deck, said later,
"Our guns just disintegrated it."[28]

Her unloading complete and her cargo in the hands of the 7th Infantry
Division, *Meredith Victory* steamed out of Inchon harbor for Yokohama.
About fifty miles from Inchon, she encountered a small boat with thirteen Koreans aboard waving a white flag. The ship stopped to render
aid but none of the ship's crew understood Korean. The ship
happened to be carrying Japanese stevedores from Yokohama, and one
of them spoke enough Korean to determine that the men were North
Korean conscripts who wished to surrender to *Meredith Victory*. The
crew gingerly disarmed the men and after consultation with the Navy,
brought them back with them to Yokohama, confining them to one of
the now-empty holds and providing them with food and water. The
ship's experience with the surrendering KPA soldiers was consistent
with the Marine's observation on Wolmi-do, where many of the KPA
troops were clearly inexperienced and poorly motivated. When

Meredith Victory arrived in Yokohama, a small boat carrying military police met the ship in the harbor and took the prisoners into custody. The sight of the prisoners being manacled at gunpoint seemed excessive to some of the crew who had already spent days with these ragged men.

Enjoying the success of the Inchon landing from the command ship USS *Mount McKinley*, from left to right: Rear Admiral James H. Doyle, attack force commander; Brigadier General Edwin K. Wright, CINCFE Operations Officer; General of the Army Douglas MacArthur, CINCFE; and Major General Edward M. Almond, Commander, X Corps.

THE LANDING at Inchon was an unqualified success. As the 1st Marine Division's *Special Action Report* (SAR) said,

"A successful assault landing was executed ... under the most adverse landing conditions in the history of amphibious operations ... The Force beachead line approximately 6 miles from landing beaches was seized within 24 hours after the main landing ... KIMPO airfield, a primary objective of the operation in the 1st Division zone of action, 16 road miles from the landing beaches, was captured 50 hours and 33 minutes after H-hour, D-Day ... The first assault crossing of the HAN River (400 yds wide at crossing site) was executed by RCT-5 [Regimental Combat Team-5], employing LVT, DUKWs, and pontoon ferries, less than five days after landing at INCHON ... The remainder of the Division crossed the HAN River without bridging and after intense fighting completed the seizure of SEOUL 12 days after the landing at INCHON."[29]

When MacArthur reinstalled Syngman Rhee in the Government House just two weeks after the landing, he was exultant, addressing Rhee and the assembled officials,

"Mr. President: By the grace of a merciful Providence our forces fighting under the standard of that greatest hope and inspiration of mankind, the United Nations, have liberated this ancient capital city of Korea."

The SAR summarized the victories, but they had indeed come after "intense fighting" in Seoul, where the Marines fought house-to-house in some areas to secure the city. By October 7, when the 1st Marine Division was relieved south and east of Seoul by advance elements of the 8th Army, which had pushed its way back up the west of Korea from the Pusan Perimeter, the division had suffered 415 fatalities, and 2,029 wounded, with another six missing in action.[30] The 7th Infantry Division had suffered 106 killed and 409 wounded, with fifty-seven missing in action.

How to follow up the success of Inchon? As the Marines were taking Kimpo and Seoul, the 8th Army had pushed through KPA lines north of Taegu and had reached Naktong by the twenty-second. As UN forces pushed the KPA northward across the perimeter, it became clear that the success of the Inchon landing had not only severed the KPA's supply lines from the north, it had also demoralized its forces.

By September 23 there were no significant concentrations of KPA troops around the Pusan Perimeter, and a week later the UN forces had pushed up to an axis almost joining Suwon and Kangnung (Gangneung), with some ROK units reaching within a few miles of the 38th parallel. On October 1, General MacArthur gave an order halting all air attacks against road, rail, bridges, or other structures south of the 38th parallel except where they were in active use by the KPA. There were still pockets of the enemy in the south, particularly north of Seoul and in the mountainous east, but the North Koreans could no longer execute a significant offensive in the south.

The question now was whether to declare victory as the North Koreans were expelled from the south, or to pursue the KPA north, destroy it, and essentially, unify the peninsula. On September 27 the Joint Chiefs of Staff sent MacArthur a top-secret message that effectively put the question to rest, much to MacArthur's satisfaction. "Your military objective," it began,

"is the destruction of the North Korean Armed Forces. In attaining this objective, you are authorized to conduct military operations ... north of the 38th Parallel in Korea, provided that at the time of such operation there had been no entry into North Korea by major Soviet or Chinese Communist Forces, no announcement of intended entry, nor a threat to counter our operations militarily in North Korea. Under no circumstances, however, will your forces cross the Manchurian or USSR borders of Korea and, as a matter of policy, no non-Korean Ground Forces will be used in the northeast provinces bordering the Soviet Union or in the area along the Manchurian border."[31]

The message continued with a convoluted discussion of what the UN commander should do in the case of actual or threatened Soviet or Chinese military involvement, including south of the 38th parallel, but it never clarified what to do if Chinese ground forces entered the battle in the north. It concluded with terms for disarming the KPA and occupying North Korea after the ostensible United Nations victory.

On September 29 Secretary of State George C. Marshall sent MacArthur a top-secret, "Eyes Only" message reinforcing the JCS instructions that said,

"Reference present report of supposed announcement by Eighth Army that ROK Divisions would halt on 38th parallel for regroupings. We want you to feel unhampered tactically and strategically to proceed north of 38th parallel. Announcement above referred to may precipitate embarrassment in UN where evident desire is not to be confronted with necessity of vote on passage of 38th parallel, rather to find you have found it militarily necessary to do so."[32]

Western diplomats at the United Nations, notably Britain and Canada, were calling on North Korea to surrender so that there would be no need to cross the parallel. The Soviet Union, as it had since US intervention began, decried US "aggression" but continued to be vague about the repercussions of UN forces crossing into the north. President Rhee, for his part, saw this as the moment to reunify Korea under his government.

On October 1 MacArthur increased the pressure on the north by having a surrender demand, addressed to Kim Il-sung, broadcast hourly from Tokyo.

"To the Commander in Chief, North Korean Forces: The early and total defeat and complete destruction of your armed forces and war-making potential is now inevitable. In order that the decisions of the United Nations may be carried out with a minimum of further loss of life and destruction of property, I, as the United Nations commander in chief, call upon you and the forces under your command, in whatever part of Korea situated, forthwith to lay down your arms and cease hostilities under such military supervision as I may direct ..."

The next day, with no word of a surrender forthcoming, on MacArthur's orders, two companies of the ROK 3rd Division crossed the 38th parallel along the eastern coast, unopposed for the time being.

After weeks of inaction in the Security Council due to the threat of a Soviet veto, on October 7 diplomacy by the US and its allies at the UN General Assembly led to a 47-to-five vote on a resolution that endorsed the military actions on the ground that would unify Korea. The language of Resolution 376(V) was far more benign than earlier resolutions, but it still began,

"Mindful of the fact ... that the unification of Korea has not yet been achieved, and that an attempt has been made by an armed attack from North Korea to extinguish by force the Government of the Republic of Korea, ..."

The Resolution recommended,

"All appropriate steps be taken to ensure conditions of stability throughout Korea; all constituent acts be taken, including the holding of elections ... for the establishment of a unified, independent and democratic government in the sovereign State of Korea ..."

In other words, the General Assembly would not prevent UN forces from destroying the KPA and by effect, the government of the Democratic People's Republic of Korea.

MacArthur had a hammer in the X Corps and an anvil in the 8th Army but their greatest combat capabilities were both on the same side of Korea, the western[33]. On September 26, before he had received authorization to operate north of the 38th parallel but expecting to receive it, CINCUNC instructed his planners to develop an operation that would enable his forces to halt the retreating KPA on the east side of the peninsula. MacArthur rejected marching X Corps across the peninsula, demanding instead an amphibious landing. A day later he had in front of him a concept for a landing at Wonsan, eighty miles almost due east from Pyongyang, that would enable X Corps to meet the 8th

Army at Pyongyang for the capture of the North Korean capital. Once Pyongyang and the territory south were fully in UN possession, the two armies could advance north, with only ROK troops advancing closer than fifty or one hundred miles from the Manchurian border, in conformance with the just-received JCS instructions. The plan was just as MacArthur had requested, and the JCS approved it on October 1.

With D-day for Wonsan initially set for October 15, the Navy and Marine planners once again had to use their training and experience to compress their planning for the embarkation, transportation, and landing, possibly under fire, into less than two weeks. The inadequate port facilities and the widely swinging tides meant that if the 1st Marine Division loaded transports in Inchon for a landing on the twentieth, there would be no time for the 7th Infantry Division to do the same. So, the decision was made for the 7th Infantry Division to travel by rail and truck south to Pusan and board transports there. As in the assault phase, the Navy and the Marines had to time their out-loading with Inchon's tides, and even loading just the Marines ended up taking from October 8 through the sixteenth. D-day was pushed back to the twentieth.

Wonsan was a natural location for a landing, and far more hydrody-namically benign than Inchon, with tidal swings on the order of a foot. The port featured extensive facilities (albeit with half destroyed by previous US bombing), good rail connections, and a forty-square-mile bay for an anchorage. The Taebaek mountain range rising behind the city created a natural barrier directly to the west, albeit with passes and roads, but to the north the coastal plain opened up towards Hamhung.

What was unknown this early in the war was the scale of the mining of harbors in the north. What would Wonsan hold? Drifting mines had been seen all around the Korean peninsula, including near Inchon before the landing, and had taken a steady toll on shipping. On September 29 the destroyer USS *Brush* had struck a mine in the waters off Tanchon, killing nine of her crew and injuring ten. The ship was able to make Sasebo on her own power the next day. The few mines at Inchon had been hastily laid and therefore easily cleared, but there was no assurance that would be the case in North Korean waters.

The US Navy leadership in Korea, including admirals Joy, Struble, and Doyle, had memories of what effective minelaying could do to stymie an invading force. Vice Admiral Struble had served as chief of staff for the US Naval Forces at Normandy during World War II and had witnessed the loss of the US Minesweeper *Osprey* on the day before the landing, and then the devastation a field of magnetic-influence mines had wrought on the invading force at Utah beach, where more than sixteen landing craft and several warships were lost.[34] The UN forces did not know at the time that after June 25 the Soviet Union had provided the DPRK with large numbers of mines, including magnetic influence mines. The North Koreans had used them to great effect to lay mixed fields of moored-contact and influence mines that would be hard to sweep.

Prior to the Inchon landing, the US Navy had won the assistance[35] in Korea of twenty Japanese minesweepers and their crews, experienced at clearing the more than nine-hundred influence mines the US had laid from aircraft in the seas between the Japanese home islands during World War II. Eight of these 136-foot long, wooden-hulled ships, US "YMS" motor minesweepers now designated "JMS" in Japanese service, were assigned to join 185-foot steel-hulled US "AM" minesweepers and their wooden sisters.

On October 10 the AMs of Mine Squadron Three, under its new commander, Captain Richard T. Spofford, started a sweep, clearing almost two dozen contact mines the first day, but unaware of the real danger. A helicopter surveying the area discovered five densely laid lines of mines ahead and the squadron shifted its focus to a channel to the north. On October 11 as the minesweepers were prosecuting three lines of mines, one the minesweepers, the *Pirate*, was broken in two by an exploding mine and sank in minutes. Five minutes later her sister ship, the *Pledge*, was sunk. Ninety-two men were killed or injured.

US Navy Commander Sheldon Kinney was commanding the destroyer *Taylor*, one of those off Wonsan tasked with protecting the minesweepers from shore fire. Four years later in *Proceedings* he wrote,

> "Once mined, you never forget. The explosive impact jars every ounce of your body ... Your bones reverberate the blow. Inert objects become lethal missiles ...A small ship doesn't last long when mined. Disintegrating TNT opens a cavern in the hull. She carries down her badly wounded as well as her dead. A live, driving vessel becomes a circle of oil and flotsam."[36]

There would be no landing at Wonsan until the mines could be cleared.[37]

The hard, dangerous work continued, with fixed-wing aircraft, helicopters, underwater demolition teams in small boats, and minesweepers working to clear a channel to the beach. [38] Using sonar and visual observation to find the mines, the Navy used gunfire, aircraft-dropped bombs, diver-delivered explosives and experimental magnetic-influence sweep gear to detonate the mines in place. Over the course of a week, two more minesweepers were lost with extensive fatalities, the ROK Navy's YMS-516, and the JMS-14, but a channel was finally cleared. The field turned out not to be a few dozen or a hundred mines thought to have been laid, but three thousand mines over four hundred square miles, following sound, Soviet doctrine to combine contact mines with influence mines to make the sweeping all the more difficult. Indeed, Soviet advisors had helped the North Koreans lay the influence mines.[39]

On October 5 the 7th Infantry, relieved by elements of the 8th Army, began their journey south, moving by road to Taegu and completing the journey to Pusan by rail. Four days later the 1st Marine Division began loading LSTs for the voyage to Wonsan. As Wonsan was still being swept for mines, the 1st Marine Division was aboard LSTs waiting for D-day to arrive, a condition they would have to suffer for two weeks as the LSTs slowly plowed through the Sea of Japan, back and forth off shore, waiting to disembark at Wonsan.

Even before the sweeping had begun, on October 9, the 8th Army had started crossing the 38th parallel in force following two days of probes across the border. By the fourteenth, the 8th Army had pushed some fifteen miles north of the parallel and less than fifty miles from Pyongyang. Kim Il-sung, seeing his capital was now threatened from the ground, ordered his army to halt its retreat and to enforce his dictum to hold the city at all costs, ordering spot executions for offi-cers and men who did not comply. Whether Kim's orders were followed or not, within a week Pyongyang had fallen to a UN force of American, British, Australian, and ROK troops, and Kim and his ministers had fled to Sinuiju, a town on the border with Manchuria.

By the time mine clearance was complete at Wonsan, the ROK I Corps had already done the first job expected of the X Corps by arriving by land and taking Wonsan on the tenth. The I Corps completed clearance of the surrounding ground by the seventeenth. When the Marines of X Corps began their landing on October 26, their second job had been done as well, since Pyongyang had fallen days before. As a result, General Almond ordered the 7th Infantry Division, still at Pusan, to perform a beach landing at Iwon, a town 150 miles north of Wonsan that had been captured by the ROK Capital Division. Since the 7th Infantry, still in Pusan, had expected to land from the harbor at Wonsan and had already loaded onto trans-ports, the change of plans meant the troops and their equipment had to unload from the transports and then back onto LSTs. The division began its landing at Iwon on the twenty-ninth and was largely ashore by November 9. The 7th Infantry Division was soon to be joined by the 3rd Infantry Division sailing from Japan, which began landing at Wonsan on November 1. Anticipating the need to supply the X Corps as it continued its drive north, the minesweeping forces were directed to start clearing Hungnam, a smaller port about forty miles north of

Wonsan and just a few miles southeast of the strategic city of
Hamhung.

———

THE *MEREDITH VICTORY* was never assigned to Wonsan. Instead, she
spent October and November shuttling supplies between Yokohama
and Pusan or Inchon, each trip taking ten to fifteen days of loading,
transit, unloading and return. Liberty in a large, urban port like Yokohama had the usual attractions for the crew—plenty of bars, shopping
for trinkets, and available companionship. Junior Third Mate Burley
Smith recalled one night on watch in the bridge as the crew hurried
down the gangplank to the delights awaiting them. Captain La Rue
had joined him on the bridge for a moment. The captain, a man
known to sightsee and have a beer ashore, but not much more,
watched the men leaving the ship and commented, "What a shame,
there they go looking for booze and women." During his Merchant
Marine career, Smith would sail with a master who traded in the black
market, one who drank excessively, one who chased skirts, and one
who committed the greatest sin a merchant mariner could commit,
falsifying a log. La Rue's discipline, bordering on asceticism, was
unlike any other master with whom he served.[40]

Meredith Victory unloading cargo in Pusan, October, 1950. Note
the soldiers with an antiaircraft gun in the foreground.

If Yokohama had its charms when the ship was in port, war-ravaged Korea had a different appeal. As the stevedores were unloading the ship during one weekend stay in Pusan in mid-October, Burley Smith, Merl Smith, and Bob Lunney decided they wanted to see the K-9 airfield, a former Japanese facility on the east bank of the Nakdong River, perhaps five miles from the harbor. That morning the trio hitched a ride on an Army vehicle out of Pusan and shortly arrived at K-9.[41] Inspecting the field, they struck up a conversation with a C-47 pilot, who offered them a ride to Suwon, his next destination, about 160 miles to the northwest in the direction of Seoul and Inchon. Passenger travel by aircraft was still a novelty for young men in 1950, and they were anxious to see the war closer to the front. So, even though Burley and Merl had watch at 2000, the three happily accepted the offer. When they landed at Suwon, they were shocked to find the airfield deserted except for a few wrecks.

Pusan East Airbase, also known as K-9, circa 1953.

If they had enjoyed the sightseeing on the ride north, they were now getting concerned about making their way back to Pusan. The mass of the KPA and the opposing 8th Army had passed through Suwon long before, but the men could still hear occasional rifle fire in the distance as troops tried to root out residual KPA and communist sympathizers who had stayed behind as guerrillas. The airfield was overseen from a large canvas tent by a sergeant who informed the men that the C-47 that had carried them to this bleak venue was the first aircraft to land at the field for three days. The pilot who had flown them from K-9 offered them a ride to Tokyo, where he was heading next, but the three officers politely declined, figuring that as much more appealing as Tokyo would have been to spend their time compared to this barren place, it was also more than five hundred miles in the wrong direction and across the Sea of Japan. The pilot and his crew said their good-byes, started their engines, and flew off to the east.

The sergeant overseeing the base had little else to suggest to the three forlorn merchant mariners than to try hitchhiking at the two-lane road that ran beside the field. Off they went to the roadside. For almost half an hour, nothing approached from either direction, not even a jeep. Finally, an M4 Sherman tank rattled towards them from the south, stopped beside them, and offered them a ride to Kimpo airfield. The field was to the north and in the opposite direction from Pusan, but it also was a place more likely to have an aircraft flying back to the south, so they climbed aboard. Burley Smith was lucky enough to get a seat, the assistant commander's position with his head sticking out through a hatch in the tank's hull, but Merl Smith and Bob Lunney were stuck riding on top.

The tank made slow progress, their trip punctuated by occasional rifle shots in the surrounding forest and the tank slowly fording rivers as they passed alongside bombed-out bridges. Hours later the tank left them at a fork in the road, the crew pointed them in the direction of Kimpo, and continued on their way to the front. It was now about 2200, the two Smiths wondering in the darkness as they walked the last few miles to the airfield what punishment would await them for missing their assigned watches when they returned to the ship.

When they reached the gate of the airfield, the guards were suspicious of the three men in khaki uniforms bearing no insignia, but they held their fire and listened to their story. Convinced that they were not saboteurs, the guards admitted them to the field, directing them to the headquarters building, a low, brick building with bombed-out windows. Despite the condition of the building, things looked more promising since, even at that late hour, they could hear an aircraft circling overhead, presumably waiting for a chance to land.

The sergeant in charge listened to their tale and studied his manifests to find them a flight south when suddenly the building was rocked by two nearby explosions. All the soldiers inside the building jumped out through the permanently open windows seeking cover. Following the soldiers' lead, the three men ran outside and took shelter under a truck. When no more explosions followed, the soldiers determined it was not a mortar attack by KPA stragglers but "Bedcheck Charlie,"[42] an intrepid North Korean pilot who flew a single-engine observation plane into the pattern for the airfield and kicked small bombs out of the cabin, closing the airfield for the night and sending the incoming aircraft back to where they had come. The three spent a cold night on cots in a canvas tent, each with a single, thin, wool army blanket for warmth.

The next morning, they finally got a ride on another C-47, this time bound south for K-9. Sitting on the fold-down bench seats along the fuselage, they joined a group of nurses being evacuated. Next to Burley Smith sat a young soldier from Tennessee whose brother had been killed during World War II and the Army, just having realized he came from a Gold Star family, was sending him away from the front. Once they were aboard, the aisle between the facing benches was filled with sacks of mail. As was so often the problem, the ceiling was low that day, but at three thousand feet, the plane somehow snaked its way around the mountains, the Buddhist cemeteries on the hilltops appearing at shoulder height. After a stop in Taegu, they arrived back at K-9, more than a day after climbing aboard their first C-47. While they should have been chewed out for missing watch and fined two days' pay, the men don't recall that they were actually disciplined, La Rue and Savastio perhaps so happy to see them back safely.

Home sweet home for Lunney, Smith and Smith after their adventure,
the Meredith Victory *at Pusan.*

To the north, the war continued as serious business. After their landing at Wonsan, a battalion of the 1st Marine Division immediately ranged south to the small port of Kojo to protect the supplies of the ROK I Corps, while the rest assembled their cold-weather gear and proceeded by truck to join the ROK I Corps in Hamhung and to spread west into the mountains near Majon-ni.[43]

With the full strength of the X Corps assembling on the northeast coast, General Almond order the components of his Corps to move north and west. He ordered the ROK I Corps to advance toward the Manchurian border along the coast and the 7th Infantry Division to push to their west north from Iwon. The 1st Marine Division was ordered to advance still further inland through Hamhung to the Chosin (Jangjin) reservoir, about sixty miles south of the Chinese border. Finally, the 3rd Infantry Division was assigned to secure the X Corps' southern and western flanks and to protect their lines of communications for resupply and evacuation of wounded through Hamhung to Hungnam and Wonsan.

What was supposed to be a rapid advance against a weakened and demoralized Korean People's Army instead soon became a battle against at least ten divisions of the Chinese People's Liberation Army.

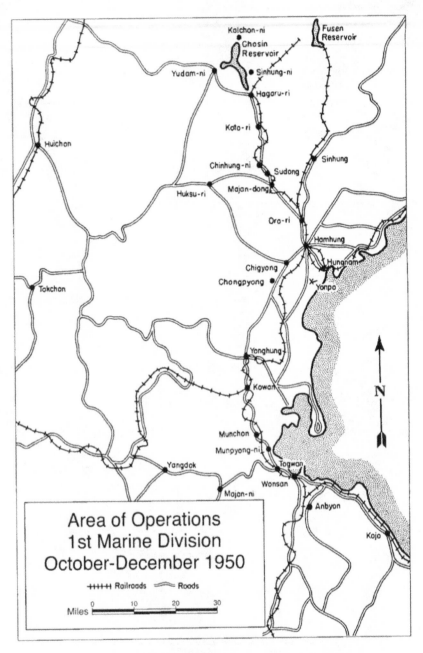

Map showing Korean locations that would soon become famous in US military history, including Chosin, Fusen, Hamhung and Hungnam.

9

CHOSIN

One of the seminal events in Leonard La Rue's life, and certainly the one for which he was best remembered, was the Hungnam evacuation in December 1950. To understand why the evacuation was necessary, we have to consider the events in Korea that fall and the reaction of communist leaders, particularly in China.

Even if by November it seemed unlikely that the Soviet Union would overtly enter the war by supplying troops, the question of potential Chinese involvement haunted the UN forces long before it actually occurred. As early as July 8, the CIA presented four scenarios for possible Soviet involvement in the conflict, the second scenario suggesting that the Soviets, "in order to prolong US involvement in Korea, give increasing material aid to the North Koreans, perhaps employing Chinese communist troops, either covertly or overtly."[1]

While more recently available sources show the PRC-Soviet relationship was more complex than the CIA memo suggested, China had its own reasons, both ideological and practical, to be concerned about the US intervention. When the KPA was successful and appeared to be pushing US forces off the peninsula brought one perspective, but when the KPA started to falter, with the prospect of US forces on the Chinese border or worse, entering Manchuria, brought another. With the KPA advance blunted, an alarmed China moved its best troops to the border.

The PRC's Premier, Zhou Enlai, had proposed China's own diplomatic approach to the Korean conflict in a meeting with the Indian ambassador to the PRC, K.M. Pannikar at the end of July. The plan called for: an immediate ceasefire; withdrawal of all US troops; and negotiations for the reunification of Korea under the auspices of an Asia-only committee consisting of the PRC, India, Burma, and Pakistan. Since the premier was silent on the withdrawal of KPA forces from below the 38th parallel, it is hard to believe the Chinese thought that the United States would agree to terms allowing a ceasefire with KPA troops occupying more than ninety percent of the entire peninsula. But the diplomatic initiative allowed the PRC to align strongly with the other countries that did not want a strong US presence in the region.

On July 31 the Soviet ambassador to the United Nations, Yakov A. Malik, announced that the Soviet Union would attend its first UN Security Council meeting since January, with Ambassador Malik assuming his turn in the rotating presidency for the month of August. The ambassador said his primary focus would be the seating of the PRC in place of Nationalist China, with the conflict in Korea secondary. If nothing else, the Soviets appeared to have learned that the use of their veto in the Security Council could be more effective than their boycott.

On October 1, as MacArthur was calling on North Korea to surrender through his radio broadcasts from Tokyo, the PRC was broadcasting its own thoughts. The Associated Press reported that, in an interview in the Soviet Union's state newspaper *Pravda*, Zhou claimed, "the American government is China's most dangerous enemy." Noting that UN forces, led by the United States, might soon be fighting North Korean forces near the Chinese border, he said that China, "cannot remain indifferent to the fate of her neighbors who have been subjected to imperialist aggression."

How seriously to take this saber-rattling? On October 9 the JCS advised MacArthur in a top-secret message,

> "Hereafter in the event of open or covert employment anywhere in Korea of major Chinese Communist units, without prior announcement, you should continue the action as, in your judgment, action by the forces now under your control offers a reasonable chance of success. In any case you will obtain authorization from Washington prior to taking any military action against objectives in Chinese territory."[2]

MacArthur had the opportunity to speak in person with President Truman and his military and foreign-policy advisors during a meeting at Wake Island on October 15. Asked to give an assessment of the situation, MacArthur told the president that he believed "formal resistance will end throughout North and South Korea by Thanksgiving." Later, when Truman asked about the chances for "Chinese or Soviet interference," MacArthur opined,

> "Very Little. Had they interfered in the first or second months it would have been decisive. We are no longer fearful of their intervention … The Chinese have 300,000 men in Manchuria … not more than 100-125,000 are distributed along the Yalu River. Only 50-60,000 could be gotten across the Yalu River … Now that we have bases for our Air Force in Korea, if the Chinese tried to get down to Pyongyang there would be the greatest slaughter."

MacArthur was confident the 8th Army would start returning to Japan by Christmas and, with the Japanese occupation coming to an end, it be available for possible redeployment to Europe to confront the Soviets there.[3]

The unanimity of views expressed on the fifteenth makes it all the more curious that, two days after the conference, CINCUNC partially relaxed the restriction against non-ROK forces approaching the Manchurian border, allowing them ten or twenty miles closer.[4] And it is more curious still that a week later the restriction was completely relaxed, allowing UN forces free reign all the way to the Yalu. The JCS protested, but when MacArthur argued that it was a military necessity, they did not force him to follow their original orders. He was intent on sending the 8th Army and the X Corps all the way to the Yalu, without restrictions on the nationality of the soldier.

With the possibility of UN forces operating right up to the border, where Chinese territory actually began was the subject of some minor confusion. On October 29, X Corp Headquarters distributed a top-secret message from CINCFE regarding the border between Korea and Manchuria to the commanding generals of the I ROK Corps, the 1st Marine Division, the 7th Infantry Division, and the 1st MAW. The message said, in part,

> "Maps curr use in Korea ... indicate different bdrys between Korea and Manchuria ... A study is being conducted to determine the legal bdry in this area. Until such time as a decision is made, it is mandatory that you take positive action to confine opns to the area established by the southernmost bdry of those indicated on maps ... above."

The border was not always in the middle of the meandering Yalu or Tumen rivers and the command did not want UN soldiers blundering into Chinese territory.

Given General Almond's loyalty to MacArthur, the X Corps *War Diary* for November 1950 almost certainly echoed CINCUNC's thinking as it listed the reasons for attacking right up to the Yalu.

> "(1) It was the most rapid and effective means of carrying out the 1947 UN Resolution for a unified Korea. (2) By quickly gaining control of all North Korean territory, the Chinese Communists' excuse for coming

to the aid of the North Korean People's Government would be removed in that the NKPG would be a government without a country. (3) It would force the Chinese Communist Government to cross an international boundary openly against UN Forces instead of being able to claim that volunteers were aiding the North Korean cause. (4) The fact of a united, well organized Korea solidly behind the UN could be expected to deter the Chinese Communist Government from unshielded intervention. (5) And finally it was generally considered throughout the capitals of the world in October and November 1950, that Communist China was not prepared to go to war with the United Nations."[5]

Whether any of the political judgments were valid is an interesting historical debate, but the fact was the PRC never gave the UN forces the time for "quickly gaining control of North Korean territory." Even as CINCUNC's strictures were being loosened with a view towards the unlikeliness of Chinese involvement, there were signs that small numbers of PRC soldiers were already in North Korea. Towards the end of October, ROK units attached to X Corps north of Hamhung in the east and units attached to the 8th Army north of Unsan in the west battled Chinese soldiers. Interrogation of captured prisoners of war (POWs) soon showed that the 42nd Army, consisting of three divisions, had crossed the Yalu at Manpojin between October 14 and 20. Later interrogations showed that the 20th Army, consisting of four divisions, crossed at the same location about three weeks later, in the first half of November. Unknown at the time, the 27th Army with its three divisions crossed into Korea on November 4, reentered China on the seventh, and crossed back into Korea on the twelfth. These were all part of the 9th Army Group of the "Chinese People's Volunteer Force" (CPVF), Chinese soldiers who would serve in Korea wearing Chinese People's Liberation Army uniforms but without the usual insignia and without the red star on their caps.

By early November, UN troops in the west under General Walker's command were heavily engaged with Chinese forces. Starting with attacks against the ROK II Corps near Unsan, the 8th Army, was struggling to maintain its advance north of the Chongchon River, having already been pushed back from advances that had reached within fourteen miles of the Yalu. The UN forces, particularly the ROK divisions, had gone too far, too fast. The KPA, their morale buoyed by the arrival of massive numbers of sympathetic Chinese communist soldiers, effectively used infiltration of the UN lines and flanking maneuvers to get behind the UN troops, destroying lines of communication with the rear and creating panic among some of the soldiers. When the 8th Army and its associated ROK units attempted to move forward again later in November, it was with much more caution.

Captured members of the CPVF. Note the lack of insignia and the warm "pajama" uniforms well suited to the cold, but also the lack of gloves.

CPVF documents captured a month later asserted that infantry in the 8th Army during this period, "abandon all their heavy weapons ... and play opossum ... Their infantrymen are weak, afraid to die, and haven't the courage to attack or defend." The report continued later, "As a main objective, one of the units must fight its way rapidly around the enemy and cut off their rear ..." The document clearly contained generalizations that were used to building the confidence of the attacking troops and it overdramatized and exaggerated the faults of UN troops. As fighting progressed, UN forces' superiority in artillery, mortars, armor, and close-air support were able to blunt many Chinese attacks.

How were those KPA and CPVF soldiers faring? A KPA prisoner captured by the 5th Marines in Chongpyong, southwest of Hungnam, on November 11 was quoted in his interrogation report,

> "All men in the 2nd Division want to surrender but are not able to since officers are watching the men closely even when going to the head. Any men caught trying to desert the NK Army are punished by death ... The unit had no food on hand. Troops are able to eat only when they are able to obtain rice from nearby villages."

Some of the Chinese POWs reported similar deprivations, one saying he had "only two meals in the three days his unit lived in the hills." As far as their motivations, many of the troops in the 42nd Army were former Nationalist soldiers and "want to surrender but they were afraid if captured by Americans they would be killed as they were led to believe by their superiors." According to their commanders, "America plans to invade China from North Korea ..." and their fight in North Korea was to prevent that.[6]

While the 8th Army struggled to conclude the war on the western side of the Taebaek Mountains, in the east X Corps had its own challenges. The I ROK Corps, with assistance from the ROK Capital Division, captured the town of Kilchu, a key crossroads town about twenty miles northeast of their landing site at Songjin, about a hundred miles north of Hungnam, where the main coast highway continued east-northeast towards the Tumen River and the Chinese and Soviet borders, and another road passed more northerly. The Capital Division continued along the coast while the remaining ROK Divisions continued north. After weeks of heavy fighting, the Capital Division captured Chongjin on the twenty-fifth. The KPA resistance stiffened further as they passed Chongjin, less than thirty miles from the Soviet border. The balance of the ROK forces to the east, the I Corps and the

3rd ROK Division, had worked their way north and captured Hapsu, about twenty miles from the border, on November 22.

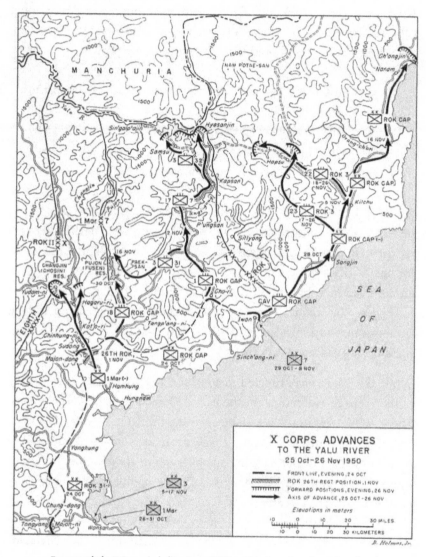

For a month the X Corps, including Army, ROK and Marine units, advanced north and west from the coast. Note the mountainous terrain, denoted by the density of the squiggles on the topographical map.

The 7th Infantry Division continued working north as the balance of its components came ashore at the beaches in Iwon. The division met occasional artillery and mortar attacks, but continued the advance to Pungsan, less than twenty miles from the border, relieving the 1st ROK Regiment on November 2. The 7th spent almost two weeks establishing its command post at Pungsan and bringing up its troops and supplies from the landing, all the while watching the KPA establish defensive positions on the high ground above the Ungi River in front of them. On the fifteenth the division infantry attacked and after moderate resistance began to cross the river. After several days of fighting, on the nineteenth the division captured the town of Kapsan, about ten miles south of the border. The push to the border came quickly, as the KPA seemed to have disappeared. The 7th approached Hyesanjin with little resistance on the twentieth, and a day later they entered the town, sited on the bank of the Yalu River, unopposed. Through the windows of abandoned houses, the Americans could see the People's Republic of China across the river.

To the 7th Infantry Division's west, the 1st Marine Division was in contact with the KPA and CPVF even before they were relieved at Wonsan by the 3rd Infantry Division. The road north out of Hamhung led through a series of towns, Oro-ri, Majon-dong, Sudong, Chinhung-ni, Koto-ri, and Hagaru-ri, before it reached an eight-mile long lake surrounded by mountains known as the Chosin (Jangjin) Reservoir, a little less than thirty miles due west of Pungsan. The Marines were ordered to relieve the elements of the ROK I Corps near Sudong, twenty-nine miles north of Hamhung, where the ROK 26th Regiment had recently suffered X Corps' first contact with the CPVF.

On November 4, the 7th Marine Regiment came under attack. Fighting back with the heavy use of mortars, they were able to capture Sudong. On the same day, the division command post was moved from Wonsan to Hamhung on the expectation that they would continue movement north to Chosin. The regiment fought its way into Koto-Ri, a further sixteen miles up the road, by the eleventh, and by the fourteenth the 7th Marine Regiment had moved up to Haragu-ri, at the southern end of the reservoir fifty-four miles up the dirt and gravel road from Hamhung. To give them a break, the 7th was relieved at Koto-ri by the 5th Marine Regiment.

Over the next few days, the 1st Marine Regiment relieved the 5th at Koto-ri, and now the 5th Marines worked their way north to leapfrog above the 7th Marine's position at Hagaru-ri, to a position about two miles up the east side of the reservoir, while the 7th worked up the west side towards Yudam-ni, a town above the very western finger of the lake fourteen miles by road from Hagaru-ri. The 7th attacked the area around Yudam-ni from the twenty-third through the twenty-fifth, securing the area by the evening of the twenty-sixth. Joining the 7th Marines for the forthcoming push north were the 5th Marines, relieved on the east side of the reservoir by elements of the 7th Infantry Division. Everything was in place for an attack northwest on the twenty-seventh.

Still west of the Marines but well to their south was the 3rd Infantry Division. The division was still unloading at Wonsan when advance elements moving west were attacked at Yonghung on the seventh and again on the next day, but both KPA attacks were repulsed. The final element of the 3rd Infantry Division, the 64th Tank Battalion, was ashore by the twenty-first. Wonsan was just ten miles from the 8th Army's area of control, and patrols were sent to make contact with the 8th Army at Hadongsan-ni, but they were unable to find their sister army on the west side of the mountains.

While CINCUNC and his staff were slow to recognize the peril developing in the Korean north, seven thousand miles away the JCS was becoming increasingly concerned. A top-secret memorandum dated November 9 sent to the National Security Council entitled "Views of the Joint Chiefs of Staff" stated,

> "The Chinese Communists are presently in Korea in such strength and in a sufficiently organized manner as to indicate that unless withdrawn they can be defeated only by a determined military operation ... It is not envisaged that the Chinese Communists and the North Koreans

could drive the presently committed United Nations forces from Korea unless materially assisted by Soviet naval and air power. In the event of the commitment of the latter, U.S. Forces should be withdrawn from Koreas as it would then be evident that World War III is imminent."[7]

A report to the National Security Council by its executive secretary on November 14 reiterated the point, concluding, "The United States should meanwhile develop its plans and makes its preparations on the basis that the risk of global war is increased."[8]

This scenario, in which Chinese or Soviet involvement precipitated a broader conflict, led COMNAVFE on November 13 to release a top-secret *Operation Plan 116-50*, contemplating the evacuation of

"UN forces, and possibly ROK forces, from KOREA to JAPAN. This situation could arise as the result of a general emergency or the outbreak of a world war ... Initial operations may consist of controlled withdrawal of forces with ships being loaded from docks in Korean harbors, along either, or both, the East and West Coasts, and escorted in convoy to Japanese harbors ... plans should be flexible enough to provide for concurrent operations from East and West Coast ports and should be based on the principle of an "assault in reverse," with provision made, as practicable, for an objective or evacuation area, and for air and gunfire support."

The plan assigned responsibilities to the land component commanders, air commanders, and naval task forces for the embarkation of the troops and their protection from land, air, and sea threats. In particular, 7th Fleet would control aircraft-carrier operations in theatre; Task Force 90 (amphibious forces) would provide the "water lift" for the evacuation, assume operational control of naval and air assets in the evacuation area, and coordinate with the ground commanders (Lieutenant General Walker and Major General Almond); and Tasks Forces 95 and 96 would provide escort, naval gunfire support, ASW and minesweeping. Within a few weeks, many of the elements of the plan would be adapted for withdrawal of X Corps from Hungnam.

As November closed, the ROK Capital Division was still advancing, albeit slowly, towards the border, but everywhere else the Chinese offensive was pushing UN forces south, or were on the verge of doing so. In the west, 240,000 men of the 13th CPVF Field Army were pushing the 8th Army back from the Chongchon River. By December 5 the UN line was south of Pyongyang, with the 8th Army destroying anything of military value in the city before abandoning it. Ten days later the 8th Army established a defensive line at the Imjin River, north of Seoul. General Walker would only have to endure the humiliation of the massive retreat for another eight days. On December 23 his jeep was involved in a traffic accident and the general was killed.

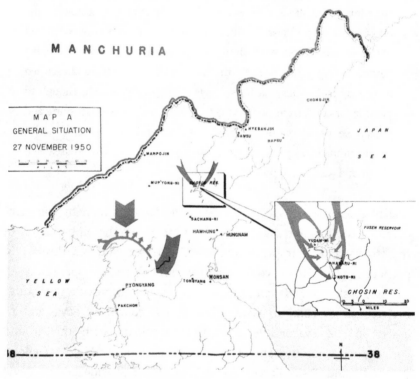

Map from the X Corps War Diary *summarizing the CPVF attacks in force against UN forces across North Korea.*

The X Corps *War Diary* summarizes what happened to the east of the Taebaek Mountains beginning on the November 27 by saying,

> "During the last week of November, which started much like the earlier part of the month, there was a complete change in the area west of the CHOSIN reservoir. The 5th and 7th Marine Regiments on the west side of the reservoir at YUDAM-NI encountered strong enemy forces. Not only was the advance to the northwest stopped, but was also cut off by Chinese units moving around the flank to our MSR[9] [the Main Supply Route]. The enemy forces were so numerous, estimated at six divisions, that they were attacking in strength as far south as KOTO-RI. Another attack was beaten off ... in the HUKSU_RI-SANGCHI-NI area approximately 25 miles southwest of the CHOSIN reservoir area. East of the reservoir, elements ... were also heavily attacked by a strong force estimated as elements of two Chinese divisions."[10] [11]

The 1st Marine Division had orders to initiate an attack northwest from positions at Yudam-ni at 0800 on the twenty-seventh in an effort to relieve CPVF pressure on the 8th Army's eastern flank. As the sun rose over a snowy landscape where the temperature had dropped to zero Fahrenheit the night before, the 5th and 7th Marine regiments performed a complex dance across terrain that would put the 7th in a position to support the 5th Marine's advance. By midmorning, the Marines were in contact with the CPVF and after a day of fighting, the 5th Marines had gained 1,500 yards to the west. The Marines now had control of the high ground around Yudam-ni and settled in for another cold night, this time with temperatures dropping to twenty degrees below zero.

As the Marines tried to keep warm and get some sleep, both nearly impossible tasks under the conditions, three divisions of CPVF crept up the hills to attack the two Marine regiments. At 2100 mortars started to rain down upon the Americans and machine guns were fired into their positions. Soon after, the heavy weapons stopped as the

Chinese assaulted the Marine positions. Both the 5th and the 7th Regiments came under attack, and the Marines fought them off with machine guns, mortars, and hand-to-hand combat. Casualties were heavy, particularly on the Chinese side, and as the initial CPVF attack faltered, the Chinese commanders brought up reserves and fought to flank the Marine positions. The fighting continued all night around Yudam-ni, and before sunrise the outnumbered Marines were forced to retreat from some of the high ground. To the south, the CPVF was attempting to cut off the Marine regiments from their supply and reinforcement to the south. Here, too, the fighting was intense, sometimes hand-to-hand. The Marines held the road.

Before dawn on the twenty-eighth, the Marines counterattacked to try to recover the high ground of the hilltops around Yudam-ni. As the sun rose over snow now blackened from battle, the Marines were still fighting uphill. Over the course of the morning, they recovered some of the lost ground, but the sheer scale of the CPVF attack made it clear that one or even two regiments of Marines would not be enough to push westward against the enemy force in place. Late on the afternoon of the twenty-eighth, General Smith ordered the advance cancelled. The Marines were now on the defensive.

Typical CPVF attack on a Marine position, 50-100 men at a time charging a smaller number of Marines dug in on high ground.

The 1st Marine Division Special Action Report for October 8 through December 15 described the typical Chinese attack.[12]

"Enemy attacks were characterized by preliminary probings by 8 to 15 men whose mission was to feel out our lines, create confusion just prior to the main attack, to draw fire and thus determine our outline and expend our ammunition. Preliminary probings were followed in 5 to 10 minutes by the main attack, with the enemy moving within small arms range in column formation before deploying as skirmishers. The brunt of the attack was aimed at the weakest point of our lines, direction often changed when strong points were inadvertently hit. The Chinese usually advanced at a walk, but sometimes at a trot or run, attempting to find a favorable point of entry into our immediate positions. Sharp hill facings were avoided in favor of gentler slopes. When the approach was channelized, he attacked while still in column. Where terrain was open, a skirmish line was used."

"Front line reports indicate that Chinese tactics also include the employment of marching fire, with submachine gun the principal weapon employed. Attacks were almost without exception accompanied by shouting, screaming, blowing of bugles and whistles and the clashing of cymbals. Few attacks were supported by mortars ... the Chinese aim was not so much the overrunning of front line positions for the sake of wiping out defenders, but primarily to gain entrance into secondary and rear areas. In those instances where the Chinese were successful in penetrating our positions, they made no attempt to stop and reorganize, but wildly continued the attack with the ultimate aim of destroying our unit integrity. Friendly counterattacks invariably caught the enemy by surprise and he was usually routed. The enemy usually broke off contact at daylight, covering his withdrawal with small groups whose mission was to draw fire away from the retreating enemy. Chinese attacks were usually launched during periods of darkness in order to minimize the effectiveness of friendly air and artillery. These attacks were excellently coordinated and well controlled."

These tactics were about to be demonstrated to the east, where the 7th Infantry Division was also suffering attacks by the CPVF. Just before the first attack, the 7th Infantry had repositioned three battalions, reinforced by a tank company, to the east side of the reservoir, two battalions coming from the north near the border at Hyesanjin, one from the south. The day of the twenty-seventh was quiet, with no probing attacks reported, but at 2250 the probing attacks began and two hours later, in the words of the 7th Infantry Division *Command Report*, "the Chinese launched a coordinated attack." The 7th's three battalions were spread out far enough that two divisions of the CPVF, the 80th and the 81st Divisions of the 27th Army, were able to flank them and attack from all sides. The casualties were heavy on both sides, with attack and counterattack, as an American position was lost and then recovered. When the sun rose, the Chinese withdrew, and the 7th regrouped, attempting to fortify their positions.

An idea of the chaos on those first days of battle can be seen in the 7th Infantry Action Report of the candid interview of Captain Robert Kitz, commander of "K" Company, 31st Infantry Battalion.[13] On November 27,

> "We arrived at the Chosin Reservoir ... my area was ... a section of the perimeter defending from the east. It was a little valley that led to the Fusen Reservoir which was several miles east of our position ... About 1930 or 2000 Colonel MacLean came into the CP [Command Post]... there was a report of 400 to 600 enemy ... six or eight miles from where we were to the northeast and we were to send a small patrol up there the following morning ... in all probability we would spend at least one more day where we were ... I prepared to hit the sack for the night. I got in my hole ... At approximately 2200 I received a call from Battalion, a flash alert ... and told everybody to double their guards for the night, which was done. About one o'clock in the morning, I heard some firing and I called Lieutenant MacFarland and asked him if he knew who was firing. He informed me that it was some one behind his positions."

The CPVF had infiltrated the 31st's positions.

Captain Kitz continued,

> "Between 1:30 and 2 o'clock ... there was considerable amount of firing just about where my machine gun section was set up. I didn't exactly know what was going on ... Perhaps someone had gotten trigger happy. I got my shoes back on and got out to check and about that time I heard a lot of firing up close and it was coming in. The cooks, of course, got up and ran out of the tents and quite a few of the ROKs working in the kitchen ... started to run ... I ... stopped them ... I tried to get them to fire back, but by this time the issue had become so confused that I couldn't tell who were ROKs and who were Chinese. There was also a lot of firing and there were Chinese coming at us ... In the meantime, 'A' Battery of the 57th opened fire on us. So we were caught in the crossfire. So I got my people back."

A few hours later (the morning of the 28th),

> "... time passed and we had about an hour to sweat before daylight. When daylight came the G---- [Chinese] pushed back and except for an occasional sniper they had more or less withdrawn ... My platoon up on the hill and one of the 'I' Company's platoons up on the hill had been overrun. They had stayed there ... our orders then were to tighten up our perimeter. We couldn't occupy all the high ground because of the distance involved. And our entire perimeter then was placed on the low ground of the valley. It was at this time that the rascals started throwing mortars at us. We dug in our positions, stayed there that night (28-29 Nov) and this second night (29-30 Nov) this thing started. It wasn't even dark yet. I didn't have time to dig my new hole when it started. When they came in they took a machine gun right on the perimeter so I didn't have any communication by that time. They knocked out my commo [communications] and I only had 60 men left in the company ... Our casualties weren't as heavy as the night before."

"The following morning (30 Nov) we were told the 32nd was coming in. They were pulling back to our positions ... which was all right with us because we felt that the more people we had the merrier it would be ... The next day we got a little small arms fire ... and a few mortar rounds thrown in. But it was the next night (1-2 Dec) that all hell broke loose, the attack started. It began early in the evening and kept going all night. There was plenty of mortars, 120s, big ones, small ones, middle ones, medium size ones. We had had some artillery on the thing. And our artillery was almost out of ammunition ... And the 50s were short of ammunition and the 40s were short ... People who fired M-1s had to conserve ammunition ... The attack lasted all night ... Our aid station was in tough shape. We got a lot of wounded. I don't know how many, but a hell of a lot."

The 31st finally got the order to withdraw, but they were unprepared for the strength and disposition of the CVPF around them. Kitz states,

"... about 11 o'clock (021100 Dec) I was told we were going to withdraw after an air strike. So we prepared for the withdrawal. There wasn't a hell of a lot we could do to prepare for it. We took what equipment we had. What we couldn't carry we put in holes and started to burn it. Destroyed what weapons we couldn't take with us. The vehicles were stripped and broken down and the planes finally got overhead and we started to withdraw."

They would have to fight their way all the way down to Hagaru-ri, but unlike the Marine 5th and 7th regiments, discipline in the battalions of the 7th Infantry Division had broken down. Captain Kitz continued,

"They were right down about 50 to 75 yards from the perimeter shooting into us, when we were pulling out. As a result the withdrawal was a little bit disorganized ... Anyhow, we got going (021300 Dec) [1300 on December 2]. Got the column moving and from then on it was a matter of moving and every time you hit a nose the G---- [Chinese] were there shooting at you ... The men were damn hard to handle. You couldn't get them to move. Maybe it was the four days they had been caught under fire that caused it, but you couldn't control them ... The men just wouldn't function as soldiers should. They didn't go up to the high ground. They were tired and wanted to huddle together and thought there was more protection in numbers and very few of them would listen to reason. They thought that standing by the trucks was the only way of getting away from the fire, when actually it was the one place where most of the fire was being directed."

After fighting all along the road, breaking through Chinese roadblocks and bypassing flaming tanks, the first men of the 7th Infantry entered Hagaru-ri in the early afternoon of the second, but the retreating force had been so decimated that soldiers were still trickling in the next day. Captain Kitz survived in part because he took the initiative. He said,

"... myself ... and a couple ... other officers ... all grabbed a small group of men that were available and pushed them up this hill ... We Banzaied the hill, the ridge and took it, knocked out a few roadblocks along the way."

Kitz returned to gather more men, both wounded and able, until he led 210 into Hagaru-ri around midnight on the second. Wounded, frostbitten, and demoralized, the three battalions had completely lost their combat effectiveness and were just trying to survive, having suffered a horrifying seventy-five percent casualty rate. Only 385 men reached Hagaru-ri in a condition to fight.

If they thought they were entering a refuge from the fighting, they were mistaken. The Chinese had infiltrated all the way south to the next town on the road, Koto-ri, about eleven miles distant, and as a result Hagaru-ri was under almost constant attack by the Chinese 58th Division and a regiment of the 59th. The 12,000-man 58th Division had the reputation as the best in the 20th Army. As at Yudam-ni, the Marines at Hagaru-ri had successfully integrated their artillery with their rifles, mortars, and machine guns, and as a result masses of CPVF soldiers were decimated whenever they were spotted by the defenders. During the day, Marine F4U Corsairs were used to drop napalm and high-explosive bombs on dug-in Chinese and on their concentrations in the open. By December 4, the 59th Division had only eight hundred combat-capable soldiers, the rest of the division either killed or injured by the Marines or fallen victim to frostbite or other ailments.[14]

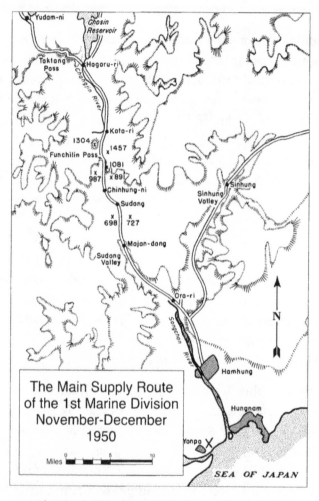

The MSR, the lifeline between the Marines at the Reservoir and resupply and reinforcement through Hungnam. It was about to become their escape route.

The Marines also had to repel constant attacks on Koto-ri and on the road running north between Koto-ri and Hagaru-ri, along which the CPVF had occupied the high ground on either side. One convoy of tanks and infantry sent from Koto-ri to augment Hagaru-ri, Task Force Drysdale, named for its commander, Royal Marine Lieutenant Colonel Douglas B. Drysdale, suffered thirty percent casualties after it was ambushed on the twenty-ninth and pinned down for two days.

While the 7th Infantry was fighting its way south from the east side of the reservoir, the Marines on the west side were holding their positions in conditions so cold that bottles of blood plasma froze and medics were afraid to cut wounded men's clothes for fear they would freeze to death. The night of the twenty-ninth began quietly, but after midnight there were localized attacks, with the Chinese driven off with few American casualties. The next day the Marines would receive new orders.

General Almond flew to Hagaru-ri to meet with Generals Smith and Barr on November 30. Speaking to his officers and seeing the wounded men and damaged equipment, he gained an appreciation for the hazard that faced his entire force, from the three battalions of the 7th Infantry on the northeast, to the two regiments of Marines to the northwest, to the constantly threatened MSR to the south. Almond abandoned his plans for the attack northwest from the area of the Chosin reservoir and urged a rapid withdrawal of X Corps forces back to Hamhung. That afternoon, X Corps headquarters issued the order for the Corps to withdraw to the Hungnam-Hamhung axis.

The CPVF made another attack that evening, long after General Almond had left, but again the preparation and the firepower at Hagaru-ri decimated the attacking Chinese. By December 1 Chinese manpower and supplies around Hagaru-ri were almost spent. Marine engineers had spent eleven days constructing a landing strip in the frozen soil at Hagaru-ri, and on that day C-47 aircraft started arriving from Yonpo Airfield outside Hungnam to carry in supplies and carry out the most seriously wounded. While the Marines had several days of rations and ammunition at Hagaru-ri, the flights added to their reserves and unburdened them from caring for those wounded who could be flown out.

General Smith had anticipated that, given the size of the enemy force opposing them, the Marines could not remain beyond their lines of supply. On November 29 he had ordered the 5th Marines to hold Yudam-ni while the 7th Marines cleared the MSR back to Hagaru-ri. Later that day he received instructions from X Corps to deploy a regiment to Hagaru-ri, which his earlier orders would facilitate. But the next day, with the movement south ordered, he modified his orders of the twenty-ninth and told both regiments both to retire to Hagaru-ri with the expectation of moving further south.

The 5th Regiment began its movement from the north and west of Yudam-ri on the thirtieth, so by December 1 the center of gravity of the force had shifted south and east. The movement involved careful coordination among the battalions of both regiments so that even as they maneuvered, they retained mutual support. The Marines then began their movement east out of Yudam-ni. As on the day before, the Marines evacuated their positions in daylight, using Marine air cover and artillery to keep the Chinese from pursuing. One battalion would move through the high ground on either side of the road to prevent the CVPF from attacking the rest of the force below. Between airstrikes and hard fighting by the infantry, the two regiments were well south of the town by nightfall.

For hours into the night, the Marines fought their way across the ridges and along the roads, inflicting horrendous casualties on the Chinese, and taking many themselves. The vehicles on the road, led by a single tank, continued to receive fire from the hillsides when it could not be suppressed by Marine infantry or air strikes, but the Marines made steady progress. To free up space in the trucks for the wounded from Yudam-ni, and the wounded yet to come, the dead Marines who had been resting in the backs of the trucks had been buried before leaving the town. The Marines fought through December 2 into December 3, making steady progress, as the first battalion formed into a column and marched into Hagaru-ri at 1900 on December 3. It was almost a day later before the last Marines arrived, the 3rd Battalion of the 7th Regiment. They had taken three days to cover the fourteen miles, and they had returned with almost all of their weapons, the major loss being nine 155-mm howitzers abandoned near the end of the march when they ran out of fuel to move them.

Breaking out from Yudam-ni.

On Saturday, December 2, the banner headline of the *San Francisco Examiner* blared, "U.N. AND CHINA IN UNDECLARED STATE OF WAR, SAYS M'ARTHUR." The sub-headline proclaimed, "500,000 Reds Now Face Allies; Enemy Resumes Big Drive," the article pointing out that this number was a considerable increase over the general's assessment of 200,000 Chinese troops earlier in the week. A few days later, the newspapers rejoiced over the news that, as the *Baltimore Sun* put it, "Two Marine Regiments Escape Trap." But despite the excitement at home, the X Corps was not out of trouble yet.

The next step of the breakout would be Hagaru-ri to Koto-ri. In setting the date for the next movement, General Smith had to balance the exhausted condition of the 5th and 7th Marines with the desire to move as soon as possible to give the CPVF the least time to fortify their positions along the MSR. December 6 was chosen as the date for the breakout from Hagaru-ri. While the men inside the perimeter appreciated the quiet nights of December 4 and December 5, they did not know why the attacks against the town had halted. As it happened, the Chinese 20th and 27th armies, badly mauled by the combat with X Corps on both sides of the reservoir, were in need of reinforcement. On November 30 the Chinese 9th Army Forces Command had ordered a fresh army of four divisions and almost forty-nine thousand men, the 26th, to march south to reinforce the 20th and the 27th. The 26th was scheduled to relieve the 20th Army and attack Hagaru-ri on December 3, but they had started a hundred miles to the north, and without trucks to transport them, the cold and snow made for slow progress. The first regiment of the 26th did not arrive until December 4, and it was not until the evening of the sixth that the 26th was ready to attack in division strength.[15]

The breakout from Hagaru-ri was preceded by a night of artillery fire along the corridor the division would start covering the next day. As in the breakout from Yudan-ni, the division could not simply march down the middle of the road and allow the CPVF to fire down on them from the surrounding heights. Instead, the breakout was another choreographed movement of mortar and artillery fire, airstrikes, infantry assaults on hilltops, and movement. A day would separate the first unit leaving the perimeter from the last, with engineers at the rear blowing up the remaining supplies and anything else in the town that could be of use to the enemy.

The X Corps had the advantages of overwhelming air superiority, with Marine Corsairs operating from nearby Yonpo airfield, as well as aircraft flying from the five US Navy aircraft carriers offshore. US and Australian Air Force aircraft provided hundreds of bomb and rocket attacks over the course of the day. At night, the Chinese launched mass-wave assaults against Marine positions in the hills, but they were repulsed. Daylight revealed an estimated eight hundred Chinese dead in front of the 2nd Battalion, 5th Marines' position alone.

The next day brought much the same pattern, with day fighting aided by air cover as long as the clear weather held, but the night bringing intense CPVF attacks. On the night of the sixth, the column on the road had to contend with roadside machine-gun positions and blown bridges, which the engineers had to repair under fire. The first Marines marched into Koto-ri at 0700 the next morning, and after a short break inside the perimeter were sent back north to provide cover for the approaching column. The last Marines, the engineers, entered the perimeter at midnight. The Marines had taken 616 casualties over the two days, including 103 men killed. The Chinese had lost more than ten times as many.

A Marine rifle company seizes the high round between Hagaru-ri and Koto-ri, essential for limiting CPVF attacks on the road below.

The more than fourteen thousand men inside the perimeter at Koto-ri now had to make the next jump twenty-five miles to Hamhung. Before the airstrip was lengthened to accept the larger C-47 transports, hundreds of the wounded had been evacuated to Yonpo using single-engine Navy TBM torpedo bombers modified to carry a few men at a time. For the rest of the X Corps that had to march out, the road to Hamhung was narrow and twisting, with a vulnerable bridge that both the 20th and the 27th CPVF armies had already blown up three times over the course of six days, and were certain to destroy again. Following intensive research and experimentation, the X Corps arranged to have 2,500-pound steel bridge sections dropped by parachute from Air Force C-119 "Flying Boxcar" aircraft. The sections would be transported by truck to the sixteen-foot gap in the road and installed under fire if necessary.

As in the successful movements before, the plan for the attack from Koto-ri to Chinhung-ni, about nine miles towards Hamhung, called for a combination of the seizure of the strategic high ground surrounding the road, air and artillery support, and the movement by road of vehicles and armor. Tanks would take up the rear of the formation since the commanders did not want the entire column stopped if one were disabled. There was not enough room on the narrow road for trucks to pass a disabled tank, but if needed, its fellow tanks at the rear could push a crippled tank off the road and continue. The 1st Battalion of the 1st Marine Regiment had patrolled the area around Koto-ri for a week, so they understood the landscape. At 0200 on a cold, snowing December 8, the first men of the 1/1 set off for their objective. The breakout from Koto-ri had begun.

Poor visibility and falling snow prevented the use of air support, so the attacking Marines relied on mortars to disrupt Chinese positions. After a day of fighting, the first objective was captured, with additional Marines and what was left of the 7th Infantry troops formed into a provisional battalion attacking south to seize additional ground towards the Funchilin Pass, where the replacement steel bridge would be placed. The snow had stopped by sunrise on the ninth. The Marines now had the benefit of close air support to add to their mortar fire, and they made steady progress. By mid-afternoon, engineers had successfully installed the bridge sections and after a minor setback due a driver's mistake, vehicles were crossing the bridge to the Hamhung side. The traffic across the bridge continued all night.

Marching out from Koto-ri. More of the same: fighting, marching, freezing, this time in a snowstorm. Since most of the fighting was at night, little was caught on film.

Following the seizure of the high ground along the MSR, CPVF opposition was surprisingly light as the last Marines in the perimeter, followed by the tanks, left Koto-ri for the last time. By this point the combinations of fierce combat and bitter cold, with temperatures the night of December 8 dropping to forty-five degrees below zero near Koto-ri, had reduced the fighting strength of the CPVF so dramatically that by December 10 the 27th Army could only muster two thousand soldiers out of the fifty thousand that had started from Manchuria, with the 20th similarly decimated. The newly arrived 26th was in better condition, but still a fraction of its strength just a week before.[16]

There had been indications that the CPVF had infiltrated the hills and towns to the west of Hamhung; indeed, the Chinese would move in force all the way to Wonsan by the end of the month, with little to show for joining their KPA brethren in the destroyed, abandoned port. But now the 1st Marine Division and the remnants of the 7th Infantry that had come down from the east side of the reservoir had the aid of the fresh troops of the 3rd Infantry, which had moved up from Wonsan a few days before to secure the Hamhung-Hungnam area. On the evening of December 5, X Corps had ordered 3rd Infantry to create a task force (Task Force Dog) at Majon-dong and just after midnight on December 7, Task Force Dog had been ordered to advance north from Majon-dong to Chinhung-ni to secure the MSR and relieve the exhausted Marines from the 1ˢᵗ Battalion, 1ˢᵗ Regiment.

As the Corps worked south, it came under occasional attack by the CPVF, costing more men, a few more trucks, and a couple of tanks, but the Marines and the 3rd Infantry (mostly the 65th Regiment) were able to fight them off while inflicting significant casualties on the Chinese.

The Marine credited with being the last to complete the breakout from Chosin had been blown off the road north of the rebuilt bridge by a Chinese anti-tank explosion and was believed by his fellow Marines to have been killed by the explosion and fall. His body had fallen down what was thought to be an inaccessible ravine and his buddies left him there. When he actually regained consciousness, he climbed back up to the road and joined a group of Korean refugees in crossing gingerly around the now-destroyed bridge (blown by the engineers) and entered Chinhung-ni to the cheers of his fellow Marines.

When the last Marine tanks rumbled onto the beach at Hungnam just before midnight on December 11, it essentially brought the last part of the breakout to a close. The Marines had taken 347 casualties during the last three days, including fifty-one killed.

––––––––

THE BATTLE of the Chosin Reservoir entered Marine legend as a great victory, earned even as the 1st Marine Division was part of a retreating X Corps. The Marines entered the Port of Hungnam for redeployment with most of their men and equipment, and though tired, were still a fighting force.

In entering combat against the United Nations forces, the Chinese had little respect for the ordinary American soldier, but had tried not to underestimate the Marines. On November 11 Chairman Mao had cabled the commander of the 27th Army, General Peng Doqing, "It is said that the U.S. 1st Marine Division has the best combat effectiveness in the American armed forces. It seems not enough for our four divisions to surround and annihilate its two regiments. You should have one to two more divisions as a reserve force." Mao had been half right. Four divisions had not been enough. But neither had six.[17] [18] [19]

Colonel Forney, in this top-secret *Special Report* written a few months after the events at Inchon, Chosin and Hungnam, commented,

> "My conclusion is that although it was not desirable from the Marine Corps point of view to operate inland in the CHOSIN RESERVOIR area, circumstances forced the Corps commander to use his best division in the area where the enemy would most probably be found. The net result of the use of the 1stMarDiv in this area was that the most dangerous area of the X Corps was taken care of by its most competent troops. It is very unfortunate that it resulted in many Marines trained to do amphibious work being lost in a land campaign in the middle of the mountains in the winter."

Forney may have had a Marine Corps bias, but he was also surrounded by Army officers and as deputy chief of staff knew the problems the rapidly augmented 7th Infantry Division faced internally. Before being subsumed into the newly created X Corps in August and landing at Inchon a month later, the 7th Infantry Division had been staffed with occupation troops from Japan and replacement troops from the US. It is doubtful the troops in occupation had kept their skills at the level of the freshly trained Marines arriving from Camp Pendleton and Camp Lejeune. The Marines also did not have to manage the large numbers of poorly trained ROK recruits added to fill out the numbers of the 7th Division. Deficiencies in training and in the ability of US and ROK soldiers to communicate with each other were painfully evident during the collapse of the 31st Infantry Battalion at Chosin. Many men fought bravely, but individual effort cannot overcome overall disorder.

Colonel Forney also observed serious deficiencies in the X Corps headquarters staff. In his report he observed,

> "Numerous orders of which the CG [Commanding General] were unaware were being issued by staff officers, many of these involved units of major subordinate commands. The type of officer involved in the issuance of these orders was usually a general staff officer highly trained in staff procedures but without mature judgement that comes from troop command ... CG of X Corps ordered, about the 15th of November, that no orders that involved elements of major commands would be issued without his specific approval, or the approval of C of S [chief of staff] ... I did not preach against the general staff system when I was with X Corps, but I could see it falling down in respect to individual staff officers acting ill advisedly."

Overall, the Marines had succeeded by: superior leadership, planning and training; far greater firepower, including Marine air; and infinitely superior logistics support. With very rare exceptions, Marines didn't panic in the face of surprise attacks or what might have seemed unlimited waves of Chinese troops, and they were generally well supplied with rations and ammunition.

In contrast, while they fought earnestly, the Chinese troops were grossly undersupplied in food and ammunition, with many soldiers going days without eating even while on the march. What they did eat might be a few potatoes or yams, or a dried wheat cake, hardly enough nourishment for men in battle. Many of the troops had inadequate cold-weather gear, so much so that the Chinese would raid American corpses for boots and gloves, along with food and cigarettes, before they would take weapons and ammunition.

An example of Chinese attrition the face of combat and cold is the 26th Army's 76th Division, new to the battlefield on December 7. Already fatigued after days of forced march, between hunger, the cold, and X Corps firepower,[20] just three days of fighting reduced the Division from fifty-four infantry companies to nine by December 10.

In total, PRC records indicate the 9th Army of the Chines People's Volunteer Force of the People''s Liberation Army suffered more than 80,000 casualties during that winter in Korea, 30,700 in combat and 50,000 from the cold, disease, and malnutrition.[21] That's not to say the Marines didn't suffer from the cold, for they surely did. Between November 27 and December 24, the Marines suffered 4,395 combat casualties, including 718 killed, but also 7,338 non-combat casualties, primarily frostbite. [22]

Perhaps the final commentary on the experience of the 1st Marine Division compared to other units of the X Corps is in the distribution of combat casualties. Over the period from November 27 to December 10, the X Corps would record a total of 705 men killed in action (KIA), 3,251 wounded in action (WIA), and 4,779 missing in action (MIA).[23] Missing included men taken prisoner, unable to return to their unit in time to be counted, or men left wounded or dead on the battlefield. This tally counted 1st Marine Division's KIA and WIA as 2,545, but just 76 MIA.

In contrast, the 7th Infantry Division casualty count shows 255 KIA and WIA, but ten times as many missing, 2,505 MIA among the US soldiers. A similar pattern is apparent among the ROK soldiers attached to the 7th Infantry, 41 KIA and WIA, but 1,560 missing in action.

And this was not simply a Marine/Army issue. Over the same period the 3rd Infantry Division, the ROK soldiers attached to the 3rd Division, and the two major ROK units integrated into X Corps, the ROK Capital Division and the 3rd ROK Division, suffered a combined 939 KIA/WIA and 581 MIA. Without doubt these losses occurred under different conditions than the hell that was east of Chosin, but the conclusion was inescapable; the 7th had lost control of their battlefield on the east side of the reservoir.

10

HUNGNAM

The port of Hungnam (Huengnam), now firmly part of the Democratic People's Republic of Korea, lies about thirty miles north of the larger harbor at Wonsan, and about six miles southeast of the center of the city of Hamhung. The harbor is at the very northeastern end of an alluvial plain that interrupts the march of mountains that dominate the eastern coast of Korea, and the port and its accompanying industry (primarily fertilizer production) were developed by the occupying Japanese before World War II. The coast bends at the town of Hungnam to the southwest, passing through the fishing village of Soho-jin into a small cape, Chakto-ri, pointing south, so that the small harbor is protected from the north and west. Through this tiny harbor would have to be shipped the bulk of the X Corps, men and machines, as it evacuated from Korea north of the 38th parallel.

By the beginning of December, Hungnam and Hamhung were quickly becoming very crowded places. General Almond had ordered the withdrawal of the 7th Infantry Division's 17th Regiment by road and rail from the Hyesnjin area along the Yalu River on November 27.[1] The first units arrived in Hamhung late on December 4 and the entire regiment was assembled at Hamhung two days later. By the time the 1st Marine Division and the remainder of the 7th Infantry had arrived from Hamhung, and the rest of the 3rd Infantry and some ROK units converged on the port city, there were approximately one hundred thousand soldiers and Marines and 18,000 vehicles in the environs.[2] They were joined by thousands, soon to swell to tens of thousands, of Korean civilians escaping the Chinese and North Korean forces.

The ruined city of Hungnam, with some some of the hundreds of thousands of tons of supplies and vehicles shipped in for X Corps's use. Now they had to be shipped back out.

In addition to accommodating people, Hungnam was an ever-expanding supply dump. There were seventeen thousand drums of motor gasoline, diesel fuel, lubricating oil, and 115/145 octane aviation gasoline to be transported. There were thousands of tons of other supplies that would have to go with the Corps: 1,800 tons of Class I (rations and other consumables and personal items); 500 tons of Classes II (individual equipment, clothing, tents, etc.) and IV (construction and barrier equipment, lumber, sandbags, barbed wire, etc.); and 3,500 tons of Class V (ammunitions, missiles, bombs, etc.).[3] Motor gas for the Corps' trucks and jeeps had been in such short supply that as late as December 5 and 6, motor gasoline was still being airlifted into Yonpo from Japan, 1,500 barrels on the fifth and 2,000 barrels on the sixth, along with 2,000 barrels offloaded from a ship at the Hungnam docks. Now it all had to be reloaded or destroyed.[4] All told, 350,000 "measurement tons"[5] of supplies were to be embarked at Hungnam, equivalent to fourteen million cubic feet.[6]

The embarkation of X Corps from Hungnam, an "Amphibious Landing in Reverse,"[7] was, like the two previous landings, Inchon and Wonsan, planned on an extremely compressed schedule. Colonel Forney, in a chapter of a confidential[8] "Special After-Action Report" entitled, *X Corps in North Korea-General*, provided some insight into the early stages of planning for the withdrawal.[9]

"On December 6th, intentions of withdrawal by the Theatre became apparent to the X Corps, because we received the NAVFE Operations Order [116-50] with task Organization which readied naval units for withdrawal of X Corps. Also a Far East Air Force Operations Order was received directing them to support the withdrawal. These were of value only in that they were of a warning nature. The detailed plans or final decision by the X Corps commander could not be given until he received information as to the missions of the X Corps in SOUTH KOREA and, in fact, whether the withdrawal would be made to SOUTH KOREA or to JAPAN."

X Corps did not have to wait long. Colonel Forney continued,

"On the 9th of December, the CG of the Corps received necessary orders which described his duties on withdrawal. These were that the X Corps would assemble in SOUTH KOREA in the USAN-PUSAN-MASAN area and report on arrival to the CG8thArmy."

With the orders in place, it was now necessary to figure out how to protect the port, the ships, and the embarking troops and their supplies from approaching PRC forces. One option was to have the 1st ROK Corps, the 1st Marine Division, the 7th Infantry Division, and the 3rd Infantry Division form into "pie-shaped sectors" so that they would withdraw in parallel. But after the battles at Chosin and their fighting retreats, their combat effectiveness was unequal, so General Almond's staff arrived at a different plan. In Colonel Forney's words,

> "The 1stMarDiv could not be refitted while occupying a portion of the perimeter and was well battleworn. The 7thInfDiv had lost two-thirds of an RCT in the Chosin Reservoir; the remaining portion of the division was having difficulties in assembling. Therefore, the Corps Commander decided to withdraw in the order: 1stROKCorps, 1stMarDiv, 7thINfDiv, 3rdInfDiv."

Tents outside Hungnam, a luxury some of the exhausted Marines enjoyed for a short time before boarding their transports.

The 3rd Infantry Division, with the only fresh troops in the Corps, was given the job of holding off the enemy while the pocket around the harbor at Hungnam slowly shrank as the soldiers, Marines and supplies were embarked.

As valuable as these troops would prove to be, the X Corps had almost lost the 3rd Infantry from Hungnam just a few days before. Colonel Forney's reported,

"On the morning of December 1, the Corps received orders for the 3dInfDiv to assemble in the WONSAN area and be prepared for further operations, possibly to join the 8th Army overland. This order was executed by the Corps Commander immediately and at the same time it was decided to send me and the Corps G-2 [the Corps intelligence officer][10] to Tokyo on the next day to explain the implications of the withdrawal of the 3rdInfDiv from X Corps. Accordingly, on the 2nd, the G-2 and I went to TOKYO by air, reported to the CofS of the Far East Theatre, Major General Doyle HICKEY, U. S. Army. By noon of the third, the Theatre HQ had released the 3rdInfDiv back to the X Corps."[11]

General Almond put his newly restored troops to good use. In Forney's words,

"The Corps Commander then ordered the 3rdInfDiv back to the HAMHUNG area and directed it to push up the MSR with the objectives of protecting the MSR, assisting the 1stMarDIv and relieving the 1stBn of the 1stMarines at the foot of the plateau."

As other X Corps units loaded, the 3rd Infantry would play a key role in the defense of the port and the men, ships, and supplies located there.

Compared to Pusan, which had multiple docks comprising more than 39,000 linear feet at which to load and unload ships, and Wonsan, which had 10,500 linear feet of piers and wharves (albeit with half having been destroyed by US bombing), the harbor at Hungnam was much smaller.[12] The four wharves at Hungnam combined provided less than six thousand linear feet, and the water depth limited the sized of ships that could be moored.[13] The whole inner harbor, from the tip of the breakwater to the innermost wharf, enclosed an area of less than half a square mile. In theory, nine destroyer-sized ships could anchor inside the harbor over the mud-and-sand bottom, but in run practice all ships would have to anchor outside the harbor. On the other hand, the tides at Hungnam were negligible compared to Inchon, with a tidal range of less than one foot, so the harbor could be used and transited at any hour.[14]

US Navy F2H-2 Banshee fighters fly over an empty Hungnam in 1953, long after the evacuation. At the lower left is the main dock with its breakwater protecting the harbor. On either side are beaches used for loading LSTs, including those with refugees. The Songchon River is visible at the upper left.

The small tidal swing also meant Hungnam could be heavily mined by the retreating North Koreans. Minesweeping commenced in early November using the minesweepers that had completed their work the month before in Wonsan. No doubt the experience gained at Wonsan on sweeping combined fields of moored-contact and bottom-influence mines paid off, and by the time of the evacuation, three swept channels were available through the minefield. One channel approached from the south, following the contour of the land by approaching first west and then north into a swept anchorage south of the breakwater. This was designated as the "South Fire Support Channel." To the north of the Fire Support Channel, the main swept channel for shipping approached from the east before joining a broad swept area north and east of the cape. To the south of this swept area was the entrance to the anchorage and the inner harbor. To the north of the main channel and following the coast north of the cape branched the North Fire Support Channel. The UN forces would put the fire-support channels to good use, particularly during the final phases of the embarkation. The channels were swept and enlarged over the course of the month to provide easier access to the anchorage and the inner harbor, particularly at night.[15]

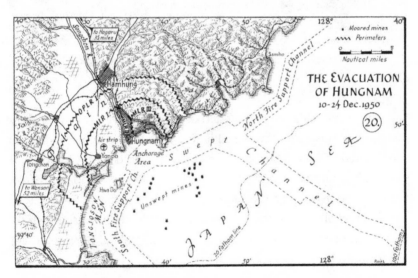

Map showing the mine-swept main channel and north and south gunfire channels. The swept area would be enlarged during the month.

Enlarging the swept channel would not help a ship blindly steaming through the remaining minefield, as the *Senzan Maru* did on December 6. The ship left Japan, her holds full of flour for X Corps' bakers, without any information on the minefield, nor a chart of the swept channel. She struck a moored contact mine just after three in the morning but made her way to the inner anchorage, her number one (forward) hold flooded and her number two filling with seawater. A day later she was still afloat, but the waters of the harbor were just two feet below her bulwarks at the bow. It soon became clear the flour in her number two hold would need to be unloaded before she could be salvaged, and stevedores from the port were sent to help unload. Free flour was offered to any USN ship that would send a working party; the rest was tossed overboard. Patched, pumped and level at the waterline, she left for Japan on the eighteenth.[16]

Senzan Maru, on the right, after she blundered into the minefield within sight of the port (visible in the background). Note the minesweeper in the foreground on the left.

So, how would this massive undertaking, the movement of all these men and all this cargo through this tiny port in just fourteen days, be coordinated? General Almond named his trusted deputy chief of staff, Colonel Forney, as control officer, with overall responsibility for the embarkation aspects of the redeployment. Reporting to Forney were an executive officer and five sections that would execute aspects of the activity and coordination: operations, liaison, loading, movement, and ration.[17]

The operations section, headed by Major Richard W. Shutt, USMC, "maintained a file of units, with their personnel strength, equipment and tonnage. Files were built around every unit within the X Corps." The liaison section, headed by Major Jack R. Munday, USMC, "furnished the Control Officer with the shipping as it became available and furnished the link between the Control Officer and the Navy for the management of the shipping within the harbor area." The loading section, headed by Major Kieran R. Highland, USMC, prepared plans for the loading of a specific unit onto a specific ship. The movement section, headed by Lieutenant Colonel Harry E. Mizell, USA, controlled the traffic carrying the unit from their temporary encampment to the staging area for loading. The ration section, headed by Captain William C. Cool, USA, provided rations for the troops as they boarded their ship.

All of these officers and their staffs were housed in a "shed in the dock area." Engineers quickly partitioned the shed into offices and installed plexiglass in place of the shattered windows. Colonel Forney commented parenthetically that, "This plastic glass was very handy that, after explosions all that was required was to tack it up; you didn't have to put together the pieces."[18] The Control Organization received other help from X Corps: the quartermaster provided ration kits for the staff; the medical officer bunks and blankets; the communications officer telephones; the transportation officer jeeps for a motor pool; and the personnel officer provided typewriters, adding machines, paper, and thirteen clerk-typists and stenographers to maintain records.

Liaison was critical, since offshore there was another key player, Task Force (TF) 90, commanded by Admiral Doyle. As the *CTF 90 After-Action Report* said,

"On 28 November, on being alerted by ComNavFE as to the possible need for future redeployment operation, CTF 90 commenced planning for the redeployment of U.N. forces in Korea either as an administrative outloading or as a general emergency. CTF 90 then prepared and issued OpOrder 19-50 to units of TF 990 for planning purposes. Basically, this plan provided for one half of the amphibious force to conduct redeployment operations on the East Coast of Korea under RADM Doyle, COmPhibGru ONE and CTF 90; the other half to conduct redeployment operations on the West Coast under RADM THACKERY, ComPhibGur THREE."[19]

The next day, November 29, COMNAVFE told CTF 90 that the perilous situation in northern Korea,

"made it desirable for ships of TF 90 to be on six hours notice either in Korean waters or at SASEBO, Japan. Accordingly, all amphibious units in Japan were directed to proceed to SASEBO"

at the far northwestern corner of Kyushu. From here, due south of the Korean peninsula, ships could easily proceed from safety to ports on either the east or west coasts of Korea. The report continued,

"On 30 November the steadily deteriorating ground situation in Korea necessitated the immediate deployment of all units of CTF 90 to Korea. The ground situation on the West Coast appeared to be more critical and amphibious units were deployed to provide for approximately two-thirds to be on that coast, except for transports which were deployed on a fifty-fifty basis. The latter was dictated by the fact that transport types are more readily usable at HUNGNAM than at INCHON."

Admiral Doyle and his staff had freshly experienced the complications that a small port with thirty-foot tidal swings meant for loading non-LST-type ships. Unlike an LST, a conventional ship was not designed to sit and load on the mud. The LSTs used at Inchon to load the 8th Army for transportation to Pusan would be available later for use at Hungnam.

Over the next week, CTF 90 staff planned the naval aspects of the embarkation and assigned mine-sweeping forces to enlarge the anchorage area off the inner port at Hungnam, create swept channels for gunfire support, and widen the swept channel between the harbor and the Sea of Japan. When the order was received on the eighth that embarkation was imminent, and then on the ninth that the redeployment would be to the Pusan area, CTF 90 had assumed the following responsibilities: coordinate the redeployment with General Almond and his staff, provide sealift between Hungnam and Pusan, control air and naval gunfire support at Hungnam, perform small-scale redeployment operations for ROK forces or UN prisoners of war as needed, protect shipping en route, and provide naval blockade and gunfire support elsewhere along the coast.

Embarked aboard his flagship, the *Mount McKinley*, Admiral Doyle commanded a fleet of more than seventy-five ships, including eight transports, eleven US Navy and twenty-seven Japanese LSTs, twenty cruisers, destroyers and other ships for gunfire support and assorted tugs, and repair and salvage vessels. In addition, he would have access to whatever time-chartered MSTS ships like the *Meredith Victory* were available in the theater, which themselves would number in the dozens.

General Almond's command diary notes that on December 10 he visited Colonel Forney at his office in the port and told him to "study and brief the shipping requirements to embark the X Corps."[20] The term "study" is a curious entry, since the *CTF 90 Action Report* and the *COMPHIBGU1 War Diary* indicated that multiple planning conferences had already been held on the ninth with representatives of the X Corps, including General Almond, culminating in a final staff conference and the approval of the loading plans that night.[21] Indeed, at 0800 on the tenth, CTF 90 officially initiated the maritime aspects of the plan.[22]

Aside from the CTF 90 staff conferences, Colonel Forney had certainly already thought about the subject. One hundred thousand soldiers and Marines might not seem like a large number, but *Operation Plan 116-50* had totaled all of the ships in theater as of November 12, transport and combatant,[23] and estimated that the use of every ship, 140 in total, would carry 100,300 personnel. Using just the cargo ships and troop transports (not the warships) would accommodate 68,250.[24] This did not include any capacity for the hundreds of thousands of tons of vehicles and supplies that needed to be embarked for a redeployment; indeed, Colonel Forney estimated before the evacuation started that they would "need shipping to move 400,000 measurement tons and approximately 15,000 vehicles, and that our personnel were, as the strength figures showed, between 110,000 and 120,000, depending on casualties and the success of their evacuation."[25]

By the date of the actual redeployment it was clear that all of these ships would not be available; indeed, half of the transports and two-thirds of the landing craft were supporting the redeployment of the 8th Army from Inchon on the other side of the peninsula. Fortunately, there was no need to load the combatants, "Dunkirk style," in a panic. According to Almond's diary entry, Forney told the general that "turn around" shipping would be needed; that is, ships that loaded early in the embarkation would be needed back in Hungnam after their initial offload in Pusan.[26]

Just as X Corps had begun to outload men and supplies, Captain La Rue and the *Meredith Victory* appeared at Hungnam on December 10, her holds filled in Yokohama with ten thousand tons of aviation fuel in barrels bound for Yonpo. *Meredith Victory* had already been at sea when the order to halt resupply had been promulgated. Given the evacuation of the Hungnam-Hamhung area and the abandonment of Yonpo, the stocks in the fuel dump at the field were more than adequate, and on the eleventh the ship was sent to unload her cargo at Pusan.[27] She was instructed to be prepared to return to Hungnam in short order.[28]

December 10 also saw the evacuation of remaining UN troops and equipment from Wonsan. Naval gunfire from the cruiser *St. Paul* and the destroyers *Hank*, *Sperry*, and *Zellars* held the KPA and CPVF at bay as the last troops and equipment were removed, with some troops flown to K-9 airfield from Kalmo Pando airfield outside Wonsan. The remaining stores on land were destroyed. The *St. Paul* and her escorts would take up station off Hungnam.

The *Zellars* and the *Sperry* stayed on to support an ongoing salvage and security operation at Wonsan. *Pledge* and *Pirate*, the two minesweepers that had been lost on October 11, contained classified cryptography materials.[29] The Navy did not want these to be compromised to North Korea, China, or the Soviet Union, so a destroyer was ordered to maintain the locations of the lost ships under constant surveillance after their sinking. It was not until December 1 that enough mines around the minesweepers could be cleared so that divers could descend the ninety-six feet to the wrecks to search for the crypto materials. By that time the hulls were already buried two-feet into the muddy bottom, so acting on orders of COMNAVFE, the two wrecks were demolished using more than a dozen tons of explosives, along with eight depth charges for good measure.

Meanwhile, the out-loading of X Corps at Hungnam was accelerating. At a given time, Colonel Forney would determine which unit should be loaded based upon the tactical requirements and the available shipping. Even though the 1st ROK Corps was ostensibly scheduled to load first, their light equipment meant that Forney felt he could "sandwich" them in between embarkations of the 1st Marine Division. Between Forney and the liaison section, incoming ships would be assigned to an open berth, a list of which was maintained by the liaison section. Liaison would provide CTF 90 with the daily shipping requirements and attempt to schedule the arrivals of shipping with CTF 90 so that ships were always available to be loaded at any available berth; that is, no berth would be allowed to stay empty for long. This also included beaches to the north and south of the wharves where LSTs could be beached and boarded.

When Forney determined that a unit should be embarked, he selected the ship and his staff informed a representative of the unit when and where they would be loaded. The movement section coordinated traffic to transport the unit to a staging area and then on to the loading area, and the ration section delivered rations to the troops as they boarded the ship. The loading section, which had prepared the plans for the unit's loading onto the ship, would send "checkers" to visit the ship while it was being loaded and provide an estimate to the operations section for when the loading would be complete. This would, in turn, generate a "chop time" (CHange of OPerational control)[30] when the ship should leave the berth and begin her voyage to Pusan. The liaison section would relay the chop time to TF 90, and the operations section would inform the next unit to be loaded where and when they would be embarked, repeating the process.

While the control officer and his staff were performing these steps on land, there was another dance at sea and in the harbor. Once the chop time arrived and the ship's lines were cast off, CTF 90 had cognizance. CTF 90 had assigned a port director on land and had staffed the liaison section in Colonel Forney's control office. Since there were no operable tug boats at Hungnam when X Corps had arrived, CTF 90 had brought two tugs, YTB-415 and YTB-420.[31] These were essential to mooring the transports as close as fifty feet bow-to-stern in winds as high as forty knots, so each tug had two crews and they operated almost continuously for the duration of the redeployment.[32] CTF 90 also provided a turbo-electric destroyer escort, the USS *Foss*, to power X Corps facilities at the port using her powerful main-propulsion generators.

A Secota-class YTB like the indispensable tugs at Hungnam.

CTF 90 assigned a beachmaster unit to manage, in coordination with the X Corps control organization and the CTF 90 liaison officer, the arrival, beaching, loading, and departure of LSTs at the beach area east of Dock 4. The eleven beaching slots were divided between Green Beach One, with space for four LSTs, and Green Beach Two, with space

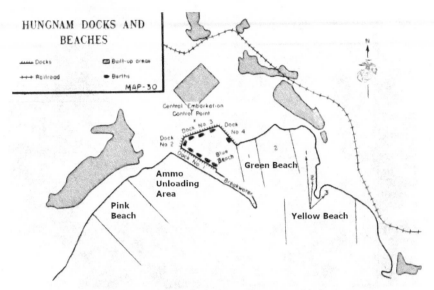

Docks and beaches used for embarkation at Hungnam, with the inner port, *Blue Beach*, in the middle.

for seven. Additional space was available at Dock Four for three LSTs to moor bow-on if more LST berths were needed. CTF 90 also provided an experienced LST pilot to aid the less-experienced crews, such as those on the Japanese LSTs, in effective beaching. Evidence of how important the LSTs and return shipping were to the redeployment was that eleven US and twenty-six Japanese LSTs beached and loaded a total of eighty-one times during the two-week period.[33] ROK LSTs provided even more lift.

Twenty-four-hour operation meant that ships had to navigate the lanes cleared in the minefield day or night. CTF 90 stationed a frigate at Buoy One of the main swept channel, which was at the entrance and near the hundred-fathom line, another frigate at Buoy Four, near the fifty-fathom line, and a third frigate at Buoy Seven, where the main channel and the northern gunfire channel met, to escort transports at night or if they were uncertain about navigating the channel. On December 18 the lighthouse on the tip of the cape at Chakto-ri lost power, and one of the YTBs was stationed there at night, close to buoy eleven, for the rest of the operation.[34]

View from Pink Beach, showing trucks, barrels of fuel and other supplies waiting to be loaded. At the right an LCM is being loaded with a crane before lightering the cargo to a waiting freighter. At the center an LST loads from the beach. The control frigate anchored near Buoy Seven is visible at the upper right.

CTF 90 was responsible for acquiring and scheduling the ships for Hungnam, so the task force maintained its own operations section to manage the comings and goings of US Military transports as well as time-chartered commercial ships like the *Meredith Victory*, including assigning anchorages and issuing docking instructions. For the military ships,[35] the operations section prepared the sailing orders, while the time-chartered ships operated under sailing orders issued by the MSTS. Because CTF 90 might not have a complete picture of the capabilities of an incoming MSTS ship, the task force borrowed a utility boat from the Army and anchored it at the entrance to the harbor so that an officer could establish first-hand

> "the loaded status of the ship, the capacity of the vessel, the amount and condition of gear and loading equipment, and the peculiarities and deficiencies of the ship if any. This information was reported immediately to CTF 90 Operations by radio. All ships were directed to be ready for

movement on immediate notice, two-hours-notice, or later notice, depending on the situation. As soon as CTF 90 Operations discussed current requirement with the X Corps Embarkation Control, a prospective docking or loading anchorage assignment was made and ships were directed to rig gear on the proper side and uncover hatches."[36]

Transports anchored outside the breakwater awaiting their turn to load at the dock, or being loaded from lighters alongside.

If the ship were sent to an anchorage instead of immediately to a berth, the master would receive instructions on whether to maintain steam to replace a ship that was imminently leaving a berth or, if not, when she should expect to be prepared to leave the anchorage. Usually, ships were placed on two-hour notice.

Since most masters were not familiar with the harbor, a highly competent US Army harbor pilot, Captain Merle R. Dawson,[37] would board the ship while the ship was still at anchor or when it reached the breakwater. The CTF 90 *Action Report* specifically praised Dawson for this skill.

The challenges of the waters around Hungnam were demonstrated already on the night of the tenth when the SS *Enid Victory*, outbound for Pusan, ran hard aground around midnight off the lighthouse on Chakto-ri east of the inner harbor.[38] After a day's work, she was refloated and the master, after sounding the bilges and holds, declared her seaworthy, leaving for Pusan on the morning of the twelfth. In fairness, *Enid Victory* was one of the first ships to sail loaded from the port, in her case with trucks and heavy equipment from the Corps engineers.

As Colonel Forney's control organization and CTF 90 planned and executed their aspects of the redeployment, the individual Army and Marine units were responsible for ensuring their men and equipment were prepared for loading. Each man carried one filled canteen and was issued "C" rations. Each Marine or soldier carried his weapon(s) and a normal combat load of ammunition and at the unit level their camp equipment, such as tents and stoves, were also embarked with them. Trucks were to have their fuel tanks three-quarters full and to carry an extra five-gallon "jerry can" on the vehicle. Drivers were to stay with their vehicles.[39]

The war did not stop just because the X Corps was withdrawing. CPVF and KPA soldiers were active and fortifying in the environs of Hamhung and Hungnam. The protection of the port demonstrated a finely choreographed effort among the four major combat elements of the X Corps as they were out-loaded. The initial disposition for the defense of the perimeter saw the 3rd Infantry Division maintaining its control to the west of the port, the 7th Infantry Division holding the northeast and the 1st ROK Corps taking position along the coast, north of the village of Soho-jin. The Marines played little role in the defense of the port, completing their movement from Hamhung to Hungnam on the evening of December 11 and staging close to the port for loading. Aside from an easily repulsed fifty-person attack on a Marine convoy that day, their fighting was done for now.

In general, the time-chartered ships were loaded at one of seven berths, four on Dock One, two on Dock Three and one on Four. In many cases, to increase the harbor's capacity, ships were double-berthed, with a second ship moored outboard to a ship moored to the dock. The outboard ship was then loaded from lighters, typically small landing craft[40] that had loaded at one of the LST beaching areas to the north of the docks. In order that the presence of a ship moored outboard did not inhibit the passage of the inner ship when she was ready to leave for Pusan, the port directors developed a technique by which the tugs could move the outboard ship to a berth alongside an adjacent ship in just fifteen minutes and resume loading.[41] The tugs would then assist the inner ship in leaving its berth.

Aerial view of Hungnam during the evacuation. Four Victory-sized ships are loading at Dock One in the foreground. Proceeding clockwise around the harbor, the destroyer escort Foss *is moored at Dock Two providing electrical power for X Corps facilities in the port. Continuing, two more ships are loading at Dock Three and another is loading at Dock Four for a total of seven. St the same time, LSTs are loading at the adjacent beaches.*

For safety, ammunition was generally not loaded at a berth, but rather at an anchorage. A small landing craft[42] would load ammunition from the beach south of Dock 1 and lighter it to the ship for loading. Much of the ammunition, particularly towards the end of the redeployment, was loaded directly onto LSTs beached at the ammunition loading area.

Military transports were also usually loaded from lighters while at anchor, with the men climbing from lighters[43] to doors opened on the sides of the ships. Their unit's ammunition (including small arms and grenades) and smaller equipment was then loaded using the ship's cranes into the holds fore and aft the berthing area of the troop ship. Vehicles and heavy equipment went separately by cargo ship. The larger troop transports, owned by the Army but manned by Merchant Marine crews and managed by the MSTS, could accommodate as many

Transports anchored at Hungnam on December 10, with the cruiser USS Rochester joining them in the foreground. The ship at the center with twin stacks is a troop transport.

LST loading from Green Beach on December 13. In the background are ships at Dock One and the *Foss* at Dock Two. *Canada Mail* is on the right at Dock Four.

as five thousand men with berthing, sanitary, and galley facilities for a long ocean voyage. Indeed, the *General Sultan* sailed with 2,381 Marines 0600 on the morning of the thirteenth and the *General Randall* sailed with 6,182 seven hours later. The last ship committed to the Marines, LST 845, sailed just before midnight on the fourteenth.[44] Some supporting elements remained for coordinating close-air support on the perimeter, and there were those Marines who supported the control organization, but the vast majority of 1st Marine Division was essentially out of Hungnam and bound for the Pusan area by December 15.

As it turned out, the decision to evacuate the Marines first was well-founded. The senior medical officer aboard the *General Collins* commented that, "seventy five (75) percent" of the troops evacuated from Hungnam "suffered one or more respiratory complaints."[45] The chaplain's report for the *Collins* said,

"On Wednesday, 13 December we sailed from Hungnam for Pusan, Korea. On board were ... 4,826 Marines. A part of those remaining who had fought their way out of the trap at the Chosen [*sic*] Reservoir. I was told later by Army personnel ashore that staging areas had been set up to receive these men when they got in, but they did not stop. They marched right on by to board small craft waiting to bring them to the ship. Sick call was a nearly twenty-four (24) hour a day project for the ship's medical department and the USN doctors attached to the Marines. Nearly every man needed some kind of medical attention."[46]

Marines boarding their transport ships from a lighter the easy way, left, via a boarding ladder, or the hard way, right, climbing a cargo net.

As Colonel Forney had planned, the South Korean forces were evacuated at the same time as the Marines. The 1st ROK Corps was divided along the coast between Hungnam and Songjin, 100 miles north. X Corps chose to embark the elements of the ROK Corps at Songjin directly, rather than load them onto southbound trains and add to the crowding at Hungnam. Despite the lack of enemy activity in the area, 7th Fleet stationed the destroyers *Maddox*[47] and *Samuel N. Moore* offshore to provide naval gunfire if the CPVF or KPA attacked.[48] The

Navy transport *Noble* loaded 3,000 ROK personnel, including hundreds of casualties and twenty-eight Korean nurses.[49] Moore-McCormack's SS *Mormacmoon*, a 7,939 gross-ton C-3 ship built in 1940, embarked five thousand 1st ROK Corps troops at Songjin, and the South Atlantic Steamship Line's SS *Southwind*, a C-2 ship built as the USS *Caswell*, embarked a further 4,800. The ROK LST BM 665 and Japanese LST Q036 loaded the Corps equipment from the beach.[50] The ships left Songjin on the morning of the tenth for Pusan.

The remaining eighteen thousand ROK personnel of the ROK 1st Corps and the Capital Division would be transported from Hungnam to Samchock, a little more than two hundred nautical miles south of Hungnam on the coast due east of Suwon.[51] On the fifteenth, the port was loading ten ships at the docks (three at outboard berths loading ROK personnel and cargo from lighters) along with the ships loading at anchor. By midday on the seventeenth, with high winds and heavy seas, the transports carrying the ROK troops, formed as Task Element 90.04 and departed for the beaches near Samchok.[52] The offloading of troops proceeded largely without event, but the vehicles and cargo were delayed because of the persistent swell from the day before.[53]

Those high winds on the seventeenth had little effect on loading in the inner harbor at Hungnam, but they wreaked havoc on the smaller vessels loading the ships at anchor. By noon the winds were blowing forty knots, and, combined with the low temperature (twenty degrees Fahrenheit), operations in the harbor were perilous. Four small landing craft[54] broke down and were blown into the minefield, but not before the men on board could be rescued. Small boat operations were temporarily suspended. Transports dragged their anchors, and the YTBs were kept busy helping drifting and disabled ships. By 1800 the winds had eased and the port returned to its normal, measured pace.[55]

THE OUT-LOADING of the 1st ROK Corps required a redistribution of X Corps forces at the perimeter, all the more critical since there was increasing enemy activity. After days of minor or desultory attacks, on December 15 the number and scale of attacks increased significantly. The 7th Infantry Regiment of the 3rd Division suffered five attacks northwest of Hamhung, and the division's 65th Regiment was attacked north of the city. A patrol by the 1st ROK Corps reported enemy contact near Taejo, about ten miles up the coast. While these attacks were successfully repelled by small-arms fire and close-air support, that same day the X Corps took the opportunity to start shrinking the perimeter, as planned, to a rough arc. "Phase 2" centered on the mouth of the Songchon River, which flowed into the Sea of Japan between Hungnam and Yonpo. The new perimeter excluded the now-emptied Hamhung, but maintained Hungnam and Yonpo within its protection. The next day, as the 3rd Infantry Division relieved the last elements of the ROK 1st Corps, the 7th Infantry withdrew to the Phase 2 lines, and by the evening of the seventeenth, the 3rd Infantry joined them patrolling the new perimeter.[56]

Now it was time for the 7th Infantry Division to embark. Elements of the 7th had begun embarking as early the thirteenth, but now the division could board in earnest and start their three-hundred nautical mile voyage to Pusan. More than half of the 18,274[57] men of the 7th Infantry Division sailed on three troop ships on the nineteenth and twentieth.[58] When the last ship carrying remaining soldiers, vehicles, and cargo sailed early in the morning of December 21, the 7th Infantry Division could finally put the trauma of Chosin behind them.

Soldiers of the 7th Infantry Division board an LCM for
passage to their troopship.

The redeployment was now entering a new stage. On the eighteenth Yonpo airfield had been abandoned, the perimeter now pulled closer to Hungnam, but not before X Corps engineers installed booby traps and mines at the field. The same day saw multiple contact with CPVF forces, starting with an early-morning attack against the 15th Infantry Regiment estimated to involve four-to-five hundred enemy soldiers. Naval gunfire and army artillery were effective at breaking up the attack, as it was for two other attacks over the course of the day. December 19 opened with "the heaviest attacks to date on the X Corps perimeter."[59] Again, intense artillery and naval gunfire, along with small-arms fire by the infantry, broke up the attack, with a POW reporting that, "an all out enemy attack in regimental strength had been reduced to battalion size [reduced by half or more] by naval gunfire before reaching the perimeter."[60]

As the 7th Infantry was completing its out-loading, the 3rd Infantry Division was beginning theirs, with the 17th Regimental Combat Team beginning embarkation on December 19. Where three divisions had held the perimeter just a week before, now three regiments would do the same, as the remaining troops made their planned withdrawal to the final phase line. The shrunken perimeter now extended five thousand yards from the center of Hungnam, on the southwest now nestling east of the Songchon River, and on the east just on the other side of Soho-jin to embrace the town with its refugees. The 7th RCT defended the western end, the 65th RCT the middle and the 15th RCT the eastern.

That afternoon, General Almond and his staff (less Deputy Chief of Staff Forney, who remained ashore as control officer) joined Admiral Doyle aboard the *Mount Whitney* and established the X Corps command post on board the ship. Operational control for the land defense of the port now rested with the commander of the 3rd Infantry Division, Major General Robert H. Soule.

Late in the evacuation, nearly every spot on the Pink Beach is occupied by LSTs and smaller landing craft. Note that the beach is now largely empty of supplies.

One of the keys to the success of the evacuation from Hungnam was the careful balance between service troops, such as the 2nd Special Engineer Battalion that operated the port and the soldiers, sailors, and Marines that operated small craft for lighterage, and the infantry and artillery that secured the port from outside. As those "trigger pullers" steadily boarded transports, more of the burden of the protection of the port fell on the ships of Task Force 77 under the control of the commander of the 7th Fleet, Vice Admiral Arthur Dewey Struble.

Naval gunfire support off Hungnam had started on December 3 with Admiral Doyle ordering the destroyer *English* to Hungnam.[61] The cruiser *St. Paul* and destroyer *Hank* joined *English* on the tenth, and after a few days the armada off Hungnam grew to include the cruiser *Rochester* and the destroyers *Borie* and *Massey*. The destroyer *Lind* also supported calls for gunfire at Hungnam before being sent with the *Massey* to cover the ROK embarkation at Songjin.[62] These ships were able to range up and down the coast, firing their five-inch guns with a range of roughly ten miles. The cruisers' eight-inch guns hurled a shell about six miles further. Between 0800 on the nineteenth and 0800 on the twentieth, the cruisers fired 316 eight-inch rounds, and the cruisers and destroyers combined fired 1,207 five-inch high-explosive rounds and 390 five-inch illumination rounds.[63] The latter were particularly valuable since they allowed soldiers on patrol or at strong points to spot and target CPVF movements at night.

Cruiser USS St. Paul *bombards targets near Hungnam on the night of December 21.*

———

THE WINDS WERE calm before sunrise on December 20 as the *Meredith Victory* neared Hungnam on her return from Pusan. The sea showed a moderate northwesterly swell as she steamed a course just west of north, twenty-three miles off the coast, almost due east of Chuncheon, far enough into the Sea of Japan that the fathometer couldn't find the bottom. The day dawned overcast but with good visibility. At 1000 Chief Mate Savastio inspected the holds and the cargo spaces, which were nearly empty except for three hundred tons of aviation fuel in fifty-two-gallon barrels that had been left by the authorities at Pusan at the bottom of Holds Two and Three. Captain La Rue inspected the officers' quarters at 1130, and afterwards he joined the officers off watch for lunch in the *Meredith Victory*'s saloon, the Merchant Marine equivalent of a navy ship's officers' wardroom.

About two hours later, after the ship had passed well offshore Wonsan, Third Mate Alvar Franzon activated the ship's degaussing coils to make her less vulnerable to magnetic-influence mines. At 1528 the bridge sighted the frigate assigned as the Harbor Entrance Control Vessel near Sea Buoy One. [64] Franzon called Captain La Rue to the bridge, and the men navigated the ship to the entrance of the swept channel. Unmentioned in the Deck Log, the ship's radioman was feeling the effects of too much Soju, the potent Korean liquor, in Pusan and had been shackled by his ankles to his bunk as *Meredith Victory* passed Buoy One at 1610.

Junior Third Mate Burley Smith stood on the bridge wing in the freezing breeze and used the Aldis lamp to communicate with the frigate by Morse code. The ship was instructed to take an anchorage, and the ship slowly made her way through the swept channel to Anchorage 46, almost dead in the center of the anchorages in the "Transport Area" south of the entrance to the inner harbor. She walked out her starboard anchor at 1947, and at 1948 the bridge rang the engine room, "All Stop."[65]

Burleigh Smith signals the Harbor Entrance Control Vessel at the entrance to the swept channel by sending Morse code using an Aldis light. Fresh out of the US Merchant Marine Academy, Smith earned the frigid duty because he remembered his Morse and was the junior-most deck officer.

WITH THE SHIP gently swinging at anchor in 50 feet of water, the deck crew began uncovering the hatches. As Smith came on watch at 2000, the deck crew were still uncovering the hatches and with the ship blacked out except for an anchor light, the men worked in almost pitch blackness. Below, the firemen and water-tenders kept steam on the boilers, the engine room ready at any time for the "Ahead Slow" bell as the *Meredith Victory* would weigh anchor and proceed to the dock. As the off-watch crew tried to sleep, shells flew overhead all night from the ships offshore towards concentrations of Chinese soldiers, ten rounds an hour from the *Massey*, nine from the *St. Paul*. The *Meredith Victory* was ready for Colonel Forney.

But Colonel Forney was not yet ready for the *Meredith Victory*. While the big troop transports *Seminole*, *Noble*, *General Bayfield*, *General Collins*, *General Sultan*, *General Breckinridge*, and *General Freeman* were loading at anchor, most for their second time in the evacuation, the *California*, *Empire Wallace*, *Alamo Victory*, *Exmouth Victory*, *Cornell Victory*, *Helen Lykes*, *Paducah Victory*, and *Kenyon Victory* were at the docks. Five LSTs were beached, loading at one of the Green beaches. X Corps' control system was working as men worked all night to load 3rd Infantry and the Corps' remaining vehicles and stores (so as not to leave anything for the enemy, Colonel Forney even found space on four Liberty Ships to load broken-down vehicles.)[66] In addition to "Anchor bearings checked frequently,"[67] *Meredith Victory*'s log entries for December 21 include, "at anchor as before awaiting orders" six times. The ship sat for the whole day after hurrying back from Pusan. She had not even been permitted the time to unload all of her cargo in Pusan, but here she sat. The captain and chief mate performed their inspections. The officers kept their watches. The crew ate their meals.

The next day, December 22, began as before, partly cloudy, cold, and with a gentle northwesterly wind. At 0650, before the sun rose, a boat[68] came alongside with "rations for 1,000 men." Forty-five minutes later, she was away, and the day went on like the previous, with holds inspected, anchor bearings taken, orders awaited. At 1520 Captain La Rue ordered a lifeboat drill to break the monotony. The abandon-ship signal blared and the men mustered at their stations and climbed into their boats. The boats were lowered into the water and the motors run and tested for five minutes before they were raised again.

Waiting at the anchorage in Hungnam for the opportunity to load. Purser Lunney on the left, Captain La Rue on the right. La Rue is wearing a camera, but it is unknown if he took any of the pictures that follow.

As the lifeboats returned to their davits, another boat was approaching, but this time it was carrying the harbor pilot, Captain Dawson, with orders for the *Meredith Victory*: she was to weigh anchor and tie up outboard the SS *Norcuba* on Dock One. Captain Dawson was aboard and in the bridge by 1530 and three minutes later on a slow bell, the ship was slowly walking up her anchor rode, the windlass on deck drawing the chain up the hawsepipe until the anchor was weighed at 1553.

With Captain Dawson on the bridge, *Meredith Victory* slowly picked her way through the anchored ships. The outer harbor was thick with ships at anchor, thirty of the eighty available anchor locations occu-

pied by ships being loaded from lighters or awaiting loading there or
at a dock. By half past the hour, Dawson had her inside the inner
harbor, and less than fifteen minutes later she was in position to moor
alongside *Norcuba*.[69] Stevedores were loading that ship from the pier
with more than twelve thousand barrels of fuel and lubricating oil.[70]

With only one of the YTBs available, the wind was pushing *Meredith
Victory* towards the dock and the ship that was already there, so
Meredith Victory let go her starboard anchor to control her bow, while
the tug took her stern. Berthing merchant ships alongside each other
was a somewhat hazardous proposition, since, unlike warships, they
did not carry fenders. The port director provided floating wooden
"camels" to hold the ships off from the dock or each other, but in this
case, whatever was between the ships was not quite adequate, and the
Meredith Victory made contact astern with the *Norcuba*. Second Mate
Albert Golembeski's log entry says, "No apparent damage to either
ship," but later that day *Norcuba*'s master sent Captain La Rue a
"Letter of Damage."[71] In any event, at 1713 she was moored fast,
boilers steaming and engine slowly turning so she would be ready to
loose her hawsers and make for sea as soon as ordered.

But what cargo was *Meredith Victory* going to add to the three hundred
tons she was already carrying? At 1730 the Deck Log only notes,
"Army officers aboard with orders to load." In later retellings, they
were described as "several Army colonels,"[72] with only one identified:
Colonel John H. Chiles, who was the X Corps G-3 (operations officer).
The others were likely Lieutenant Colonel Mizell, head of the control
group's movement section, either Colonel Gustave W. Oberlin, the X
Corps civil affairs officer or his deputy, Lieutenant Colonel Leon W.
Korschgen, and a representative or two of the 2nd Engineer Special
Brigade, which was responsible for supporting the actual loading.
Once settled in the saloon, the colonels told Captain La Rue and his
officers that the cargo was not to be soldiers or trucks or ammunition
or C-rations or any of the other thousands of items X Corps had
already crammed into 135 shiploads by the time *Meredith Victory* tied
up alongside *Norcuba*. Instead, her cargo would be civilian refugees.

THE PROBLEM of refugees did not suddenly appear on December 22. Whether they were fleeing the privations of North Korean society, the approaching Chinese troops who frequently either conscripted or killed military-age males as they crossed Korean territory, or simply trying to escape the violence of war, the December evacuation of X Corps troops had been accompanied by mass movements of Korean civilians south, in the direction of the UN forces and away from the communists. Anyone who was suspected of cooperating with the UN troops, including local government officials, policemen, or men hired by the X Corps as laborers, were at risk of summary execution.

The Corps attempted to prevent the flow of refugees from hindering its military operations. *X Corps Operation Order No. 9*, dated December 5, included the command, "No movement of civilians into or out of X Corps defense area. Permit no refugees to enter the outpost area."[73] There must have been previous communications on the subject, because on December 4 the 7th Infantry Division noted a communication from X Corps that instructed,

> "Commanders will take positive action to prohibit movement of refugees on MSR as well as their movement toward the HAMHUNG-HUNGNAM area. Refugees will be diverted and instructed to move to their homes or to small villages or towns of the countryside."[74]

In addition to the risk of civilians impeding military operations or maneuver by their presence, there was also a concern about who might be using the refugees for cover. Sabotage and guerrilla activities had already been a major problem for UN forces south of the 38th parallel. The official *X Corps Chronology* entry for December 5 comments, "Control of 'refugees' continued to prevent infiltration within our lines of enemy troops (quotation marks in the original.)"[75] On the seventh the concern was even more plain:

"Because of the danger of infiltration, all units are complying with additional instructions to divert all refugees from entering our positions and to pick up and place in POW channels all males of military age. The problem, in addition to infiltration of possible North Korean soldiers and saboteurs, of caring for, feeding and segregating tens of thousands of refugees during defense preparations and during imminent attack by large Chinese Communist Forces makes diversion of refugees from other area imperative. Movement south of civilians presently in the HAMHUNG-HUNGNAM area would also be beneficial."[76]

The situation became more acute on December 11, with "Attempts of refugees to enter HAMHUNG area increasing and require considerable effort of all units to divert them from assigned area."[77] The Marines had even found large numbers of refugees at the end of their convoy from Koto-ri. An estimated fifty thousand refugees attempted to board the last train between Hamhung and Hungnam to cover the last few miles to what they hoped would be further passage south to safety, either via rail or ship.

Finally, on December 13 the X Corps civil affairs section assumed primary responsibility for refugees since the Marines were almost embarked and 7th Infantry was starting. On that day, the chief of the X Corps civil affairs section, Lieutenant Colonel Moore, met with the US liaison to the 1st ROK Corps to seek their assistance in preventing refugees from entering the X Corps perimeter. Individual X Corps units would still need to deal with refugees already in their areas.

On December 16, the 7th Division reported,

"The rumor that civilians would be evacuated to the south by sea from HUNGNAM has caused a large influx of refugees. During the period the 1st Bn, 31st Inf was on refugee control, they turned back 6,000 persons from entering the Division defensive area."[78]

The civil affairs section of the *X-Corps Command Report* commented,

"As areas were abandoned by withdrawing troops, effective civil control was lost. Immediately thereafter columns of refugees appeared moving away from advancing CCF [Communist Chinese Forces]. The control of these refugees was absolutely essential in order that their number not complicate the already tremendous problem of evacuation. To control refugees from a military point of view it was necessary to turn away evacuees trying to enter the defense perimeter. Within the defense perimeter civilians were restricted to their own areas to prevent clogging of the limited available road net."[79]

The control group's Operations Officer Major Schutt estimated that there were now thirty thousand refugees awaiting evacuation.[80]

All of this being said, the X Corps balanced military necessity with humanitarian compassion remarkably well. General Almond's policy was, "the evacuation of all civil officials and their families, prominent citizens and all other loyal citizens for which shipping was available."[81] Whether X Corps promulgated this policy among Korean civilians or not, almost the entire Hamhung and Hungnam city government and police forces quit their jobs and joined their countrymen in flight.[82] Refugees converging on Hungnam were directed to the village of Soho-jin, where military police from US and ROK units provided security and civil affairs personnel provided food. X Corps personnel organized the refugees into groups of a hundred, and a member of each group was chosen to lead the group and keep it together. Every group was interrogated in an attempt to detect North Korean or Chinese soldiers or potential spies or saboteurs in the group. Suspects were separated and detained as prisoners of war, while the rest were maintained at Soho-jin until they could be evacuated.

General Almond's refugee policy, and the welfare of the refugees themselves, benefited enormously from an unlikely source. Hyun Bong

Hak was a native of Hamhung and the son of a Presbyterian minister who had fled south with his family in November 1945 following the communist takeover of the north. Already a graduate of Yonsei University Medical School in Seoul, after completing additional training at the Medical College of Virginia in Richmond, the twenty-eight-year-old physician had returned in March 1950 to practice medicine in the new Republic of Korea. When the war broke out, Dr. Hyun joined the Korean Marines, and ended up assigned to X Corps, eventually becoming a translator and an advisor to General Almond's staff on civil affairs.[83] [84]

When Dr. Hyun arrived in Hamhung with the X Corps, he reconnected with "old friends, my parents' friends and other civic leaders." Before the final retirement of UN forces from Hamhung, he helped organize the evacuation by train of thousands of Christians and government officials most likely to be imprisoned or killed by the communists. The balance of the refugees walked the few miles to Hungnam, hoping to be evacuated by ship.[85]

Dr. Hyun Bong Hak.

With the time fast approaching when the Korean civilians would be abandoned to their fate with the oncoming CPVF, Dr. Hyun prevailed upon his boss, Colonel Chiles, to evacuate the remaining civilians by ship. According to Dr. Hyun in an interview more than thirty years later, Colonel Chiles had replied, "Doctor, this is war, and in war the military comes first. Don't ask for the impossible."

The doctor would not take "no" for an answer and pursued the matter with no less than General Almond. Almond had taken a liking to the young doctor who shared the general's affection for his native state (Almond was born in Luray, Virginia, and studied at the Virginia Military Institute in Lexington, Virginia) but his initial reaction was negative. After meeting with Almond, Hyun discussed the matter with Colonel Forney, and the control officer conceded that, based on the pace of the embarkation, he could make cargo shipping available for the refugees.[86] With Forney's blessing in hand, Hyun was able to re-engage General Almond and receive the general's concurrence to embark refugees.[87]

The actual evacuation of refugees by ship from north of the 38th parallel began on a somewhat ad hoc basis. On December 5, Japanese LST Q067 left Wonsan for Pusan carrying nine hundred POWs, 650 ROK Navy personnel, and five hundred Korean civilians.[88] The SS *Lane Victory* loaded 7,009 refugees from Wonsan on the tenth and offloaded them at Pusan before rushing back to Hungnam to load Marines on December 14.[89] The *ROK War Diary* was probably alluding to the *Lane Victory* when it recorded on the tenth, in the context of oil and fresh water supplies available for replenishing ships, that

> "In the evacuation of refugees when some ships were hauling several thousand civilians, the shortage of food supplies and water posed tremendous problems for the master of the ships in controlling the refugees on board and in forcing them to conserve the small rations of water available to them."[90]

On December 12 a flotilla of fishing boats, fifty-five sail and two motor, loaded with an unknown number of refugees, left Soho-jin for the south. They painted red rectangles on the sides of their hulls so that UN naval forces would not confuse them with vessels smuggling weapons to KPA guerrillas below the 38th parallel. On the same day, one of the ROK LSTs that had been planned to carry refugees, BM 661, instead left Hungnam with five hundred tons of cargo, along with nine hundred patients and the staff of the 15th ROK field hospital.[91]

On the fifteenth it was reported that ROK FS 669[92] was leading a convoy of "six small vessels en-route to Hungnam" to pick up refugees when, as they were seeking shelter at Sokcho because of bad weather, one struck a mine and sank with fourteen of her crew. At the same time, forty small craft heading south, possibly among those that had left Soho-jin a few days earlier, joined them for shelter in the port.[93] A later entry in the *War Diary* indicates that the FS 669 would be used by the ROK 1st Corps for their redeployment. None of these ships appear in X Corps or CTF 90 records of the redeployment.

Desperate to escape oncoming communist forces, an unknown number of refugees sought refuge south in small boats.

Where they eventually landed on the coast and how many soldiers or refugees they carried is not known, but it shows that the Koreans were making an effort to evacuate their countrymen, even if the effort at that point was completely inadequate for the scale of the problem.

The largest recorded sea movement of refugees from the Hungnam area before the *Meredith Victory* and the other ships of December 23 involved an ill-fated ROK LST, the BM 8501. The ship was already beached and loading on the eleventh, assigned to the control of the commanding general of the 1ˢᵗ ROK Corps, General Kim Paik Il, who ordered it filled with refugees along with "Political Prisoners."[94] On December 16 she was pulled from the beach by the two YTBs and was immediately forced to anchor due to engine problems and a fouled port propeller shaft. Divers cleared the shaft and after minor repairs to her engines, she moved to a dock to take on additional refugees.

A line of refugees, many carrying their sole remaining possessions, wait patiently to board a Korean LST. Military policemen (MPs) are present alongside the line, but there is no disorder for them to address.

When BM 8501 attempted to clear the dock on the seventeenth, both of her screws became fouled again. The next morning the YTBs took her alongside the repair ship *Askari*, anchored in the inner harbor, and divers from *Askari* and the repair ship *Conserver* set to work clearing the screws. Eleven divers worked in stages to clear the shafts, and it was not until early on the morning of December 19 that her port screw was cleared of eight turns of 1-1/8-inch steel wire that had wrapped around the shaft and fouled the propeller. The starboard

shaft was still so fouled with manila rope that the effort to clear it had
to be abandoned in the interest of time.

And time was becoming critical, both in the port and aboard the ship.
On December 17 CTF 90 reported, "conditions aboard LST
deplorable-many sick and several dead or dying, critical shortage of
food. Rendered all assistance possible including repairs and furnishing
food."[95] The entry credits the BM 8501 with carrying "7,441 Korean
refugees ... including women and children."[96] Reportedly, there were
limited amounts of rice and fish aboard, but they were totally inadequate to support the men and women essentially trapped on the ship,
some for as many as six days, while the ship was loaded and then
repaired. Ships in the harbor baked and provided the LST with 1,500
loaves of bread and masses of cooked rice to provide some sustenance
to the denizens of BM 8501, and the ship took on twenty-six thousand
gallons of potable water from *Askari*. Eight tons of Army rations were
also delivered to the ship.[97]

No doubt CTF 90 was almost as happy as the refugees when BM 8501,
propelled by one engine, finally made for sea at dawn on December
19. She was escorted by another ROK LST, 665, and the attack transport *Diachenko*. It took the ships the better part of a day and a half to
make the 150-nautical mile voyage to Mukho, on the coast north of
Samchock. Eight hundred refugees disembarked there, with the
balance continuing aboard the 8501 to the island of Koje-do (Geoje-
do), off the coast at Pusan, where she would remain for a few days.[98]

Based on X Corps estimates, Colonel Forney's organization had
planned for the evacuation of twenty-five thousand refugees. Even as
the number of soldiers to be evacuated at Hungnam waned, the mass
of refugees grew so much that by the third week in December, Forney
estimated he had fifty thousand refugees, with more arriving. In
Forney's words, "By the 23rd of December, the last day, I could see my
way clear to bringing in three Victory ships and two LSTs, and on
these I out-loaded 50,000 refugees."[99]

BACK ABOARD THE *MEREDITH VICTORY*, in the retelling Colonel Chiles asked Captain La Rue whether he would be willing to carry refugees.[100] The ship's orders from the MSTS directed the ship to take any cargo that an agent of the US Government required, but the ship was not set up for carrying thousands of human beings. The former quarters of the Naval Armed Guard on the quarterdeck would normally accommodate twenty-eight persons at most. The ship would have to carry the refugees in her holds, without galley or sanitation facilities for any but the crew.

Meredith Victory was not the first time-charter to carry refugees; *Lane Victory* had that distinction with her evacuation of civilians from Wonsan almost two weeks earlier and Moore-McCormack's *Mormacmoon* had also carried civilians along with ROK troops. But Captain La Rue and his crew could see the crowds of refugees in the direction of Soho-jin. According to Purser Bob Lunney, Colonel Chiles and his colleagues described the defense situation around Hungnam, the fact that the Marines and the 7th Infantry had already redeployed, and the fact that thousands of civilians were trying to escape the oncoming communists. Without hesitation Captain La Rue said, "We'll do what we can."[101] Chief Mate Dino Savastio recalled La Rue saying, "We will take all you have."[102] Regardless of the wording, La Rue agreed, to transport an unprecedented number of refugees.

The decision made, both sides had work to do. The bosun and his deck crew turned to and prepared the hatches and the ship's cranes for loading. With the *Meredith Victory* on the outer berth, she would normally have been loaded from lighters, but instead the 2nd Engineer Special Brigade built a wooden causeway over the *Norcuba* over which refugees could board the *Meredith Victory* directly from the dock.[103] It was not until late that evening, 2130, that refugees began boarding the ship and loading into number five hold, the furthest aft. The deck crew carefully lowered the men, women, and children into the hold using large wooden pallets hung from a ship's crane. A half hour later the crew began loading hold number four. Those refugees that were able began loading the other three holds via ladders from the deck.[104]

Refugees waiting to board Meredith Victory, *with some happy faces visible.*

Refugees crossing the Norcuba *to board the* Meredith Victory
December 23, 1950.

Another view of the refugees boarding Meredith Victory. *Note the bundles carrying clothes and valuables.*

Refugees in one of Meredith Victory's *holds.*

The decks filled quickly as the holds reached capacity around sunrise. Chief Mate Savastio monitors the boarding of the refugees, perhaps futilely attempting to count them.

By 0330 the next morning, December 23, holds two and five were filled with refugees, but loading continued at the other three. Number four was filled by 0500 and just before sunrise the forward hold, number one, was filled. As the sun rose dim behind the clouds, the effort turned to loading the deck. Old men and women and children, mothers with babies carrying them on their backs in the traditional *podaegi*, continued their procession across the wooden causeway. The pictures of the refugees aboard *Meredith Victory* are consistent with Colonel Forney's comment that in his "personal judgement" among all the refugees, "no more than 10,000 were men of a category that could be used in the armed forces of KOREA."[105]

Crew members were impressed by the stoicism of the men and women, many of whom had traveled miles on foot, slept on the frozen ground, barely eaten, all while carrying their children or what little belongings they could as they fled for their lives. Whether crammed into what would soon become a fetid hold or shivering on deck, they heard not one complaint.

The loading was not without incident. More than once the crew witnessed a refugee's sole possessions, a bundle of clothes, a suitcase, or a sewing machine, tumble into the harbor. There was no time to try to recover it, and the sad civilian would continue on his way onto the ship. Worse was a mother who dropped her baby and before she could pick him up, someone in the crushing crowd stepped on the baby and killed him. La Rue, conscious of rumors among the Koreans that they were going to be dumped into the sea, resisted Army calls for a sea burial for the unfortunate child. He ordered his crew to give the father "an hour to bury his child ashore."[106]

By mid-morning it was clear that *Meredith Victory* would soon board all of the refugees she could handle. At 1030 Captain Dawson came aboard, and at 1110 the last refugee crossed the wooden bridge across the *Norcuba*. Just after 1130 the two YTBs working fore and aft pulled the *Meredith Victory* away from the *Norcuba* and slowly spun her stern west so that the ship would be bow-on to the entrance to the harbor. By noon she had cleared the breakwater and left the pilot on one of the tugs. The bridge activated the degaussing coils, and the ship accelerated as it crossed the swept channel. By 1448 she had reached Buoy One and a half an hour later, *Meredith Victory* secured her degaussing coils as she left the minefield behind and turned south for Pusan.[107]

Refugees pack the deck of the Meredith Victory.

Even as *Meredith Victory* was finishing loading, the SS *Virginia City Victory* was being told to weigh anchor and prepare to go alongside the *Norcuba*. *Virginia City* had been built by Henry J. Kaiser's Permamente Metals at Richmond, California, and delivered to the Maritime Commission in January 1945. She had served with a series of shipping lines under bareboat charter, and was now in Korea under a charter with the New York and Cuba Mail Shipping Company.[108] Whether Colonel Chiles and the other officers had the same conversation with her master as they had with Captain La Rue, by early afternoon she was alongside *Norcuba*, taking *Meredith Victory*'s place and loading refugees.[109] She would continue loading until about 2200 that evening.[110] Sometime that afternoon the SS *Madaket*, a C-2 transport built in 1945 and now owned by the Waterman Steamship Company, took a place at the dock. She likely took the berth where the recently departed SS *Rider Victory* had finished loading men and equipment of the 3rd Infantry Division. *Madaket*, too, began loading refugees.[111]

Her decks covered with refugees, the Meredith Victory *approaches a naval vessel as she leaves Hungnam for the last time.*

THAT MORNING, as the *Meredith Victory* was making thirteen knots on her voyage to Pusan, several LSTs were still loading refugees. But there were to be no more time-chartered transports after *Virginia City, Norcuba, Madaket,* and the *Provo Victory,* the latter loading not refugees, but X Corps equipment, left the harbor around midnight on the twenty-third.[112] [113] Admiral Doyle had established December 24 as "Dog-Day," the date when the redeployment would be complete, and on the twenty-second, CTF 90 had ordered that all shipping be clear of the docks by 2200 on December 23.[114] The LSTs loading refugees were instructed to retract from the beach by 0600 on the twenty-fourth. The purpose was to free up multiple embarkation locations to support the rapid loading of the remaining forces defending the port. When the final embarkation occurred, it needed to be fast and effective to stay ahead of the CPVF forces massing outside. With almost no X-Corps facilities left to power, the USS *Foss* disconnected her electrical connections to the port and steamed out early in the morning of the twenty-fourth to establish an anti-submarine patrol near the entrance to the swept channel.[115]

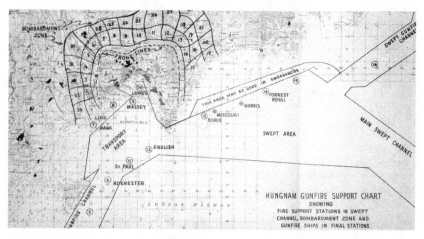

Gunfire Support Chart from the CTF 90 Action Report showing the final locations of the fire-support ships. The numbers denote bombardment zones for targeted and harrasing fire before the entire port became a free-fire zone.

As the redeployment's finale neared, the destroyers *Forrest Royal*, *English*, *Lind*, and *Norris* joined the other naval guns, with the *Forrest Royal* anchoring just off the ten-fathom line in the broad, swept area joining the northern gunfire channel with the main channel going east and the approach to the harbor opening west. Following the ten-fathom line south and west were the *Norris* and the *Borie*. The *English* anchored on the ten-fathom line off Chakto-ri, with the *St. Paul* to her southwest and the *Rochester* anchored where the south gunfire channel joined the transport anchorage. The destroyers *Massey*, *Lind*, and *Hank* anchored close to shore in five fathoms of water from just south of the harbor breakwater to the mouth of the Songchon River. They would assume the role of the 3rd Infantry's artillery.

The destroyers and cruisers had some help from even bigger guns. At 0750 on the morning of the twenty-third, the battleship *Missouri*, with Vice Admiral Struble embarked, had entered the swept channel at the outer sea buoy and by 1002 was anchored due east of Hungnam north of Chakto-ri, between the destroyers *Borie* and *Norris*.[116] With the perimeter so compressed, the twenty-four-mile range of her sixteen-inch guns was hardly necessary, but her one-ton, high-explosive shells were certain to hold enemy forces at bay when they heard them roar from the sky, and they would pulverize any remaining structures on which they landed.

Battleship USS Missouri *fires one of her 16-inch guns at a target near Hungnam on the night of 23-24 December. In the distance are visible rockets launched from the decks of three LSMR rocket-equipped landing craft near or within the harbor.*

By the morning of December 24, Christmas Eve, there were still nine thousand men of X Corps ashore, and the three regiments of the 3rd Infantry Division still had their west-to-east distribution, defending a perimeter roughly four thousand yards from the port. At 0900, as the *Meredith Victory* was steaming south six miles east of the Kanjol-ap peninsula, midway between Ulsan and Pusan, the final phase of the Hungnam redeployment began. The rate of naval gunfire had been increasing. From 0800 on the twenty-second to 0800 on the twenty-third, the Gunfire Support Group had fired 402 eight-inch rounds, 2,927 high-explosive five-inch rounds, and 366 five-inch illumination rounds.[117] On December 23 the ships tripled their rate of fire.

There is a maxim in amphibious warfare that a major purpose of fire onto the landing beach is "to keep the enemy's head down" and prevent them from forming an attack. The destroyers, cruisers, and battleships anchored near the port where now doing just that, creating a situation so chaotic and dangerous that only the most fool-hardy enemy commander would order his soldiers forward into the port. In addition to the harassing fire distributed over the area outside the perimeter, specific troop concentrations were targeted by naval gunfire and by aircraft called in by spotters on the ground.

With the remaining transports and most of the LSTs withdrawn, there were now seven landing sites from which to embark the remaining soldiers of the 3rd Infantry. Two battalions from each of the three regiments began withdrawing to the beach, leaving each regiment's remaining battalion to provide cover. The 7th Regimental Combat Team embarked LSTs on "Pink Beach," well to the southwest of the breakwater, beyond the ammunition-loading beach. This allowed the 7th RCT to embark without movement to the east, protecting the 3rd Infantry's flank and speeding the loading process. The slope of the beach ruled out the use of LSTs, so the troops boarded smaller landing craft[118] to take them to ships at anchor.[119]

As 1100 approached, H-Hour, the final embarkation began. The covering forces, the last three battalions, began to load at Pink, Blue and Yellow beaches. The embarkation proceeded smoothly until 1210, when the evacuation of Pink Beach was shattered by a series of explosions at two ammunition dumps. Three men were killed and thirty-seven wounded in the explosions, which damaged five landing craft on the beach and possibly capsized another six.[120] The explosions were attributed to human error rather than enemy action, and the embarkation continued. At 1405, Blue Beach, the inner port, was reported clear. Troops were still embarking at Pink and Yellow beaches.

There was one more gift the X Corps left for the oncoming Chinese and North Korean forces—the demolition of the port facilities. Before the redeployment began, the Army 8224th Engineer Construction Group had completed a study that proposed to destroy all locomotives and railroad rolling stock, and nearby track and tunnels north of the Hungnam, drop the bridges at Hamhung and Oro-ri, and demolish all port facilities, wharves and cranes.[121] Yonpo Airfield would be cratered through an aerial bombardment once the field was no longer needed, and naval gunfire would be used on the port.

The destruction had begun on December 7 with the cratering of a road by the 3rd Infantry.[122] The 3rd Infantry blew another bridge on the tenth and the 1st Marine Division blew three more bridges between the tenth and the fifteenth. With the out-loading of the Marines, the Army finished the job. Starting on the sixteenth, a bridge was blown almost every day, sometimes more than one, as the defensive perimeter shrank, until the fourteenth bridge was blown on the twenty-first. Over a two-day period starting on December 17, 36 locomotives and 300 freight cars were destroyed. The ROK Capital Division did their part, destroying six railroad tunnels between the fifteenth and the eighteenth.

The final explosion, destroying the inner harbor, was captured in all of its destructive glory by dozens of photographers and became, along with crowds of refugees, the iconic picture of the Hungnam evacuation. The Army's 10th Engineering Brigade placed thousands of pounds of TNT in and around the buildings of the port. Navy underwater demolition teams placed charges around docks and underwater

Passing explosive charges from a pier side landing craft for the final destruction of the dock facilities. The men are standing on demolition charges each equivalent to twenty pounds of TNT.

structures.[123] When the charges were detonated, the resulting eruption was augmented, in Colonel Forney's word, by, "400 tons of ground ammunition, about 400 tons of frozen dynamite that was too dangerous to handle, and about 250 tons of thousand-pound bombs," along with two hundred barrels of gasoline.[124] Along with what the ships had accomplished with their gunfire, this guaranteed the CPVF 27th Army would enter Hungnam to find nothing of military value.

The final destruction of the port of Hungnam, December 24, 1950. The men of the high-speed transport USS Begor (APD-127) had a ringside seat.

The timing of the demolition seems very close to the "all clear" on the beach. The timeline may have been forced by the danger of refugees flooding into the now-abandoned port area, which would have either precluded its demolition or caused massive civilian deaths. CTF 90 had received reports of civilians moving onto Green beach. The last of the three LSTs assigned for evacuating civilians, the Japanese Q074, had completed loading, missing the deadline but leaving the beach with thousands of refugees. Both recollections and contemporaneous reports indicate there were still thousands of refugees in the vicinity of the beach, hoping for an evacuation that would never come.[125]

As the fleet began to disperse, the ships moved for open water through the main channel across the minefield to the Sea of Japan and CTF 90 destroyed all of the remaining buoys marking the main and north gunfire channels. The destroyer *Endicott* had already gotten a head start on the south channel.[126] Whoever followed the UN forces into Hungnam by sea would have to re-sweep the area for mines or else take their chances.

———

MEREDITH VICTORY WAS APPROACHING Pusan on Christmas Eve as the last battalions of the 3rd Infantry Division were boarding their landing craft. Considering the massed human cargo, the trip had been surprisingly uneventful. Five babies were born aboard the ship, with Chief Mate Savastio or Captain La Rue performing the function of midwife in the infirmary. The crew named the newborns "*Meredith Victory* Kimchi One" through Five.

One other event stood out in the retelling of the voyage. While off the Korean coast, the crew discovered to its horror that a group of refugees had started a fire in one of the holds in order to keep warm, but the fire was on top of the drums of aviation fuel *Meredith Victory* still carried. Furious gesticulation by the crew convinced the Koreans to extinguish the fire.[127] The crew's quick action probably saved thousands of lives, and potentially, the ship. Unknown to the *Meredith*

Victory was that *Mormacmoon* had experienced a similar near-cata-strophe a few days earlier. Having loaded her holds with 2,800 refugees, along trucks and cargo of the 7th Infantry Division, some of the civilians had climbed into the trucks and started their engines for warmth, despite explicit instructions not to. By the time the crew discovered the running trucks, fifty men had been overcome by fumes and had to be carried to the deck. All survived, thanks to careful moni-toring of the cargo holds and prompt action by the crew.[128]

Hopeful refugees on the deck of the Meredith Victory *as she approaches Pusan.*

A series of course corrections earlier on the twenty-fourth had brought *Meredith Victory* from her south-southeast heading earlier to west-north west as she made the turn around the bottom of the Korean peninsula. At 1240 she reduced her speed as she began to enter the approaches to the harbor, passing north of Oryukdo Island as she coasted towards the breakwater. Watching the fathometer, La Rue maneuvered the ship to a spot in six fathoms of water where she could temporarily anchor to await docking orders. At 1321 *Meredith Victory* let go her starboard anchor and let three shots of anchor chain (270 feet) hold her to the shallow, muddy bottom outside the port.

The refugee-crowded deck of the *Meredith Victory* made an impression on those who saw it. The master of the troop transport USS *Sergeant*

Truman Kimbro (the former Victory ship *Hastings Victory*), Captain Raymond Fosse, recounted,

"When we first saw that Victory ship, we couldn't figure out what in the world it had on deck. From a distance it was simply a dark, solid mass. As the ship came nearer, we could see it was human beings. They were packed so close you wondered how they could breathe. And there wasn't a sound from them. They just stood there, silently, waiting. Even the babies and children were strangely quiet. Unless you saw it, you wouldn't believe it."[129]

The "dark, solid mass" Captain Fosse saw at Pusan.

At 1506 a Naval officer boarded *Meredith Victory* with orders for the ship. Whoever the young officer was, he had the unfortunate task of telling Captain La Rue that the ship could not unload her human cargo at Pusan, but would have to do so at Changsungpo, Koje-do (Jangseungpo, Geoje-do), a small bay on the southeast side of an island about thirty nautical miles from where they were anchored. Geoje-do is a large island, separated at its closest point by just a quarter mile from the land of the peninsula. Today it is home to a quarter-million people on its 148 square miles, but in 1950 it was largely empty, a wooded rock jutting dramatically out of the sea like so much of the Korean coast. The US Army's 3rd Logistical Command had built refugee camps on the island where the *Meredith Victory*'s passengers could be housed and fed. In the coming months, the refugee camp would be joined on the island by a POW camp.

The diversion to Koje-do should not have been a surprise to the *Meredith Victory* and her passengers stuffed into her holds and crammed onto her deck. On December 20, the 8th Army, which had operational control of Pusan, had sent a priority message to X Corps saying, "Request prior notification movement of refugees. Pusan overcrowded. Request refugee ships be scheduled to Kojo Island."[130] The message was marked for action to the "Corps Control Off" (Colonel Forney) and for information to others, including the civil affairs officer.

On the twenty-second, the Commander Fleet Activities, Pusan, advised that "Landing the 25,000 refugees at Pusan for transshipment to Koje-do would seriously interfere with military movements in the port, which was already congested due to the rapid turn around vessels."[131] No ROK vessels were available to support the movement of refugees from Pusan to Koje-do or anywhere else they could escape the chaos of the hundreds of thousands of US and ROK soldiers and their equipment now trying to flow through Pusan and its environs. At the time *Meredith Victory* sailed on the twenty-third, CTF 90 had requested she be diverted to Changsungpo, to be unloaded there "by ROK LST's and native craft" while at anchor.[132] Apparently, that message was never conveyed to Captain La Rue before *Meredith Victory* arrived in Pusan.

The one consolation the officer could offer before he left just a half an hour after he boarded would be for the ship to dock temporarily at Pusan. There she could offload seventeen wounded soldiers (and one Chinese spy in ROK uniform) *Meredith Victory* had embarked with the refugees and who had stayed in the Armed Guard berthing on the quarter deck. More importantly, La Rue hoped he could obtain some food and water for the refugees.[133] More than three hours after the officer disembarked, the *Meredith Victory* received orders to dock, but not until a few hours later. She and her thousands of refugees would have to wait a little more.

The refugees had now been on the ship for more than a day. The deck crew turned to, partially uncovering the hatches, allowing the men, women, and children below a little more ventilation to relieve the foul air. The ship could provide no sanitary facilities for them, and nature compelled many of them to relieve themselves in the holds, choosing the corners of each deck for the purpose when they could make their way.

At 2024 the pilot came aboard and the *Meredith Victory* began weighing anchor. Less than half an hour later, she was passing the breakwater to the inner harbor. With just one tug to help her dock, she again used her anchor to hold her bow as the tug pushed her stern to the pier and she made it fast, then walked out the chain as the tug pushed her bow alongside. At 2130 she was fast at Berth Ten, Pier Two. Two hours later, the wounded soldiers were taken ashore down the narrow gangplank.[134]

That Christmas Eve, Captain La Rue, reflecting on the plight of his passengers, wrote in *Meredith Victory*'s deck log,

> "The nearness of Christmas carried my thoughts to the Holy Family—how they, too, were cold and without shelter. Like the crucified Christ, these good people suffer through the actions of guilty men."[135]

Clearly, now it was time to attempt some relief for the civilians. La Rue prevailed upon the authorities in Pusan to provide food and water for his passengers, who had now been aboard for at least a day and a half.[136] It was early on the morning of Christmas Day, the sky cold, clear and starlit, when port personnel began bringing rice and water aboard. US and ROK Army Military Police (MPs) guarded the gangway and decks to prevent refugees from disembarking and provide some measure of crowd control, but the Koreans were peaceful, appreciative. As the sun rose on a clear morning, the first clear sky the men of the Meredith Victory had seen in days, they finished feeding the refugees and took aboard pallets and bridles for lifting them from the holds when they reached Changsunspo.

At 0935 on the twenty-fifth, Christmas Day, the pilot re-boarded Meredith Victory, and she began her undocking. A half hour later, she had let go all of her lines, the tug pulling the stern from the dock, the anchor windlass heaving on the anchor chain to the pull the bow away. Meredith Victory advanced on her anchor and weighed it, with the tug swinging her stern to starboard so she would face the harbor entrance. At 1019 she was on her own, heading for the breakwater, and a few minutes later the pilot stepped aboard the tug, and the ship was again under the command of Captain La Rue, bound for Koje-do.

Meredith Victory picked her way through the tiny islands, that crossed its path as she steamed towards freedom for her passengers. At 1244 she reduced her speed as she approached the anchorage at Changsungpo. Twenty-five minutes later she was anchored in a hundred feet of water, awaiting the craft that would disembark the refugees. Whether or not the port officials in Pusan knew that the wait would be long and thought there might be aboard discontent and possibly a riot, they had dispatched MPs with the ship to patrol the decks and maintain order. Still, the passengers were quiet aboard Meredith Victory for the rest of the afternoon and evening, as the next few log entries note variations on, "Vessel anchored as before awaiting LSTs to discharge refugees."[137]

It was at 0820 the next morning, December 26, that the string of log entries was broken, as the luckless BM 8501 came along the port side to take on the refugees. She and her ROK sister, LST 665, had reached Koje-do with their loads of refugees, the 8501 claiming 10,500 aboard, more having been loaded at Mukho, and the 665 claiming nine thousand.[138] The two ships had been ordered to remain to help offload the refugee-bearing transports when they arrived, and they had already offloaded three thousand from the *Yoneyama Maru* and six thousand from the *Torbata Maru* a day or so before.[139]

Refugees gather their belongings and prepare to disembark at Koje-do.

With the LSTs alongside, now the challenge was getting the refugees from one ship to the other. An empty, un-ballasted LST had about seventeen feet of freeboard, putting her main deck that distance above the water. Fully loaded, the *Meredith Victory*'s freeboard was about eleven feet, which would have made it quite a climb onto the LST. But the weight of all the refugees aboard *Meredith Victory* was certainly less than a thousand tons, so she, too, was largely unloaded and her main deck was actually a few feet above the LST's. After a little improvisation on the part of both crews, the refugees were able to use lumber to climb up over the *Meredith Victory*'s bulwarks and then, with assistance, down onto the deck of the BM 8501, which they began doing at 0915.

At 0930, LST BM 665[140] came alongside BM 8501 and the refugees began to cross from one ship to the other to load her as well. The MPs and the crew assisted as the men and women handed children across the gap between the ships, perhaps twenty feet above the water, before crossing over themselves. Occasionally a small parcel would fall into the sea, perhaps the only physical possession a refugee might have. There was no time for emotion; he or she just continued passage to the 8501 and, they hoped, freedom. The anchorage was not particularly calm, but despite the movement of the ships, not one person was lost to the sea. Indeed, thanks to the babies born over the preceding two days, *Meredith Victory* arrived with more civilians than when she had started.

Refugees crossing Korean LST BM 8501 to board Korean LST BM 665.

As the refugees slowly made their way across the decks of the three ships, the men of the *Meredith Victory* operating her cargo windlasses slowly replenished the crowd on the decks with new refugees happy to be lifted from the holds. By 1320, LST 665 was full, and she left BM 8501's port side. An hour and a half later, all of the refugees had left the *Meredith Victory*. The crew searched the ship looking for any strag-

glers, or worse, any who were unable to leave, but they found none. At
1455, the BM 8501 backed her engines (or perhaps just one, if her
starboard screw was still fouled) to pull away and, continuing her
string of bad luck, dented *Meredith Victory*'s hull near the bow.
Whether she had the same difficulties when she later unloaded
Virginia City Victory and *Madaket* is unknown. By 1510 *Meredith Victory*
had weighed anchor and started maneuvering onto a course back to
Pusan to discharge the Army MPs and await further orders. She was
back at anchor outside the harbor three hours later.

Koje-do in the background as LST BM 665 prepares to pull away and land the refugees.

The ship swung at anchor for the rest of the night. It was not until
1540 on December 27 that the MPs boarded a small boat and left for
Pusan. Still, the *Meredith Victory* waited, the officers and men passing
the time with their duties on watch, or reading a book or playing cards
or chess. After a full day at anchor, the pilot boarded the ship from a
tug at 0900 on the twenty-eighth. At 1003 she weighed anchor and
made for the breakwater and the port within. Half an hour later, she
was docking as before, the anchor controlling the bow, a tug at the
stern. The pilot in Pusan must not have had the skill of Captain

Dawson at Hungnam, for under the Pusan pilot's command, *Meredith Victory* struck the dock forward of the deckhouse with enough force to merit an entry in the ship's log.

With the refugees safely disembarked and the ship at its berth, Captain La Rue could now tour the holds of his emptied ship. After three days with thousands of people confined, the sanitary conditions below decks were such that Second Assistant Engineer Harding H. Petersen was quoted as saying that when the holds were opened, one could, "chop holes in the air with an axe."[141] In addition to the remnants of its human occupation, the master saw piles of weapons left behind by some of the refugees, presumably KPA deserters.[142]

In the afternoon, five gangs of laborers boarded to help clean the ship and unload the remaining cargo from Holds Two and Three. But there was only so much the cleaners were allowed to do, and one of them was not throwing human waste overboard from the ship at dock.

When the *Meredith Victory* arrived in Sasebo a day or so later, she would not be allowed into the harbor, her stench preceding her, along with the fear of disease. The crew were forced to shovel the two feet of human waste from the corners of the holds into fifty-five-gallon gal drums which were then lifted onto deck and dumped overboard into Sasebo bay. After the crew used the fire mains to hose-down the holds and pumped the bilges, the SS *Meredith Victory* started back for the United States. Even with quicklime sprinkled throughout the holds, the ship was considered too unsanitary to carry cargo back to the US.[143]

11

LEGEND

The X Corps' fighting retreat from Chosin and the subsequent redeployment from Hungnam were major news back home in the United States. The headline on the *Spokane Daily Chronicle* for Christmas Day declared "205,000 Evacuated from Hungnam." Stories about the holiday had to take a back seat. Three stories on the front page covered the evacuation, with one entitled, "Navy Reports Evacuation is Flawless Operation." The article noted that in "two weeks allied naval units removed 105,000 troops, more than 100,000 civilians, 17,500 vehicles and 350,000 tons of supplies." Admiral Doyle was quoted as saying, "Everything clicked. No one will ever say we were pushed off the beach. They never laid a glove on us. Naval air and surface power saw to that." CONNAVFE Vice Admiral Joy called it the "most perfect withdrawal in history." He continued,

"Hungnam was Inchon in reverse from a naval point of view. While we never had to do it before, we proved that when all elements of naval, air and surface power are brought to bear we can redeploy an army by sea from a contested area with as little loss as we can in landing one. It was a simple matter of putting reverse English on amphibious doctrine developed during World War II ... Nothing was left for the enemy-not even port facilities."

Turner gleefully recounted the demolition of the port facilities in detail, right down to the destruction of the buoys.

President Truman, in Independence, Missouri, for the holiday, called the successful evacuation, "the best Christmas present I could have. I say 'well done' to General MacArthur and General Almond."

On January 6, 1951, Commander, Task Force Ninety sent a memorandum to the commander of the Military Sea Transportation Service, Western Pacific on the subject, "MSTS Ships at Wonsan and Hungnam, Korea, Performance of." In it CTF 90 recognized seventeen of the fifty-one time-chartered vessels who participated that were "noteworthy for the high caliber of their performance during the evacuations of Wonsan and Hungnam, Korea." These were the: *California, Choctaw Victory, Madaket, Southwind, Robin Gray, Robin Kirk, Helen Lykes, Beljeanne, Lane Victory, Meredith Victory, Virginia City Victory, Mormacmoon, Hunter Victory, Rider Victory, Belocean,* and *Carlton Victory.* Two other ships, the SS *Exmouth* and the British steamer *Empire Marshall* were singled out as "especially worthy of commendation for the all round cooperation and outstanding seamanship displayed by their masters and crew."[1]

While the LSTs that participated in the evacuation stayed in the 7th Fleet operating area and were busy supporting ongoing military operations in Korea, many of the commercial freighters soon returned to the United States. *Meredith Victory* left Sasebo a few days after the New Year and sailed to Seattle, arriving on January 20, the *Virginia City Victory* arriving in San Francisco Bay about the same time.

Word of *Meredith Victory's* accomplishment at Hungnam had apparently preceded her. Burley Smith recalled a US Nay lieutenant boarding the ship in Seattle and asking for any photographs taken of the evacuation, promising to return the film after it was developed. Burley gave the anonymous officer two roles he had taken, and never saw the film again.[2] On January 23 the Associated Press filed a story from Seattle saying,

"The freighter *Meredith Victory* arrived here yesterday and crew members told of rescuing 14,000 North Korean civilians from the battered Hungnam beachhead in one trip aboard their jam-packed ship."

The article continued,

"the vessel was converted into a floating maternity ward while taking the Hungnam refugees to a camp on an island off South Korea. First Mate D. S. Savastio ... was a busy man during the trip. He delivered one baby and answered emergency calls until five mothers were taken to the first aid room, which served as a maternity ward for five babies born the first day. 'There I stood with babies all around and something happening every minute,' said Savastio."

On February 16 the *New York Times*, reporting on a press conference detailing the Military Sea Transportation Service's activities during the first six months of the war, devoted three paragraphs of an eight-paragraph story to the *Meredith Victory*. The article stated, "an aide recited the story of what amounted to a mass migration of native Korean population in one small ship." The article continued,

"Late in December ... thousands of refugees were forced toward the coast ... One ship, a Victory type cargo ship named the *Meredith Victory*, loaded 14,000 Koreans into cargo holds and removed them in one voyage to safety in the south."

Nine days later the *New York Times* news service distributed a more extensive version of the story. Datelined February 25, the article began,

"Details of one of the most fantastic of all overseas movements of human beings were disclosed here Sunday by officials of the Moore-McCormack Lines and the Military Sea Transportation Service.

"The incident involved the evacuation of 14,000 Korean refugees from Hungnam on a single cargo ship and the vessel's three-day voyage to a South Korean island. So unbelievable is the episode that, although it occurred Dec. 22-25, officials of the steamship company and the transportation service refused to admit its veracity for many weeks pending an investigation."

The article stated, incorrectly, that the "vessel arrived in Hungnam Dec. 21 to evacuate civilians," and that the "skipper offered to take as many civilians as he could fit in the hull and superstructure," No refugees were allowed in the "house" which would have rendered operation of the ship impossible. The article continued, commenting that, as far as was known, the 14,000 passengers were the "largest number ever carried on a single voyage of a commercial ship with the exception of the *Queen Mary* and *Queen Elizabeth*." The article expanded on Savastio's quote in the AP story, adding, "Before these people disembarked I had lost count of the number of births."

Other newspapers picked up both the AP and *New York Times* stories, and Moore-McCormack's internal *Mooremack News* was only too happy to report as well. On March 26, 1951, Maryland US Sen. Herbert R. Connor asked for and received unanimous consent to enter the March 1951 *Mooremack News* into the Congressional Record for the First Session of the 82nd Congress. In addition to repeating Chief Mate Savastio's quote about "babies all around and something doing every minute," the *News* quoted the *Philadelphia Bulletin*,[3] whose story took particular joy that the master of the ship was a Philadelphia native.

Charles Regal, editor of the "Down the Hatch" column in the *Seattle Post-Intelligencer*, lauded the accomplishment of the *Meredith Victory*. Regal, who had served in the Merchant Marine before becoming a reporter, gushed,

"Man of the year in this, man of the year in that. How about ship of the year? As far as Down the Hatch is concerned, 1950's outstanding merchant ship was the steamship *Meredith Victory*, the ship that on December 22 evacuated 14,000 Koreans in one load."

He continued,

"That surely was the largest number of persons ever taken aboard a freighter of any size, and it may be the largest load ever taken by any ship. The *Queen Mary* (81,235 gross tons) reportedly averaged ten to twelve thousand troops during the war."

The two Cunard liners, *Queen Mary* and *Queen Elizabeth*, were the largest troop-carrying ships of the war, indeed the largest ships period. Moore-McCormack, to its credit but certainly not wanting to be corrected in the press by a competitor, contacted Cunard White Star Lines, who said the most either ship carried during World War II was 15,000. No matter. Even a casual reader appreciated the drama of the *Meredith Victory* carrying almost as many people as a ship nearly ten-times her size.

Meanwhile, the general story of the refugee crisis in Korea was receiving considerable attention from the press. The February 10, 1951, issue of *The Saturday Evening Post* carried a story by William L. Worden entitled "The Cruelest Weapon in Korea." The article was replete with pictures of refugees crossing southward, including bare-legged women wading across the freezing Taedong River and lines of men, women, and children waiting to board an LST in Hungnam. Composed well before the MSTS press conference, the story did not explicitly discuss the Hungnam evacuation but it did describe the plight of refugees in Korea as hapless escapees from communist rule, whose numbers may inadvertently shelter spies and guerillas.

The *Post* reached nearly seven million households in the 1950s, so two months later, when Ashley Halsey Jr. wrote of the "Miracle Voyage off Korea" in the magazine's April 14, 1951, "Report to the Editors" section, the ship's story gained considerable fame. In six hundred words, Vance's article, complete with a photograph of the refugees packed onto the deck of the *Meredith Victory*, appears to be the earliest, detailed, published account of the voyage, and established at its start the heroic nature:

> "In the painful annals of war, commonplace ships, like ordinary men, sometimes render supreme services of which no one dreamed them capable. The *Meredith Victory* ... was one of those ships ... when she steamed into Hungnam for the big evacuation in December. She emerged as one of the most heroic vessels of the Korean struggle."

The author described the arrival of the ship in Hungnam and the subsequent loading of the refugees. He included poignant details, presumably gathered from interviews with the crew, of a "man who brought only his violin," a woman boarding "with her sewing machine her head," and a family "shoving a piano aboard, until told the space was needed for people." Vance told of the *Meredith Victory*'s cooks boiling rice and the crew passing it among the refugees in "large, galvanized garbage cans," and the capture of a Chinese spy who snuck aboard disguised as a Korean MP. The article closed with,

> "When the *Meredith Victory* pulled into Pusan, Captain LaRue's log entry was one of the most original since Noah grounded on Ararat: 'Five births, no deaths, enroute. Disembarked 14,005 persons safely."

Whether this was an embellishment to the story or related to a log entry when the ship returned to Pusan from Koje-do is unknown. The extant copy of the deck log omits this remark.

James Finan published a similarly detailed account of the voyage in the September, 1951, issue of *Naval Affairs*, the Fleet Reserve Association's magazine. The article was condensed into two pages in November, 1951's *Reader's Digest*, reaching millions more readers, including many outside the United States. Dramatically told, Captain

La Rue tells Savastio, "Start 'em aboard. And let me know when the count reaches ten thousand."

Perhaps the apex of the press coverage came on December 22, the first anniversary of the *Meredith Victory*'s berthing alongside the *Norcuba*. Writing in *The Tablet*, the newspaper of Brooklyn, New York's Roman Catholic Diocese, the Rev. J. J. Murphy, O.M.I., the port chaplain of Seattle, lyrically recalled the events of a year before in an article entitled "Twasn't Much of a Christmas." The author called La Rue "a sterling Catholic" and indirectly quotes him many times, but only directly quotes Chief Mate Savastio, adding to the suspicion that Savastio was the source in Seattle of the original accounts of the evacuation. There is in fact no evidence that La Rue ever spoke to the Associated Press in 1951, only by phone to James Finan and to the editors of *Mooremack News* before heading back to sea. *Mooremack News* also reported that they had received a copy of La Rue's "personal memoir" of the "Hungnam trip."[4] That document, almost certainly lost with the rest of Moore-Mccormack's files, appears to have provided much of the details often quoted in later press accounts.

WHILE THE PRESS publicized *Meredith Victory*'s achievements, life went on for the merchant mariners. Just as La Rue and the *Whittier Victory* had established a routine with regular passages from New York to the South America, now the master led *Meredith Victory* on a routine of voyages between the west coast of the United States and Japan and Korea. With the ship finally clean enough to carry cargo again, she sailed for the western Pacific.

The next few voyages illustrate the circuits La Rue and his crew, with Dino Savastio still as chief mate but a new group of junior officers aboard, would take the *Meredith Victory*. On June 23 she sailed from Portland, Oregon, for Pusan, Korea. She sailed from Pusan on July 11 for Yosu, Korea. She discharged her cargo in Yosu and sailed on

August 1 for Sasebo. On August 3 she sailed for San Francisco, completing her voyage on August 16.

On August 23, 1951, *Meredith Victory* sailed from San Francisco again for Pusan, Korea, and after a brief stay left Pusan for Inchon on September 11. She sailed from Inchon for Kunsan, Korea, on September 20, where she discharged the bulk of her cargo, and on the thirtieth sailed from Kunsan for Sasebo, Japan.

During this leg of the voyage, Captain La Rue was faced with a decidedly non-routine event when two sailors reported a theft. From the log:

> "While in the port of Kunsan, Korea, September 29, 1951, Frederick L. James, A.B. and Stanley L. Strauss, Dk. Utility, report to Chief Mate that the sums of $10.00 and $30.00 respectively were missing from their lockers. F. James stated that he had missed $15.00 previously and suspected Harry T. Stewart, O.S., his roommate of the theft. Because of his suspicion James copied the serial number of an American $10.00 bill which he left in his working clothes. At approximately 1815 hours same day, a search of Stewart's room was made ... The marked $10.00 bill was found crumpled up into a perfume box, also a wallet which had been reported missing on the previous port (Inchon) by U.S. Army Private W.F. Bald (money was missing from wallet)."

Added almost as an aside, but clearly the most worrying, the log continues, "Also found in Stewart's locker was a .22 caliber revolver and ammunition for same." Recognizing the severity of this situation, La Rue called for the local provost marshal to come aboard when the ship arrived in Sasebo on October 1. The provost marshal interrogated the sailor and took him off the ship and into custody. Stewart was returned to the ship on *Meredith Victory*'s sailing for San Francisco on October 3 and was presumably either held in irons or kept under close observation until he was arrested when the ship arrived in port on the nineteenth.

That was not the end of the adventures for the *Meredith Victory*'s crew on this voyage. Whether it was thanks to Seaman Stewart trying to get revenge on one of his accusers or otherwise, the log reports when the *Meredith Victory* arrived on the nineteenth,

> "While in the port of San Francisco ... Stanley S. Strauss, dk. Utility, left the ship at noon without permission and was apprehended by U.S. Customs Inspectors carrying a quantity of marihuana. Strauss resisted arrest and refused to turn over the marihuana and when requested by Customs officers, instead he swallowed the narcotic and was taken into custody and placed under hospital arrest ..."

———

IF THE POPULAR accounts of the rescue of the refugees tailed off by the end of 1951, the official recognition did not. On January 2, 1952, Vice Admiral William McCombe Callaghan, commander of the Military Sea Transportation Service, wrote to Albert V. Moore, the president of Moore-McCormack lines. Congratulating him of the one-year anniversary of the rescue, he told Moore,

> "Captain LaRue and his crew have written a chapter in American merchant marine history which will long stand as one of the most brilliant. What the *Meredith Victory* accomplished at Hungnam has served to remind the world that the American merchant marine has always been more than equal to its responsibilities in times of emergency."[5]

Captain La Rue received the first of many personal honors when the Propeller Club of Seattle[6] made him their dinner guest on February 21, 1952, while the *Meredith Victory* was in port. When La Rue took the microphone, he told an audience that included the president of the American Bureau of Shipping and the deputy commander of the MSTS,

"We are grateful to God for having given us the privilege along with the other United Nations of assisting our Korean neighbors. It is my sincere hope-my prayer-that what happened to the people of Hungnam will never happen to your families or mine."

In the words of the Moore-McCormack's manager in Seattle, C. J. Gravesen, "He brought the house down." The commander of the Northern Pacific Area of the MSTS, Commodore M. E. Eaton, presented Captain La Rue with a commendation from Vice Admiral Callaghan. Walter Green, the president of the American Bureau of Shipping, presented La Rue with a plaque to hang aboard the *Meredith Victory* commemorating the rescue "... in Recognition of Outstanding Performance by Master and Crew in Evacuating Over 14,000 Refugees from Hungnam, Korea in December, 1950 ..." Before the ship left on its next voyage, the Catholic Archbishop of Seattle, the Most Rev. Thomas A. Connolly, presented La Rue with a crucifix from the Holy Land blessed by Pope Pius XII and a letter of appreciation from the Catholic mission in Yosu (Yeosu), Korea, located about forty miles west of Koje-do.[7]

Captain La Rue receives an award from the Propeller Club of Seattle, as well as a crucifix from the city's archbishop.

Whether or not Captain La Rue knew at the time of the February honors in Seattle that his time aboard the *Meredith Victory* was coming to a close, La Rue soon repeated what he had done with *Whittier Victory* almost four years earlier. On June 5, 1952, the *Meredith Victory* steamed to Olympia, Washington, to join the Reserve Fleet. There, the legendary ship would rest until reactivated fourteen years later for service in another Pacific war.

———

HOW MANY REFUGEES did the *Meredith Victory* actually carry and did she, in fact, carry the most of any ship? While some accounts have Chief Mate Savastio counting the refugees as they boarded, surviving officers assert that, given the masses boarding across the causeway, it would have been nearly impossible to obtain an accurate count. It is more likely that the count corresponded to some degree of counting as refugees boarded or were lowered into the holds, combined with estimation.

With that in mind, it is important to address the question of whether the ship could have even accommodated fourteen thousand human beings objectively. Prior to the evacuation, COMNAVFE's *Operation Plan 116-50* had estimated the personnel capacity of a Victory ship at 1,400.[8] The origin of that number is not referenced, but it likely resulted from dividing the total deck area in the cargo holds by a required area per soldier.

Without the detailed ship plans, it is not possible to calculate the exact area of the holds, but for each hold we can use the Victory ship's bale capacity,[9] depth of the hold and the number of decks in each hold to estimate it. With the pontoon hatches in place, as they were for *Meredith Victory*'s voyage from Hungnam, we can estimate an area for the refugees of about 40,000 square feet in the holds, and another approximately 15,000 square feet available to them on deck (including on top of the hatches at the weather deck). That translates into roughly four square feet per refugee (assuming 10,000 below and another 4,000 on deck), consistent with photographs, crew recollections, and printed accounts like the February 25 story from the *New York Times* news service that commented, "Virtually all the refugees were forced to stand throughout the three-day voyage, none able to move more than a foot or two in any direction." Four square feet is just enough area for a small adult to sit, cross-legged, so there were certainly some opportunities to sit as well as stand. We also know that the refugees were able to move enough that they could attend to their bodily needs. But it was certainly a painful several days.

More challenging are the recollections regarding the number of refugees on the LSTs. Aside from the deckhouse above the main (weather) deck and the accommodation and galley areas on the second deck, which would likely be off-limits to the refugees, the only places to accommodate civilians would be the third ("tank") deck and the main deck forward of the house. The tank deck of an LST was just 8,500 square feet. The main deck provided another 11-12,000 square feet. If the reports were correct that as many as 10,500 Koreans were loaded onto a single LST, the two square feet per person was truly standing-room only!

Did the *Meredith Victory*, in fact, carry the most refugees? At least five contemporaneous US military documents discussed the evacuation of civilian refugees from Hungnam. The *CTF 90 After Action Report* does not break down the ship totals, saying only,

> "On 23 December loading operations continued satisfactorily and loading of merchantmen was completed by midnight. Three merchant ships were loaded with refugees and sailed to Koje Island." The report credits the evacuation of "91,000 Civilian Refugees."[10]

The *X-Corps Command Report* for December, 1950,[11] included this from the chief of staff, Colonel John S. Guthrie, US Army, in his "Summary of Chief of Staff Journal":

> "In view of the short travel time involved in the transporting of personnel to ports in South Korea, it was possible to load fantastic numbers of personnel on all ships (refugee). For example, the MEREDITH VICTORY, normally a cargo carrier, sailed with 14,500

aboard, and LST 668 carried 10,500. A total of 98,100 refugees were evacuated by sea from the X Corps zone."

The *War Diary of ROK Navy and Commander Naval Forces South Korea (CTG 95.7)* commented that on December 10 "... it became apparent that the redeployment of forces from Hungnam had begun. However, no operations plan had been received from CTF 90, and the extent of the operation was unknown to this command." The next paragraph begins, "The known factors were the approximate size of the Tenth Corps with the added number of refugees to be taken out of Hungnam..." The *War Diary* mentioned several small civilian boats carrying refugees in addition to the LSTs and merchant ships loading at the port. At 1230 on the twenty-third, it reports,

"Time chartered Meridith [*sic*] Victory departed from Hungnam loaded with 14,000 refugees bound for Pusan. CTF-90 requested she be diverted to Changsungpo, Koje Island (Lat. 34-51.7N, Long. 128-43.8E). Upon arrival she was to anchor outside the harbor for offloading by ROK LST's and native craft."

The *War Diary* continued,

"On the 23rd of December, the time chartered vessels, Virginia City Victory with 6,000 civilian refugees and Madaket with 7,000 refugees left Hungnam for Kojedo."[12]

Colonel Forney, in his *Special After-Action Report*, commented,

"By the 23rd of December, the last day, I could see my way clear to bringing in three Victory ships and two LSTs, and on these I outloaded 50,000 refugees."

He described the ramp that Army engineers had built across the *Norcuba* and said, "In this way we got over 12,000 refugees on one ship." If he is only crediting that number to one ship, he almost certainly had to be talking about the *Meredith Victory*.[13] Interestingly, in the same reference he says, "On the LSTs we always got at least 5,000," which would seem a more realistic number than ten thousand.

Major Richard W. Schutt, USMC, Colonel Forney's plans and operations officer, wrote his own after-action report, saying that the planning assumed twenty thousand civilians would be evacuated. On December 21 he noted,

> "A tabulation showed that over 41,000 civilian refugees had been evacuated to date with more thousands gathered at the small fishing village of Sokojin, on the right flank of the beach perimeter."

He noted that two days later,

> "In spite of the fact that over 40,000 refugees had been embarked, many thousands still remained to go. At no time had they presented a major problem, except for the solution of getting them all out. On this day it was found that an excess of shipping now existed and three AK[14]'s and three LST's were able to be designated for this use. As a matter of interest approximately 14,000 persons were loaded on each AK type ship, and 9,000 to 10,000 on each LST ... By 2400 all AK type shipping was cleared of the dock area and only several LST's loading refugees and Corps supplies remained."

Major Schutt concludes his report with a summary, in which he totals the number of refugees as "91,100 (probably a low figure)."[15] Major Schutt's numbers would total more than seventy thousand refugees embarked at the end of the evacuation, at least twenty thousand more than Colonel Forney credited.

Outside of Colonel Forney's files, the most exhaustive report is the *Headquarters X Corps Special Report on Hungnam Evacuation*. The report commented enthusiastically,

"The Commanding General's policy to evacuate all civil government officials and their families together with as many other loyal non-communist citizens as shipping space would allow was successful far beyond the highest estimates of the officers involved concerning this problem. In addition to the military evacuation, 98,100 refugees, not including babies on mothers' backs, were transported out of the X Corps area by sea."[16]

The report then goes on to give a breakdown by ship, which is summarized in the Table below along with data from the other sources.[17]

Ship	X Corps	CTF 95.7	Forney	Schutt	Loading Rpt	Loading Date
Lane Victory (Wonsan)	7,000				7009	12/10
LST BM 8501 (ROK)	4,300[i]				4,000[ii]	12/16
Yonayama Maru	3,000				3,000	12/20
Torbata Maru	6,000				6,000	12/20
Madaket	6,400	7,000		14,000+/-	6,400	12/23
Meredith Victory	14,500		12,000+	14,000+/-	14,500	12/23
Virginia City Victory	14,000	6,000		14,000+/-	14,000	12/23
LST BM 668 (ROK)	10,500				10,500	12/20
LST BM 666 (ROK)	7,500				7,500	12/20
LST BM 661 (ROK)	9,400				9,400	12/20
LST 059 (SACJAP)	8,000			8-9,000	8,000	12/23
LST 081 (SACJAP)	4,000			8-9,000	4,000	12/23
LST 074 (SACJAP)	3,500			8-9,000	3,500	12/23
Total	98,100				98,109	

The difference between the "7009" for the *Lane Victory* and the other totals rounded to the nearest hundred or thousand probably reflects the differences in the conditions in the two ports. Fewer than 21,000 soldiers and just 635 vehicles were loaded in Wonsan and Songjin, so there was time to count the refugees as they boarded the *Lane Victory* on the sixth and seventh of December.[18] The crush of refugees and the chaos of their boarding suggests a much less accurate count at Hungnam. Whatever the exact number, Colonel Forney implied that one ship carried an unusually large number of refugees. The totality of the evidence is that the SS *Meredith Victory* was that ship.

WHILE CAPTAIN LA Rue and the *Meredith Victory* were in the lime-light, Vice Admiral Joy was singing the praises of Rear Admiral Doyle, and Major General Almond was receiving his third star, a less famous hero of Hungnam was on his way to his next assignment. Colonel Forney, who had so distinguished himself as X Corps deputy chief of staff and as the control officer for the embarkation at Hungnam, remained in Korea for a few more months. He then returned to San Diego and the organization from which MacArthur's staff had appropriated him, the Troop Training Unit of the Pacific Fleet's Amphibious Training Command. Apparently on track to receive his first star, he temporarily held command of the Troop Training Unit until relieved by Brig. General John T. Selden.

In 1951 the commandant of the Marine Corps ordered Colonel Forney to Paris, France, to teach the first entering class that November at the new NATO Defense College, just founded in the City of Light. Forney was to meet with the commandant on September 5, before flying to Paris on the seventh. On September 3 Forney and his wife boarded an overnight American Air Lines flight from San Diego to Chicago, with a planned connection to another flight leaving Chicago for National Airport in Washington, DC, on the morning of the fourth. Their San Diego flight ended up arriving an hour and a half late, and they missed their connection. American sent them to United Airlines, but there was no space on the flight for the two passengers, and the Forneys were put on a later Capital Airlines Flight to D.C.

In the confusion, Colonel Forney's briefcase was lost during the transfer from American to United to Capital. Forney spent hours at National Airport inquiring with American and United regarding the case. When he received a call at his quarters at 2200 that evening, the good news was that an American Air Lines agent in Chicago had found the briefcase. The bad news was that the case was now in the possession of another agent, this one working for the Federal Bureau of Investigation.

The American Air Lines agent who found the case had opened it in order to find an address for the owner. Inside the briefcase were personal papers, Forney's will, some War Bonds, a street guide to Paris, an English-French dictionary, and a Catholic Daily Missal. Unfortunately, it also contained a stack of classified documents, including top-secret dispatches and operations orders, the top-secret COMNAVFE *Operation Plan 116-50*, secret operations orders, and various documents classified "Confidential." Colonel Forney had planned to present these documents to the Commandant as part of his report on the Hungnam evacuation. When the American Airlines agent saw the classified documents, he had immediately called the FBI, who in turn contacted the Ninth Naval District. The Office of Naval Intelligence (ONI) would soon take possession of the wayward case and its contents.

ONI performed an investigation, interviewing Forney and the American Air Lines employees who had contact with the briefcase and the material inside. At the conclusion of the investigation, the commandant of the Marine Corps, General Clifton B. Cates, sent a memorandum to the chief of naval operations, Admiral William M. Fechteler,[19] with the subject "Possible compromise of classified material." The commandant's memo concluded with four points:

> "Compromise is possible but not probable, Colonel FORNEY was negligent in allowing himself to become separated from this material, For such negligence the Commandant of the Marine Corps intends to issue a letter of censure to Colonel Forney, Recommend no further action."

Forney did get to Paris and teach at the NATO Defense College. After he returned from Paris, he served in the Office of the Secretary of Defense and later as USMC advisor to the Republic of Korea's Marine Corps. When he retired in June 1959, Forney was honored with the "tombstone rank" of brigadier general for his twenty-eight years of distinguished service in and out of battle, marred only by the letter of censure that ensured he would never again be promoted while on active duty. He had earned a Bronze Star during World War II, and two Legions of Merit and an Air Medal in Korea.

Brigadier General Edward H. Forney, USMC (Ret.).

Brig. General Edward H. Forney, USMC (Ret.), was serving as public safety advisor for the US Agency for International Development in Saigon, Vietnam, in the midst of his third war in the Pacific, when he was diagnosed with cancer. He died in San Francisco on January 22, 1965.[20]

PART III

MONK

12

LIFE ON LAND

When he signed off the *Meredith Victory* on June 7, 1952, Captain La Rue was ready for a rest. The first two years of the Korean War had been a constant circuit across the Pacific, with cargo delivered in a war zone and all the attendant stresses he had endured for four years in World War II. So, it was not surprising that he now took a four-month vacation, resting, reading, praying, and visiting family in Philadelphia. Leonard's sister Irma, who had been living in the house on Disston Street with her husband Frank since their mother's passing in 1945, had lost her husband to a heart attack in late June 1950, just before her brother took command of *Meredith Victory*. It appears that their brother, Paul, lived in the house as well. Irma's twin, Isabelle, lived nearby with her husband, John T. Hanigan, as did Maurice and his wife, Jesse.

After a few months of rest, La Rue took his final command, the SS *Mormactide*, on October 20, 1952. The *Mormactide* had been built for the Maritime Commission as a 7,954 gross-ton C-3 transport by Ingalls Ship Building Corporation in Pascagoula, Mississippi, in April, 1941. She was initially operated by Moore-McCormack Lines, but in September, 1942, she was taken over by the Navy Department and renamed USS *Lyon* and operated as a Navy transport for the duration of the war. Surviving intact, Moore-McCormack took her back into her fleet in May 1946 and assumed bareboat-charter of the renamed *Mooremactide* in November of the same year.[1]

SS Mormactide.

Captain La Rue assumed command of the *Mormactide* in Los Angeles. The previous year the ship had been on a regular route from the Atlantic coast down to Brazil and back. With the Korean War still raging, La Rue now took the ship on the routes he had steamed the *Meredith Victory*, from US Pacific ports to Japan and beyond. On the morning of November 6, the *Mormactide* sailed for Yokohama. She spent nearly a month in Japan and Korea, returning to the US on January 6, 1953, when she tied up at a berth in San Francisco. After a few days she was down the coast, and on February 10 *Mormactide* steamed out of San Pedro for Yokohama. She made a fast turnaround, for this time she was back in Los Angeles after just a month. She sailed again from Los Angeles on April 16 for Pusan and was back in the US on May 19, this time docking at the Oakland Army Terminal where the *Meredith Victory* had loaded trucks and tanks for Inchon almost three years earlier.

The major involvement of UN forces in Korea ended with the signing of the Armistice on July 27, 1953. Three years of fighting had cost the lives of 54,246 American soldiers, sailors, airmen, and Marines. The ROK lost 59,000 fighting men killed and 291,000 wounded.[2] The People's Republic of China lost 183,018 killed and more than 800,000 wounded.[3] KPA losses were probably comparable to those of the PRC. Unknown millions of Korean civilians were killed or displaced. Every part of Korea, North and South, had been wrecked to some degree, whether from the simple traffic of men and tanks or from the massive firepower from both sides that turned stones to dust. For all of the destruction it unleashed by invading in 1950, the Democratic Peoples' Republic of Korea actually lost fifteen hundred square miles of territory in the armistice.

Moore-McCormack Lines' official portrait of Captain Leonard P. La Rue.

La Rue sailed back and forth across the Pacific a few more times over the next year in command of *Mormactide*, bringing back war materials and supplies. Then, on July 12, 1954, the SS *Mormactide* arrived at the US Army Base in New Orleans, Louisiana, having passed through the Panama Canal on its way from Yokohama. The man who signed the Immigration and Naturalization Service's "Statement of Master of Vessel Regarding Changes in Crew Prior to Departure" was not Leonard P. La Rue but "A. Swanson." The box where the form asks,

"Seamen left in hospital (or died)" has a number "2" entered, and on the crew list the line with "Leonard P. La Rue" and "Master" is stricken through with a heavy pencil line. Captain August Swanson had relieved Captain La Rue as master in Pusan on May 19, 1954, and La Rue had been left behind in the US Army hospital in Yokohama.

In later interviews, Leonard La Rue denied that there was any one event that caused him to abandon his Merchant Marine career and choose a new vocation. He told Bob Mitchell of the *Newark News* that his vocation was, "just something that always seemed to be there."[4] But he also said his time in the hospital in Japan offered another opportunity to consider his life and life in general. La Rue had two operations, culminating in the removal of an infected kidney, and spent weeks in the hospital.

As La Rue recuperated in the hospital, he had time to think, read and reflect. He got to know some of the patients and was touched by the death of a two-year-old boy he had befriended.[5] At some point he read *The Seven Storey Mountain*, Thomas Merton's 1948 autobiography about his search for faith, his conversion to Roman Catholicism, and his subsequent decision to enter a Trappist monastery and leave the outside world behind. In the book, Merton describes his first thoughts when he entered the monastery, "Brother Matthew locked the gate behind me and I was enclosed within the four walls of my new freedom."

The captain got to know the Catholic chaplain at the hospital and discovered that the chaplain was a member of the Benedictine Order. He recalled his friendship with Father Lautenschlager, the Swiss Benedictine missionary from Bahia, Brazil, whom he sailed home from Trinidad on the *Whittier Victory* eight years before. He asked the chaplain more about the Benedictines and religious life in general. After further study, he resolved to try life as a Benedictine monk. When he returned to the United States from Japan, La Rue requested a six-month leave of absence from Moore-McCormack Lines and entered the St. Paul's Abbey in Newton, New Jersey, sixty miles west of New York City and a hundred miles north of his hometown, Philadelphia.[6]

Leonard La Rue had been raised with a strong Catholic faith, and unlike some men who spent their lives at sea, he had not lost it. While he never directly imposed his faith on his officers and crew (aside from occasionally inviting ones he knew were Catholic to join him ashore for Mass), his crew always knew him to be sober, fair, and moral. Both Bob Lunney and Burley Smith, who combined sailed with dozens of masters in their Merchant Marine careers, recalled captains who drank, who traded in black-market goods, who falsified their deck logs or who carried on with women while in port or, in one notorious case, with the young daughter of his passengers. In their experience, Captain La Rue was the only captain who did not show these human frailties. As Burley Smith put it, "The skipper is a God-like creature on the ship; La Rue didn't play it like that."[7]

Their opinion seems to have been widely shared. Crewman Sam Graham said of La Rue in 1956,

> "The man was a born seaman and a saint. He seemed to know when to take his ship off of one course and put her on another to avoid rough weather. We all knew he said prayers every day and many of his shipmates joined him. I never heard him use a curse word the whole time I was with him. He never took the name of God in vain."[8]

Dino Savastio, La Rue's chief mate on the Meredith Victory and later a master, port director and vice president for Moore-McCormack, told another Mooremack captain that,

> "the captain [La Rue] was a very competent one and a nice one to work for…a very serious, thoughtful guy…quite religious, never adopting a sailor's profane vocabulary, but just a regular 'nice guy.'"

Savastio also relayed to his interlocutor that,

"when they would be in a port on a Sunday without cargo operations, the captain would come down to his cabin and say, 'OK, Dino, get ready because we have to go to Mass.'"[9]

In a letter to his old shipmate, Bob Cochran, two years after his time in the hospital, La Rue described his thoughts around leaving the sea and joining the Benedictines. Writing on Palm Sunday, March 25, 1956, La Rue told Cochran,

"You know, Bob, our Lord has recommended the single life to those who can stand it, but it takes the assistance of the sacraments for an individual to live a virtuous life. Particularly in any traveling profession. So many on ships toss aside all morality and make a mess of their lives...and it certainly is not worth it. The one thing that can help us is the Mass and holy communion. The more we attend Mass, the more we receive communion, the more Christlike we can become and the more masses will speak for us on out judgement day. Our Lord wants us to be daily communicants and if you have never done so... you don't know what you are missing until you do it. It will completely change your whole life and put things in their proper perspective."

"After we laid the Whittier up, I started going to mass and receiving daily on my vacation. My inspiration for this was an old woman in her 80's whom I've never met but I heard about her as she is the mother of one of our neighbors at home. She walks miles to attend daily mass and has been doing so for a long time...all her life I suppose. Anyhow, I said to myself, 'If that old lady can do that...La Rue get your lazy rear end out of that bed instead of sleeping in in the morning and get to mass.' I guess that's one of the reasons why I'm here at the abbey."

"We certainly had some fine shipmates back in those days and it was great sailing south in quest of the sun. I could have gone on and spend the rest of my days going to sea...and accumulating what would have been a fairly substantial sum of money but...'What does it profit a man to gain the whole world and lose his soul?' Each day I'm here I

realize what a great blessing it is and it surprises me to know that out
of millions...the good Lord picks a worm like me!"[10]

In the Roman Catholic Church, religious orders are groups of men or
women committed to prayer and service, according to the founder's
charism, or spirit. The man later known as St. Benedict of Nursia was
born in Italy around AD 480 in what is today the Umbrian town of
Norcia. Almost all of what we know of the man is thanks to a hagiographic biography in the second book of the *Dialogues* by Pope St.
Gregory the Great, written in 593, about fifty years after Benedict's
death.

Tradition holds that Benedict was well-born and had traveled to Rome
for his studies but he was horrified by the dissolution and corruption
he saw there among the general populace of the city, as well as among
his teachers and fellow students. Benedict decided to leave Rome and
pursue a spiritual life of isolation as a hermit. He settled in a cave in
Subiaco, in the upper Aniene valley, about fifty miles east of Rome,
and lived there for three years. His reputation as a holy man grew
among the shepherds and others living in the vicinity of the cave, now
known as the *Sacro Speco* ("Holy Grotto").

While Benedict reputedly had no interest in establishing a religious
order, his apparent sanctity and his reputation for performing miracles
led others to request his help in organizing both lay and religious
communities. As a result, Benedict founded more than a dozen
monasteries, most famously the great monastery at Monte Cassino, in
the rugged mountains about eighty miles south of Rome[11].

In these communities, "monks" (from the Greek *monakhos*, meaning
"alone") lived in isolation from the larger society under vows of
poverty, chastity, and obedience. Some monks would pursue additional studies and be ordained priests in order to celebrate Mass and
perform sacraments. It was for the monastic community of Monte
Cassino that St. Benedict famously composed a list of precepts by
which the monks should live. *The Rule of Saint Benedict (Regula Sancti*

Benedicti), an essay describing how monks should live faithfully, whether alone or in community, comprised seventy-three chapters concerning topics ranging from "What kind of man an Abbot ought to be" to "How the monks are to sleep." *The Rule of St. Benedict* became the basis for much of both male and female monastic life for the next fifteen centuries.

The groups of monks organized by St. Benedict eventually coalesced into a religious order, *Ordo Sancti Benedicti* in Latin, the Order of Saint Benedict, abbreviated as "OSB." The Order of St. Benedict, comprising congregations of priests and brothers, and separately, congregations of sisters, functions differently from other Roman Catholic religious orders by maintaining a relatively non-hierarchical structure. There is no "superior general" or senior leader at the international, national, or even regional level. Benedictine Congregations form abbeys, physical locations where monks or sisters live, work, and pray in community. The head of the abbey, the abbot or abbess, is elected by the abbey's monks or sisters, respectively. Among a monk's vows are obedience to the authority of his abbot, who assigns him work, decides when he can leave the abbey and where he is allowed to go, and even any punishment due. On the other hand, decisions at the congregation level are made more or less democratically among the assembled abbots.

It was just a short time after he entered the St. Paul's Abbey as a guest that La Rue decided he had found his true vocation. He requested to join the order and was admitted as a postulant, the first stage in joining the Order of Saint Benedict, on Thanksgiving Day, November 26, 1954.

St. Paul's Abbey had been founded in 1924 by the Congregation of Missionary Benedictines of Saint Ottilien in Oberbayern, Germany. The abbey grew quickly, so that by the time La Rue had joined in 1954, St. Paul's hosted forty monks in the low hills of northwestern New Jersey. The men lived and worked in a great, grey granite building built in 1932 that stretched along US Route 206, less than a dozen miles east of the Delaware River.

St. Paul's Abbey, circa 1954.

Within a few weeks, La Rue had resigned his position as a master at Moore-McCormack Lines. In his letter of resignation to Captain H. S. Mayo, his superintendent at Moore-McCormack, La Rue explained his reasons for choosing a new path for his life.

"My stay in the hospital proved to be climactic in that it resolved me upon a course of action to settle two absorbing questions: 1. What is the real purpose of life? 2. What am I doing about it? Going to sea had many facets which were enjoyable but each of us in his own manner must walk the Road into Eternity alone, and I feel certain that for me the Road stretches from here onward ..."[12]

La Rue concluded in a reflective vein,

"I shall miss all the good friends ashore and afloat and if I have wronged or injured anyone in any way, I hope I shall be forgiven. So, then it is goodbye, Captain, to you and to all hands. It was a wonderful 12 years."[13]

Certainly, the rhythm of life in a monastery agreed with him, reflecting the order he had experienced as a young officer, with regular periods of activity separated by times of rest or introspection. The motto of the Benedictines is *"Ora et Labora,"* "Prayer and Work," where the work is intended both as a sacrificial offering as well as a means of supporting the abbey. The monks rose at five thirty in the morning, and started their communal prayers ("vigils and lauds") twenty minutes later. They attended Mass, and after Mass they ate a simple breakfast and worked until their midday communal prayer around noon, which was followed by lunch. The monks worked through the afternoon and rejoined for communal prayer ("vespers") in the later afternoon, followed by supper. The day ended with a final communal prayer ("compline") before the monks went to sleep, preparing to repeat the cycle the next day.

Monks from St. Paul's walking with a visitor on their agricultural land across the highway from the abbey.

The monks shared an easy camaraderie. Just as no secular relationship is always sweetness and roses, no one living in a religious community will claim that they always appreciate their fellow religious man's or woman's quirks. But that would have been no surprise to La Rue, since even though as master he had enjoyed his own cabin and office aboard ship for a decade, he still shared his meals and much of his time awake with almost a dozen other officers and a few dozen crewmen. La Rue was not a glib back-slapper, but the pictures from ports in South America and the recollections of his officers show him to be personable even if somewhat reserved.

Men and women joining religious orders frequently take on a new name to signify their break with their past. La Rue chose the name "Marinus," not, as was sometimes reported, because he had been a merchant mariner, but as a male version of the name "Mary," the mother of Jesus. As a postulant Marinus had not technically made a commitment to the Benedictines, but on Christmas Eve, December 24, 1955, he was admitted as a novice, at which time he began formal training for life as a monk.

A year later, on Christmas Day, December 25, 1956, Marinus made his "simple" vows. Men and women in Catholic religious orders typically take vows of chastity, poverty, and obedience. The Benedictines extend these concepts by taking vows of obedience, stability (the commitment to stay at the monastery where the vows are made), and "conversatio morum" or "conversion of life." The latter calls on the monk to strive continually to improve his personal behavior and faithfully live his monastic vocation.

Marinus blended well with the other monks and enthusiastically did as he was asked by the abbot. He first worked in the abbey's refectory, setting the table, clearing the plates, and washing the dishes and glasses after meals. Next, he was assigned to help care for the abbey's nine hundred chickens, certainly a new experience for a man who had only lived in a city or on a ship. When carrying the food for the chickens became too much for his hernia, he was assigned other work, including trimming the hedges around the monastery and shaping the conifers the abbey would sell each year as Christmas trees.

Brother Marinus La Rue, OSB, outside the abbey.

For decades Marinus served the Abbey as its bell-ringer, waking the monks for their morning prayer with the sound of a bell and the loud Latin proclamation, *"Benedicamus Domino"* ("Let us bless the Lord"), to which the monks would respond, *"Deo Gratias"* ("Thanks be to God"). Marinus would then call, *"Laudetor Jesus Christus"* ("Praised be Jesus Christ)," to which the bleary-eyed monks would respond, *"In saecula saeculorum. Amen."* ("For ever and ever. Amen.") As his classmates at the Nautical School had observed in 1934, Marinus loved to sing, and at Mass or during the praying of the office, he sang hymns with gusto, never understanding why his fellow monks occasionally did not share his enthusiasm.[14] He also served as night porter, answering the door to the abbey if the doorbell were rung late at night, after the monks had gone to sleep following compline.[15]

Celebrating a monk taking vows, St. Paul's Abbey chapel, circa 1960.

In December 1959, Marinus sent a Christmas card to his old ship-mate, Bob Cochran, and his wife. The printed message inside said, "A sincere wish of true happiness on Christmas that will continue with you through the New Year." Inside, Marinus wrote to his friend, "Making my final vows at the Christmas midnight mass. Will remember you then and especially ask that Our Lady of Fatima will have good news for you in the New Year." La Rue had a special reverence for that 1917 appearance of the Virgin Mary to three young children in Fatima, Portugal, that included, among other things, a plea for prayers for the conversion of Russia. Marinus made his solemn or "perpetual" vows on December 25 and joined his brothers as a full member of the Benedictine community. He had now committed himself to live as a monk for the rest of his life.

13

GALLANT SHIP

Bob Lunney joined Merl Smith and Burley Smith on the train back to New York after the *Meredith Victory* reached Seattle in January, 1951. Merl and Burley resumed their Merchant Marine careers on other Moore-McCormack ships, but never again sailed with Captain La Rue. Bob Lunney also sailed with Moore-McCormack in 1951, but in September he finally made it to Cornell University Law School, albeit a year later than he had planned. As he had in college, every summer between semesters he sailed with Moore-McCormack and when he graduated in June, 1954, he did the same while looking for a job. In February, 1955, he went to work as an assistant US attorney for the Southern District of New York, a prestigious position in an office that launched many a political career, including those of Elihu Root, Thomas E. Dewey, and Rudolph Giuliani.

The story of Captain La Rue and the *Meredith Victory* was again very much alive in the press thanks to stories about La Rue's new vocation. The autumn 1955 edition of Moore-McCormack's *Mooremack News* reported that Captain Leonard P. La Rue had decided to leave the sea permanently and join the Benedictine Order at St. Paul's Abbey under the name Brother Marinus. A number of news services reported the story and newspapers around the country picked it up, including the *New York Times*. The Republic of Korea's president, Syngman Rhee, an avid reader of the *Times*, read with interest the story on page twelve of October 17, 1955's newspaper, with the headline, "Rescuer of 10,000 now Benedictine" and sub-headline, "Shipmaster Hero of Koreans at Hungnam Has Become a Brother in the Order." The article by Joseph J. Ryan began,

> "The heroic shipmaster who snatched 10,000 Korean refugees from the beaches of Hungnam only hours before the Chinese Communists overran the port in 1950 has walked the bridge of a ship for the last time. Heeding a call far stronger than the sea, Captain Leonard P. La Rue has laid aside his sextant and charts and donned the robes of a Brother at St. Paul's Abbey ..."

The paragraphs that followed recalled the circumstances of the rescue and La Rue's journey to his vocation.

President Rhee responded immediately, since he had been seeking the man who had rescued so many Koreans during the evacuation.[1] He immediately set in motion the process to award Marinus the second highest decoration his government could grant, the "Order of Military Merit Ulchi, with Gold Star." Just two months after Rhee had seen the article in the *Times*, on December 21, the ambassador of the Republic of Korea, His Excellency You Chan Yang, pinned the medal on Brother Marinus' plain black suit before a small crowd at the Korean embassy in Washington. In attendance were three men for whom Leonard La Rue and Brother Marinus had worked: Emmet J. McCormack, Chairman of the Board of Moore-McCormack lines; Vice Admiral Francis Compton Denebrink, Commander of the Military Sea Transportation Service, for which *Meredith Victory* had served during the Korean War; and his new "boss," the Rev. Charles Coriston, OSB, the abbot of St. Paul's Abbey.

Presentation of the Korean "Order of the Military Gold Star" at the Korean Embassy, Washington, DC.

In a quiet voice, Brother Marinus accepted the award and asked to say a few words, which were captured by the news men and women in attendance. Bess Furman, writing in the *New York Times* the next day, quoted him as saying,

"It was like a scene of Dante's Inferno. The once fine city of Hungnam was a mass of devastation and wreckage. It was gasping in its death throes. There was the fire of the fleet, the bombing and strafing, the artillery and rocket fire. Prior to the time when we entered the harbor, we had no idea of the cargo we would carry. Five unshaven, disheveled Army colonels came aboard. Captain, we need your assistance. Zero hour is fast approaching. Thousands of men, women, and children are here. We have to get them out. Will you help us?

"That heart-rending plea needed no reply. It had been answered twenty centuries ago: 'Whatsoever you do to the least of these you do unto me,'"

quoting the Gospel of St. Matthew, Chapter 25, Verse 40. zHe continued,

"We were credited with taking 14,000 in a single lift. Some had to be left behind. What their fate was is better left to the imagination. Many times I have wondered if we faced such a catastrophe what would our reaction be. Would we face up to it as did these brave people?"

Brother Marinus told the audience that he was accepting the award on behalf of all of the officers on the ship and then, reflecting his strong anti-communist feelings, he turned to the ambassador and said, "I hope all countries whose liberties have been stolen from them by the Communists will once more be free and independent."

A few months later, Marinus confided his discomfort in the attention to his friend Bob Cochran, writing,

"I don't know whether or not the article you read mentioned about me receiving an award from the Korean Ambassador not long ago, anyhow, knowing Jack Brady [La Rue's chief engineer on the Meredith Victory] as well as I do, I know he would 'kid' the ears off me as he used to lampoon Admiral Lee, of Moormack, for going down to Washington and 'assuming the angle' for another decoration."

Elsewhere in the letter he commented, "Actually, Bob, the main reason for all this ballyhoo, aside from the interest that may accrue to the Merchant Marine or Mooremack, is the fact that there is such a tremendous need for religious vocations throughout the world."[2] Marinus' awards provided positive publicity for men choosing religious vocations, particularly among the Benedictines.

After the award in Washington, Brother Marinus returned to the abbey for prayer, study, and work, but he was back in the newspapers by the middle of 1956. Again, trading his monk's habit for his plain black suit, on May 25 he accepted the first annual "Tradition of the Sea" award, presented by the New York Board of Trade in a ceremony aboard the Moore-McCormack freighter SS *Mormacsurf* at Pier 32 on the Hudson River. In remarks aboard the ship, Korean Consul

Yongchin Choi said, "Captain La Rue's heroic action will never be forgotten in Korea."[3]

Brother Marinus receives the "Tradition of the Sea" award from the New York Board of Trade.

THE US GOVERNMENT was to take considerably more time than Korea's two-month span for recognizing La Rue and the men of the *Meredith Victory*. On November 5, 1956, Assistant US Attorney Lunney sent a letter to the "Medals and Awards Section" of the US Maritime Administration (MARAD), the successor to the US Maritime Commission.

"Dear Sirs: In view of the recent enactment of Public Law 759 on July 24, 1956, I would like to recommend for appropriate recognition the distinguished and meritorious service of the S.S. Meredith Victory during the Korean War."

The letter goes on to recount the ship's reentry into service, the loading of war materials in Oakland, the service at Inchon, and, in Lunney's words, the "epoch-making evacuation" from Hungnam.

The letter concludes,

"Our brave captain, Leonard P. LaRue, who has since joined the Benedictine Order as a monk, was awarded a high Korean decoration in 1955 for the vessel's exploits. Various publications including the 'Readers Digest' and 'Saturday Evening Post' have reprinted accounts of our Hungnam Evacuation. The above is but a synoptic account of our experience and I would be only too willing to submit any further information you may desire."

Lunney did not have to wait long for a reply. On November 9, H. C. Walker, Chief of the Seaman Services Section of the Division of Office Services at MARAD, wrote Lunney that he had

"read with great interest your account of the performance of the S. S. *Meredith Victory* and her crew ... The Seamen Services Awards Committee, appointed to review Public Law 759 and submit recommendations, is being given your letter for its consideration and you will be informed of its findings as soon as possible."

Public Law 759 of the 84th US Congress was passed to "authorize medals and decorations for outstanding and meritorious conduct and service to the United States Merchant Marine." The first section of the law authorized the Secretary of Commerce to award, with the concurrence of the Secretary of the Treasury, "A merchant marine distinguished service medal" for "any person serving in the United States merchant marine who distinguishes himself by outstanding act, conduct or valor beyond the line of duty," as well as a "merchant marine meritorious service medal ... for meritorious act, conduct or service in line of duty, but not of such outstanding character as would warrant an award of the distinguished service medal."

The second section authorized, "a distinctive service ribbon bar to each master, officer or member of the crew of any United States ship who serves or has served after June 30, 1950, in any warm or national emergency proclaimed by the President or by Congress." The third section authorized the Secretary of Commerce, with the concurrence of the Secretary of the Treasury, "a citation as public evidence of deserved honor and distinction to any United States ship or to any foreign ship which participates in outstanding or gallant action in marine disasters or other emergencies for the purpose of saving life or property."

At the time of Bob Lunney's letter, Walker's Seaman Services Awards Committee was concerned not with the actions of a ship in 1950, but of one in 1956. On July 25, a day after Public Law 759 took effect, the Swedish-American Line's SS *Stockholm* knifed into the side of the Italian Line's SS *Andrea Doria*, the pride of the Italian merchant fleet, in the waters south of Nantucket Island. Before the *Andrea Doria* sank to the continental shelf less than twelve hours later, 1,663 passengers and crew members had to be rescued. Among the ships that responded to the disaster, the United Fruit Company's SS *Cape Ann*, the troopship USNS *Private William H. Thomas*, and the French Line's SS *Ile de* France participated in the rescue, the *Ile de France* herself rescuing almost half of the survivors. The *Stockholm* took on most of the balance, although it was hard to imagine she might be honored for her rescue role in a disaster she had helped cause.[4]

The dying Andrea Doria, *left, and the* Stockholm, *missing much of her bow.*

After receiving H.C. Walker's letter, Bob Lunney followed up with a letter to Walker on March 4, 1957. Internal memoranda at MARAD indicate that Lunney also wrote to his Congressman, Paul Fino, highlighting the lack of action on the part of the Administration. On June 7, 1957, A. A. Hart, Chief of the Office Services Division wrote, "The

attached letter from Mr. James R. Lunney, dated November 5, 1956 ...
was discussed with the Medals Awards Committee ... No action was
to be taken pending conclusions with respect to the ANDREA DORIA
citation then under consideration."

The memo continued, "On June 5, 1957, New York Congressman Paul
Sino's [sic][5] office advised by telephone that Mr. Lunney had written
stating he had not been informed of an action taken on his request."
After explaining the amount of activity MARAD was expending to
administer Public Law 759, particularly in the context of the Andrea
Doria, "the secretary was very understanding and said rather than
send the letter to Maritime, the Congressman would prepare a reply to
Mr. Lunney."[6] Bureaucratic protection assured.

The next paragraph provided insight into the initial thinking of the
Awards Committee:

"From Mr. Lunney's account, it would appear that this particular
voyage of the MEREDITH VICTORY was more or less of a routine
nature, and that probably most ships delivering cargo to Korea had like
or similar experiences. Too, there is no indication that the ship
participated in or displayed outstanding or gallant action in a marine
disaster or other emergency for the purpose of saving life or property,
as required under Public Law 759 for an award of a Gallant Ship
citation."

Here, Hart is likely referring to the initial service of the ship through
Inchon, as well as the hazards of the minefields, the action onshore,
etc., that Lunney noted in his letter.

On the other hand, the memo continued,

"The extent of any action of the vessel that could be considered in any
way as unusual or exceptional was in connection with evacuating
military and civilian personnel. In view thereof, and following
discussion wherein it was generally believed that the Committee

would draw its conclusions from the letter statements, no effort has been made to obtain substantiation of the facts as given. Should the Committee desire official substantiation, processing of the case will be started immediately. Conversely, should the Committee vote against recommending a citation for the MEREDITH VICTORY, a letter will be prepared advising Mr. Lunney of the Committee's findings."

Discussion continued inside MARAD regarding *Meredith Victory*'s eligibility as a Gallant Ship. In August, 1957, the administration's general counsel ruled that the language of Public Law 759 did not allow for retroactive awards. MARAD's H. C. Walker sent Bob Lunney a letter to that effect on August 14, saying, "Therefore, despite the outstanding action in which the MEREDITH VICTORY participated, the Seaman Services Award Committee regrets there is no authority for considering this vessel for any award pursual to Public Law 759." There was a further exchange of letters between Lunney and MARAD regarding retroactivity, but as far as MARAD was concerned, the matter was closed.

Outside of MARAD, however, as the result of Lunney's prodding, House Resolution 10156, "A Bill to Provide Appropriate Public Recognition of the Gallant Action of the Steamship Meredith Victory in the December 1950 Evacuation of Hungnam, Korea," was introduced in the 85th Congress on February 19, 1958. MARAD must have been informed that the bill would be submitted because on January 21, H. C. Walker sent a letter to William T. Moore, the president of Moore-McCormack Lines and the son of founder A. V. Moore, with a copy of the proposed legislation and a request for "copies of all authentic information in your possession, particularly log entries and statements of the Master and/or members of the crew."[7]

Regardless of how Moore responded (he would presumably have been highly enthusiastic for the positive publicity), on February 17 Walker forwarded to the Merchant Marine Awards Committee the verbatim description of the event that Bob Lunney had provided more than a year earlier. Two days later the committee considered the bill and recommended that MARAD support it, but they added,

> "The Committee, however, recommends that the bill be amended to make provision for an award, in accordance with our policy, of the Merchant Marine Meritorious Service Medal to the Master of the vessel at the time of the action."

Brother Marinus would receive still another honor.

Within a month, the Secretary of Commerce, Sinclair Weeks, was corresponding with both the Director of the Bureau of the Budget, Maurice H. Stans, and the Secretary of the Treasury, Robert B. Anderson, seeking their concurrence, which he received.[8] On April 24 Secretary Weeks wrote Congressman Herbert C. Bonner of North Carolina, the chairman of the House Committee on Merchant Marine and Fisheries, to recommend "favorable consideration of the bill with an amendment hereinafter suggested," the addition of the Meritorious Service Medal for Captain LaRue. But H.R.10156 never made it to the floor of the House for a vote before the 1958 election, and in February 1959, Secretary Weeks was repeating the process with Chairman Bonner, now on behalf of H.R. 2533 in the 86th Congress.

On May 20, 1958, the Republic of Korea again recognized the events of the Hungnam evacuation, this time with a Presidential Unit Citation. After La Rue had been honored with the Korean Order of Military Merit and the US Congress had passed Public Law 759, Bob Lunney had contacted the Korean Embassy with a similar package of information about the activities of the *Meredith Victory*, requesting recognition for the officers and crew. On June 27, 1958, the Consul General of the Republic of Korea, D. Y. Namkoong, presented Lunney with the award in a ceremony at the Korean Consulate on East 80th Street in New York. The award was ostensibly received on behalf of all of the officers and men of the *Meredith Victory*, although the brief *New York Times* article announcing the award carried the unfortunate headline of "Korea to Decorate Second Hungnam Hero" and described of

Lunney "his medal and citation" without mentioning the more general nature of the honor.

Bob Lunney receives the Korean Presidential Unit Citation from the Korean Consul in New York on behalf of the officers and men of the Meredith Victory.

The Citation read, "The President of the Republic of Korea takes pleasure in citing The Officers and Crew of the Steamship Meredith Victory who participated in the evacuation of Hungnam, Korea in December of 1950." It continued,

"The Meredith Victory entered the port of Hungnam on the evening of 22 December 1950 where thousands of civilians waited by the water front, the last avenue of escape from the threat of annihilation by invading enemy forces. Answering an appeal from the United Nations Forces, then under great pressure from overwhelming communist forces, the Officers and Crew of the Meredith Victory spared no effort in accepting on board their 7,636 ton cargo-freighter 14,000 men, women and children and transporting them down the coast to safety.

"The arrival of the Meredith Victory in Pusan after a three-day voyage though dangerous waters was a memorable occasion for all who participated in this humanitarian mission, and is remembered by the people of Korea as an inspiring example of Christian faith in action.

"By this citation the Officers and crew of the Meredith Victory who participated in the evacuation of Hungnam during the period 22 December to 25 December 1950 are entitled to wear the Presidential Unit Citation Ribbon."

As 1959 began, the bills in Congress to honor the *Meredith Victory* were finally advancing from committee to votes on the floor, with House Resolution 2533 introduced in January to replace the expired HR 10156, and New York Senator Jacob Javits introducing Senate Bill 2185 in August. On March 15 Chairman Bonner's committee reported the bill out favorably, the House approved it on the 21st, and HR S.2185 was approved by acclamation in the Senate on March 31. The bill was signed by President Eisenhower the same day, becoming Public Law 86-398. The law provided for the awarding of the Gallant Ship designation to the SS *Meredith Victory*, a ribbon bar to each officer and crewman, and the Meritorious Service Medal for the master, as the MARAD had requested.

The text of the Unit Citation for SS *Meredith Victory* naming her a Gallant Ship was written within MARAD and borrowed extensively from Bob Lunney's original letter to the Administration in 1956, but apparently, in the interest of drama, it managed to embellish many of the facts of the ship's accomplishment. The Citation read,

"At the height of the epoch-making evacuation of Hungnam, Korea, by the United Nations Forces in December, 1950, the Meredith Victory was requested to assist in the removal of Korean civilians trapped and threatened with death by the encircling enemy armies. Most of the military personnel had been pulled out and the city was aflame from enemy gunfire. Despite imminent danger of artillery and air attack, and while her escape route became more precarious by the hour, "the MEREDITH VICTORY, her tanks full of jet fuel, held her position in the shell-torn harbor until 14,000 men, women and children had crowded the ship. One of the last ships to leave Hungnam, the MEREDITH VICTORY set her course through enemy mine fields, and although having little food and water, and neither doctor nor interpreter, accomplished the three-day voyage to safety at Pusan with her human cargo, including several babies born en route, without loss of a single life.

"The courage, resourcefulness, sound seamanship and teamwork of her master, officers and crew in successfully completing one of the greatest marine rescues in the history of the world have caused the name of the MEREDITH VICTORY to be perpetuated as that of a Gallant Ship."

Each of the forty-seven officers and men of the *Meredith Victory* received this text within a letter from the Office of the Administrator at MARAD, dated April 29, 1960. The letter included the Gallant Ship Unit Citation Bar that could be worn on their uniforms and it closed with the note that the crew member

"is congratulated upon the performance of a service which was in keeping with the highest traditions of the Unite States Merchant Marine, and I have directed that a copy of this award be made a part of his service record."

On April 13, 1959, Bob Lunney, finally hoping to see the results of his plentiful correspondence, had written to MARAD requesting information on when and where the Gallant Ship presentation would occur. The administration responded the following week that they anticipated the ceremony to take place in New York, at a date and time to be determined.

The ceremony actually occurred more than a year later in Washington, D.C., at the Propeller Club of the United States, Port of Washington, in the National Press Club building, at noon on August 24, 1960. The *Washington Post* published an article on the twenty-first headlined, "Ex-Ship Captain, Now in Monastery, To Be Honored for War Heroism,"

with the sub-headline "Rescued 14,000 Refugees." Like the citation
that would be awarded, the article mixed fact with fiction, saying,
"Small crash boats shuttled loads of refugees to LaRue's ship, which
had accommodations for just 12 passengers." It did credit Sen. Javits
for introducing the bill in 1959 "to give the action public recognition."
There was no mention of the earlier efforts in the House of Representatives.

The bronze citation affixed to the Gallant Ship award to the SS Meredith Victory.

Secretary of Commerce Frederick H. Mueller presided over the cere-
monies and in remarks before unveiling the plaque he tied the actions
of the *Meredith Victory* and her crew to the ongoing fight against
communism.[9] He began,

"Our purpose here today is to honor a gallant, generous act, executed
under enemy fire in Korea in December 1950 … In 1953, President
Eisenhower secured an Armistice in Korea and the war ended. Today,
no Americans are dying in distant battles.[10]

"But the times are still perilous. Wise, strong and brave leadership is
vital. Remembering the heroic deeds of those gray days in Korea tends

to focus our attention on the dangers posed by Communism-then and now.

"The great challenge of our time is the survival and ultimate victory of freedom-the call to save freedom from Red slavery-from those who boast that eventually Communism will dominate the world.

"It is significant that by commemorating this gallant ship, the SS MEREDITH VICTORY, her brave captain and her courageous crew, we honor those who were pioneers in saving people from Communist terror. Let us be dedicated to a similar purpose."

Secretary Mueller then read the citation to the assembled Merchant Mariners, dignitaries, and press.

Before the actual presentation of the Service Bars to the officers in attendance and the Meritorious Service Medal to Captain La Rue, the secretary read from remarks written for the occasion by Admiral Arleigh Burke. Burke, who ten years prior had played a significant role in the success of CTF 90 as the Chief of Naval Operation's hand-picked deputy chief of staff for CINCNAVFE's Vice Admiral Joy, was himself now Chief of Naval Operations, the Navy's most senior leader. Burke said,

"I was in Hungnam in late December and I have vivid memories of the conditions which existed at that time in that much battered port. In those days we were evacuating our troops and we in the Navy had guaranteed to supply all the artillery necessary to prevent a successful Communist attack on the Hungnam perimeter while our ground forces were loaded out.

"I remember the thousands of woebegone Koreans who were hungry, destitute and fearful, but who at the same time had the strong desire for freedom and the willingness to make sacrifices for freedom. This is a very powerful desire which is so prevalent in all peoples who have suffered under a dictatorship in which liberty is suppressed and in which there is no human dignity or respect.

"That these people might live in freedom and that they might have hopes that their children could also live in freedom, required great effort and drastic measures by sympathetic men. The captain, the officers and crew in MEREDITH VICTORY were sympathetic men; they did take the desired drastic measures; they were successful, and as a result of their extraordinary efforts many people are now free who otherwise might well be under the Communist yoke. Many unknown Koreans owe the future freedom of their children to the efforts of these men whom you are honoring on August twenty-fourth."

Since the *Meredith Victory* had reentered the Reserve Fleet on June 30, 1952, this time in Olympia, Washington, the actual presentation of the Gallant Ship plaque was to the head of MARAD, Vice Admiral Ralph E. Wilson. Admiral Wilson accepted it with the expectation that, "at an appropriate time it be prominently affixed to the SS MEREDITH VICTORY and forever be preserved among our Merchant Marine's honored memorabilia."

The crew receive their citations and ribbons from Secretaty Mueller. behind a seated Brother Marinus. From left, Bob Lunney, William Jarrett, Albert Golembeski and Major Fuller. Dino Savastio is to Lunney's right, out of the picture.

Following the presentation of the plaque, it was time for the officers and crew in attendance to receive their citation bars. Representing a distribution of the officers and crew, the men receiving their citations and ribbons in person were: the ship's steward, Major M. Fuller; Second Mate Albert W. Golembeski; Able-bodied Seaman William R. Jarrett; Chief Mate Dino Savastio; and the persistent purser, James Robert Lunney.

Brother Marinus receives his Merchant Marine Meritorious Service Medal from Secretary Mueller.

The last award was to Brother Marinus, the former Captain La Rue. Unbeknownst to the other attendees, Marinus had been reluctant to attend the ceremony but he was obedient to his abbot, who had instructed him to appear.[11] Secretary Mueller presented the Meritorious Service Medal to the thin, soft-spoken man wearing the same black suit he had worn at the Korean embassy in 1955, saying, "It is with pride that I present the Merchant Marine Meritorious Service Medal to Brother Marinus, a man of courage and conviction, a man who, unlike the Communist aggressors he met in Korea, walks humbly before God." In a soft voice, the strongly anti-communist Brother Marinus followed the theme set by Secretary Mueller, saying, "No one can appreciate the importance of stopping communism unless he has been at a place like Hungnam." He closed his brief remarks by speaking of the "wonderful feeling when one surrenders himself to the love of the Lord."[12]

Marinus says a few words after receiving his award.

One man who could not be at the event sent his congratulations via a telegram to the Secretary of Commerce. Whittier College's most famous alumnus said,

> "I greatly appreciate this opportunity to express, through you, my deep admiration and appreciation to Brother Marinus, former master of the SS Meredith Victory, for the magnificent leadership he gave to the entire crew of that gallant ship which enabled them to save 14,000 South Koreans from communist slavery in the evacuation from Hungnam in Dec. 1950. This outstanding humanitarian achievement will live long and gloriously in the annals of history. Kind regards, Dick Nixon."[13]

If Marinus had finished his service at sea, the *Meredith Victory* had not finished hers. With another war in the Pacific raging in 1966, this time in Vietnam, fifteen hundred miles southwest of Korea, the ship was again reactivated from its rest in the Reserve Fleet at Olympia, Washington.[14] Joining 160 other cargo ships, many Victory's like the *Meredith*, she was reactivated in Seattle, but unlike the others, her reactivation would be accompanied by a ceremony with the "Gallant

Ship" plaque that Secretary Mueller had presented on her behalf to Admiral Wilson. Washington's own US Senator, Warren G. Magnuson, chairman of the Senate Commerce Committee, presented the plaque to the master and crew of the newly reactivated ship. The bronze and mahogany trophy had been hanging in a hallway at the Department of Commerce for more than six years.

Brother Marinus was invited to attend the ceremony but declined, this time with the consent of his abbot. Instead, he wrote a letter to be read at the ceremony.[15] Addressing the new officers and men of the *Meredith Victory*, he said,

"Within the monastic walls of our Benedictine Monastery, located in the colorful hill country of Northern New Jersey, word has been conveyed to me of the reactivation of the SS Meredith Victory.

"During the Korean War, I enjoyed the privilege of sailing in this vessel. At present, and for the past twelve years, I have been holding down a berth in another vessel, namely the Barque of Peter.

"Though approximately sixty miles separated the Monastery from the sea (jokingly, we say the beach is a little wider here) the news of the reactivation re-kindles a host of vibrant and treasured memories-memories of a Gallant Ship and her complement utilized in a gallant mission of mercy and justice. Distance cannot separate us from cherished recollections of the Meredith Victory and the men who constituted her complement.

"Once again, in a National crisis, the Meredith Victory will be engaged in an effort to help stem the scourge and evil of communist aggression.

"May she and all who serve in her be successful in their endeavor!

"Please convey to the Master, Officers, and Seamen of the Meredith Victory my sincere congratulations in their new assignment. May they always uphold the highest traditions and ideals of our Country and our Merchant Marine.

"Wishing them God speed and all blessing. Sincerely, in Christ, Brother Marinus, O.S.B., Ex-Master, SS Meredith Victory."

The SS *Meredith Victory* dutifully carried supplies for the soldiers and Marines in Vietnam for three and a half years under MSTS charter with American President Lines. On January 30, 1970, she entered the Reserve Fleet at Suisun Bay, California, near where the Sacramento and San Joaquin Rivers meet as they reach for San Francisco Bay. When she left the fleet this time, it would not be for service in her fourth war. The massive army and Marine forces deployed for the Gulf War in 1991-92 had their own, modern roll-on/roll-off ships and combat transports to carry them across the oceans. Instead, on October 1, 1993, she was sold for scrap to the Nishant Import and Export Company of the United Arab Emirates.

While the rest of the ship lives on as imported cars or structural steel or razor blades, one very important item survives. Following Admiral Wilson's commitment years before, the "Gallant Ship" plaque of the SS *Meredith Victory* today hangs in a place of honor in the American Merchant Marine Museum, located on the grounds of the the United States Merchant Marine Academy in Kings Point, New York. The plaque shares a small room dedicated to the ship's achievements at Hungnam and to the honor of Captain Leonard Panet La Rue.

The Meredith Victory's Gallant Ship *plaque at the American Merchant Marine Museum.*

14

THE CAUSE

The Gallant Ship award presentation was the last time Brother Marinus appeared in public. At the same time Congress was considering the Gallant Ship award, the alumni of La Rue's *alma mater*, the Pennsylvania Nautical School, nominated Brother Marinus for their second-annual "Jamoke Pot" award. Named after nautical slang for a pot of coffee, the award was made to alumni members for "attaining outstanding personal achievement, and particularly, to those members making their achievement in the maritime field." Marinus wrote to alumni president Ed Blake, thanking him for the nomination but politely declining:

"I want to thank you and the membership for your words of congratulations, your kind interest and sentiments. Rest assured, all of you maintain an irreplaceable affection in my heart and memories and daily, along with your loved ones, are remembered in my communions and prayers … In regard to the idea you mentioned in honoring me, I would prefer to be left out of the picture entirely. Instead, I humbly suggest that if the alumni wish to do something in this regard that the chalice you mention or placque [*sic*] or other idea you may have in mind, may be dedicated to the men who have passed on."

Within St. Paul's Abbey, the life of prayer and work was proceeding so robustly that the monks planned a new complex of buildings to replace the current abbey building, nearing thirty years old. On February 11, 1961, Marinus wrote his friend, Bob Cochran, asking for support,

> "In a few days now here at Newton, we are going to begin construction of a new monastery as the present facilities are no longer adequate and are lacking in many respects.
>
> "I am sending you a booklet telling a little of our story and the reason for our expansion plans.
>
> "In order to carry out this program, we must appeal to our families and friends wherever they may be for help … It is mortifying to have to do this, but such mortifications are good for us … serve to humble us. The servant should not be above the Master."

It must indeed have been mortifying for Marinus, who as Leonard La Rue had not asked his family for anything since graduating from the Nautical School. Marinus closed with a typical prayer for his friend, "All here remember you and your loved ones in our prayers. God bless you and may you become the saint He wants you to be."[1]

The brochure Marinus sent told that the original monastery had been built for thirty-five monks, but now had to house fifty-one. Some of these men were seminarians who took high school- and college-level courses in preparation for full acceptance into the Benedictine community and subsequent missionary work. The new complex, to be built across US 206 from the current abbey on part of the land farmed by the monks, would feature a much-enlarged chapel and refectory, separate wings for the monks and the seminarians, as well as a wing for up to one hundred lay Catholics to stay while attending abbey-sponsored religious retreats. The estimated cost of the construction was $850,000. The Benedictines hoped to have $350,000 on hand at the time of groundbreaking, March 20, 1961, the eve of the Feast of St. Benedict on the twenty-first.[2]

Whether Marinus raised any money from his friends outside the monastery, we do not know, but the new complex was built on schedule and opened in 1962.

Even in the heady days of the 1950s and 1960s, the Abbey always needed income, and without a parish there was no Sunday collection to rely upon. Fees charged for religious retreats helped. Every December the abbey sold Christmas trees, with families arriving in station wagons armed with saws and warm clothing to traipse the abbey property in search of the perfect fir or scotch pine for their living room. But the largest source of income was the kindness of outsiders who made donations to support the monks and the overseas missions they populated once trained at the abbey.

Brother Marinus at the gift shop's snack bar in 1988, where he entertained a cadre of the abbey's neighbors.

Brother Marinus did his part supporting the finances of the abbey starting in the spring of 1959 by running the abbey's gift shop.

Marinus replaced another monk, Fr. Anthony Ashcroft, who left to work in the St. Ottilien Congregation's missions in Africa. The gift shop sold religious articles and books, along with snacks and drinks for travelers on a part of the highway that did not have many restaurants. During the monks' apple harvest, the store sold the fruit by the bushel.

Marinus always had a pot of "jamoke" hot and ready for travelers for sale at ten cents a cup, and over the years he accumulated a group of regular visitors from the Newton area who would stop by to share a cup of coffee with the aging monk. They discussed religion, the weather, politics, but the one topic Marinus never discussed was Hungnam. Not until years later, when he died and they read his obituary in the newspaper, did they realize their quiet friend had been pivotal to the rescue of fourteen thousand of their fellow human beings. Marinus never talked about it because he had left Hungnam and the rest of his past behind when he became a Benedictine. His humility and his commitment to his vows prevented him from reliving the event.[3]

Marinus in front of his beloved hedges in 1989.

Perhaps one of the few times Marinus came close to discussing Hungnam was in his 1978 Christmas card to Bob Cochran. Marinus alluded to his time on the *Meredith Victory*, asking, "Did you know Jack

Brady-Chief Engineer for Mooremack?" He continued, "He passed away during the past year and was buried in Venezuela. He was my Chief on the Korea run." Then Marinus turned back to the more mundane, the work of the abbey. "We are carrying on here selling firewood and had a two week logging operation last fall. All O.K. and doing well." Marinus closed as he always did, with a blessing for his friend, "God love you and keep you in his care. Merry Christmas, Brother Marinus."

A frail Marinus, now eighty-two, in the courtyard of the new abbey in 1996.

As Marinus entered his late seventies, his health started to fail. His dedication to the abbey gift shop was admirable (his brother monks recalled the path he had worn in the grass between the main entrance of the abbey and the entrance to the gift shop, a straight line from door to door), but his management increasingly left much to be desired. The shop was disorganized and dusty, and sales were not keeping pace with previous years. The abbot took the occasion of closing the gift shop for renovation to gently ease Marinus into retirement.[4] The elderly monk sounded wistful as he wrote to Bob Cochran before Christmas in 1991, "Gift shop will be closed after Christmas for

2 or 3 months. There will be refurbishing, etc. I will be replaced by a lady hired from the outside. Don't know what the future will be but will carry on."

Marinus had worked in the gift shop for more than thirty years and had taken his vow of "stability" seriously. He turned down offers from friends to come and stay with them, and he never asked to go on a vacation outside the abbey or to travel except to attend a family funeral. He never learned to drive. If he needed to get to a doctor's appointment, he would either walk along US 206 to get there or another monk would drive him. Other than that, he never left the abbey. He continued trimming hedges around the property, and helped to farm the abbey's all-important Christmas trees. As he had done since the mid-1960s, he continued ringing the morning bell, waking the monks and calling them to prayer, and he continued his service as night porter.

Christmas of 1996 brought Marinus a joyful occasion when he cele-brated his fortieth anniversary as a Benedictine and renewed his vows at a special Mass. Marinus was presented with a "Jubilarian Staff," a man-height ceremonial staff with a cross carved at the top. By tradi-tion, the Jubilarian Staff would be presented at a monk's fiftieth anniversary, but Abbot Justin Dzikowicz did not believe Marinus would survive to his fiftieth anniversary, having joined late in life and not being in the best of health, so he elected to honor him a decade earlier.[5]

Perhaps this was the high point in Marinus' life at St. Paul's. Over the course of the next year health problems began to hobble the old monk. In May 1997, he resigned his post as bell-ringer, and in June he was forced to retire as night porter. Marinus' gait had become unstable and his vision was now poor enough that he could not read. An earlier cataract surgery had been unsuccessful in restoring his vision. That month he moved from the room he had occupied since the new abbey had been constructed into a room in the abbey infirmary. Marinus was unable to work, and now only left his room to attend Mass and eat in the abbey refectory.

In 1999, as the fiftieth anniversary of the Hungnam evacuation approached, Marinus received requests for interviews made through the new abbot, Fr. Joel Macul. Korean newspapers were avid to remember the event, and the journalist and author William H. "Bill" Gilbert began writing the first book in English telling the story of the rescue of the refugees from Hungnam, *Ship of Miracles*. Abbot Macul spoke with Gilbert on several occasions, but Gilbert never spoke with Marinus. Even if he had been willing to talk about a subject he had avoided discussing for almost forty years, he would not have been able. After suffering from cataracts and painful arthritis in his spine that had confined him to a wheelchair, Brother Marinus was now showing signs of dementia.

Brother Marinus La Rue died in his sleep at seven in the morning on October 14, 2001. A Vigil for the Dead was held on the evening of October 16, with his brother monks in attendance joined by members of the local Korean Catholic community. The next morning the abbey celebrated a Mass of Christian Burial for Marinus in the abbey church, and again members of the Korean Catholic community attended, and even served as pallbearers. In his homily during the Mass, Abbot Macul said of Marinus that he

"left the sea with all its drama and heroic opportunities for the intimacy of a daily sustained relationship with the Lord and his Mother ... he believed he was joining the inhumanity he had witnessed around the world to the saving humanity of Christ."[6]

After the funeral, Marinus was buried in the Christ the King Cemetery behind the abbey, a short walk down a hill from what is today a fruit orchard.

Among the mourners that day were Bob and Joan Lunney, who drove over from their home in New York, as well as a Korean-American named Peter Kim, who had been an 11-year-old boy when he joined 14,000 others aboard the *Meredith Victory* in 1950. For years Kim had lived within a dozen miles of the abbey, but he had only discovered how close he was to the former Captain La Rue the summer before when they were introduced by a Korean-American priest of the Archdiocese of Newark. That fifty-year reunion was a joy for Peter Kim, but Marinus barely knew he was there.

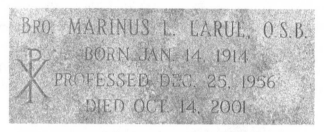

Brother Marinus' headstone in the abbey cemetery.

Coming fifty years after the original coverage of the Hungnam evacuation, Bill Gilbert's book and the obituaries that followed Brother Marinus' death exposed thousands of new readers to the story. On October 20, *The New York Times* placed La Rue's obituary at the top of page A11, next to that of a Princeton University philosopher and above those of a film actress and a renowned herpetologist. Featuring the iconic formal "headshot" of La Rue in his master's uniform and white cap, over eighteen paragraphs the *Times* recounted the evacuation in detail and described his journey to his new vocation. The obituary closed with a quotation from one of La Rue's interviews almost five decades earlier, "... God's own hand was at the helm of my ship."

The *Times* was not the only newspaper to report the death. The *Los Angeles Times* carried a long obituary two days after its New York namesake, placing theirs at the top of page A9. Under the sub-heading "Military mission of mercy that saved 14,000 souls," the *Guardian* newspaper of London, England, carried an extensive obituary on December 19. The abbey's local newspaper, the Morris County *Daily Record*, carried a long obituary of Marinus on the same page as that of a victim of the September 11 attacks on the World Trade Center two months earlier.

Wire services distributed the obituary widely, basing it on a release by the abbey. The publication of Marinus' obituary in the *Tampa Tribune* on October 21 was followed nine days later by a long letter to the editor by local artist Glenwood Sherry. Sherry must have either read Gilbert's book or a more extensive obituary, because under the title, "Heroic Humanitarian," he detailed La Rue's part in the rescue.

Marinus' decline and death were paralleled within the fortunes of the abbey. After the second Vatican Council in the early 1960s, all Catholic religious orders saw declines in men and women entering religious life and the Benedictines were no exception; the last monk had entered St. Paul's Abbey around 1975.[7] By the late summer of the year 2000, the monastery community had decided that the remaining monks were unable to continue operating the monastery and would leave St. Paul's. Most would go to other monasteries, while one or two would move into assisted living. Fortuitously, the leadership of the congregation to which the abbey belonged, St. Ottilien in Germany, approached another of their constituent abbeys, the Abbey of Saints Maurus and Placid in Waegwan, South Korea, about the possibility of sending monks to St. Paul's. After several visits by monks from Waegwan, an agreement was completed on October 19, 2001, for monks from Korea, all significantly younger than the population currently at St. Paul's, to move to New Jersey and reinvigorate the abbey.

While the Koreans would certainly have been sympathetic to their *confreres* in any event, the connection between Korea and the monks at St. Paul's was particularly strong. Indeed, the 140 monks at Waegwan owed the existence of their abbey in part to the work of a monk from St. Paul's. Fr. Timothy Bitterli, OSB, had been serving as a missionary in Korea before the Korean War and had lived with Korean Benedictines at their abbey in Tokwon, near Wonsan. Fr. Bitterli left Tokwon to return to St. Paul's before the suppression of the monastery by the North Korean government in 1949 and the subsequent war. The suppression of the monastery, which began in May with the arrest and imprisonment of all of the monks and sisters, eventually claimed the lives of twenty-eight monks and eight sisters. In 1951 Bitterli returned to the ROK to gather the remaining monks who had fled south and help them form a new monastery at Waegwan, just north of the city of Taegu (Daegu). The abbey was officially founded in July 1952, and after the armistice in 1953, St. Ottilien's Arch-Abbey sent 20 German monks to help construct the abbey buildings.

Another affinity was, of course, Brother Marinus, who died less than a week before the Waegwan Abbey agreed to send their monks to St. Paul's. The Korean monks were well aware of his role in rescuing fourteen thousand of their countrymen. Indeed, one of the monks at Waegwan, Fr. Antonio Sun-geon Kang, had been born at Hungnam on April 2, 1950 and had been evacuated as a baby along with his parent aboard the *Meredith Victory* that fateful December.

Over the years following their arrival in 2001, the Korean Benedictines added religious art from Korea to the abbey, silk panels and statuary depicting saints and holy scenes in the styles of Asian, rather than European, artists. They also displayed awards to the late Brother Marinus. Hanging in the entrance to the refectory to this day is a great, glass-covered gold frame enclosing a pair of golden medals in the pattern of a sunburst, one hanging from a pink silk ribbon. The citation reads in English and Korean, "The Great Meritorious Service Medal," and continues,

"Presented Posthumously to LEONARD P. LaRUE, Captain, THE S.S. MEREDITH VICTORY.

"This is to certify that the Great Meritorious Service Medal is presented on behalf of all the members of the Korean Veterans Association, in grateful recognition of the contribution to the Heungnam Evacuation Operations as Captain of the S.S. MEREDITH

VICTORY, which saved many Korean soldiers and civilians during the Korean War in 1950."

The citation is dated February 23, 2006, and signed by General Sang-Hon Lee, ROK Army, Retired, the chairman of the Korean Veterans Association.

The "Great Meritorious Service Medal" awarded by the Korean Veterans' Association.

Years later, the Korean government itself made several more post-humous remembrances of Captain La Rue, Brother Marinus. On June 28, 2017, as his first official duty on landing in the United States, South Korean President Moon Jae-in traveled to the US Marine Corps base in Quantico, Virginia. There, in front of the Marine Corps Museum's octagonal bronze-and-granite monument commemorating the battle of the Jangjin (Chosin) Reservoir, the president gave a gracious speech extolling the bravery of the Marines and the importance of their sacrifice to US-Korean relations.

Central to the speech was a recounting of Huengnam and of his own personal contact with the evacuation,

> "My parents were also among the refugees aboard the SS *Meredith Victory* at that time.
>
> "...Loaded with a whopping 14,000 refugees, ... The voyage was a perfect success without a single death.
>
> "...It was the greatest humanitarian operation in history.
>
> "Two years later, I was born on Geoje Island where the SS *Meredith Victory* disembarked the refugees. Had it not been for the...the success of the Hungnam evacuation, my life would not have started. I would not even exist today."

President Moon, center, in front of the monument. The Commandant of the Marine Corps, General Robert Neller, is to his left. Third and fourth from the left are Bob and Joan Lunney. Second from right is Ned Forney, grandson of Colonel Edward H. Forney, USMC.

On June 1, 2018, a year after President Moon had made his speech to the assembled dignitaries and US Marine veterans at Quantico, the Korean ambassador to the United States, Yoon-je Cho, traveled to St. Pauls abbey. At the front of the abbey, along the path Marinus walked daily to the gift shop, the ambassador joined in the ceremonial placement of a monument to the monk and the planting of a memorial Winter Hawthorn tree.

Ceremonial placement of the Korean government's memorial to Brother Marinus at St. Paul's Abbey. Ambassador Yoon-je Cho at the center, the current abbot of St. Paul's, Rev. Samuel Kim, OSB, at the far left, and Bob Lunney is to the ambassador's left.

한국, 1950년 겨울, 기적의 항해,
마리누스 수사님께 존경과 감사의 마음을 바칩니다.

WITH RESPECT AND GRATITUDE FOR BROTHER MARINUS
WHO, IN THE WINTER OF 1950, KOREA
LED THE VOYAGE OF MIRACLE

PRESIDENT OF THE REPUBLIC OF KOREA

MOON JAE-IN

JUNE 1, 2018

Inscription on the memorial at St. Paul's Abbey.

Another honor had been awarded closer to the time of the Korean Veterans' Meritorious Service Medal, this time by an American group. The "Star of the Sea Award" was awarded by the Apostleship of the Sea of the United States of America (AOS USA), the professional association of Catholic maritime ministers and Catholic seafarers. Today, the organization is perhaps best known for providing Catholic chaplains for cruise ships.

The award, which is not made every year but only when the AOS USA seeks to acknowledge "special actions in the maritime industry," requoted the familiar highlights of the *Meredith Victory* story, ending with,

> "Four years later, Captain LaRue laid down his sea bag and took up the habit of a Benedictine brother, and the name Brother Marinus at the Abbey of St. Paul in Newton, New Jersey. For the next 47 years he dedicated his life to prayer, service to the community and those who visited the abbey's gift shop. In recognition of the great Christian seamanship of Captain Leonard LaRue, and the dedicated life of prayer and hospitality of Brother Marinus, the Apostleship of the Sea of the United States of America bestows this very special honor."

The award, dated August 4, 2004, was signed by the senior cleric associated with the Apostleship in the US, The Most Reverend Curtis Guillory, and by the President of the Apostleship of the Sea of the USA (AOS USA), the Reverend Sinclair Oubre.

Sinclair Oubre grew up in Port Arthur, Texas, ninety miles east of Houston on the Texas-Louisiana border. The city can lay claim as the home of the largest oil refinery in the United States, as well as being the birthplace of singer Janis Joplin and NFL coach Jimmy Johnson.[8] Oubre recalls as a small child seeing "buildings" moving through town. These were actually the deckhouses of the tankers that plied the channels and canals fed from the Sabine Pass off the Gulf of Mexico to reach the refineries of Gulf Oil, Atlantic Refining, and Texaco. If he had been born a few decades before, he might well have seen young Able Seaman Leonard La Rue strolling the streets of Port Arthur as La Rue's first ship, the SS *Francis E. Powell*, filled with Texas crude and refined products for the trip north. So inspired was he that, even though he felt a vocation to the priesthood, he also joined the Merchant Marine, sailing as an ordinary seaman during college. In 1993 he gained the rating as an Able Seaman and continued sailing on ships and ocean-going tugs throughout the Gulf of Mexico as time permitted long after his 1986 ordination as a priest of the Diocese of Beaumont, Texas.

Father Oubre first became formally associated with Catholic maritime ministry in 1988 as director for the Diocese of Beaumont. In 2001 he was elected the President of AOS USA, a position he held through 2013. Early in his tenure, Father Oubre happened upon the book *Ship of Miracles*, and after reading it was intrigued enough by the story to ponder how it related to the apostleship's mission to mariners as well as his own vocation within AOS USA. He proposed to his board awarding the "Star of the Sea" award posthumously to Brother Marinus, a proposal the board readily approved. About a decade later he saw the documentary film *Ship of Miracles*, based on Gilbert's book and produced by filmmaker R. J. McHatton. Again, in between his daily pastoral duties, the priest pondered the story of Marinus and his place in the mission of the apostleship.

On October 28, 2016, Father Oubre attended the annual Admiral of the Ocean Seas dinner in New York City. Following the dinner, he took the opportunity to visit Bob Lunney in nearby Bronxville, staying with Bob and his wife, Joan, for the weekend. While with the Lunneys he passed the hours listening to the retired lawyer and mariner's reminiscences and he viewed his extensive collection of documents and memorabilia related to the Hungnam Evacuation, the *Meredith Victory*, and Captain La Rue/Brother Marinus. His time with Lunney crystalized Father Oubre's belief in the exemplary life of Captain La Rue and in 2016, at Oubre's urging, the AOS USA board passed a resolution supporting a "Cause for Sainthood" for Brother Marinus, Leonard La Rue.

The Catholic Church's process for declaring a decedent a saint has varied over the Church's 2,000-year history, but the current process, codified in the 1983 revision to the Code of Canon Law, begins with an investigation by the bishop of the diocese in which the candidate died. Normally, five years must have passed between the candidate's death and the initial inquiry, although the pope can waive this period in extraordinary circumstances. The diocese forms a committee to receive testimony as to the candidate's "heroic virtues" and whether the candidate lived with faith, hope, and charity and exhibited prudence, justice, temperance, and fortitude. The bishop assigns an individual known as a "postulator" to lead the investigation.

The first approach to the bishop of the diocese in which Marinus died, the Diocese of Patterson, New Jersey, was made on behalf of AOS USA by board member Rev. Dennis Donovan in 2016. On April 28, 2017, Father Oubre sent a letter to The Most Reverend Arthur J. Serratelli, the bishop of Paterson, asking for the opportunity to discuss the Cause with him. The two clerics met soon after and on May 9, 2017, Bishop Serratelli officially notified Father Oubre by letter that he would sponsor the Cause, beginning the informal process before an official decree.

Now the hard work began. Over the course of the year, Father Oubre obtained official statements of support from the AOS USA, the Council of American Master Mariners, The American Merchant Marine Veterans, the Commodore Barry Club of Brooklyn, and the New York chapter of the Navy League. On October 12, 2017, Father Oubre and Bob Lunney met with Bishop Serratelli and his staff for a first-hand account of the events of December 1950. Following the October meeting, Bishop Serratelli consulted with the bishops of neighboring diocese for their opinions on the Cause for Brother Marinus, and received uniformly positive reactions. Father Oubre continued working with the diocesan staff to gather information about Marinus/La Rue, enduring a false start with the first postulator, based in Rome, with whom the communication was exceedingly difficult, before Bishop Serratelli appointed a priest of his diocese, Father Pawel Tomczyk, postulator, greatly smoothing the process.

March 25, 2019 represented the end of the very beginning. On that date, Bishop Serratelli signed a decree, which began,

> "On January 29, 2019, the Postulator, Rev. Pawel Tomczyk, on behalf of the Apostleship of the Sea of the United States of America, requested the instruction of the Cause for the Beatification and Canonization of

the Servant of God, Brother Marinus LaRue, O.S.B., in the Diocese of Paterson."

The decree continued,

"Therefore, I, Most Rev. Arthur J. Serratelli, Bishop of Patterson, decree that the informative process for the Beatification and canonization be officially opened to study the heroic virtues and reputation of Holiness of Servant of God, Brother Marinus LaRue, O.S.B."

Bishop Serratelli honored Brother Marinus tremendously by naming him a "Servant of God," an honor the man himself would have strenuously rejected, but much, much more will be required for Leonard La Rue, Brother Marinus, OSB, to be declared a saint of the Catholic Church. Indeed, it is sadly unlikely that any of the men who served with La Rue will live to see him declared "Venerable," the next stage in canonization. Before the COVID-19 pandemic made travel hazardous, particularly for elders, the tribunal had planned to host Burley Smith and Merl Smith to testify in person, but that will instead need to be performed via video conference (Bob Lunney had already testified in person). Other testimony and the overall work of the committee will need to be performed in a similar fashion, at least until the pandemic subsides.

Once Postulator Tomczyk completes the work of the historical and theological commissions, their reports will be delivered to the Congregation for the Causes of the Saints at the Vatican in Rome. After the postulator's reports are summarized by the staff of the congregation into a document called a *Positio*, a committee of nine theologians will review the *Positio* and vote on whether the candidate lived a life of heroic virtue. If a majority of the nine vote in favor, the *Positio* is reviewed by cardinals and bishops who are part of the Congregation. If these clerics concur, the congregation will present the Cause to the pope. If the pope concurs, the Congregation would then declare the candidate "Venerable Marinus La Rue, OSB" All of this takes time, between the legitimate analysis and documentation, and the sometimes opaque whims of Vatican bureaucracy. "Rome was not built in a day," and one does not become a saint overnight.

If Marinus is declared Venerable, the next step on the road to canonization would be Beatification. This step requires the Congregation's verification of a miracle occurring after Marinus' death directly that is attributable to prayers requesting his intercession for the relief of, for example, a severe illness or infirmity. Catholic doctrine admits the possibility that members of "The Communion of Saints" can intercede with God on behalf of the living. A miraculous event, that is, an event with no natural explanation, following intercessory prayer to such an individual, is taken as strong evidence that he or she is indeed in heaven. Needless to say, the investigation of such a miracle is exhaustive and time consuming. But with a successful result, the candidate would be declared "Blessed Marinus La Rue" and could be the subject of public veneration in the Diocese of Patterson and the community of Benedictines, but not in the wider Church. The most recent American to achieve this status is Blessed Michael McGivney, the parish priest who founded the Knights of Columbus in 1882, beatified on October 31, 2020,.

Canonization, the Church's unambiguous declaration that the candidate is assuredly with God in heaven, requires the Congregation's verification that an additional miracle has occurred thanks to intercessory prayer following Beatification. Again, the verification process is lengthy and far-reaching. As of this writing, there are just eleven American Saints, with an additional American woman and two American men declared Blessed (including Father McGivney), and thirteen American men and women declared Venerable. The last Saint of the Americas to be canonized, Junipero Serra, was beatified in 1988 but only canonized twenty-seven years later. The last few Americans to be canonized were Venerable for twenty to forty years before being named Blessed, and about a dozen years beyond that before canonization

Perhaps then, it is appropriate that we close this tale of Captain Leonard Panet La Rue, Servant of God Brother Marinus, OSB., with the Diocese of Patterson's official "Prayer for the Cause of Captain La Rue/Brother Marinus," composed by Father Oubre and approved by Bishop Serratelli:

God, our Father, Creator of the seas, Protector of refugees, and all those in need,

You called Captain Leonard La Rue to recognize Your Son Jesus Christ in the faces of Korean refugees, and led him as Brother Marinus to a life of prayer and service in the tradition of St. Benedict.

May his life be an inspiration to us, and lead us to greater confidence in Your love so that we may continue his work of caring for the people of the sea, welcoming those who are refugees from war, and deepening all the faithful in their prayer and work of service.

We humbly ask You glorify Your servant Captain Leonard La Rue/Brother Marinus on earth according to the design of Your holy will.

AMEN

GLOSSARY

AB: Able Seaman

AH: Convoy from Curacao to Halifax, Nova Scotia

AOS USA: Apostleship of the Sea, United States of America

Bulwark: Side of a ship above the upper or weather deck

C-1A: US Maritime Commission cargo ship, 412 feet long

C-2: US Maritime Commission cargo ship, 459 feet long

C-3: US Maritime Commission cargo ship, 492 feet long

C-4: US Maritime Commission cargo ship, 520 feet long

CHOP: Change of operational control

CINCFE: Commander in Chief, Far East Command

CINCPAC: Commander In Chief, Pacific Command

CINCPACFLT: Commander in Chief, Pacific Fleet

CINCUNC : Commander in Chief, United Nation Command

COMNAVFE: Commander, Naval Forces, Far East Command

COMPHIBGRU : Commander, Amphibious Group

CPVF: Chinese People's Volunteer Force

D-Day: Date scheduled for a military event to occur

DPRK: Democratic People's Republic of Korea (North Korea)

DUKW: Amphibious wheeled vehicle carrying up to 24 troops

EC2-S-C1: Emergency Cargo, 400-449 ft. long, steam (Liberty ship)

Fathom: 6 feet of depth

Fathometer: Acoustic device for measuring water depth

G-2: Army intelligence officer, also refers to intelligence product

GN: Convoy from Guantanamo, Cuba, to New York

GUS: Convoy (slow) from Gibraltar to United States

GZ: Convoy from Guantanamo, Cuba, to Panama Canal

HA: Convoy from Halifax, Nova Scotia, to Curacao

H-Hour: Time scheduled for a military event to occur

HMCS: His (Her) Majesty's Ship (Royal Canadian Navy)

HMS: His (Her) Majesty's Ship (Royal Navy)

HX: Convoy from Halifax, Nova Scotia or New York to Liverpool, UK

JCS: Joint Chiefs of Staff

K-9: Pusan East Air Field, Pusan

K-27: Yonpo Air field, Hungnam

KN: Convoy from Key West to Norfolk or New York

KPA: Korean People's Army, the army of the DPRK (North Korea)

KS: Convoy from Norfolk to Key West

LCVP: Landing Craft, Vehicle, Personnel (36 ft long)

Lighter: Boat or small ship used to load or unload a larger ship

LSM: Landing Ship, Medium (203 ft. long, 34 ft. wide)

LSMR: Landing Ship, Medium, Rocket (LSM equipped to fire rockets)

LST: Landing Ship, Tank (large landing ship)

LSU: Landing Ship, Utility (113 ft. long, 32 ft. wide)

LVT: Landing Vehicle, Tracked (amphibious, carrying up to 24 troops)

MARAD: United States Maritime Administration

MCE: Maritime Commission, Emergency (hull number)

MCV: Maritime Commission, Victory (hull number)

MS: Motor Ship

MSR: Main Supply Route

MSTS: Military Sea Transportation Command

NCSORG: Naval Control of Shipping Organization

NG: Convoy from New York to Guantanamo, Cuba

NK: Convoy from New York to Key West

NSC: National Security Council

ON: Convoy from Liverpool, UK, to Boston or New York

OSB: *Order Sancto Benedicti*, Order of Saint Benedict

PLA: People's Liberation Army, army of the communist party of China

PQ : Eastbound convoy from the UK/Iceland to Murmansk, Russia

PRC: People's Republic of China (communist China)

QP: Westbound convoy from Russia to Iceland/UK

RCT: Regimental Combat Team (augmented regiment, 4-5,00)

ROK: Republic of Korea (South Korea)

SAR: Special Action Report

SOS: Distress call via Morse code

SS: Steam Ship

Turn to: Appear for duty

U-boat: *Unterseeboot,* German submarine

UGS: Convoy from the United States to Gibraltar (slow)

USCG: United States Coast Guard

USN: United States Navy

USNR United States Naval Reserve

VC2-S-AP2: Victory, cargo, 400-449 ft. long, steam (Victory ship)

WAT : Convoy from Key West to Aruba and Trindad

Weigh Anchor: Raise anchor from the sea bottom

YTB: Harbor Tug, Large

ZG: Convoy from Panama to Guantanamo, Cuba

ACKOWLEDGEMENTS

There are many people who made this book possible and deserve to be thanked. This project never would have started without Bob Lunney, who has been stalwart for seventy years retelling the story of the *Meredith Victory*, both in print and in person, in the US, Asia and Europe. Without his note in *Proceedings* that February, I probably never would have heard of La Rue, Marinus or Hungnam. Among other documents, Bob was able to provide a copy of the *Meredith Victory's* "Smooth Log" from the dates of the Hungnam evacuation. Like Bob Lunney, *Meredith Victory* officers Burley Smith and Merl Smith have been hugely helpful in providing additional context for life in 1950s Merchant Marine, as well as describing specific events and operations aboard the *Meredith Victory*.

In addition to the men who were there, many curators and archivists have contributed to this work. Professor Joshua M. Smith of the United States Merchant Marine Academy at King's Point, New York, curator of the Academy's American Merchant Marine Museum, kindly searched the museum's archives for files related to the *Meredith Victory*, Captain La Rue and Brother Marinus, and provided resources for the duplication of some of their contents. Pat Weeks, curator of the archives at the Independence Seaport Museum in Philadelphia, Pennsylvania, was hugely helpful in making available the archive's collection of the files from the former Pennsylvania Nautical School. These files included the yearbook from La Rue's graduating class at the Nautical School, along with student and school correspondence and other documents.

Several federal agencies were very helpful in promptly responding to Freedom of Information Act (FOIA) requests. The US Coast Guard provided Leonard La Rue's official file, including his license applications. The Maritime Administration provided their entire file on the deliberations surrounding various awards to the *Meredith Victory* and her crew, including "Gallant Ship." Many thanks to Maritime Administration historian Barbara Voulgaris, Kim Strong, Scott Perquita, and FOIA officer T. Mitchell Hudson, Jr.

While some contemporaneous references, such as many newspaper articles, are now available online, many are not. My thanks go to Shirley Moore at the Fleet Reserve Association for searching the association's collection of *Naval Affairs* magazines for an article on La Rue and Hungnam from 1951.

The bulk of the sources that contributed to this book came from the US National Archives and Records Administration (NARA). Archivists at NARA locations in New York, NY, Philadelphia, PA, and San Bruno, CA, pulled the US Coast Guard *Official Logs* of ships on which La Rue sailed, along with other documents. The dozens of unnamed archivists at the main NARA location in College Park, MD, were supremely helpful during my week there. In addition to pulling dozens of banker's-box-sized "Federal Records Containers," they provided other support, including chasing down an errant box containing US Marine Corps records I was seeking, and in another case, suggesting the use of WW II US Navy Armed-Guard logs and reports as a proxy for missing ship's logbooks. Thanks go to Desiree Allen in Atlanta; Nathanial Wiltzen in Boston; Chris Killillay in Washington, DC; Kelly McAnnaney in New York; Grace Schultz and

Stephen Charla in Philadelphia; and Russell Hill, Amy Reytar, and Nathanial Patch in College Park. There are many more whose names I haven't remembered from their NARA badges.

I must thank the monks of St. Paul's Abbey: Reverend Samuel Kim, OSB, the current abbot; as well as former abbot Reverend Joel Marcul, OSB, and the recently-deceased Brother Luke O'Connell, OSB. Father Samuel was kind enough to spare an hour or two on his busiest day of the year, the Saturday of the annual Christmas tree sale, in order to give me a tour and introduce me to Brother Luke. Brother Luke and Father Joel were the last monks to remember Leonard La Rue when he lived among them and have been generous with their recollections.

Reverend Sinclair Oubre, JCL, has been kind enough to share his research into the early life of Leonard La Rue, as well as his motivations in pursuing canonization for the man. Father Sinclair was willing to submit to a telephone interview even as he was getting sick from COVID-19. Reverend Pawel Tomczyk of the Diocese of Patterson has helped by providing additional information about the ongoing Cause for Sainthood.

Finally, I wish to thank my wife, Jane, and my children and grandchildren for allowing me all the time they did, tucked away in my office or traveling for research, when I could have been with them.

Please note that the exact origin of the images of refugees aboard the *Meredith Victory* is unclear. Both Burley Smith and Merl Smith recall taking photographs, with Burley's film "borrowed" by the US Navy and never returned.

SELECTED BIBLIOGRAPHY

The following are suggested for the reader who would like to learn more about the events in this book that surrounded the life of Leonard La Rue. The titles are arranged in chronological order roughly corresponding to how they relate to the events of his life.

John A. Butler. *Sailing on Friday: The Perilous History of America's Merchant Marine.* Washington, DC: Brassey's, 1997.

Edward A. Turpin and William A. MacEwen. *Merchant Marine Officer's Handbook.* New York: Cornell Maritime Press, 1943.

Terry Hughes and John Costello. *The Battle of the Atlantic.* New York: The Dial Press, 1977.

Justin F. Gleichauf. *Unsung Sailors: The Naval Armed Guard in World War II.* Naval Institute Press. Annapolis: Naval Institute Press, 1990.

John T. Mason, Jr. *The Atlantic War Remembered.* Annapolis: Naval Institute Press, 1990.

Dan van der Vat. *The Atlantic Campaign.* New York: Harper and Row, 1988.

Bernard Edwards. *The Road to Russia, Arctic Convoys 1942.* South Yorkshire: Pen and Sword Maritime, 2015.

William Geroux. *The Ghost Ships of Archangel, The Arctic Voyage that Defied the Nazis.* New York: Viking, 2019.

Bob Ruegg and Arnold Hague. *Convoys to Russia, 1941-1945.* Kendal, UK: World Ship Society, 1992.

David Irving. *The Destruction of Convoy PQ.17.* New York: Simon and Schuster, 1968.

Jurgen Rohwer. *The Critical Convoy Battles of March 1943.* Annapolis: Naval Institute Press, 1977.

Arthur Herman. *Freedom's Forge, How American Business Produced Victory in World War II.* New York: Random House, 2012.

L. A. Sawyer and H. W. Mitchell. *The Liberty Ships, The History of the 'Emergency' Type Cargo Ships Constructed in the United States During World War II.* Cambridge, MD: Cornell Maritime Press, 1970.

Herman E. Melton. *Liberty's War. An Engineer's Memoir of the Merchant Marine, 1942-1945.* Annapolis: Naval Institute Press, 2017.

Frederic C. Lane. *Ships for Victory, A History of Shipbuilding under the U.S. Maritime Commission in World War II.* Baltimore: The Johns Hopkins University Press, 2001.

L. A. Sawyer and W. H. Mitchell. *Victory Ships and Tankers.* Cambridge, MD: Cornell Maritime Press, 1974.

Capt. Walter W. Jafee. *The Lane Victory, The Last Victory Ship in War and Peace.* Palo Alto: Glencannon Press, 1997.

D. M. Giangreco. *Hell to Pay, Operation DOWNFALL and the Invasion of Japan, 1945-1947.* Annapolis: Naval Institute Press, 2009.

Micheal Clodfelter. *Warfare and Armed Conflicts: A Statistical Reference to Casualty and Other Figures, 1618-1991.* Jefferson, NC: McFarland and Company, 1992.

Harry G. Summers Jr. *Korean War Almanac.* New York: Facts on File, 1990.

Lynn Montross and Captain Nicholas A. Canzona, USMC. *U. S. Marine Operations in Korea 1950-1953. Volume I. The Pusan Perimeter.* Washington, DC: Historical Branch, G-3, Headquarters, U.S. Marine Corps, 1954.

Lynn Montross and Captain Nicholas A. Canzona, USMC. *U. S. Marine Operations in Korea 1950-1953. Volume II. The Inchon-Seoul Operation.* Washington, DC: Historical Branch, G-3, Headquarters, U.S. Marine Corps, 1955.

Roy E. Appleman. *South to the Naktong, North to the Yalu, United States Army in the Korean War (June-November 1950).* Washington, DC: Center of Military History, United States Army, 1961.

Malcolm W. Cagle and Frank A. Manson. *The Sea War in Korea.* Annapolis: Naval Institute Press, 1957.

Commander Eugene Franklin Clark, USN. *The Secrets of Inchon.* New York: G. P. Putnam and Sons, 2002.

William B. Breuer. *Shadow Warriors: The Covert War in Korea.* New York: John Wiley and Sons, 1996.

Lynn Montross and Captain Nicholas A. Canzona, USMC. *U. S. Marine Operations in Korea 1950-1953. Volume III. The Chosin Reservoir Campaign.* Washington, DC: Historical Branch, G-3, Headquarters, U.S. Marine Corps, 1957.

Gregory K. Hartmann and Scott C. Truver. *Weapons That Wait.* Updated edition. Annapolis: Naval Institute Press, 1991.

Tamara Moser Melia, *Damn the Torpedoes, A Short History of U.S. Naval Mine Countermeasures, 1777-1991.* Contributions to Naval History Volume 4. Washington, DC: Naval Historical Society, Department of the Navy, 1991.

Joseph R. Owen. *Colder than Hell, A Marine Rifle Company at Chosin Reservoir.* Annapolis: Naval Institute Press, 1996.

Hampton Sides. *On Desperate Ground: The Marines at the Reservoir, the Korean War's Greatest Battle.* New York: Doubleday, 2018.

Xiaobing Li. *Attack at Chosin. The Chinese Second Offensive in Korea.* Norman, OK: University of Oklahoma Press, 2020.

Glenn C. Cowart. *Miracle in Korea: The Evacuation of X Corps from the Hungnam Beachhead.* Columbia, SC: University of South Carolina Press, 1992.

Shelby L. Stanton. *America's Tenth Legion, X Corps in Korea, 1950.* Novato, CA: Presidio, 1989.

Gordon L. Rottman. *Landing Ship, Tank (LST) 1942-2002.* Oxford, UK: Osprey Publishing, 2005.

Bill Gilbert. *Ship of Miracles: 14,000 Lives and One Miraculous Voyage.* Chicago: Triumph Books, 2000.

NOTES

1. Philadelphia

1. United States Circuit Court, Massachusetts District, *Petition*, October 2, 1900.
2. *Register of Enlistments, United States Army.*
3. United States District Court, Eastern District of Pennsylvania, *Petition*, May 29, 1905.
4. Theodore Irwin. "God's Skipper." *Coronet*, Vol. 40, No. 1, (1956) 34-38.
5. Letters written by Cadet Wilson Rittenhouse Edwards, Class of 1929 to his mother, in the collection of the archives of the Independence Seaport Museum, Philadelphia, PA.
6. United States of America, *Shipping Articles*, OMB 1624-0006 (Washington: Office of Management and Budget, 2018).
7. His license represented the most senior position he could hold. Available employment sometimes meant he would serve at a rank inferior to his license.
8. Leonard P. La Rue, *Particulars of Sea Service.*
9. Edward A. Turpin and William A. MacEwen, *Merchant Marine Officers Handbook*, (New York: Cornell Maritime Press.1943).
10. Ensign E. D. Henderson, USNR, *Summary of Statements by Survivors of SS Cranford, US Freighter, 6096 GT, Owner Lykes Brothers*, Memorandum for Files, Navy Department, Office of the Chief of Naval Operations (1942).

2. War

1. *The Story of Moore-McCormack*, Moormack News, Moore-McCormack Lines, June, 1951.
2. Rear Admiral Robert C. Lee, "Mr. Moore, Mr. McCormack-and the Seven Seas," *American Newcomen*, 15th Newcomen Lecture, New London, CT, October 16, 1956.
3. Records of the US Maritime Commission, US National Archives and Records Administration, College Park, MD.
4. A note on tonnage: Deadweight tonnage is the number of "long tons" (2,240 lbs) that must be added to a ship to take her draft from "light" to her "load line." It expresses the total weight of cargo, fuel and stores that the ship can carry. Gross tonnage is not actually a measure of weight but an expression of the volume of the ship and is equal to the volume of her hull in cubic feet divided by 100. The displacement of the ship is the weight of water in long tons displaced by its hull, which is the weight of the ship and all her contents.
5. Maritime Commission Records.
6. She would remain known as *Mormacmar* until late in the war, when the United States Maritime Commission, the successor to the Shipping Board formed under terms of the Merchant Marine Act of 1936, would transfer her in March of 1945 to

the Soviet Union under Lend Lease and she would be renamed *Belinsky*. The Soviets returned her in August after the war ended. She was scrapped in 1946.

7. Maritime Commission Records.

8. Micheal Clodfelter, *Warfare and Armed Conflicts: A Statistical Reference to Casualty and Other Figures, 1618-1991*, (Jefferson, NC: McFarland 1992).

9. *Historical Statistics of the United States, Colonial Times to 1970*, (Washington, DC: US Department of Commerce, 1976).

10. *Historical Statistics*.

11. *Escort Manual*, Office of the Chief of Naval Operations, Division of Fleet Training (1941).

12. Maritime Commission Records.

13. Gregory K. Hartmann and Scott C. Truver, *Weapons That Wait*, Updated edition, (Annapolis: Naval Institute Press, 1991).

14. *General Instructions for Commanding Officers of Naval Armed Guards in Merchant Ships, Fourth Edition*, OPNAV 23L-2, Department of the Navy, (Washington, DC: US Government Printing Office,1944).

15. Commandant Fifth Naval District, *Port Directors Report Arming of Merchant Vessels SS Mormacmar,* June 1, 1942.

16. Maritime Commission Records.

3. Murmansk

1. Adding to the absurdity of the missing monument to allied merchant mariners, Australia features a monument to the lost sailors of the Murmansk run in a park north of Brisbane, almost 9,000 miles away.

2. *German Fleet Disposition*, Navy Department, Office of the Chief of Naval Operations (1942).

3. Bob Ruegg and Arnold Hague, *Convoys to Russia, Allied Convoys and Naval Surface Operations in Arctic Waters 1941-1945*. (Kendal, UK: World Ship Society, 1992), 20.

4. Ruegg, *Convoys*, 22.

5. Ensign Harrison R. Smith, USNR, *Armed Guard Unit Aboard SS Mormacmar report of* 4-2-42.

6. Smith, *Armed Guard Unit*.

7. Bernard Edwards, *The Road to Russia, Arctic Convoys 1942*, (South Yorkshire: Pen and Sword Maritime, 2002), 17.

8. Bernard Edwards, in *The Road to Russia, Arctic Convoys 1942*, claims, "At the height of the attack, her Armed Guard gunners found themselves running out of ammunition and broke into the cargo to replenish their guns. On arrival in Murmansk, the Soviet authorities demanded that the *Mormacmar's* gunners be court martialed for 'stealing ammunition belonging to the Soviet Union.' It required the intervention of the US Consul to halt this ridiculous farce." Ensign Smith's report is silent on this matter.

9. Naval Message, ALUBMA LONDON to OPNAV, May 31, 1942.

10. Naval Message, ALUBMA LONDON to OPNAV, May 27, 1943.

11. Soviet commander of the "Red Banner Northern Fleet," Admiral Arseniy Grigoriye-vich Golovko.

12. Banak, Finmark, Norway, on the south end of a fiord opening onto the North Cape, about 180 miles west-northwest of Murmansk.
13. Naval Message from COMNAVEU London to OPNAV, May 1, 1942.
14. Ensign Harrison R. Smith, USNR, *Homeward Voyage, Murmansk, U.S.S.R. to Reykjavik.* May 8, 1942.
15. Idem, *Completion of Homeward Voyage.* May 27, 1942.
16. Vice Chief of Naval Operations, *Recommendation for Suitable Awards, U.S. Navy Armed Guard, SS Mormacmar, Gross Tons 5453.* July 7, 1942.
17. John C. Donovan, *SS Mormacmar-Trial of Robert McElroy, Boatswain, Francis W. Durbin, A.B. and Andrew Mahin, A.B., re Misconduct of Crew at Iceland, March 17, 1942,* Memorandum in the files of the US Maritime Commission dated June 30, 1942, National Archives and Records Administration, College Park, MD.
18. The men were fortunate in a sense, since they could have been Court Martialed. Being on shore for longer than 30 days also rendered them eligible to be drafted, although it is unlikely they were.
19. Donovan, *SS Mormacmar-Trial.*

4. Around The World

1. Lieut. (JG) Hiram Royal Mallinson, USNR, *Report of SS Mormacmar, outward bound voyage from New York, N.Y. to Calcutta, India,* December 15, 1942.
2. *United States Naval Administration in World War II History of Convoy and Routing,* Naval History and Heritage Command.
3. Describing action on June 27, the Armed Guard report says that, "At dusk, a burning tanker (not in our convoy) was sighted on the horizon, and appeared to be sinking." The only ship sunk in the vicinity close to that date was the tanker Rockefeller, but records show that she was actually torpedoed mid-day on the 28th and drifted for twelve hours before sinking, so Lieutenant Mallinson probably inadvertently conflated the dates as he composed his report six months after the actual events.
4. The typed report says "August 1" but unless the report was retrospective it must be September 1.
5. Same, the report says "August 3." In this case, war records show she was unsuccessfully attacked on September 3.
6. Records of the US Maritime Commission, US National Archives and Records Administration, College Park, MD.
7. Maritime Commission Records.
8. L.W. & P. Armstrong, Inc. v The Mormacmar, 196 F. 2d 752 (2nd Circuit 1952), Filed May 12, 1952.
9. Different US Coast Guard records identify the date of the end of his service on Mormacmar as April 18th.
10. F. V. Westerlund, Letter "To Whom it May Concern," April 17, 1943.

5. Liberty

1. *Historical Statistics of the United States, Colonial Times to 1970*, (Washington, DC: US Department of Commerce, 1976).
2. Arthur Herman, *Freedom's Forge: How American Business Produced Victory in World War II*, (New York: Random House, 2012).
3. L.A. Sawyer and W. H. Mitchell. *The Liberty Ships* (New York: Cornell Maritime Press, 1970).
4. Sawyer, *The Liberty Ships*.
5. Sawyer, *The Liberty Ships*.
6. Records of the US Maritime Commission, US National Archives and Records Administration, College Park, MD.
7. Maritime Commission Records.
8. *Ship Card, Joseph M. Medill*, US Navy.
9. Some records give the ship's gross tonnage as 5,028, since she was constructed as a C1-A shelter-deck, rather than a C1-B built to scantlings, but the USN ship cards and British Admiralty records classify the ship with the higher number.
10. "Nordberg Diesels Power Ship *Mormacdale*," *The Log*, Vol. 37, No. 3, March, 1942,16-22.
11. Lieut. Thomas F. Dalton, USN, *Report of Homeward Voyage of M.S. Mormacdale from Persian Gulf to Philadlephia*. September 2, 1943.
12. Ensign William H. Egli, USNR, *Smooth Copy of the Armed Guard Log of the Motor Ship Mormacdale (gross tons 7100) with respect to a passage from Norfolk, Virginia on September 18, 1943, to Milne Bay, New Guinea, to San Pedro, California where the voyage ended April 23, 1944*.
13. The records do not show this to have been a regular GZ convoy.
14. SS *Henry Miller*, like the *Smith Thompson*, was built by the California Shipbuilding Corporation. As an illustration of how many were being built, between the 10/42 and 12/43 completions of the respective Liberty ships Calship completed 184 others.

6. Victory

1. Samuel Elliott Morrison, *The Two Ocean War*, (Boston: Little, Brown and Company, 1963).
2. D.M. Giangreco, *Hell to Pay: Operation DOWNFALL and the Invasion of Japan, 1945-1947*. (Annapolis: Naval Institute Press, 2009).
3. After the war, when the Armed Guard was no longer needed, these would be useful accommodations for paying passengers.
4. One of Whittier College's most famous alumni was, on the day Whittier Victory was placed in service, an obscure US Navy lieutenant who had just returned from service in the Pacific. Richard Milhous Nixon graduated *summa cum laude* from Whittier in 1934, the same year Leonard La Rue graduated from the Philadelphia Nautical School.
5. The 44th Victory that Calship built, the SS *Lane Victory*, is afloat at Berth 39 in San Pedro Harbor, California, and maintained as a volunteer-operated museum.

6. L. A. Sawyer and W. H. Mitchell, *Victory Ships and Tankers* (Cambridge, MD Cornell Maritime Press.,1974), 48.

7. "Bond Buyers May Inspect Four New Ships at Calship," *San Pedro News-Pilot*, June 25, 1945, 2.

8. The letter was actually written by Hungarian physicist Leo Szilard, who was active in nuclear research and had patented the idea of a nuclear chain reaction in 1934. Einstein signed the letter and Szilard arranged for economist Alexander Sachs to present the letter to the president in person.

9. Fermi, a brilliant professor at the University of Rome, used his trip to Stockholm to receive the 1938 Nobel Prize as the opportunity to escape fascist Italy with his two children and his wife, Laura, who was Jewish and therefore subject to Italy's new racial laws.

10. "2 Catholic Chaplains Rushing to Bedside of Dying Mother in Hub," *The Boston Globe* March 31, 1946, 1.

11. Men and women in Catholic religious orders, such as the Benedictines, Dominicans, or Franciscans, while following all the dictates of the Catholic Church, adopt a particular mission based upon the precepts for the order's founder. For Benedictines, it is a combination of prayer and work within their community, "Ora et Labora."

12. In a 1956 interview in *Coronet* magazine, the quote is rendered, "This, my son, is no vocation for you."

13. "Ship Sued for $20,000," *The Vancouver Sun*, February 20, 1948, 16.

14. Captain La Rue's US Coast Guard file shows no evidence of administrative penalty.

15. Unlike the cargo ships on which he served, the passenger liner's second in command was referred to as "Staff Captain," so the First Mate was actually the third in command.

16. While the three were considered sister ships, the Uruguay, the first built, was slightly shorter and featured twelve boilers of slightly lower pressure than the eight boilers in her sisters. As a result, she was slightly less economical to operate and passengers in cabins adjacent to the engineering spaces suffered from bulkhead surfaces that were so hot they could not be touched with a bare hand and which therefore rendered sleep in the tropics an impossibility. Those cabins, like all the tourist-class cabins, had no air conditioning.

17. Records of the US Maritime Commission, US National Archives and Records Administration, College Park, MD.

7. War Again

1. Germany officially surrendered to the Allies in Reims on May 7, but the Soviets, in possession of Berlin, insisted after the Reims ceremony that the German high command surrender in Berlin, in the presence of Marshall Zhukov, so a second Act of Surrender was signed there on May 9.

2. Commander in Chief Army Forces Advance Tokyo Japan to War Department, Number CAX 52058, September 18, 1945.

3. G-2 refers to a US Army division's intelligence staff. The term is also used as Army shorthand for any military intelligence product.

4. Transliterating Asian words into English is always a challenge. Older references render this place as "Whanghai."
5. He had less than a year to mourn the division of his country. Kim Koo would be assassinated on June 26, 1949, possibly on Rhee's orders.
6. Guomindang is the more contemporary Pinyin transliteration of what was formerly called, in English, the Kuomintang, abbreviated "KMT."
7. *A Report to the President by the National Security Council on The Position of the United States with Respect to Korea*, NSC-8, April 2, 1948.
8. *Consequences of US Troop Withdrawal from Korea in Spring, 1949*, Central Intelligence Agency, ORE 3-49. February 29, 1949.
9. *A Report to the President by the National Security Council on The Position of the United States with Respect to Korea*, NSC-8/2, March 22, 1949.
10. Later in the column Zausmer cites British historian Arnold J. Toynbee as guessing that the length of the cold war would be 50 years, a remarkably accurate assessment.
11. *Current Capabilities of the Northern Korean Regime*, Central Intelligence Agency, ORE 18-50, June 19, 1950.

8. Inchon

1. *Classified Teletype Conference*, Number DA TT 3425, Department of the Army, Staff Communications Office, June 25, 1950.
2. Blair House, across Pennsylvania Avenue from the White House, was being used as the President's residence while the latter was undergoing a complete renovation from 1948 to 1952.
3. It appears the first use of this phrase in the US press was not associated with the march of communism but rather with a military coup in Peru during July 1962, which had followed similar coups in Argentina, Brazil, Ecuador, and El Salvador. Less than a month later, Senator Barry Goldwater referred to the "'falling domino' thesis in an opinion piece about the fall of Laos causing the fall of Thailand, Cambodia, South Vietnam, and Malaya to communists.
4. United Nations Security Council Resolution 82 (1950), June 25, 1950.
5. United Nations Security Council Resolution 83 (1950), June 27, 1950.
6. France had begun its own campaign against communist insurgents in Indochina, and at the same time the US was mobilizing for war in Korea, it was also providing the first aid to the French in their fight, eight C-47 cargo planes delivered on June 30. This presumably marks the first tiny step in the US military involvement in Vietnam.
7. Neither North nor South Korea were admitted as members of the UN General Assembly until September 17, 1991. The Republic of Korea held observer status at the UN starting on the date its government was recognized, December 12, 1948. The DPRK, because it rejected the legitimacy of UN action in Korea, didn't seek and obtain observer status until 1973.
8. The 24th's commander, Major General William F. Dean, stayed with his men until the last convoy leaving the city. His jeep subsequently got separated and after tending to wounded men, he was captured and held prisoner by North Korea for

more than three years. He received the Medal of Honor on his return to the United States.

9. Roy E. Appleman, *South to the Naktong, North to the Yalu, United States Army in the Korean War (June-November 1950)* (Washington, DC: Center of Military History, United States Army, 1961).

10. In a later correspondence Colonel Forney advised a colleague that the top-secret classification "by Headquarters, USMC, was to prevent criticism of other services from becoming public."

11. Developed in 1942, the "Landing Ship, Tank" was a 327-foot, 50-foot beam ship with doors at the bow enclosing a ramp-connected deck inside. The hull and ballast system were designed so that the bow could be driven onto the shore and "beached," allowing the vehicles within the ship to drive right onto the shore at a landing. Those vehicles could be up to 20 M4 Sherman tanks, twenty-nine two-and-a-half-ton trucks, seventeen LVTs, an amphibious tracked vehicle capable of carrying up to twenty-four troops, or a combination thereof. Powered by two 900-horsepower General Motors 12V-567 diesel engines, their cruising speed was a leisurely nine knots, hence their nickname, "Large, Slow Targets." More than a thousand were built before the end of World War II.

12. Doyle later said admiringly of Forney, "Forney had a characteristic that particularly fitted him to Almond's staff: he could get along with anyone-and without compromising himself." Vice Admiral James H. Doyle and Arthur J. Mayer, *December 1950 at Hungnam*, Naval Institute Proceedings, Vol. 105, No. 4, p. 44, US Naval Institute, Annapolis, MD (1979). The comment hints at the prickly dynamic among the flag and general officers of 7th Fleet, CINCFE, 8th Army and X Corps. For an excellent description see Donald Chisholm, *Negotiated Joint Command Relationships: Korean War Amphibious Operations, 1950*, Naval War College Review, Vol. 53, No. 2, Article 5, Naval War College, Newport, RI (2000).

13. Eniwetok, now rendered Enewetak, is a loop of coral, an "atoll," fifty miles in circumference that forms some forty small islands. It is most famous today for the more than forty US nuclear weapons tested there between 1948 and 1958 and the resulting radioactive contamination of the atoll and surrounding Marshall Islands.

14. It is possible that La Rue and the *Whittier Victory* passed just a few hundred miles from his future command, the *Meredith Victory*, while the former was on its way to San Francisco and the latter was in Guam.

15. Bill Gilbert, *Ship of Miracles: 14,000 Lives and One Miraculous Voyage*, (Chicago: Triumph Books, 2000).

16. Naval Control of Shipping ORGanization, "the control exercised by naval authorities of movement, routing, reporting, convoy organization, and tactical diversion of allied merchant shipping." (US DOD)

17. Unlike the classical rhumb line, a course of constant compass bearing from the origin to the destination, a great circle, an arc that stretches towards the pole in the middle, is the shortest distance between two points on a sphere and requires "waypoints" to navigate.

18. *Official Log, SS Meredith Victory*, July 11th, 1951.

19. Michael Helbig, private communication provided by Rear Admiral J. Robert Lunney, USNR, July 30th, 2020.

20. LSU, Landing Ship, Utility, a 113-foot-long, 32-foot-wide vessel with a ramp-type bow door designed to beach like an LST. The designation had been "LCM" (Landing Craft Utility) but it was changed in 1949 to LSU, and changed back in 1956.
21. LSMR, Landing Ship, Medium, a 203-foot-long, 34-foot-wide ship with bow doors like an LST, but smaller, faster and more maneuverable. The "R" designation means it was equipped to fire 1,000 five-inch rockets from its deck in salvo.
22. LVTs, an amphibious tracked vehicle capable of carrying up to twenty-four troops
23. H. J. Burley Smith, interview with the author, December 16, 2019.
24. LSMRs
25. LVTs
26. LCVPs, Landing Craft, Vehicles, Personnel, a 36-foot-long, diesel-powered boat with a ramp at its blunt bow for disgorging its contents onto the beach, capable of carrying thirty-six troops, a small vehicle, or five tons of cargo.
27. LVCPs
28. Gilbert, *Ship of Miracles.*
29. *First Marine Division, FMF, Special Action Report Inchon-Seoul, 15 Sept 50-7 Oct 50.*
30. Lynn A. Montross and Captain Nicholas A. Canzona, *US Marine Operations in Korea 1950-1953, Volume II, The Inchon-Seoul Operation* (Washington: Historical Branch, G-3, Headquarters US Marine Corps, 1955).
31. Joint Chiefs of Staff, *Outgoing Classified Message,* Department of the Army, Staff Message Center. Number WCL 30453, September 27, 1950.
32. George C. Marshall, *Outgoing Classified Message,* Department of the Army, Staff Message Center, Number JCS 92985, September 29th, 1950.
33. The analogy is intentional. MacArthur was unhappy with what he viewed as lethargic performance by 8th Army until its breakout following the Inchon landing.
34. Tamara Moser Melia, *Damn the Torpedoes: A Short History of U.S. Naval Mine Counter-measures, 1777-1991,* Contributions to Naval History Volume 4, (Washington, DC: Naval Historical Society, Department of the Navy, 1991).
35. The minesweepers were actually obtained, thanks to the efforts of Rear Admiral Arleigh "31-knot" Burke, whom Chief of Naval Operations Admiral Forrest P. Sherman had been sent to Tokyo as Deputy Chief of Staff to Vice Admiral Joy. Sherman wanted Burke to be his eyes and ears, particularly with respect to the feasibility of the Inchon operation. See Chishlom.
36. Commander Sheldon Kinney, USN, "All Quiet at Wonsan," *Proceedings,* August, 1954, 862.
37. In words that would be quoted often during the "tanker-war" of the 1980s and the Persian Gulf war of 1992, Rear Admiral Allan E. "Hoke" Smith, commander of Task Force 95 (the advance force for the landing), lamented, "We have lost control of the seas to a nation without a navy, using pre-World War I weapons, laid by vessels that were utilized at the time of the birth of Christ."
38. Details of the sweep operation can be found in Cagle and Mason, *The Sea War in Korea.*
39. Malcolm W. Cagle and Frank A. Mason. *The Sea War in Korea.* (Annapolis: Naval Institute Press,1957).
40. Smith, Interview.
41. Smith, Interview.
42. According to Harry G. Summers, *Korean War Almanac,* Facts on File Books, New York (1990), a Bedcheck-Charlie pilot flew either a Yakovlev YAK-18 or a Poliarkov PO-2

biplane carrying one or two small bombs. Militarily insignificant, they nevertheless were effective at harassing troops and in one case, President Syngman Rhee. The planes flew too slowly (around 100 knots) for the UN jet fighters to shoot them down, but US Navy Lieutenant Guy P. Bordelon flying the much slower, propeller-driven F4U Corsair, shot down five of of them in less than three weeks in 1953, putting their activities to an end. The Armistice ending hostilities in Korea was signed less than two weeks later.

43. Lynn A. Montross and Captain Nicholas A. Canzona. *US Marine Operations in Korea 1950-1953, Volume III, The Chosin Reservoir Campaign.* (Washington, DC: Historical Branch, G-3, Headquarters US Marine Corps, 1957).

9. Chosin

1. *Consequences of the Korean Incident,* Intelligence Memorandum No. 302, Central Intelligence Agency, July 8, 1950.
2. Joint Chiefs of Staff, JCS Message Number 93709, October 9, 1950.
3. Omar N. Bradley, *Substance of Statements Made at Wake Island Conference on 15 October 1950, Complied by General of the Army Omar N. Bradley, Chairman of the Joint Chiefs of Staff, From Notes Kept by the Conferees from Washington.*
4. Appleman. *South to the Naktong.*
5. "Drive to the Yalu: CCF Counter Attack," *War Diary X Corps,* Monthly Summary, 1 Nov 1950 to 30 Nov 1950, 3.
6. *First Marine Division, FMF, Special Action Report Wonsan-Hamhung-Chosin, 8 Oct 50-15 Dec 50.* Annex IV to Annex Baker.
7. *Views of the Joint Chiefs of Staff,* November 9, 1950, 1.
8. *A Report to the National Security Council by the Executive Secretary on United States Course of Action with Respect to Korea,* NSC 81/2, November 14, 1950, 2.
9. MSR=Main Supply Route, the land route by which the troops would be augmented and resupplied and the wounded evacuated.
10. The following pages only summarize the action around the Changjin Reservoir and are not intended to be exhaustive. For more detail and the stories of the brave men who fought this epic battle (on the UN side), see Joseph R. Owen. *Colder than Hell.* Naval Institite Press. Annapolis, MD. 1996, or Hampton Sides. *On Desperate Ground.* Doubleday, New York. 2018.
11. *X Corps War Diary,* 23.
12. *First Marine Division, FMF, Special Action Report Wonsan-Hamhung-Chosin, 8 Oct 50-15 Dec 50,* 35
13. "Section 3, Personal narrative reports of individuals regarding action at CHOSIN RESERVOIR, Transcript of recorded statement by Captain Robert J. Kitz, 0-1287896," *Action Report of the 7th Infantry Division from 21 November 1950 to 20 December 1950 from Hyesanjin to Hungnam Outloading.*
14. Xiaobing Li, *Attack at Chosin: The Chinese Second Offensive in Korea,* (Norman, OK: University of Oklahoma Press, 2020).
15. Li, *Attack at Chosin.*
16. Li, *Attack at Chosin.*
17. Professor Xiaobing Li's recent book, *Attack at Chosin,* provides fascinating insight from the Chinese perspective into the intelligence, communications, and logistical shortcomings that contributed to the Chinese army's failure to destroy X Corps.

18. Apparently, the US Army agreed with Mao. In a June 1951 letter, Colonel A.H. Butler of the Marine Corps Board at Quantico asked Forney whether the Corps commander or his senior staff had expressed sentiments similar to the statement in his report that, "the best division in the X Corps was 1stMarDiv, and it would be assigned the most dangerous sector, that is, the sector along the boundary of the X Corps and in that area which most of the enemy were expected to be encountered." Forney replied that the X Corps Chief of Staff, Major General Clark L. Ruffner, had told him that twice, that the "overriding consideration was that the best division would have to operate on the exposed flank where most of the enemy were expected."

19. Li, *Attack at Chosin.*

20. In the aforementioned letter Colonel Butler asked Forney to respond to their finding that, "the primary reason for the highly successful evacuation from the HUNGNAM perimeter was the fact the action of the 1stMarDiv and supporting air, plus non-battle attrition, so decimated the CCF divisions that the Chinese were unable to launch an attack against that perimeter in anything greater than company strength ... did you at any time hear the Corps Commander or any of his principal staff officers or commanders express this view?" Forney replied, "The thought did occur to staff later, but I can recall no specific individuals. I and other of X Corps staff were mystified at the time, 9-24 DEC, by lack of CCF aggressiveness, and considered it was occasioned by their fear of our artillery and naval gunfire and by the fact that the X Corps was obviously pulling out. At the time I and most others believed that the divisions defeated by the 1stMarDiv were to be passed through by fresh troops who would hit our perimeter."

21. Li, *Attack at Chosin.*

22. Lynn A. Montross and Captain Nicholas A. Canzona, *US Marine Operations in Korea 1950-1953, Volume III, The Chosin Reservoir Campaign,* (Washington, DC: Historical Branch, G-3, Headquarters US Marine Corps, 1957).

23. *Command Report. Headquarters X Corps Special Report on Chosin Reservoir, 27 November to 10 December 1950. P 97.*

10. Hungnam

1. *Command Report, Period From: 1 December 1950 Through: 31 December 1950.* Headquarters, 7th Infantry .

2. Major Richard W. Schutt, USMC, *The Amphibious Withdrawal of the U.S. X Corps from Hungnam, Korea* (undated).

3. Schutt, *Amphibious Withdrawal.*

4. *Command Report, Headquarters X Corps Special Report on Chosin Reservoir, 27 November to 10 December 1950,* 81.

5. A "measurement ton" is actually a unit of volume equivalent to forty cubic feet. That volume of seawater displaced by the ship weighs about 2,560 pounds.

6. *Headquarters X Corps, Special Report on Hungnam Evacuation, 9-24 December 1950,* 2.

7. Lynn Montross, "The Hungnam Evacuations: Amphibious Landing in Reverse," *Marine Corps Gazette,* December 1951, 18-37,

8. Unlike Forney's other report, this one was classified confidential presumably because it did not involve "criticism of other services."

9. Colonel Edward H. Forney, USMC, *Transcript of Special Report, Colonel Edward H. Forney, USMC. Special After-Action Report by, Deputy Chief of Staff of the X Corps, 19 August to 31 December 1950.*

10. X Corps Intelligence Officer (G-2), Lieutenant Colonel William Glass.

11. Forney, *Transcript of Special Report*, 3.

12. Pusan may have had plenty of dock space for the upcoming movement of the X Corps, but it was limited in how quickly men and materiel could be moved out of the port. COMNAVFE estimated the port could unload 39,850 long tons (2,240 pounds) per day, but the three railroad tracks leaving the port could together only support 8,500 long tons per day if they had adequate locomotives and rolling stock, and the roads about the same with adequate trucks. The port's limitations meant that some Marines would offload at the port of Masan to the west, and some Army units at Ulsan to the northeast. Even then the port became so over crowded that by the end of the redeployment refugees were not allowed to be offloaded at Pusan.

13. Annex "C", Brief of Port Information on Korean Ports, *COMNAVFE Operation Plan 116-50*, Commander Naval Forces, Far East, Tokyo, Japan. 9 November 1950. Pp C-13-22, C-26-30, C-36-41.

14. Annex "C", Brief of Port Information.

15. *Commander Amphibious Group One, United State Pacific Fleet, War Diary, December 1950*, 16.

16. *Amphibious Group War Diary,* 10-44.

17. Forney, *Transcript of Special Report*, 8.

18. Forney, *Transcript of Special Report*, 10.

19. *Commander Amphibious Group One (CTF 90) Action Report, Hungnam Redeployment, December 1950*, 1.

20. "Extracts from the Commanding General's Diary 27 Nov-10 Dec," *Command Report. Headquarters X Corps Special Report on Chosin Reservoir, 27 November to 10 December 1950*, 26.

21. *Amphibious Group One War Diary*, 16.

22. *Amphibious Group One War Diary,* 19.

23. Cruisers, destroyers, frigates, mine sweepers, landing craft, and fast transports (ex-destroyers).

24. "Annex "D", Vessel Planning Data," *COMNAVFE Operation Plan 116-50*, Commander Naval Forces, Far East, Tokyo, Japan. 9 November 1950, D-1.

25. Forney, *Transcript of Special Report*, 10.

26. "Commanding General's Diary 27 Nov-10 Dec," 26.

27. Rear Admiral J. Robert Lunney, USNR, interview with the author, September 26th, 2019.

28. *Commander Amphibious Group One (CTF 90) Action Report, Hungnam Redeployment, December 1950.* P 11.

29. *(CTF 90) Action Report*, 5.

30. CHange of OPerational control. When the control of a unit passes to the next authority, in this case, CTF 90.

31. YTB: Harbor Tug, Big. YTB-415 was named *"Secota"* and 420 was the *"Wallacut."* Fleet records show them as 100 feet long, 237 tons and 1200 horsepower, although the CTF 90 Report rates them at 390 tons. *Secota* survived until 1986 when she sank following collision with the stern plane on the submarine USS *Georgia* (SSBN-729) with the loss of two of her crew.

32. *(CTF 90) Action Report*, 14.
33. *(CTF 90) Action Report*, 16.
34. *(CTF 90) Action Report*, 30.
35. These were primarily troop transports of three varieties: APA: Attack Transport (primarily for troops); AKA: Cargo Ship, Attack (primarily for cargo); APD: High Speed Transport (converted destroyers or destroyer escorts).
36. *(CTF 90) Action Report*, 13-14.
37. In this case, "Captain" was Dawson's Merchant Marine rank, equivalent to the military rank O-6, rather than an Army captain, O-3.
38. *Amphibious Group One War Diary*, 20.
39. *1st Marine Division Embarkation Order No. 3-50*. PP 3-5.
40. Usually LSUs.
41. *(CTF 90) Action Report*, 15.
42. Either an LSU or an Army DUKW, six-wheeled, amphibious vehicle capable of carrying up to five thousand pounds of personnel and cargo on land or water.
43. LCVPs or LSUs.
44. *Assignment of Shipping* (undated), found in file for Forney's *Transcript of Special Report.*
45. *Voyage Number 4, Medical Officer report of.* 15 January 1951.
46. *Chaplain's Voyage Report for Period 21 November 1950 to 10 January 1951.*
47. The *Maddox* played a more important historic role fourteen years later when it engaged three North Vietnamese motor torpedo boats on August 2, 1964, in what came to be known as "The Gulf of Tonkin Incident." The attack on the Maddox became the premise for greatly increased US involvement in the Vietnam War.
48. *Commander Amphibious Group One, United State Pacific Fleet, War Diary, December 1950.* P 11.
49. *Amphibious Group One War Diary*, 13.
50. *(CTF 90) Action Report*, 39.
51. *Amphibious Group One War Diary*, 31.
52. *Embarkation Progress Report, Period of 1800 16 Dec to 1800 17 Dec 1950*, found in file for Forney's *Transcript of Special Report.*
53. *Amphibious Group One War Diary*, 39.
54. LCMs, "Landing Craft Medium," like at LCVP but about twenty feet longer.
55. *Amphibious Group One War Diary*, 41.
56. *Headquarters X Corps, Special Report on Hungnam Evacuation, 9-24 December 1950.* P 14.
57. As of the date of X Corps Embarkation Order 3-50.
58. *Loading Progress Report, Period of 1800 18 Dec to 1800 19 Dec. Embarkation Progress Report, Period of 1800 19 Dec to 1800 20 Dec.* Forney Files. US National Archives and Record Administration, College Park, Md.
59. *Headquarters X Corps, Special Report on Hungnam Evacuation, 9-24 December 1950.* P 14.
60. *Amphibious Group One War Diary*, 14.
61. *Amphibious Group One War Diary*, 6
62. *Amphibious Group One War Diary*, 16.
63. *Amphibious Group One War Diary*, 49.
64. The HCEV that day was either the *Sausalito* (PF-4) or the *Glendale* (PF-36).
65. *Deck Log, SS Meredith Victory.* Wednesday, 20th December 1950.
66. Forney, *Transcript of Special Report*, 12.
67. Bearings are taken to make sure the anchor is holding fast to the bottom and the ship is not drifting.

68. LCM B46

69. *Norcuba* was a Liberty ship launched by Bethlehem Steel's Fairfield yard in October 1943 as the "SS Stage Door Canteen" to honor, "the stage door canteens which offer servicemen free refreshments and dancing as a morale-building venture." She was on a time-charter with the North Atlantic and Gulf Steam Ship Company.

70. Handwritten note found in file for Forney's *Transcript of Special Report*, US National Archives and Records Administration, College Park, MD.

71. The CTF 90 *Action Report, Hungnam Evacuation*, states, "No damage was done to merchant ships during the entire operation, in spite of the rush, darkness and poor weather conditions."

72. Bill Gilbert, *Ship of Miracles: 14,000 Lives and One Miraculous Voyage*, (Chicago: Triumph Books, 2000.

73. *X Corps Operation Order No. 9.* 5 December 50.

74. "Daily Chronological Summary of Operations 1 December 1950 through 31 December 1950," *Command Report, 7th Infantry Division, Operation in Korea, From 1 December 1950 to 31 December 1950*, 11-12.

75. Chronological Summary, 14.

76. Chronological Summary, 20.

77. Chronological Summary, 27.

78. *Command Report, Period From: 1 December 1950 Through: 31 December 1950*. Headquarters, 7th Infantry, 41.

79. *Command Report for December 1950*, Headquarters X Corps, 3.

80. Schutt, *Amphibious Withdrawal*, 6.

81. *Headquarters X Corps, Special Report on Hungnam Evacuation, 9-24 December 1950*. P 23.

82. *X Corps Special Report*, 24.

83. Bong Hak Hyun, Letter to Father Marinus, December 12, 1960.

84. Myung Oak Kim, "Savior of the People," *Philadelphia Daily News*, December 24, 2004, 7-9.

85. Hyun, Letter to Father Marinus.

86. Kim, "Savior of the People."

87. After the war Dr. Hyun married and returned to the United States, where went back to medical school at the University of Pennsylvania (in order to obtain a US medical license) and taught and practiced medicine in the US for twenty-seven years. In 1999 a Korean Broadcasting Service documentary dubbed him the "Korean Schindler" and his role in facilitating the evacuation of refugees from Hungnam was recognized in the Korean and Korean-American communities. In 2016, nine years after his death, a statue of Dr. Hyun was erected outside the former home of the Yonsei University Medical School he had attended almost seventy-five years before.

88. *Amphibious Group One War Diary*, 9.

89. *Loading Progress Report, Period of 1800 13 Dec to 1800 14 Dec. Embarkation Progress Report, Period of 1800 19 Dec to 1800 20 Dec.* Forney Files. US National Archives and Record Administration, College Park, Md.

90. *War Diary of ROK Navy and Commander Naval Forces South Korea (CTG 95.7)*, December 1950, 10.

91. *War Diary of ROK Navy* 11. Also: *Assignment of Shipping*.

92. A former US Army AKL, a small cargo ship 177 feet long of 345 deadweight tons.

93. *War Diary of ROK Navy* 13.

94. *War Diary of ROK Navy* 11.

95. *Amphibious Group One War Diary*, 41.

96. Colonel Forney's *Embarkation Progress Reports* show only one entry for BM 8501, that for the period 1800 Dec. 15th to 1800 Dec. 16th, and lists for the ship "Embarked 4,000 civ & 300 political POWs." The difference between CTF 90's number and Forney's could have been refugees embarked while at the dock after leaving the beach.

97. *Commander Amphibious Group One (CTF 90) Action Report, Hungnam Redeployment, December 1950*, 68.

98. *War Diary of ROK Navy*, 16.

99. Forney, *Transcript of Special Report*, 16.

100. Rear Admiral J. Robert Lunney, USNR, interview with the Author, September 27th, 2019. Also in Gilbert.

101. Lunney interview.

102. Captain Edward, J. Pierson, private communication to Rev. Sinclair Oubre and Rear Admiral J. Robert Lunney, USNR, January 6, 2018.

103. Lunney interview. Also: Forney, *Transcript of Special Report*, 16.

104. *Deck Log, SS Meredith Victory*, Friday, 22rd December 1950, and Saturday, 23rd December 1950.

105. Forney, *Transcript of Special Report*, 15.

106. Warren Hall. *Dedicated Skipper.* "The American Weekly." December 18, 1960

107. *Deck Log, SS Meredith Victory*, Friday, 22rd December 1950, and Saturday, 23rd December 1950.

108. *Vessel Status Card*, US Maritime Administration.

109. Handwritten pencil notes on the typewritten record *Ships Present as of 221200I* found in Forney's files note the *Meredith Victory* "going alongside Norcuba 1st" and for Virginia City "alongside Norcuba 2nd." The *Assignment of Shipping* gives the dates loading began and the date and time completed.

110. *Assignment of Shipping*.

111. *Assignment of Shipping*.

112. The *Assignment of Shipping* lists the following time-chartered ships leaving port on the 23rd: *Hunter Victory; Clarksburg Victory; Robin Gray*, all before the *Meredith Victory*. Sailing after: *Morgantown Victory; Lafayette Victory; Rider Victory; Carleton Victory; Provo Victory; Virginia City Victory; Norcuba*; and *Madaket*. The *Shiano Maru*, which provided berthing for the Japanese stevedores working at the port for X Corps, left that evening also. The *Madaket* may have been the last non-LST transport to leave, probably passing the breakwater well after midnight.

113. *Assignment of Shipping*.

114. *Amphibious Group One War Diary*, 52.

115. *(CTF 90) Action Report*, 58.

116. *COMSEVENTHFLT Deck Log*. Entry for Saturday, 23 Dec. 1950. Also: "Hungnam Gunfire Support Chart," *(CTF 90) Action Report*.

117. *Amphibious Group One War Diary*, 54.

118. LCVPs and LVTs.

119. *(CTF 90) Action Report*, 23.

120. *(CTF 90) Action Report* 67.

121. *Engineer Study-Demolition Plan Hungnam Area.* US Army, 8224th Engineer Construction Group.

122. "Demolition Table, Hamhung-Hungnam Operation," *Headquarters X Corps, Special Report on Hungnam Evacuation, 9-24 December 1950.*

123. *Amphibious Group One War Diary*, 59.

124. Forney, *Transcript of Special Report*, 14.

125. Major Richard W. Schutt, *The Amphibious Withdrawal of the U.S. X Corps from Hungnam, Korea*, 9. US National Archives and Record Administration, College Park, Md.

126. *Amphibious Group One War Diary*, 58.

127. Rear Admiral J. Robert Lunney, Interview with the Author, September 27th, 2019. Also in Gilbert.

128. *Moormack News*, Moore-McCormack Lines, March, 1951.

129. As told to Seattle Post-Intelligencer reporter Charles Regal. Quoted in the *Mooremack News* of March, 1951, in turn quoted in the *Congressional Record* for legislative day Monday, March 26, 1951.

130. *Headquarters X Corps, APO 909 US Army, Incoming Message.* Number G 35288 KCA, December 20th, 1950.

131. *War Diary of ROK Navy* 18.

132. *War Diary of ROK Navy*, 18.

133. Rear Admiral J. Robert Lunney, USNR, interview with the author, September 26th, 2019.

134. *Deck Log, SS Meredith Victory*, Sunday, 24th December 1950.

135. This passage in the log is claimed in later interviews with La Rue. It does not appear in the extant copy of the *Meredith Victory*'s "Smooth log", the edited, typed copy of the deck log. It may actually have been written in La Rue's personal journal.

136. Leonard. P. La Rue and Lester David. "I Witnessed a Christmas Miracle," *This Week Magazine*, December 11, 1960, 11.

137. *Deck Log, SS Meredith Victory*, Tuesday, 26th December 1950.

138. *War Diary of ROK Navy*, 19.

139. *War Diary of ROK Navy*, 19.

140. *Meredith Victory*'s Deck Log repeatedly identifies this ship as LST Q636. There was no Q636 in theater, all of the Japanese LSTs having hulls numbered "Q0XX"; i.e., with two digits after the zero. This was almost certainly the 665.

141. James Finan, "Voyage from Hungnam," *The Reader's Digest*, November, 1951, 111-112.

142. James Finan, "Last Voyage from Hungnam," *Naval Affairs,* September, 1951, 9. Also: Merl Smith, private communication with the author.

143. H. J. Burley Smith, interview with the author, December 16, 2019.

11. Legend

1. Commander Amphibious Group One, United Stated Pacific Fleet, Memorandum A4-3, Serial: 28, January 6th, 1951.

2. H. J. Burley Smith, interview with the author, December 16, 2019.

3. A daily evening newspaper that ended publication in 1982 after 134 years.

4. *Moormack News*. Moore-McCormack Lines. June, 1951, 7.

5. *Moormack News*. Moore-McCormack Lines. March, 1952, 5.

6. The Propeller Club was founded in 1922 as a venue for maritime professionals to meet to discuss industry issues. Regional chapters are referred to as "Ports." Even

today, with the decline of the US maritime industry, the Seattle, Washington Port claims almost two hundred members.

7. *Moormack News*, 5.

8. "'Annex "D,' Vessel Planning Data," *COMNAVFE Operation Plan 116-50*, Commander Naval Forces, Far East, Tokyo, Japan, 9 November 1950, D-1.

9. The volume of the holds for rigid cargo that cannot conform to the curvature of the hull or fit between the ship's structural elements. The volume available for cargo that does not follow these constraints is called, aptly, "grain capacity."

10. *Commander Amphibious Group One (CTF 90) Action Report, Hungnam Redeployment, December 1950*, 10.

11. *Command Report for December 1950*. Headquarters X Corps, 3-4.

12. *War Diary of ROK Navy and Commander Naval Forces South Korea (CTG 95.7)*, December 1950, 18.

13. Colonel Edward H. Forney, USMC, *Transcript of Special Report, Colonel Edward H. Forney, USMC. Special After-Action Report by, Deputy Chief of Staff of the X Corps, 19 August to 31 December 1950*, 16.

14. AK was the designation for a military cargo ship (a United States Ship, operated by a military crew), with many of them during this period Victory-type ships. Major Schutt is no doubt using the designation as shorthand to differentiate them from LSTs. We know from other sources there were no AKs left at Hungnam by this point.

15. Major Richard W. Schutt, USMC, *The Amphibious Withdrawal of the U.S. X Corps from Hungnam, Korea*, (undated), 9-10.

16. *Headquarters X Corps, Special Report on Hungnam Evacuation, 9-24 December 1950*, 4.

17. The *X Corps Special Report* identifies BM 8501 as "BM 501" carrying refugees from Sonjin. Both CTF-90 and the ROK Navy War Diary record this ship at Hungnam. No record the author found showed it at Sonjin loading refugees. The report probably means ""Soho-jin." Also the 4,300 number must be included in the tallies and the Loading Progress Report of 20 December shows 4,300 "refugees," but the Embarkation Report shows that 300 were "political POW's" and the remaining 4,000 are identified as "civilians." It also does not jibe with CTF-90's number of 7,441 for the ship.

18. *Commander Amphibious Group One, United State Pacific Fleet, War Diary, December 1950*, 12

19. Admiral Sherman had died on July 22, 1951, of a heart attack while on official travel in Naples, Italy.

20. Obituary. "General Edward H. Forney." *Daily News*. January 23, 1965.

12. Life On Land

1. *Vessel Status Card*. "Mormactide." Maritime Administration.

2. Harry G. Summers Jr. *Korean War Almanac*, (NY: Facts on File, 1990), 75-77.

3. Xiaobong Li. *Attack at Chosin; The Chinese Second Offensive in Korea*. (Norman, OK: University of Oklahoma Press, 2020).

4. *Moormack News*, Winter, 1955-56, Moore-McCormack Lines, 8.

5. *Moormack News*, 8.

6. *Moormack News*, 8.

7. H. J. Burley Smith, interview with the author, December 16, 2019.
8. Harry P. Moore, "God-Fearing Sea Captain Now a Monk," *The Virginian-Pilot The Plymouth Star*, March 18, 1956, 2-C.
9. Captain Edward, J. Pierson, private communication to Rev. Sinclair Oubre and Rear Admiral J. Robert Lunney, USNR, January 6, 2018.
10. Letter to Bob Cochran, dated "Palm Sunday, 1956," in the archives of the American Merchant Marine Museum, Kings Point, NY.
11. During WW II, the great redoubt of Monte Cassino, high on a hillside with a commanding view of two river valleys leading towards Rome, presented such a potential advantage for occupying Germans that the Abbey was bombed to rubble by the US Eighth Air Force on February 15, 1944. Unknown to the Allies, the Germans had agreed with the abbot not to use the abbey for military purposes, so the only fatalities in the bombing were several hundred Italian civilians who had sought refuge there. Ironically, German officers had also offered to remove the abbey's treasures of artwork and manuscripts to the Vatican for safekeeping and did so, using their own military resources to accomplish the feat in 1943. After the bombing, German paratroopers used the remains of the abbey to great advantage against the advancing Allies. The abbey was rebuilt after the war and re-consecrated in 1964.
12. *American Weekly*, December 18, 1960.
13. Harry P. Moore, "God-Fearing Sea Captain Now a Monk," *The Virginian-Pilot The Plymouth Star*, March 18, 1956, 2-C.
14. Rev. Joel Macul, OSB, private communication with the author, July 16, 2020.
15. Rev. Joel Marcul, OSB, interview with the author, February 19, 2019.

13. Gallant Ship

1. *Moormack News*, Winter, 1955-56, Moore-McCormack Lines, 8.
2. Letter to Bob Cochran, dated "Palm Sunday, 1956," in the archives of the American Merchant Marine Museum, Kings Point, NY.
3. "Tradition of Sea Award is Given," *The Tablet*, June 2, 1956, 1.
4. SS *Ile de France*, SS *Cape Ann* and USNS *Pvt. William H. Thomas* were the first post-WW II ships awarded Gallant Ship citations. The awards were made on October 23, 1957, in recognition of their service to the passengers and crew of the *Andrea Doria*.
5. The Congressman's name was actually Paul Albert Fino, Republican, of New York's 25th Congressional District.
6. Memo from Chief, Division of Office Services to Chief, Office of Property and Supply. Subject: SS. Meredith Victory-Application for Ship Citation Pursuant to Public Law No. 759, 84th Congress, Maritime Administration. Washington, DC, June 7, 1957.
7. The letter is dated "January 21, 1957," but the "1957" is almost certainly a new-year typo.
8. In 1972, Maurice Stans would resign as Commerce Secretary to serve as Finance Chairman for the campaign to re-elect Whittier College-graduate President Richard M. Nixon. In 1975 Stans would plead guilty to three counts of campaign-finance violations and pay a $5,000 fine. Nixon, of course, suffered a more serious fate.

9. Press Release, Office of the Secretary, Department of Commerce, for Release at 12:00 noon, August 24, 1960.
10. According to US Government records, five Americans providing military assistance to the Republic of Vietnam were killed there during 1960.
11. Rev. Joel Marcul, OSB, interview with the author, February 19, 2019.
12. Helen Delich Bentley, *The Baltimore Sun*, August 25, 1960, 6.
13. Press Release, Office of the Secretary, Department of Commerce, For Release at 12:00 noon, August 24, 1960.
14. Six years would, unfortunately, make quite a difference in Vietnam—6,350 Americans died there in 1966.
15. US Department of Commerce, Maritime Administration, Memorandum to Pacific Coast District from Acting Administrator, August 24, 1966.

14. The Cause

1. Letter to Bob Cochran, dated February 11, 1961, in the archives of the American Merchant Marine Museum, Kings Point, NY.
2. For centuries the Catholic Church celebrated the date of Benedict's passing, March 21st, as his feast day. The 1969 revision of the Church calendar following Vatican II moved the date to July 11, when it is celebrated now.
3. Rev. Joel Marcul, OSB, interview with the author, February 19, 2019.
4. Macul Interview.
5. Macul Interview.
6. Michael Wojcik. "Bishop Opens Cause for Sainthood of World War II and Korean War Veteran. *The Beacon*. March 28, 2019.
7. Rev. Joel Macul, OSB, *Dear Friends of St. Paul's Abbey*, December, 2001.
8. Port Arthur, Texas, may be proud of its most famous daughter, but the feeling was not always reciprocated. In her song "Ego Rock," Joplin sang, "...I just had to get out on the Texas plane, baby, Lord it was bringing me down. I been all around the world, but Port Arthur is the worst place I've ever found."

ABOUT THE AUTHOR

Philip Lacovara was born and raised in Washington DC. A graduate of the University of Chicago and Boston College, he trained as a physicist and worked as a researcher in US Government, university, and private research laboratories. Two decades ago, he tried his hand at business and founded companies in optical sensors and communications, and in renewable energy. After successful exits from his companies, he turned his hand to writing and publishing. *The Mariner and the Monk* is his first work of non-fiction. He divides his time between San Diego, CA and Tucson, AZ, where he is a doting grandfather.